Programming Reality

Film and Media Studies Series

Film studies is the critical exploration of cinematic texts as art and entertainment, as well as the industries that produce them and the audiences that consume them. Although a medium barely one hundred years old, film is already transformed through the emergence of new media forms. Media studies is an interdisciplinary field that considers the nature and effects of mass media upon individuals and society and analyzes media content and representations. Despite changing modes of consumption—especially the proliferation of individuated viewing technologies—film has retained its cultural dominance into the 21st century, and it is this transformative moment that the WLU Press Film and Media Studies series addresses.

Our Film and Media Studies series includes topics such as identity, gender, sexuality, class, race, visuality, space, music, new media, aesthetics, genre, youth culture, popular culture, consumer culture, regional/national cinemas, film policy, film theory, and film history.

Wilfrid Laurier University Press invites submissions. For further information, please contact the Series editors, all of whom are in the Department of English and Film Studies at Wilfrid Laurier University:

Dr. Philippa Gates, Email: pgates@wlu.ca
Dr. Russell Kilbourn, Email: rkilbourn@wlu.ca
Dr. Ute Lischke, Email: ulischke@wlu.ca

75 University Avenue West
Waterloo, ON N2L 3C5
Canada
Phone: 519-884-0710
Fax: 519-884-8307

PROGRAMMING REALITY
Perspectives on
English-Canadian Television

Zoë Druick and Aspa Kotsopoulos
editors

Wilfrid Laurier University Press
WLU

This book is published with the help of a grant from the Canadian Federation for the Humanities and Social Sciences, through the Aid to Scholarly Publications Programme, using funds provided by the Social Sciences and Humanities Research Council of Canada. We acknowledge the financial support of the Government of Canada through the Book Publishing Industry Development Program for our publishing activities.

Library and Archives Canada Cataloguing in Publication

Programming reality : perspectives on English-Canadian television / Zoë Druick and Aspa Kotsopoulos, editors.

(Film and media studies series)
Includes bibliographical references and index.
ISBN 978-1-55458-010-1

1. Television broadcasting—Canada. 2. Television programs—Canada. 3. Television broadcasting policy—Canada. 4. Television broadcasting—Social aspects—Canada. 5. Canadian Broadcasting Corporation. 6. Canada—Cultural policy. I. Druick, Zoë II. Kotsopoulos, Aspa, 1966– III. Series.

PN1992.3.C3P76 2008   302.23'450971   C2008-902715-9

Cover photo: Actor Nicholas Campbell in *Da Vinci's Inquest*. Image courtesy of Haddock Entertainment. Cover design: Blakeley Words+Pictures. Text design: Catharine Bonas-Taylor.

© 2008 Wilfrid Laurier University Press
Waterloo, Ontario, Canada
www.wlupress.wlu.ca

∞

This book is printed on Ancient Forest Friendly paper (100% post-consumer recycled).
Printed in Canada

Contents

List of Illustrations

Acknowledgements

An anthology is by nature the product of many minds and many hands. This one benefited not only from the contributions of its authors but also the dialogue that the project promoted with editors, colleagues, and students across Canada.

We would like to acknowledge Danielle Deveau, Fiona Jeffries, and Cassandra Savage for invaluable assistance with research and manuscript preparation, and Jacqueline Larson and Lisa Quinn, hard-working and dedicated editors, past and present, at Wilfrid Laurier University Press. We also acknowledge our anonymous readers for their keen insights, which added immeasurably to the manuscript.

Our gratitude goes to Chris Haddock for granting permission for the cover image from *Da Vinci's Inquest*.

We are extremely pleased to be able to highlight in this collection some of the exciting work being done on Canadian television across the country in a range of academic disciplines, much of it by emerging scholars. It has been satisfying to have so many people confirm our view that an anthology on Canadian television has been long overdue.

Zoë Druick and Aspa Kotsopoulos
Vancouver and Ottawa

The views reflected in this collection do not represent those of the Canadian Radio-television and Telecommunications Commission (CRTC).

ZOË DRUICK
ASPA KOTSOPOULOS

Introduction

Programming Reality: Perspectives on English-Canadian Television is a collection of original interdisciplinary articles that explores the television that has thrived in the Canadian regulatory and cultural context: namely, programs that straddle the border between reality and fiction. Predating the current interest in reality television, these hybrid realisms have been a part of the medium since its inception. Seen through a wider lens, the current proliferation of shows grouped under the category of reality-based programming provides an opportunity to reconsider the complex mediation of reality that television performs within the Canadian context. Each of the contributions to this collection is also a reminder of the significant relationship of television to nation building in Canada—to the imaginative work involved in thinking through the relations that constitute nations, citizens, and communities.

Historically, a strong communications perspective has informed the study of English-language Canadian television, with few exceptions.[1] When communications scholars have turned their attention to Canadian television, they have most often done so from the perspective of state regulation and international dependency, the result of a strong tradition of political economy.[2] By contrast, television studies in the United States and the United Kingdom have long combined perspectives drawn from political economy and cultural history with audience studies and analyses of television content.[3] But a fresh chapter in Canadian television studies is now being written. New publications examining the content that emerges from the political-economic context shaping television production in Canada are appearing in greater numbers than ever.[4] Programming Reality is a part of this emerging trend.

The collection focuses on English-language Canadian television because the imperatives guiding this programming's texts are markedly different from those of their French-language counterparts. A look at the weekly ratings tells the story: where the top twenty shows in English-language Canada are usually made in the US with the occasional exception, the top twenty programs in Quebec are French-language ones made in Canada. From the perspectives gathered in this volume, a detailed picture therefore emerges regarding the cultural and political-economic specificities that inform the imaginative work of television production for English-speaking Canada.[5]

From the Massey Commission (1951) to the establishment of the Canadian Television Fund (1998), the Canadian state, much like other small-market nations, has associated television with policies of nation building. In *Documentary Television in Canada*, David Hogarth notes that the high point of Canadian television regulatory ambition occurred between the mid-1960s and the mid-1980s, when the CBC held sway over a clearly defined public broadcasting sector.[6] As contributions to this volume by Hogarth, Aspa Kotsopoulos, Mary Jane Miller, and Jen VanderBurgh indicate, CBC dramas and docudramas achieve a certain maturity during this period, striving to interpret citizenship issues to a broad national audience.

The early 1980s mark a neo-liberal ideological shift, signified in part by an increased policy emphasis on globalizing Canada's media industries and cultural output, which profoundly altered the role of the CBC. These policy objectives, outlined in the mandate of the 1982 Federal Cultural Policy Review commissioned by the Liberal government, were introduced the following year in a document titled *Towards A New National Broadcasting Policy*.[7] Marc Raboy notes that the purpose of the report was to enhance the private sector's ability to create high-quality television that Canadians would watch and that could be exported globally, and says the report "endorsed a new economistic thrust and made recommendations to shift the emphasis in public funding from the CBC to the private sector."[8]

Following up on the report's recommendations, in 1984 the Conservative government inaugurated a series of budget cuts to the public sector, including the CBC, as well as a new set of directions in Canadian television policy. As a result, the CBC began eliminating its in-house production in 1984 and changed from a producer to a patron of Canadian programming. Thanks to these policy initiatives, including the 1983 creation of the Canadian Broadcast Program Development Fund—part of the transformation of the Canadian Film Development Corporation into Telefilm Canada in 1984—which gave direct subsidies to independent television producers, Canadian productions experienced growth.

In the mid-1980s, the CBC also instituted a five-year plan to "Canadianize" its schedule as a means to set itself apart from the private broadcasters and their Americanized schedules.[9] A 1994 decision by the Canadian Radio-television and Telecommunications Commission (CRTC) reaffirmed this mandate in a review of the CBC's licence.[10] By providing services and programming that the private Canadian broadcasters did not, the argument went, the CBC would make itself relevant to Canadians as a public broadcaster connecting the regions, reflecting the nation, and serving its citizens. A number of the contributions to this volume speak to the CBC's renewed commitment to Canadianization through programs such as *Canada: A People's History* (Dick), *The Greatest Canadian* (Rak), and the "hockeymentary" phenomenon (Foster).

That commitment acquired urgency as a crisis of national unity followed the 1995 referendum in which the citizens of Quebec voted narrowly against declaring sovereignty and separating from Canada. Marusya Bociurkiw's analysis of English-Canadian news coverage at the time reminds us of the heightened sense of collective trauma that seemed to surround this event, transforming it into a family melodrama for the nation. The *Heritage Minutes*, discussed in this collection by Katarzyna Rukszto, are a definitive response to anxieties about Quebec's possible separation from the rest of Canada and were funded secretly by the federal government, a fact revealed in the Gomery Inquiry's investigation of government sponsorship. At a time when citizenship in Canada seemed increasingly uncertain, the *Heritage Minutes* turned history, an important aspect of informed citizenship, into miniature affective moments of heritage with an appeal to feelings of belonging to the Canadian family. Several contributions to this collection speak to that moment in Canadian politics as informing, either explicitly or implicitly, various examples of programming. Zoë Druick notices a profound shift in Canadian news parody, from the disruptive margins of *CODCO*, with its subversive critique of institutions, in the 1980s to the cohering centre of *This Hour Has 22 Minutes*, with its safe legitimization of national narratives, in the 1990s.

What these and other contributions also reveal is that the 1990s mark a period of transition in the Canadian television industry in which the policy directions of the preceding decade come to bear fruit, a trend that continues into the new century. The results of these policy changes are reflected in this collection with chapters on independent productions such as *Da Vinci's Inquest* (Lowry), created for the CBC and exported internationally, and *Moccasin Flats* (McCullough), made for APTN, as well as *Train 48* (Matheson), produced for CanWest. Essays in this collection reflect the CBC's continuing and historic role in Canadian television production, but with one-quarter of *Programming Reality* devoted to productions not made for the CBC, the collection also mirrors the new production landscape in the wake of policy shifts in the 1980s and 1990s.

The establishment of the Canadian Television Fund in 1998 continued investment in independent television production, and also offered the bonus of "visibly Canadian elements" for productions meeting certain cultural criteria, such as biographies of Canadians or stories about Canadian events. Although that bonus was eliminated in 2003, the CTF still maintains a commitment to productions with recognizable Canadian content. Such policy initiatives would seem to encourage and support the hybrid realism that this book explores. Similarly, a 1999 CRTC decision has had major repercussions for dramatic production in Canada. The decision to widen the definitions of primetime and priority programming made it possible for Canada's broadcasters to meet their Canadian content quotas with relatively inexpensive light documentaries.[11] These programs are either adapted from global formats—such as Britain's *Pop Idol*, which private network CTV morphed into its blockbuster success, *Canadian Idol* (Byers, Chapter 5)—or they are simply cheaper to produce than traditional dramatic fare and trade on their cachet as representations of "real life."

Indeed, policy seems to have created or encouraged new modes of production, such as global formats and international co-productions, as we see through the 1990s to the present, and these changes are mirrored in this book.[12] As well, the explosion in cable and specialty channels in Canada and the US created a new appetite for content, while federal funding for independent television production increased. Despite the increase, however, many independent producers wishing to make programs with high production values began to seek international partners.[13] Each of these factors contributed to unprecedented growth in independent television production and helped shift Canada from a "television importer" to a "television exporter" in the 1990s.[14]

The transformation of the popular *Degrassi* franchise—from a gritty co-venture between the CBC and PBS to a glossy teen drama for CTV and an American specialty channel—attests to changes in the televisual environment (Byers, Chapter 11). More and more, Canadian creators routinely make programs for more than one national market, with implications for not only the kinds of stories that are told but also the ways they are told.[15] Glen Lowry speculates that the transformation of *Da Vinci's Inquest* into *Da Vinci's City Hall* was partly the result of such pressures. Where *Inquest* dealt with narrative arcs rooted in a specific locale with a unique history—Vancouver's impoverished Downtown Eastside—*City Hall* became a generic, exportable tale of a new mayor's encounters with the vicissitudes of power. The implications of storytelling for more than one national market are also explored in Kirsten Emiko McAllister's contribution on the miniseries *Human Cargo*. She identifies the development of a new transnational genre, the "geopolitical complicity drama," which addresses the interconnectedness of world events and economies, and their impact on individuals seemingly far removed from each other by geography. Many of the articles in this book touch on the effects of new policies, new television economies, and new political realities.

Neo-liberal-era television has added a new facet to the discourse of citizenship in Canada with a new form of market populism found across a range of shows made possible by new technologies. In her analysis of *The Greatest Canadian*, Julie Rak discusses the harnessing of celebrity discourse and historical biography in order to glamorize and popularize the past for an audience accustomed to showbiz glitz. The added dimension of audience participation, in which viewers can vote online or by cellphone for the "greatest Canadian," situates the series within a market populism we have seen demonstrated in reality programming in recent years. Rak argues, however, that while such appeals to audience involvement may be populist and may claim to address a nation of citizens, they are not particularly democratic. As Michele Byers finds in her study of *Canadian Idol* (Chapter 5), populist appeals to who is best suited to "stand for" Canada can legitimate regressive notions of who belongs, or, conversely, does not belong, to the national family. In another vein, in her analysis of Canadian news parodies, Druick considers the implications of using crowd-pleasing humour to comment on the news. While satire has a long tradition as political commentary, skits that rely on imitation or practical jokes have great popular appeal but questionable political effectiveness.

These new forms of addressing citizenship, funded by public–private partnerships, speak to economic and ideological shifts of the past twenty-five years. In her analysis of CBC flagship dramas set in Toronto, Jen VanderBurgh suggests a direct correlation between the receding public sector and the increasing ambivalence toward public institutions shown by protagonists in series such as *Seeing Things* and *This is Wonderland*. During this time, the citizenship project, as epitomized in the mandates of the CBC and the NFB, was challenged by the private sector's market populism and by neo-liberal arguments against public sector spending. Kotsopoulos discusses the implication of these pressures on the CBC's approach to historical miniseries and the kinds of citizen engagement these productions encourage—and discourage, too. She examines how the tensions between citizenship and entertainment arising from this context have affected the CBC's institutional mode of address with respect to the narrative treatment of history and the subsequent formation of a national mythology.

Changes in the television environment, such as the move toward privatization and globalization since the 1990s, also parallel the emergence and development of so-called reality television. In the UK, docusoaps and emergency shows emerged from a loosened interpretation of the public service mandate in the 1990s.[16] In the US, the rise of reality television, by way of lifestyle and variety programming, resulted from declining network audiences and the expanding cable dial in the same period.[17] Although reality television can be explained by transformations in the political economy of television, however, the fascination it holds as a concept in both popular culture and the academy is linked to its claims to documentary reality, to its foregrounding of ordinary people, and to its emphasis on confession.

Despite its proliferation on the Canadian airwaves, not much exists yet in the way of Canadian-made reality television. As we write, the CBC is changing its programming mandate to increase emphasis on fact-based content with its new Factual Entertainment division and its recent acquisition of a controlling interest in the Canadian Documentary Channel. Canadian television may be poised to chart a new route between recent developments in British and American television. As the research in this book shows, reality–fiction hybrids have a long tradition in Canada. We believe that analyses of reality television today can benefit from a deeper understanding of television's history and the ways in which new forms are the complex result of the pressures of policy, the marketplace, and popular culture.

Inflecting the Dialogue

One of the most influential concepts in Canadian television studies comes from Mary Jane Miller's "Inflecting the Formula," which offers a framework referred to more than once in this book. In her comparison of the contemporaneous legal dramas *L.A. Law* (for American network television) and *Street Legal* (for the CBC), Miller argues that Canadian television drama may use the same formats as their American counterparts, but key differences remain. One notable difference is that Canadian shows are, according to Miller, less reliant on stereotypes and formulas and as a result demand more thoughtful engagement from their audiences. Not only must viewers work harder to activate meanings from the texts, but the narratives tend to be more ambiguous or open-ended.[18]

Miller's notion of Canadian television realism, a paradigm she uses in her chapter in this volume on how Canadian dramatic series have negotiated the thorny topic of Native residential schools, is both supported and challenged by other contributions to this collection. John McCullough praises the Aboriginal series *Moccasin Flats* as a "socio-political milestone" for its radical blending of neo-realism with political modernism and its refusal to provide easy solutions to the tough situations facing First Nations youth in downtown Regina. Byers (Chapter 11) makes similar claims about *Degrassi*, pointing out that the series often featured stories dealing with complex issues facing teenagers that worked well in the Canadian context but were edited to eliminate ambiguity and controversy for American broadcast. But Hogarth's historical analysis of the CBC's early forays into dramatic reenactment challenges the assumption of a more realist Canadian style. He shows that the CBC considered fantasy, spectacle, and desire as important means by which to induce excitement abo't Canada in viewers and did not consider the use of visual pleasure and the solicitation of emotion as any less real or less effective than other forms of fact-based television.

While Miller's theory may once have applied more neatly, recent American television dramas challenge her claims as producers and networks strive for more and more novel forms of viewer engagement.[19] Moreover, many contributors to this volume identify unambiguous forms of national storytelling that contradict the open-endedness thought to be typically Canadian. For instance, the monumental series *Canada: A People's History* would appear to represent a deviation from Miller's historical insights. According to Lyle Dick, the seventeen-episode production, largely composed of reenactments, is far from open-ended in its telling of Canadian history. On the contrary, the series pushes forward an unambiguous interpretation of Canadian history as one of benevolent nationalism, sidetracking any stories or interpretations that might trouble this single overarching narrative. Bociurkiw identifies a similar nationalist narrative at work in news coverage of the 1995 Quebec referendum, which univocally supported a unified Canada. Other contributions to this volume also trouble the idea that there is a distinctively Canadian way to tell a story, either because the Canadian programs in question have been adopted from an international format (Byers, Druick, Matheson, Rak) or because the issues dealt with— immigration, First Nations rights, global capital—are inherently transnational (Lowry, McAllister, McCullough).

For this reason, *Programming Reality* in part thinks reality television in Canada into a longer set of conventions and practices for reality-based forms that are contextually specific and necessarily in dialogue with international trends. For instance, Derek Foster's chapter on the "hockeymentary" *Making the Cut* is an example of the way in which a national pastime comes to be re-envisioned for television as a result of genre trends while still perpetuating core myths about Canada. Similarly, Sarah Matheson discusses the low-budget soap opera *Train 48*, adapted for a Canadian audience from a successful Australian format, as a creative response to financial constraints. According to Matheson, the series self-consciously adopts codes and conventions from reality television that are both popular and inexpensive, in ways that "encourage a different engagement with the form." Examining the kinds of generic transformations that these authors highlight contributes new perspectives on the connection between Canadian television's political economy, its texts, and its audiences.

Reflecting the complexities of the English-Canadian televisual landscape, the book is divided into three parts: "Narrating Nation," "Making Citizens," and "Mapping Geographies." Although issues of citizenship and location run through many of the articles, this division highlights the particular tendencies of Canadian television programming. They also allow readers to chart historical tensions between publicly and privately funded television, as well as changing notions of citizenship.

The chapters in Part One, "Narrating Nation," confront the general theme that the media contribute to the formation of imagined communities.[20] Telling stories about a nation, notes Homi Bhabha, is an indispensable aspect of the nation's existence.[21] Although national stories come in many forms, the use of television for the formation of a national public is distinctive because it is connected to its provenance as a regulated public service. The contributions here show that television has not only narrated the nation in ways that monumentalize it through recourse to Canada's past, but it has also operated at the level of the ordinary through reference to current events and sports. Elsewhere, Michael Billig argues that, with a few spectacular exceptions, most nationalism occurs at this banal or everyday level.[22] Practices are so obvious that they become invisible, like a flag hanging in front of a public building. His argument distinguishes between *explicitly* national stories that may include historical events, important figures, or moments of national crisis and the *implicitly* national ones that may be found in hockey programming, current affairs, news parody, and even in talent shows. The two types of national stories complement one another. Shows explicitly focused on nation building paradoxically call the nation into question, if only momentarily, by historicizing it; they are essentially self-conscious. Banal nationalism, on the other hand, naturalizes the nation and takes it for granted, thereby making the case more surreptitiously. Both kinds of nationalism are apparent on English-Canadian television.

In a way that brings to mind Tony Bennett's *Culture: A Reformer's Science*, Part Two, "Making Citizens," explores an array of programming that engages questions about the relationship between public policy and citizenship. Adopting a Foucauldian perspective, Bennett argues that policy is "inescapably normative" in the sense of "bringing about a reformation of habits, beliefs, values—in short, ways of life."[23] As the four contributions to this section show, this activity can take on many guises, from the seemingly benign to the downright destructive. Yet by no means has this activity been monolithic. On the one hand, several television programs discussed here exemplify a social-mission tradition with dramatic offerings meant to help Canadian youth negotiate the complex contemporary realities affecting them or to draw attention to the ongoing impact of oppressive colonial practices on First Nations communities. On the other hand, discourses of marginalization, otherness, and exclusion are amply represented on Canadian television screens and carry with them normative notions of citizenship. This normativity is contextually defined across the cases studied here. But a common thread between these chapters is attention to the mutual interaction of entertainment and information, of pleasure and reason, and of affectivity and rationality that characterize the televisual address of reality–fiction hybrids.

The chapters in Part Three, "Mapping Geographies," demonstrate the degree to which Canadian television has served as a technology for constituting national geographies. Cognitive maps are often affective, rendering visible the significance of places, as well as sentiments of belonging and attachment. As Fredric Jameson notes, one of the key problems with visualizing change in a global capitalist economy is the difficulty of imagining or mapping the whole.[24] While traditional forms of Canadian art, such as landscape painting, have tended to dwell on a colonial myth about Canada's vast and largely unpopulated wilderness, television has been an important site for processing the experiences of urban Canada, where the vast majority of the population lives and on a daily basis engages with the forces of global capitalism at the local level. The essays in this section identify the degree to which television acts as a mapping device, allowing audiences to envision an urban Canada and to make sense of the relationship of everyday citizens to world events and global economies. Whether focused on the commuter train, the neighbourhood, or the family, the studies here all grapple with the significance of the local and the communal in grounding experiences of the political and the transnational.

The contributors to *Programming Reality* illustrate that the theme of citizenship runs through much Canadian programming, even in the most unlikely places. That is because, as Peter Dahlgren reminds us, television "has become, for better or worse, the major institution of the public sphere in modern society."[25] Television has been an important part of how people have been able to see locally and globally at once.[26] Over the past half-century, television has loomed large in discussions about modern society and politics as a technology for informing and activating citizenship. Television and mass democracy have grown up hand in hand. Yet in more recent years, television has been accused of destroying the possibility of citizenship by transforming reality into a spectacular media event, infecting other social spheres with its media logic, and subordinating the values of the public sphere to commercial interests.[27]

A number of convergences in the 1990s have changed the primary relationship between television and modern citizenship. Television's role as the primary tool of national citizenship is in question. Although not a mass medium in the way television is, the Internet has been taking both the attention and the flak formerly reserved for television. The Internet is currently the medium thought to have the greatest potential for contributing to political democracy and civic engagement, and, as such, policymakers and media analysts have turned with fascination toward this new medium. Along these lines, democratic communications researcher and former journalist François Demers has assessed the state of Canadian television studies: "Television in Canada has become ordinary and accepted. It is no longer the fascinating object it once was in daily life. Logically, with the advent of the Internet, the old medium is less of a priority for the research community. In the Canadian case, this lack of fascination with the medium itself has been complemented by the exhaustion of the paradigm of cultural sovereignty, which, while still dominating the scholarly discourse regarding television, is in fact showing severe signs of fatigue."[28]

As television loses its lustre as an exciting and threatening new medium and becomes either residual or remediated, it also leaves behind its pride of place in policy and media studies.[29] The groundbreaking new work gathered here demonstrates that television's uncertain present marks a moment of opportunity for the field of television studies, when anxious concern about the future can be transformed into fruitful reflection on the past. If the cultural sovereignty paradigm is exhausted and television is going to neither single-handedly make nor destroy the Canadian nation, then the medium's existence as a multifaceted policy object and site of textual creativity is liberated for other kinds of analysis and uses. We hope that the original and diverse studies included in this volume will contribute to this exciting new phase in Canadian television studies.

Notes

1 Collins, *Culture, Communication and National Identity*; Miller, *Turn Up the Contrast*; Rutherford, *When Television Was Young*. Note: We have adopted the term "English-Canadian" to differentiate from Québécois or French Canadian. Although the Canadian population is composed of many groups speaking multiple languages, English still constitutes the language of national public discourse on TV outside Quebec, and for this reason we utilize the somewhat outmoded but still descriptive term "English-Canadian."

2 Innis, *Empire and Communications*; Peers, *The Public Eye*; Smyth, *Dependency Road*.

3 Ang, *Watching Dallas*; Feuer, *Seeing Through the Eighties*; Fiske, *Television Culture*; Gitlin, *Inside Prime Time*; Hartley and Fiske, *Reading Television*; Liebes and Katz, *The Export of Meaning*; Morley, *Family Television*; Spigel, *Make Room for TV*.

4 Hogarth, *Documentary Television in Canada*; Tinic, *On Location*; Beaty and Sullivan, *Canadian Television Today*; Urquhart and Wagman, "Considering Canadian Television."

5 Raboy, *Les médias québecois*.

6 Hogarth, *Documentary Television in Canada*, 69.

7 Canada, *Report of the Federal Cultural Policy Review Committee*; Canada, *Towards a New National Broadcasting Policy*.

8 Raboy, "Public Broadcasting," 187.

9 Canada, *Report of the Task Force on Broadcasting Policy*, 9–11

10 CRTC, CRTC Decision 94–437.

11 Tolusso, "CRTC TV Policy."

12 See Sinclair et al., *New Patterns*; Hoskins et al., *Global Television*.

13 Attallah, "Canadian Television Exports," 175–87.

14 Attallah, "Canadian Television Exports," 189.

15 Tinic, *On Location*.

16 Dovey, *Freakshow*.

17 Magder, "The End of TV 101." See also Biressi and Nunn, *Reality TV: Realism and Revelation*; Hill, *Reality TV: Audiences and Popular Factual Television*; Holmes and Jermyn, *Understanding Reality Television*; Kilbourne, *Staging the Real*; Murray and Ouellette, *Reality TV: Remaking Television Culture*; Paget, *No Other Way to Tell It*.

18 Miller, "Inflecting the Formula."

19 Sconce, "What If?"

20 Anderson, *Imagined Communities*.

21 Bhabha, *Nation and Narration*.

22 Billig, *Banal Nationalism*.

23 Bennett, *Culture*, 91. See also Lewis and Miller, *Critical Cultural Policy Studies*.

24 Jameson, "Cognitive Mapping."

25 Dahlgren, *Television and the Public Sphere*, x. See also Corner, *Television Form and Public Address*.

26 Morley and Robins, *Spaces of Identity*, Peters, "Seeing Bifocally."
27 Boorstein, *The Image*; Dayan and Katz, "Defining Media Events"; Doyle, *Arresting Images.*
28 Demers, "Canadian Television," 660.
29 Acland, *Residual Media*; Bolter and Grusin, *Remediation.*

References

Acland, Charles, ed. *Residual Media*. Minneapolis: University of Minnesota Press, 2007.

Anderson, Benedict. *Imagined Communities: Reflections on the Origins and Spread of Nationalism*, 2nd ed. New York: Verso, 1991.

Ang, Ien. *Watching Dallas: Soap Opera and the Melodramatic Imagination*. London: Methuen, 1985.

Attallah, Paul. "Canadian Television Exports: Into the Mainstream." In *New Patterns in Global Television: Peripheral Vision*, edited by John Sinclair, Elizabeth Jacka, and Stuart Cunningham, 162–91. Oxford: Oxford University Press, 1996.

Beaty, Bart and Rebecca Sullivan. *Canadian Television Today*. Calgary: University of Calgary Press, 2006.

Bennett, Tony. *Culture: A Reformer's Science*. London: Sage, 1998.

Bhabha, Homi, ed. *Nation and Narration*. London: Routledge, 1990.

Billig, Michael. *Banal Nationalism*. London: Sage, 1995.

Biressi, Anita and Heather Nunn. *Reality TV: Realism and Revelation*. London: Wallflower Press, 2005.

Bolter, Jay David and Richard Grusin. *Remediation: Understanding New Media*. Cambridge, MA: MIT Press, 1999.

Boorstein, Daniel. *The Image: A Guide to Pseudo-events in America*. New York: Atheneum, 1961.

Canada. *Report of the Federal Cultural Policy Review Committee*. Ottawa: Ministry of Supply and Services, 1982.

———. *Towards a New National Broadcasting Policy*. Ottawa: Department of Communications, 1983.

———. *Report of the Task Force on Broadcasting Policy*. Ottawa: Ministry of Supply and Services, 1986.

Canadian Radio-television and Telecommunications Commission. CRTC Decision 94–437, "Canadian Broadcasting Corporation." Ottawa, 1994.

Collins, Richard. *Culture, Communication and National Identity: The Case of Canadian Television*. Toronto: University of Toronto Press, 1990.

Corner, John. *Television Form and Public Address*. London: Edward Arnold, 1995.

Dahlgren, Peter. *Television and the Public Sphere: Citizenship, Democracy and the Media*. Thousand Oaks, CA: Sage, 1995.

Dayan, Daniel and Elihu Katz. "Defining Media Events: The High Holidays of Mass Communication." In *Television: The Critical View*, 6th ed., edited by Horace Newcomb, 401–20. Oxford: Oxford University Press, 2000.

Demers, François. "Canadian Television: The Exhaustion of a Domestic Paradigm?" *Journal of Broadcasting & Electronic Media*, December 2003: 656–61.

Dovey, Jon. *Freakshow: First Person Media and Factual Television*. London: Pluto, 2000.

Doyle, Aaron. *Arresting Images: Crime and Policing in Front of the Television Camera*. Toronto: University of Toronto Press, 2003.

Feuer, Jane. *Seeing Through the Eighties: Television and Reaganism*. Durham, NC: Duke University Press, 1995.

Fiske, John. *Television Culture*. London: Routledge, 1987.

Gitlin, Todd. *Inside Prime Time*, rev. ed. London: Routledge, 1994.

Hartley, John and John Fiske. *Reading Television*. London: Methuen, 1978.

Hill, Annette. *Reality TV: Audiences and Popular Factual Television*. London: Routledge, 2005.

Hogarth, David. *Documentary Television in Canada: From National Public Service to Global Marketplace*. Montreal and Kingston: McGill-Queen's University Press, 2002.

Holmes, Su and Deborah Jermyn, eds. *Understanding Reality Television*. London: Routledge, 2004.

Hoskins, Colin, Stuart McFadyen, and Adam Finn. *Global Television and Film*. New York: Oxford University Press, 1997.

Innis, Harold. *Empire and Communications*. Toronto: University of Toronto Press, 1972.

Jameson, Fredric. "Cognitive Mapping." In *Marxism and the Interpretation of Culture*, edited by Cary Nelson and Lawrence Grossberg, 347–60. Urbana: University of Illinois Press, 1988.

Kilbourne, Richard. *Staging the Real: Factual TV Programming in the Age of Big Brother*. Manchester: Manchester University Press, 2001.

Lewis, Justin and Toby Miller, eds. *Critical Cultural Policy Studies: A Reader*. Oxford: Blackwell, 2003.

Liebes, Tamar and Elihu Katz. *The Export of Meaning: Cross-Cultural Readings of Dallas*. New York: Oxford University Press, 1990.

Magder, Ted. "The End of TV 101: Reality Programs, Formats, and the New Business of Television." In *Reality TV: Remaking Television Culture*, edited by Susan Murray and Laurie Ouellette, 37–56. New York: New York University Press, 2004.

Miller, Mary Jane. *Turn Up the Contrast: Canadian Television Drama since 1952*. Vancouver: University of British Columbia Press and CBC Enterprises, 1987.

———. "Inflecting the Formula: The First Seasons of *Street Legal* and *L.A. Law*." In *The Beaver Bites Back? American Popular Culture in Canada*, edited by David H. Flaherty and Frank E. Manning, 104–22. Montreal and Kingston: McGill-Queen's University Press, 1993.

Morley, David. *Family Television: Cultural Power and Domestic Leisure*. London: Comedia, 1986.

Morley, David and Kevin Robins. *Spaces of Identity: Global Media, Electronic Landscapes and Cultural Boundaries*. London: Routledge, 1995.

Murray, Susan and Laurie Ouellette. *Reality TV: Remaking Television Culture*. New York: New York University Press, 2004.

Paget, Derek. *No Other Way to Tell It: Dramadoc/Docudrama on Television*. Manchester: Manchester University Press, 1998.

Peers, Frank W. *The Public Eye: Television and the Politics of Canadian Broadcasting, 1952–1968*. Toronto: University of Toronto Press, 1979.

Peters, John Durham. "Seeing Bifocally: Media, Place, Culture." In *Culture, Power, Place: Explorations in Critical Anthropology*, edited by Akhil Gupta and James Ferguson, 75–92. Durham, NC: Duke University Press, 1997.

Raboy, M. "Public Broadcasting." In *The Cultural Industries in Canada*, edited by Michael Dorland, 178–202. Toronto: Lorimer, 1996.

———. *Les médias québecois: presse, radio, television, inforoute*. Montreal: Gaetan Morin, 2000.

Rutherford, Paul. *When Television Was Young: Primetime Canada, 1952–1967*. Toronto: University of Toronto Press, 1990.

Sconce, Jeffrey. "What If? Charting Television's New Textual Boundaries." In *Television After TV: Essays on a Medium in Transition*, edited by Lynn Spigel and Jan Olsson, 93–112. Durham, NC: Duke University Press, 2004.

Sinclair, John, Elizabeth Jacka, and Stuart Cunningham, eds. *New Patterns in Global Television: Peripheral Vision*. New York: Oxford University Press, 1996.

Smythe, Dallas. *Dependency Road: Communication, Capitalism, Consciousness and Canada*. Norwood, NJ: Ablex, 1981.

Spigel, Lynn. *Make Room for TV: Television and the Family Ideal in Postwar America*. Chicago: University of Chicago Press, 1992.

Tinic, Serra. *On Location: Canada's Television Industry in a Global Market*. Toronto: University of Toronto Press, 2005.

Tolusso, Susan. "CRTC TV Policy." *Playback*, June 28, 1999. Available at www.playbackonline.ca/articles/magazine/19990628/26004.html. Accessed December 20, 2007.

Urquhart, Peter, and Ira Wagman. "Considering Canadian Television: Intersections, Missed Directions, Prospects for Textual Expansion." Introduction to special issue edited by Urquhart and Wagman, *Canadian Journal of Film Studies* 15 (1) (Spring 2006).

PART ONE

Narrating Nation

DAVID HOGARTH

Reenacting Canada

The Nation-State as an Object of Desire in
the Early Years of Canadian Broadcasting

Recent backlashes from as far afield as Europe, Australia, and Canada against television reenactments and dramatizations can make it easy to forget just how important these types of programs have been in defining public service broadcasting, not only as a medium of truth but as a medium of beauty.[1] The truth value of dramatizations has been widely considered elsewhere, with Canadian research focusing on various types of "sociological journalism" designed to edify viewers when adequate factual material was not available.[2] But in this chapter, I want to consider these programs as something else entirely—not just as make-do vehicles for "actual" sounds and images, but as techniques to create spectacles that viewers might long to see. Here I focus on the hopes expressed by producers in the early years of Canadian television that dramatizations might make the nation an object of audiovisual pleasure.

In doing so, my aim is to call into question the usual association of public broadcasting with social realism and sober modernity. We often hear that early pundits and policymakers valued Canadian broadcasting for its careful and considered deployment of sounds and images in the pursuit of truth. But I would argue that these views—famously expressed by the Massey Commission, which presided over the introduction of Canadian television in 1952—were rather at odds with actual broadcast practice at the time.[3] By the early 1950s, broadcast journalists were quite adept at staging, rehearsing, and revamping interviews; aurally and visually enhancing location material; and making free and generally enthusiastic use of dramatizations of historical events and current affairs. More than just a substitute for truth gone missing, these programs were integral efforts to "bring the country alive," as one producer of the day put it, and even to make it the "stuff of dreams."[4] In this chapter, then, I want to examine dramatizations as fantasyscapes and consider what they tell us about public service broadcasting, specifically about its "modern" past and its "postmodern" future as it attempts to reconfigure itself as a purveyor of spectacle as well as learning in a digital age.

Dramatizations as Fact

Given their prominence in early public broadcasting schedules, dramatizations are somewhat neglected in media histories and memoirs. In hindsight, at least, Canadian broadcasters tended to give pride of place to their undramatized work—that is, to the "as found" sights and sounds they recorded across the country without the benefit of staging or artificial enhancement. In broadcasters' memoirs, on-the-fly actuality looms large.[5]

But program schedules and production documents suggest that producers also took pride in the way they managed to dramatize and reenact factual material and thus make it more compelling for their audiences. Indeed, for all the attention given to real-life recording, reenactments and dramatizations were arguably the true foundation of Canadian broadcast realism. Dramatico-musical information programs were a staple on radio in the late 1920s, as were reenacted histories, dramatized farm broadcasts, and fictionalized war reports in the decades that followed. Radio public affairs producers made frequent use of poetry, drama, and theatre after the war, and so did their television counterparts in the early 1950s. Most of these shows enjoyed the enthusiastic support of policymakers, pundits, and educational authorities across the country. And many received awards for public service excellence in Canada and the United States.[6]

Clearly, much of this programming was designed to be factual if not actual. That is, it was primarily intended to *credibly* represent Canada, and more specifically to realistically depict the nation in a way that suited public broadcasters at the time. In this sense, dramatizations had distinct advantages over actuality reporting in the factual realm. First, many of the programs were seen to represent Canada in all its variety, from a range of perspectives. Composite characters and their stories were used to investigate issues of the day, such as mental health, racism, and business cycles, in a reliable and representative way. Dramatized characters meant to be typical, such as "Joe Alcoholic" and "Mr. Down and Out"—sometimes the pseudonyms were less apocryphal—could be viewed from various positions, either intimate or diagnostic, and in this sense they were often considered to be more revealing than any particular stories or angles on them. Designed to display the deep patterns of everyday life, these programs employed a range of techniques that apparently uncovered not just surface facts but

Canada's core and essence. Dramatizations worked, for instance, to construct national averages. Experts were regularly consulted to help create composite characters and stories, free of the random realities and scattered truths—the dreaded anomalies—of actuality reporting. At the CBC, scripts were often checked with social scientists, and radio shows like *Cross Section* worked to "present all sides of various controversial topics."[7] Other programs drew their authority from the everyday experience of "average Canadians," with the writer of the CBC Radio program *In Search of Ourselves* "trotting downstairs" to talk to his landlady to research a story about menopause for a national broadcast.[8] In these cases, dramatizations were chiefly valued as useful illustrations of "life as it is." "Accuracy is an absolute must," declared one producer at the time. "To give misleading information in these programs would be terrifying."[9] Dramatizations can thus be understood as a convenient epistemological device and a plausible barometer of the national broadcaster's mood and development.

At the same time, dramatizations served to fulfill more political aspects of the CBC's social realist agenda. Dramatized productions could be appreciated by both anglophone and francophone audiences in a way pure actuality could not because they could be produced in twin versions for each community, thus bringing together a national audience. They also brought together French and English producers, thus serving as symbols of cross-cultural collaboration in Canadian programming.[10] And they allowed the corporation to deliver "comprehensive" programming in the most cost-efficient way, with drama documentaries, film features, and live reports all funnelled into one show "accommodat[ing] a great many different program areas and ideas."[11] Finally, and crucially, dramatized programs allowed the CBC to explore the more remote reaches of Canadian life, past, present, and future. Historical reenactments enabled the network to investigate the undocumented past that was no longer available for conventional reportage. Contemporary dramatizations let the CBC investigate the lives of contemporary Canadians who were sometimes reluctant to speak on air.[12] And future-oriented material allowed producers to consider scenarios facing the nation in years to come. In this way, reenacted television programs explored the various time–space trajectories of the nation in apparently credible and comprehensive ways.

Dramatizations were thus anything but "frivolous" or "fantastic" from a public broadcaster's point of view. These shows were considered solid pedagogical tools and listening in was, by some accounts, never meant to be a pleasant or diverting experience. Many producers saw dramatizations and reenactments as purely instructional and essentially at odds with entertainment per se. Some claimed to have no time for "frilly conventions" and the idle pastimes of fiction.[13] Others frowned upon neat dramatic resolutions of any kind. And a good many regarded escapist pleasures with disdain. If CBC audiences found the gloomy topics and dangling storylines hard to take and harder to follow—and some audience studies suggested they did—their complaints were often dismissed as "misunderstandings" of real life as it was translated for the airwaves. Producers hoped that viewers would get used to the rigours of social realism and, in time, come to appreciate actuality in its purest—and most austere—form.[14]

Dramatizations as Fantasy

But there was another way of seeing dramatizations. These productions were also part of an enormously ambitious effort to make the nation appealing in broadcast form. That is, beyond being workhorse vehicles for truth, dramatizations were produced and promoted as sensual texts whose sights and sounds might evoke pleasures altogether different from those of the known, the familiar, or even the epistemologically warranted. Dramatizations and reenactments might be faithful reproductions of the real, but they could also be fantasyscapes, fact-based story worlds that viewers would long to inhabit and experience in the fullest, most sensual sense of the word.

Dramatization as such had its own technologies and techniques. In the 1930s, special workshops were established to train actors in real accents and rhythms of Canadian speech. In 1938, a sound effects department was set up in Toronto to archive and create material for use in more conventional actuality reports. And in the decade that followed, CBC technicians developed specialized equipment for playback and mixing of actual and simulated material. Even before the appearance of television, a full-fledged lexicon of dramatization had emerged at the CBC, conceived as something more than a mere instrument of recorded actuality or factual transmission.

This lexicon was designed to make Canada not just familiar but fascinating, as production documents of the time make clear. Actors were encouraged to develop characters that audiences would "want to spend time with." Writers were urged to develop "intriguing storylines," gloomy or not, sometimes taking their cues from daytime radio dramas, the much-reviled antithesis of actuality in its purest form. And producers were taught to guide listeners through diverse segments of the new actuality package, helping them make the switch "from information to drama and back again" as occasions required.[15]

Producers of all types drew upon varied backgrounds to enliven dramatizations in these ways. Writers in the Talks and Public Affairs Department,
where many of the shows were produced, flaunted their backgrounds in
journalism and theatre. Arthur Hiller was both a playwright and clinical
psychologist who valued plausibility, instructing his players in the "emotions aroused by the lines themselves."[16] Frank Willis billed himself as a
singer, writer, poet, and documentarist who aimed for smooth "effortless
transition[s]" between drama and actuality reportage. And Thom Benson was a self-styled topical dramatist, "fascinated by narratives in real
form."[17]

Other producers worked to both document and embellish Canadian life,
and they apparently saw little contradiction between reportage and seductive storytelling. Beginning in the late 1930s, story editors used standard
boom microphones to represent main storylines and specialized cardioid
microphones to signal flashbacks, guiding listeners through what one
supervisor called "robust and profound, multi-layered tales of Canada."
Musicians enhanced the listening experience with musical scores that created "emotional emphasis" in "short sequential form." And sound engineers worked to "augment existing sounds to create a more fulfilling
experience."[18] These techniques were designed not only to deliver information but also to attract and accommodate audiences to new story worlds
in pleasurable ways.

Dramatizations were thus designed to "paint a picture in sound," as producers of the time put it. Programming of this type would instruct listeners, but it would also "involve [them] so that they share the experiences
being presented," according to the script editor of the radio show *Cross
Section*.[19] Clearly, CBC producers wanted audiences to immerse themselves in Canadian actuality, rather than simply learn from it in a detached,
civic-minded fashion. In this way, they used these dramatizations to inspire
new types of affective citizenship.

Televised Dramatizations

In the realm of television, we see the same efforts to psychically engage
Canadians. Like its radio counterpart, televised actuality has been generally viewed not as alluring or affective programming, but as a backup vehicle for factual recording where truth, for whatever reason, has gone missing.
But such an epistemologically-oriented approach fails to account for prevailing understandings of technology and the marketplace in the early
1950s—understandings that led producers to seek out entertaining information in a variety of forms.

To begin with, public broadcasters desperately sought to attract mass audiences to factual material in the early years of television. Indeed, programmers not only had to attract viewers for their own fact-based programming, but they had to win many more viewers over from competing US fare. The CBC thus searched in the early 1950s for factual shows that would have higher ratings potential than conventional actuality programs.[20] To be sure, breathless accounts of the day suggested that actuality could do the trick, with live or recorded as-found material hopefully amassing—and amazing—a new Canadian mass audience. Television documentarists promised a master view of Canada with an array of cameras and lenses "do[ing] for the TV image what binoculars or small telescopes do for the spectator's vision."[21] Other producers offered a more lyrical perspective and a new "poetry of the tripod."[22] Even lowly current affairs shows promised viewers a compelling on-screen experience, with a CBC *Newsmagazine* feature on arts schools, for instance, positioning its cameras outside windows, on the pavement, and on toy wagons to give viewers the impression they were "going in there" with reporter Harry Rassky.[23] In programs like these, cameras were concealed, seamless narratives constructed, and viewers "delegated" to the televisual gaze—in theory, at least.

But most of these efforts never came to much. Field reporters may have made better use of camera stands and dolly shots, but, by their own admission, many of the images were "flat."[24] It was not just that the recording equipment of the day was immobile—even fixed shoots were a challenge. Winter filming was a logistical nightmare throughout the 1950s, requiring jerry-rigged generators to prevent freeze-ups. Summer projects often had to shut down when dampness ruined cable connections and darkness shut down picture range. Even stay-at-home reports were problematic, as Canadians tended to be more cowed than compelling as speaking subjects. One interviewee for the 1959 documentary special *This Electronic World*, for instance, described the recording equipment that had invaded his apartment as a "revelation to the layman" that left him sadly "stuck for words" the moment filming began.[25] The sights and sounds of the Canadian wilderness could sometimes be secured with less fuss—here were the captive subjects many documentarists dreamed of—but even this material tended to be "fuzzy, choppy and still" by the time it reached the screen.[26] This was hardly captivating stuff, and certainly not very fertile ground for immersive spectatorship. CBC producers themselves acknowledged that factual television would have to be something more than actual in an as-found sense if it were to retain its interest for a Canadian audience.

Thus, by default, dramatization emerged as a foundational form of Canadian actuality. Not surprisingly, the CBC made early efforts to feature it prominently in the factual television schedule, just as it had in its radio lineups. In April 1952, before Canadian television went on the air, the corporation hired American broadcast consultant Gilbert Seldes to give a ten-day workshop on "fact and fiction" programs, based on his book *Writing for Television*. Seldes insisted television actuality must combine many techniques—demonstration, dramatization, and discussion—and utilize "the entire range of the documentary image" to keep viewers tuned in.[27] Dramatization, he argued, was an essential tool in the television actuality kit. Careful reenactment, for instance, alerted viewers to important themes and undercurrents. It positioned the audience in relation to images on screen. And it rarely "lost" its viewers or left them to find their own meanings in the material being presented. The precision and economy of dramatized sounds and images was vital in guiding viewers through the multidiegetic spaces—studios, field locations, and attendant modes of address—of the new tabloid information shows.

CBC producers were apparently persuaded by Seldes's theories of audience engagement. Even pedagogically-minded stalwarts like Eugene Hallman acknowledged that televised actuality would need to proceed "more along the lines of the theatrical newsreel than sound news." TV pictures, he noted, had a "high emotional and a low intellectual appeal," and simply offering viewers a factual record of Canadian life would not suffice.[28] Hallman's colleagues in sales and marketing tended to agree. Indeed, early experience in a more or less competitive North American broadcast market suggested viewers tended to drift off and tune out when it came to conventional reportage. By 1954, for instance, four television affiliates had stopped carrying *Scope*, a heavily promoted series from the Talks and Public Affairs Department, because viewers were apparently dissatisfied with its "egghead" approach to current affairs and its "cold, conceptual way of dealing with everyday topics," as one disgruntled supervisor put it.[29]

Not that dramatized material was particularly adventurous by contrast. We should keep in mind that restrictions on sounds and images, dramatized or not, were severe indeed in the early 1950s. Technical journals like *Radio* decreed that television depictions must be carefully deployed so as not to lose the viewer. Producers should avoid disorienting jump-cuts. They should make frequent use of dissolves, fades, and rapid transitions to provide an image with "vitality." They should employ close-ups, simple sets, and careful framing to suit limited screen resolutions. And they should back this material up with sounds that "underline the image in a tangible way."[30]

But, staid or not, dramatizations were seen to suit television's emerging realist aesthetic—its aesthetic of involvement—in a way that conventional actuality reporting did not. Dramatized sounds and images had the advantage over their as-found counterparts of being carefully planned and executed on location and thereby employed to the best effect. Their sounds and images could be composed in studio conditions in the most effective ways possible. Their sets and shots could be matched to the presumed exigencies of the small, flickering screen image. And their segments could be carefully edited as part of a seamless narrative that presumably encouraged viewers to lose themselves, as well learn from, actuality on the air.

None of these techniques were available to conventional actuality producers of the time. Post-production manipulation of sound and images was virtually nonexistent in the early days of television, leaving dramatizations and reenactments as the only space of actuality where broadcasters could exert true audiovisual control. A new generation of producers thus used these innovations to construct a new rhetoric of the real that would benefit from their own experience in broadcasting. CBC *Graphic* producer Sidney Newman dramatized events on location, inspired by his earlier work in New York as part of an NBC "live theatrical programming" crew. Thom Benson was more familiar with the studio because of his experience with Canadian theatre and television drama. Alan King filmed wherever circumstances warranted, enjoying his freedom to portray real-life stories without worrying about "credibility." Dramatization producers thus drew upon a number of genres and geographical traditions to depict Canada in vivid and novel ways to make viewers feel that "what they are seeing on screen is really here."[31]

These efforts become clearer when we examine some of the shows themselves in more detail. In a February 5, 1958, edition of the CBC's *Close-Up*, for instance, Frank Willis tells a tale that is almost impossible to imagine in as-found form—at least in a neat and compact package like the following.

"Our reporters at the ready in *Close-Up*," Willis announces, "a program designed to stimulate opinion." Instead of handing things over to the field crew, Willis continues to speak from the studio. "And now a story we have seen before, which this reporter believes is worth another look." The camera cuts to an image of a woman, liquor bottle in hand, sitting alone at the kitchen table. "It's Christmas time again. No family in sight. No friends. Problems at work." A shot appears of a quarrel with a colleague, followed by another image of the kitchen again. "Sadness—nothing but sadness. What can we do to help her?"

This is a signature piece for Willis, who often set the scene for dramatized segments in an authoritative way, speaking for himself, for the characters, for his show, and for the viewers at home. As dated and overbearing as his approach may now seem, it was viewed as a major advance in "personalized journalism" at the time. In the view of one supervisor, he was a "major motivating factor for viewer interest" who, by speaking for an array of subjects, brought "the story together and the viewer along with him."[32] In Willis's stories, as in many others, hosts encouraged viewers to "get involved" with the stories of the nation, guiding them through the varied diegeses of televised actuality.

Jo Kowin's dramatized work for the show *Explorations* was quite different in that it eschewed narration of any kind, but it too encouraged viewers to identify with their fellow Canadians in a lasting way. Kowin's aim was to construct portraits not just of "deep social significance" but with "frank visual appeal." Her self-styled "thought-sync" productions differed from scripted, studio-based projects, with the producer visiting her subjects at home, encouraging them to discuss their problems on a "very personal level," and drawing up a list of possible visuals, ambient sounds, and spoken phrases to set the stage for "reenactments of a most intimate kind." Kowin thus set out to dramatize in a "direct and moving way the thoughts, sensations and aspirations" of Canadians across the country.[33] In this way, viewers were encouraged to intimately identify—beyond a conventional actual engagement—with the characters they were seeing on screen. For all the differences, Willis and Kowin share a commitment to inform and involve viewers, with at least equal emphasis on the latter.

Programs like these thus remind us that, in its golden age, Canada's defining public medium was more than just a vehicle of information or social realism. It was also a full-fledged apparatus of desire designed to invoke new modes of attachment to the nation in all its represented forms. This dual emphasis is evident in actuality programs themselves and in the ways they were promoted by producers and pundits of the time. It is worth emphasizing that neither Willis nor Kowin nor their colleagues expressed much concern about the truth value or realism of their work. Their supervisors similarly made no efforts to graphically mark the shows as interpretation or entertainment. And critics routinely applauded the projects for their illumination of Canadian life, with little further epistemological discussion. Anxieties about the inherent dishonesty or manipulativeness of dramatized actuality were heard in the 1950s, but not nearly as loudly or as often as they were in the decades that followed, when the interpretive power of journalists came to be more widely debated in Canadian cultural discourse. Dramatized segments were sometimes scrutinized in program documents, periodically critiqued in press reviews, and occasionally flagged in the shows themselves, but usually much more casually than they were in the "infotainment" age that followed.[34]

In fact, in the first decade of Canadian television, producers, pundits, and policymakers tended to focus more on the pleasures than the plausibilities of dramatized programming. Beyond being fakes, dramatized shows were feared to be "non-events," as one supervisor put it in 1955, calling into question not just the integrity of their production methods but the relevance of their subject matter—the nation-state and its doings.[35] Whatever the style or approach, producers feared that actuality television might reveal Canada to be not just an elusive object of representation but a dull one: a nowhere land, a place of lugubrious landscapes and silent subjects, a place to be ignored and not just misunderstood. In this view, widely shared at the height of the public service era, television's job was to provide not only a convincing image of Canada but a captivating one, offering not just the cerebral joys of recognition but the more sensual pleasures of discovery. This was a new subject for television's roving eye—a land waiting to be explored, inhabited, and dramatically enhanced as the occasion required.

Conclusion

Rethinking dramatizations and reenactments requires us to rethink public service broadcasting, "post-public television," and more specifically the distinction that is often made between the "information" and "infotainment" eras. Clearly, categorical periodizations like these are of limited use in understanding Canadian factual broadcasting. After all, as Emily West has pointed out, information is an ongoing concern in the "infotainment" age as broadcasters seek out new forms of popular and journalistic evidence to credibly represent the nation.[36] By the same token, entertainment was a constant preoccupation in the golden age of "information" as public service producers sought out dramatic styles to make the nation not just convincing but compelling—a sight to be seen, heard, and pleasurably experienced in audiovisual ways. In this respect, current efforts to purvey beauty as well as truth through public broadcasting may be less novel or particular to the digital age than some observers have made out.[37] Public broadcasters made extensive efforts to make the nation spectacular in the 1950s, and these efforts should make us question not just the traditional binaries used to explain Canadian broadcasting over time but some of the categorical assumptions we make about television today.

Notes

1 I am using these terms the way they were used in CBC production documents in the 1940s and '50s. At the time, "reenactments" were seen to be firmly grounded in actual events or testimony, while "dramatizations" were understood to be based more loosely on historical fact, often without the benefits of transcripts or eyewitness accounts but usually with the help of expert consultants. For the sake of brevity, I sometimes use "dramatization" as an umbrella term. See Hogarth, *Realer Than Reel.*

2 Hogarth, *Documentary Television in Canada.*

3 Canada. *Report of the Royal Commission on National Development in the Arts, Letters and Sciences, 1949–1951*(the *Massey Report*).

4 Boyle, *Appendix B.*

5 For a broadcaster's history of Canadian dramatizations, see Stewart, *From Coast to Coast.* For academic accounts, see Feldman, "The Electronic Fable," 41; and Miller, *Turn Up the Contrast.*

6 *CBC Times,* 19–25 May 1950, 2.

7 *CBC Times,* 6–12 August 1948, 11.

8 *CBC Times,* 21–27 May 1951, 5.

9 *CBC Times,* 6–13 March 1954, 2–4.

10 Hallman, PG 1–13, pt. 2.

11 See Hogarth, *Documentary Television in Canada,* 86–88.

12 While some "average" Canadians were willing to serve as off-the-record consultants, most were too shy to speak on air. "They're very stiff, and sometimes distrustful," complained one producer, who noted that even actual interviews had to be rehearsed or reenacted many times over. "It's not easy bringing passion to the surface." See Boyle, *Appendix B.* Reenactments were thus more than a second-best documentary material. They were instead an acknowledgement that Canada—as imagined by its broadcasters—only emerged through stimulation and even outright simulation.

13 Dilworth, PG 1–13, pt. 2.

14 Dilworth, PG 1–13, pt. 2.

15 Boyle, *Appendix B.*

16 *CBC Times,* 7–13 November 1954, 6.

17 *CBC Times,* 22–28 December 1957, 4.

18 *CBC Times,* 22–28 December 1957, 4.

19 *CBC Times,* 25–31 May 1952, 2.

20 See Hogarth, *Documentary Television in Canada,* 159.

21 *CBC Times,* 26 February–3 March 1953, 1.

22 *CBC Times,* 26 February–3 March 1953, 1.

23 *CBC Times,* 23–29 August 1953, 5.

24 Gillis, "Talks and Public Affairs," 9.

25 *CBC Times,* 2–8 January 1960, 30.

26 Boyle, *Appendix B,* 2.

27 Seldes, *Writing for Television,* 192

28 CBC Agenda, PG 1–13, pt. 2.

29 CBC Minutes, PG 1–13, pt. 2.

30 Wright, "For Better Cutting on Television."
31 *CBC Times*, 13–19 January 1957, 5.
32 McDonald, CBC Memorandum, PG 1–13.
33 Kowin, *Explorations*, PG1, pt. 1.
34 See Hogarth, *Documentary Television in Canada*, 86–88.
35 Hallman, PG 1–13, pt. 1.
36 West, "Selling Canada to Canadians."
37 Wheatley, "The Limits of Television."

References

Boyle, Harry. CBC National Conference, Outside Broadcasts Department, 27 November–1 December 1961. *Appendix B*, CBC National Archives Papers, RG 41, series A-V-2, vol. 851, PG 1–13, pt. 3.

Canada. *Report of the Royal Commision on National Development in the Arts, Letters and Sciences, 1949–1951* (the *Massey Report*). Ottawa: King's Printer, 1951.

CBC National Program Office Meeting, Agenda, 17–18 November 1953: 8. CBC National Archives Papers, RG 41, series A-V-2, vol. 988, PG 1–13, pt. 2.

CBC National Program Office Meeting, Minutes, 2–4 March 1953: 3. RG 41, series A-V-2, vol. 988, PG 1–13, pt. 2.

CBC Times, 6–13 March 1954: 2–4.

CBC Times, 7–13 November 1954: 6.

CBC Times, 13–19 January 1957: 5.

CBC Times, 19–25 May 1950: 2.

CBC Times, 21–27 May 1951: 5.

CBC Times, 22–28 December 1957: 4.

CBC Times, 23–29 August 1953: 5.

CBC Times, 25–31 May 1952: 2.

CBC Times, 26 February–3 March 1953: 1.

CBC Times, 2–8 January 1960: 30.

CBC Times, 6–12 August 1948: 11.

Dilworth, Ira. CBC Internal Memorandum, *Explorations*, 5 March 1959: 1. CBC National Archives Papers, RG 41, series A-V-2, vol. 988, PG 1–13, pt. 2.

Feldman, Seth. "The Electronic Fable: Aspects of the Docudrama in Canada." *Canadian Drama* 8 (1983): 41

Gillis, H. "Talks and Public Affairs." *Radio*, April (1958): 9.

Hallman, Eugene. Documentary Series. CBC Internal Memorandum, 9 December 1955. CBC National Archives Papers, RG 41, series A-V-2, vol. 988, PG 1–13.

Hogarth, David. *Documentary Television in Canada: From National Public Service to Global Marketplace*. Montreal and Kingston: McGill-Queen's University Press, 2002.

Hogarth, David. *Realer Than Reel: Global Directions in Documentary*. Austin: University of Texas Press, 2006.

Kowin, J. CBC Internal Memorandum, *Explorations*, 26 August 1956: 2. CBC National Archives Papers, RG41, series A-V-2, vol. 895, PG1, pt. 1.

McDonald, P. CBC Internal Memorandum, 24 February 1958: 1. CBC National Archives Papers, RG 41, series A-V-2, vol. 876, PG 1–13.

Miller, Mary Jane. *Turn Up the Contrast: CBC Television Drama since 1952.* Vancouver: University of British Columbia Press and CBC Enterprises, 1987.

Seldes, Gilbert. *Writing for Television.* New York: Doubleday, 1952.

Stewart, Sandy. *From Coast to Coast: A Personal History of Radio in Canada.* Toronto: CBC Enterprises, 1985.

West, Emily. "Selling Canada to Canadians: Collective Memory, National Identity and Popular Culture." *Critical Studies in Media Communication* 19 (2002): 212–229.

Wheatley, Helen. "The Limits of Television." *European Journal of Cultural Studies* 7 (2004): 325–39.

Wright, Harold. "For Better Cutting on Television." *Radio*, January (1954): 16–17.

Filmography

Radio Programs
Cross Section (CBC, 1946–56)
In Search of Ourselves (CBC, 1948–52)
Wednesday Night (CBC, 1947–63)

Television Programs
Close-Up (CBC, 1957–63)
This Electronic World (CBC, 1959)
Explorations (CBC, 1956–63)
Graphic (CBC, 1956–57)
Newsmagazine (CBC, 1952–81)
Scope (CBC, 1954–55)

LYLE DICK

Representing National History on Television

The Case of *Canada: A People's History*

The proliferation of public history in the past decade included the expansion of historical productions into electronic media, enabling authors to reach larger audiences than ever before. Alongside treatments of local or regional topics, national history became a focus for major television series sponsored by public broadcasting corporations in various countries. These included the BBC's sixteen-part documentary series *A History of Britain*, narrated by the well-known historian Simon Schama, and recent additions to Ken Burns's canon of historical film productions in the United States. In Canada, the CBC broadcast its seventeen-part series *Canada: A People's History* in 2000 and 2001. These productions have employed varying forms, including non-fictional documentaries, historical dramas, and assorted hybrids under the rubric of docudramas, comprising an enormous shift in the ways of presenting historical information to the public. This chapter will explore some of the issues arising from the application of particular narrative forms in just one of these historical television productions—the CBC's *Canada: A People's History*.

Canada: A People's History was the largest production to date on Canadian history. Its impact and legacy flowed from an unprecedented scale and convergence of television and book production, sales of numerous products, and marketing. These efforts included CD-ROMs, children's books, documentaries on specific historical topics, a documentary on the making of the series, and a book, *Making History*, by executive producer Mark Starowicz. The series has been frequently broadcast on CBC Television and other networks. But amid the ubiquitous airing of episodes, display and selling of books and videos in stores, stocking of school and university library shelves, and use of these products in high school and post-secondary school courses, the actual form and content of this production has received inadequate critical attention relative to its presence on the Canadian historical landscape. This chapter identifies some of the operative narrative forms of *Canada: A People's History* and their implications for understanding authorial intention and audience reception. The series reveals much about the specific circumstances, time, and place of its production, so the chapter will also seek to place its particular forms—narrative structures, images, music—and content—topics, personalities, and events—within the specific historical and cultural contexts of its production.

The CBC's Objectives for *Canada: A People's History*

While it is difficult to find a concise statement of objectives for this series, the CBC's intentions can be gleaned from various remarks by its producers and executives and their interpretation of their mandate under Canada's Broadcasting Act of 1991. The clearest statement appears on the CBC History Home Page in the section titled "Canada: A People's History—Merchandise." Beneath sales promotions for VHS and PAL tapes, DVDs, books, CDs, "Kids' Books," T-shirts, coasters, and playing cards, it states: "*Canada: A People's History* chronicles the human drama that is Canada's journey from past to present. Diaries, letters and archival documents tell the stories of those who shaped this country, in their own words. Using historical re-enactments, dazzling photography and digital special effects, *Canada: A People's History* presents Canada as you've never seen it: a riveting account of our history, through the eyes of the people who lived it."[1] The emphasis on presenting Canadian history as the story of "those who shaped this country" confirmed the makers' preoccupation with narrating a story of building the nation-state of 1867. Their objective was consistent with one of the main components of the CBC's mandate as set out in the Broadcasting Act of 1969: to "contribute to the development of national unity and provide for a continuing expression of Canadian identity." The updated 1991 version of the act reiterated much the same objective in its reference to the CBC's role of building a "shared national consciousness and identity."[2] Mark Starowicz, the series' executive producer, expressed similar objectives in his assessment of the audience's response to his production. In an interview published in 2002, Starowicz observed that in his historical series, "There is a profound streak of wishing to maintain Canadian sovereignty."[3]

The series can also be placed within the economic and cultural contexts of the mid- to late 1990s, when the CBC was experiencing a number of pressures associated with the extension of cable TV networks in North America, increasing penetration of Canadian television markets by American channels, and a diminishing revenue base from advertising and government appropriations. Throughout the 1990s, the corporation sustained a series of cutbacks. Between 1994 and 1998, its core funding was reduced by about one-third, from $1.6 billion a year to about $1.1 billion, and by 1999, it was reported to have stabilized at $800 million.[4] In the same period, heightened nationalism in Quebec, culminating in the narrow referendum result in 1995, shook the confidence of Canada's national cultural institutions about the future of the federal state and their role within it. In an atmosphere of crisis, the documentary unit of CBC-TV discerned the potential to propose a large-scale television series on Canadian history, which was readily endorsed by the corporation's executives and televised in seventeen parts in 2000 and 2001.[5] The project also included the production of two large books summarizing the narrative line of the TV production, as well as numerous other product lines, affording opportunities to generate revenues and boost ratings while enhancing patriotism.[6]

Documentary Form

For the series' producers, a key step was determining an appropriate form to fulfill their objectives. Film scholar Bill Nichols has identified four modes of representation in the making of documentaries: expository, observational, interactive, and reflexive.[7] Within each of these modes, documentaries position themselves between two poles of representation: narrative, encompassing chronology, moral and ideological argument; and realist, or techniques of mimetic verisimilitude. For the CBC series, Starowicz and his team drew on both forms of representation, placing this series within the category of docudrama, which has been defined as "a mode of representation that ... combines categories usually perceived as separate: documentary and drama."[8] The producers followed in the tradition of earlier CBC docudramas, especially *The National Dream*, a miniseries adaptation of Pierre Berton's books on the building of the Canadian Pacific Railway, in presenting extended sequences of third-person voice-over narration, alternating between on-camera narration by actors representing historical figures and dramatized reenactments of episodes from Canadian history. Both series focused on the heroic role of famous historical players and dramatizations of stories associated with their subject.

In formal terms, the book's authors sought to present history diachronically, as a procession of events in linear sequence from a selected point of departure to an end point, in this case 1990. Such an approach is familiar to many Canadians and has been a staple of historical writing from the early national histories of the post-Confederation era to the Canadian

Centenary Series, a more scholarly version of the national narrative published by McClelland & Stewart between 1962 and 1988.[9] For the CBC, the decision to take a "narrative" approach represented a deliberate rejection of a trend toward thematic or synchronic approaches represented in more recent academic scholarship of the past twenty years. In his foreword to the series' books, Starowicz asserted a need for "a narrative cleansing of Canadian history." He explained: "We have bleached the dramatic narrative out of Canadian history and reduced it to social studies units in our schools," adding, "This is a narrative work, not an academic work."[10] In a panel discussion on visual history, CBC producer Gene Allen, director of research for the series and the book, observed that "most television producers are deeply attached to the narrative mode, to telling the audience what happened, and what happened next, and how it turned out." Asserting that "this narrative orientation is shared at an almost instinctive level by the dozens of different people I've worked with over that time," he added, "We talk among ourselves about maintaining the suspension of disbelief, about making the audience feel as if they're inside the story as it unfolds."[11] For the authors of *Canada: A People's History*, verisimilitude, or the representation of "real-life" events in narrative form, and maintaining the suspension of disbelief were the keys to presenting Canadian history successfully to a general audience.

To realize their goal, the authors relied on a single overarching story, a largely sequential treatment of selected events to illustrate the emergence and development of the modern nation-state from the pre-contact era to the present. Within this structure, selected stories from a variety of observers were included as testimonials and quoted to reinforce the main narrative line. The CBC's website informs us that for the television series, Starowicz heeded advice to broadcast the same story on both the French- and the English-language networks. "So the co-production, with one story, one executive producer, and one team was born."[12] The principle of presenting "one story" also applied to the book: for each of its component narratives, a single version—the version supporting the plot and the overriding narrative objectives—was advanced. The book's focus on "one story" of a single "people" was reinforced by the narration, a story as told by a single voice. Throughout the narrative, the story was revealed by an impersonal and authoritative narrator whose statements were almost invariably structured as declarations and rarely as questions. The focus on "one story" was reinforced by the timeline on the series' website, which was presented as a linear progression covering 15,000 years from a single point of view. This approach contrasted with the BBC's *History of Britain*, which presented five different timelines: a British timeline, but, reflecting the different histories of its constituent nationalities, also English, Scottish, Welsh, and Northern Ireland timelines.[13]

Starowicz and his team also explicitly rejected the use of commentators. In the CBC's video documentary on the making of the series *Making History*, the narrator stated, "Although there are dozens of historians behind the scenes, one of the surprises for viewers is the conspicuous absence of on-screen academics." Gordon Henderson, senior producer of *Canada: A People's History* elaborated: "I think one of the really cool things about the series is that we don't have historians that come on, analysts that come on with a tie and a tweed jacket and a bookcase behind, explaining what we just saw, giving you perspective. I mean, I'm all for perspective, but I'd rather see the narrative driven, I'd rather see the story kept alive. We want to avoid history class—we want to keep telling stories." Accordingly, the producers attempted to chart the human history of Canada in chronological sequence from its early, pre-contact origins to the year 1990. In *Making History*, Starowicz explained his decision to take a narrative approach:

> There are a lot of ways you could do the history of Canada. You could do it thematically, or, you know, one episode on labour, or another episode on women, or another episode on ethnic groups. We chose to do it chronologically, which is quite a challenge, I mean, the history of Canada begins about 20,000 years ago. And why? Because the central unifying idea of Canadian history is, once there was nothing here, so that's why we chose to do it as the growth of an entire United Nations of peoples, because that's the story in the end, and that's why we decided to go back 20,000 years and begin when there was nothing.[14]

The producers divided the narrative into seventeen episodes treating historical periods of varying lengths. Apart from its opening episode, the narrative segments resembled the temporal divisions selected for the Canadian Centenary Series, with similar turning points and time frames in both. The principal difference was that the first book of the centenary series began with early Viking approaches and concluded in 1632 in the era of New France, while the CBC's opening episode was devoted to both the pre-contact and early post-contact history of Aboriginal peoples.[15] As well, the centenary series included some books with overlapping chronologies treating different areas of the country, while the CBC series largely avoided simultaneous stories that did not feed into the main narrative line, a single chronology of the advent of Western societies in northern North America from early beginnings to the present.

The selected entry point for the first episode was the arrival of Aboriginal peoples in northern North America from Asia, presumed to have occurred around 15000 BCE, while the segment concluded in the post-contact era, around 1800 CE. It culminated in John Jewitt's well-known and highly embellished story of the alleged massacre of the crew of the ship *Boston* by members of the Mowachaht Nation, ending with a dramatization of Chief Maquinna shedding tears over Jewitt's departure for the United States. This sentimental vignette served a narrative purpose, as it set up a flash-forward to a report that Maquinna, in his later years and "hobbled by rheumatism," was still welcoming traders to his people's shores. The final, resonating message of the first episode was that Aboriginal peoples invited Europeans to Canada and that First Nations' histories functioned mainly as a prologue to the arrival and future dominance of the Western newcomers. Much of the balance of the narrative replayed the familiar history of European trade, occupation, settlement, and constitutional and political developments, culminating in Confederation and the establishment of a transcontinental nation by the end of the show's first season. Following the traditional division of Canadian history into pre- and post-Confederation eras, the second season's episodes charted the fulfillment of the new nation-state up to 1990.

Genre

Genre is an important category of analysis in literary criticism. Defined as a "literary type or class," it encompasses such well-known categories as tragedy, comedy, romance, satire, and epic.[16] Starowicz characterized *Canada: A People's History* as an epic, so this analysis will consider some of the implications of his choice of genre.[17]

Two current definitions of the epic include, "a long narrative poem, on a grand scale, about the deeds of warriors and heroes" and "a long narrative poem on a great and serious subject, related in an elevated style, and centred on a heroic or quasi-divine figure on whose actions depends the fate of a tribe, a nation, or the human race."[18] E.M.W. Tillyard identified four typical formal components of classical epic: high literary merit and high seriousness; breadth and inclusiveness of subject matter; rigorous control and a conscious will to maintain unity of the content; and a capacity to express the feelings and values of its age.[19] The epic has been a preferred genre for national histories, which centre around the founding and peak periods in the history of a nation or people.[20] In Canada, a fully realized national epic was not developed until the Canadian Centenary Series, whose framework was largely replicated in *Canada: A People's History*.[21]

Literary theorist Mikhail Bakhtin has provided a useful alternative way of looking at the genre. He distinguishes between the epic's orientation to an "absolute past," characterized by remoteness from the historical past or present, and the "zone of familiar contact," a kind of open-endedness to the present that he associated with novels.[22] For Bakhtin, the term "epic" signifies more than a genre. He argued that it is also an expression of a distinctive orientation to historical time and place, one in which the past is presented as whole, complete, and sealed off from revision. Bakhtin held that it was also possible for an epic work to present the past in familiar time; that is, to approach the past with indeterminacy and open-endedness, thus avoiding the monological closure that often characterizes the genre.[23]

The open-endedness described by Bakhtin does not apply to *Canada: A People's History*, however. In its emphasis on the heroism of its protagonists and the salvation of the nation, and its preoccupation with a presumed unity and coherence of history, it displays characteristics typical of the traditional epic. By situating the narrative within an absolute past, it displays a remoteness from the actual contingency and possibility of history, and closes off the possibility of substantive change in the future. Rather than engage the actual diversity of voices and perspectives on Canadian history, the producers opted for the valorization of selected historical figures and their perspectives, which they presented as models for advancing the series' overriding political objectives of shoring up the nation-state in its contemporary travails.

Plot

A key aspect of literary form is the plot, defined simply as the structure of actions in a dramatic or narrative work. *Canada: A People's History* was plotted as the inexorable progress, through many challenges, of Canadians from different origins to their collective realization as a "people" within the nation-state of 1867. The vehicle through which the action was advanced was the dramatization of a succession of confrontations, including pre-contact wars between Aboriginal peoples, conflicts between European and First Nations people following contact, wars between nations competing for North America, battles between Canada and the Métis in 1870 and 1885, World War I and II, and assorted internal political confrontations culminating in the faceoff between Pierre Trudeau and René Lévesque in the first sovereignty referendum of 1980 and wrangling over the patriation of the Constitution in 1981. Each of these conflicts was shown to find resolution in its own era or, through flash-forwards, to anticipate a future resolution.

At another level, the plot functioned as a vehicle for advancing core meanings embedded in the series' basic structure. The first season's episodes presented a sequence of developments prefiguring the future nation-state, while the second season charted the fulfillment of the new country's promise in its first 123 years following Confederation. Responding to perceived challenges to the nation-state in the 1990s, the plot highlighted 1967 as a peak moment of unity and patriotism selected to represent the promise of the country's future fulfillment. In this schema, both Expo '67 and Pierre Trudeau, who emerged as prime minister in its wake, were invoked as symbols of national achievement and leadership to help shore up the nation-state.

Characterization

Since the plot relies on characters to carry out the action, characterization is another key element in the construction of a literary work. The principal character is typically the protagonist, or hero, often pitted against an adversary of comparable weight, the antagonist. Through the interplay of these characters, much of the dramatic action is carried and viewer interest sustained. For *Canada: A People's History*, the collective hero of the work is the Canadian people from earliest times to the present, supported by a number of representative individuals from different social groups.

These representative individuals were meant to enlist audience identification with personalities drawn from Canadian history, but they were in all cases selected for inclusion to the extent that their reported words were seen to reinforce the larger narrative thrust of the series. Heroic status was accorded those individuals considered to have moved history toward the unity of the modern nation-state. In the pre-Confederation era, the cast of supporting heroes consisted largely of politicians and military leaders whose actions were shown as anticipating or contributing to the unification of 1867. For the period following Confederation, the series advanced the story through the stories of individuals seen to promote the cause of national unity in the first 123 years of the constituted nation-state. Particularly highlighted were Sir John A. Macdonald, presented as the leading unifier in the making of the nation-state in 1867, and Pierre Trudeau, shown as fulfilling a similar role in maintaining the integrity of the nation-state near the end of the narrative. Both the images and narrative material on Trudeau were ubiquitous in the last two segments of the series, as well as in the books prepared to accompany and supplement the production. Periodically, the roles of these and other leading figures of federalism were set off by the introduction of antagonists seeking to thwart the inexorable momentum of the nation-state toward unity.

Apart from colourful anecdotes about the historical figures, characterization was largely given short shrift. Other individuals were referenced to the extent that they reinforced the main narrative line, but all played supporting roles to the central action as played out by heroic figures from the nation-building tradition of Canadian history.

Theme

Separate from but related to the plot is the theme of a work. As Northrop Frye noted, the plot answers the question "How is the story going to turn out?" while the theme is concerned with the question "What is the point of this story?"[24] In this respect, *Canada: A People's History* displays three mutually reinforcing themes.

First, the stories selected for narration indicated the producers' preoccupation with finding a unifying theme for Canadian history. Mark Starowicz discerned a unifying thread in the theme of refuge, asserted to be "at the core of the Canadian identity."[25] The series introduced this theme in the opening episode, when the narration highlighted a Salish creation story bearing a superficial resemblance to the hypothesized Bering Sea migrations of Aboriginal people from Asia to North America. By including Aboriginal people in the theme of refuge, the authors implied that they were immigrants like other Canadians, effectively diminishing alternative national aspirations based on indigenous occupation. The series storyline replayed the refuge theme in other segments throughout the series, culminating in the producers' peroration in the epilogue following the final segment: "Fifteen thousand years ago, the first travellers came to this continent, which became the destination for countless generations, a place where a million epic journeys ended and a million new stories began." The idea of refuge as a putative defining feature of Canada was reinscribed in the prologue to Episode 17, featuring the story of a refugee fleeing the killing fields of Cambodia, for whom Canada offered both a safe haven and hope.

A second dominant theme of this series was revealed in its presentation of Canadian history as a succession of conflicts. The emphasis on conflict was in keeping with contemporary approaches to journalism in Canada, as well as executive producer Mark Starowicz's penchant for reducing current affairs to confrontations between the diametrically opposed, as in his successful newsmagazine program, *The Journal*, in the 1980s. In various interviews about the production, Starowicz asserted his view that Canadian history was just as exciting as its American counter-part. For example, he said, "It is a thrill for viewers to find out that it is not the Americans alone who have the great stories such as revolution, civil war, and the taking of the west."[26] To make history exciting for view-ers, the producers' approach was to seek out sensational episodes from Canada's past, such as battles and massacres in earlier periods and politi-cal confrontations in the modern era, and reenact or narrate them, dram-atizing them to lure viewers away from competing American docudrama products being broadcast on rival networks. And, like its competitors, the CBC series relied especially on the most common type of television fictional drama—melodrama.[27]

The third theme the series highlighted was the importance to the coun-try of unity in the face of successive perceived threats to the constituted nation-state. In the first episode, devoted to Aboriginal peoples' history, the storyline presented an allegory with a coded message for its audience. The narrator related the story of a legendary Huron sage named Dekanaw-idah, who was said to have convinced the Iroquoian nations "to form a union to govern a crowded landscape." According to this story, each nation "shall contribute an arrow to form a single strong bundle ... So joined, these arrows represent the Confederacy solidarity." Dekanawidah is then said to warn "that if any arrows are withdrawn from the bundle that represents the power of their solidarity," the entire confederacy would be weakened. As in other didactic representations of thematic material, the narrative message was underscored visually, in this case by the reenactment of an unsuccessful attempt by a First Nations man to break the bundle of arrows, followed by footage of the successful breaking of a single arrow. The mes-sage was unmistakable—"United we stand; divided we fall."

In its narrative trajectory, the series began with unity, followed with divi-sion, and concluded with the reassertion of unproblematic unity by the end of the narrative, set in the present. As Starowicz summarized, "The genius of Canada is the constant search for equilibrium, where no one ever fully gains the upper hand."[28] The interpretation of overriding equilibrium sug-gested the capacity of the nation-state to accommodate all groups and aspirations. After its treatment of the constitutional crisis of 1980–81, the narrative included selected episodes from political confrontations that had emerged by 1990, including the Oka Crisis, the depletion of cod stocks in Atlantic Canada, and the political battle between Alberta and Ottawa over the National Energy Program. Largely untreated were other struggles in process at the end of the story, such as the status and rights of First Peo-ples, racial minorities, women, people with disabilities, lesbian, gay, trans-gendered, and bisexual people, the homeless, the unemployed, and others.

A few inspiring stories, such as Mary Eberts's campaign to secure women's equality rights in the Charter of Rights and Freedoms, Elizabeth May's environmental crusade, and Baldej Sikh Dhillon's quest to wear a turban as part of his RCMP uniform, were cited as parables of inclusiveness. Where the experience of minorities did not reinforce such a sanguine conclusion, the narrative simply omitted them from the story, thereby maintaining the desired harmony and coherence for this epic representation of Canadian history.

Music and Sound

The makers of *Canada: A People's History* made extensive use of sound, and especially music, which in non-fiction television has often been employed to achieve an organic unity.[29] For such productions, musical themes have been used to create moods, evoke particular eras, and signal to the audience the continuing presence of historical developments associated with earlier iterations of the thematic material. In the Wagnerian tradition, the CBC producers attempted to integrate narrative and music, with leitmotifs introduced to represent recurring characters or concepts in the narrative. The initial entry of melodic material linked an early concept with future stories or events introduced by the same melody, while subsequent iterations evoked earlier stories or events and heroic associations represented by these leitmotifs.

For *Canada: A People's History*, the score by Claude Desjardins and Eric N. Robertson eschewed the music of folk or popular culture and instead featured new pop-symphonic material written specifically for this production. Driving the narrative forward was the principal subject, introduced with swelling strings at the beginning and conclusion of each episode, accompanying the narrator's patriotic words. Simultaneously, a sense of urgency was connoted by a base line of beating drums as the narrator summarized a new chapter in the building of the nation, anticipating confrontations to come in the ensuing episode. In the narration accompanying many of the pre-1867 episodes, it was stated that these confrontations would challenge the future of existing European societies in northern North America; in other words, the nation-to-be. For episodes dealing with periods after 1867, the confrontations would challenge the constituted nation-state. For more sombre sections of the narrative, the music modulated to muted passages played by solo violins, while in the sections featuring military topics, drums were prominent.[30] While several complementary melodies were employed, the principal subject was ubiquitous throughout, as its swelling strings contributed a cosmetic coherence when

the historical facts failed to unify. Meanwhile, the homogeneously romantic score figuratively expressed the overriding importance of "the people"
over individual or vernacular expression.

Images

In addition to the dramatic reenactments, Starowicz's team displayed historical still images, including paintings and photographs, throughout the
series. They also relied on and enhanced through artificial colouration
numerous historical images for the accompanying two volumes of the
book released as part of the project. However, for television, they particularly favoured moving images, including dramatic reenactments for the
pre-film periods and video footage from the television age. In the selection of both still and moving images, they showed a fondness for presenting confrontations in history, including military conflicts through battle
reenactments, which are prominent in the early episodes of the series.
With the journalist's eye for compelling visuals, the CBC team also selected
still images that highlighted drama, which they equated with confrontation, usually between forces supporting the development of the nation-state
and their adversaries.

Just one example was the highlighting of an 1870 illustration of the
execution of Thomas Scott at Red River in the segment titled "A Single
Act of Severity." A propagandistic image from the *Canadian Illustrated
News*, it represented the execution as a murder, reinforcing a stereotype
of the Métis participating in the Northwest Resistance as cold-blooded
killers (Figure 1).[31] Here, the image provided a backdrop to the segment
title and reappeared in a sequence of still images presented to carry the
story. For the series, the illustration served a dual purpose—it provided
a dramatic image of the Red River Resistance and also reinforced the
unifying thread of the narrative by marginalizing forces considered to
oppose the forward advance of the nation-state.[32] The Scott image also
figured prominently in the series' books, which featured two reproductions of this tableau: a full-page rendering used as the signature image of
the chapter titled "Confederation" and a second reproduction accompanying the text's discussion of the "Red River Rebellion."[33] For the
chapter's title page, the image was cropped and blown up to focus more
directly on the killer and victim. As with most other illustrations in the
book, the authors attempted no critical pictorial analysis, nor was there
an acknowledgement that they had artificially coloured and manipulated
the image, as it was presented as a realistic treatment of the past without explanation or context.

Figure 1. "The Tragedy at Fort Garry, March 4, 1870," *Canadian Illustrated News*, 23 April 1870, 1.

Within the larger narrative, the Scott image served a useful function in foreshadowing the final images of First Nations violence in sensationalized treatments, in both video and book versions, of the Oka Crisis of 1990. In the television series, the presentation of a version of the Oka Crisis near the end of the concluding episode focused on this single episode of confrontation as representative of the state of relations between European and Aboriginal Canadians in the present. In the books, the treatment of the standoff was even starker, illustrated with a montage of images featuring three photographs of masked Mohawk Warriors, the major image being that of a warrior brandishing a rifle atop the barricade at Kanesatake.[34]

The television series also included considerable film footage on twentieth-century events, including images of Canadian soldiers involved in the First and Second World War, although these shots rarely presented close-ups of violence or actual suffering. For the episodes dealing with the period after World War II, historical images and reenactments were largely supplanted by television footage of historical events and personalities, including familiar images from the CBC's archives used in numerous other TV documentaries. The videotaped material included such well-known clips as Pierre Trudeau's famous exchange with a reporter outside the Parliament buildings during the October Crisis of 1970— stock footage for many CBC political documentaries on this period. The reporter asks, "How far would you go?" to which the determined prime minister responds, "Just watch me." Use of this clip served various functions, including reinforcement of the stature of the series' principal hero and also a valorization of the CBC's assumed role, not only in bringing the news to Canadians but in actually "making history," the title of both the CBC's documentary video and Starowicz's own book on the making of the series.

Conclusions

While referencing a variety of groups in Canadian society, the plot and thematic structure of *Canada: A People's History* subordinated distinctiveness and difference to an overriding goal of promoting unity and coherence in the country's history. In every historical era, official forces, forerunners of the dominant culture to which the CBC belongs, were highlighted as protagonists preserving society from the putative chaos represented by their adversaries. In the pre-Confederation era, the protagonists were politicians and military leaders whose actions anticipated the unification of 1867, as contrasted with Aboriginal peoples, who were

presented as the major threat to the nation-to-be.[35] Following Confederation, a heroic role was accorded individuals promoting the cause of
national unity in the first 123 years of the constituted nation-state, set off
by adversaries periodically seeking to thwart the inexorable momentum
toward unity. Overall, the CBC's approach was to combine techniques of
verisimilitude and authorial assertion to channel the audience toward the
desired conclusions.

To what degree did the CBC producers succeed, through this series, in
expressing the feelings and values of their own era? A clue may be found
in published reports on its initial reception. Following the first season, the
Carleton University Public History program compiled unsolicited survey
data indicating that *Canada: A People's History* was particularly well
received by anglophone audience members favouring patriotic representations of history.[36] In his book *Making History*, even Starowicz acknowledged that the series found a cool reception among francophone reviewers.
The analysis of the series' storyline and images leads back to the specific
historical circumstances of the production of *Canada: A People's History*.
Its production coincided with a concerted effort to shore up the federal
structure in the years following one of its greatest political challenges since
Confederation—the Quebec referendum of 1995. Only a year later, the
Supreme Court of Canada delivered its decision in the Delgamuukw case,
which affirmed Aboriginal title to land. Starowicz recently acknowledged
that the series reveals much about the political context of the mid-1990s.
As with the series' and books' narrative structure, his comments suggest
an overriding concern at that time with responding to perceived challenges to the federal state.[37]

My review of these books elsewhere identified a particular preoccupation with stereotypical textual and visual depictions of Aboriginal peoples
in the narrative.[38] For a brief moment, the series' monolithic narrative
appeared to salve a longing among traditional anglophone Canadians for
greater coherence in national history and identity after the political challenges of the 1990s. Yet this very unity and coherence was achieved through
marginalizing the history of various groups considered to be outside the
mainstream in order to advance the historical role of the traditional nation-
state and its proponents.[39] Both the form and content of this series raise
significant questions about the role of history, and quasi-official historical
television productions, in Canada's body politic.

Notes

1 At http://history.cbc.ca/history/webdriver?MIval=GENcont.html&series_id=4& episode_id=99&chapter_id=1&page_id=1&lang=E (accessed December 28, 2007).

2 Broadcasting Act, 1991, 3(1)(m)(vi). Available at http://www.crtc.gc.ca/eng/LEGAL/ BROAD.htm.

3 Clark, "Engaging the Field." Available at www.quasar.ualberta.ca/css/Css_36_2/ ARengaging_the_field.htm (accessed December 28, 2007).

4 Saunders, "The CBC"; "Remaking the CBC (2)."

5 In his book on the making of the series, Starowicz has related his rationale for using the referendum to seek support for the project. He wrote: "The shock of the referendum was not the genesis of the Canadian History project. I had been actively talking about the idea for years, and in the documentary unit, we hoped it would be the next project for the *Dawn of the Eye* team. But until now, I had zero confidence I could sell it in the acrid climate in the CBC. I began to think that now might be the moment to make the formal move. The shock of the referendum, I was betting, would change the climate in the CBC, because it had given us all a brush with history" (Starowicz, *Making History*, 28).

6 In assessing the project, Gene Allen, senior producer and director of research for the project, stressed the extent of book sales and increased television ratings as benchmarks of success. Allen, "The Professionals and the Public," 381.

7 Nichols, *Representing Reality*, 32–33.

8 "Docudrama."

9 Dick, "A Growing Necessity for Canada"; Berger, *The Writing of Canadian History*, 2–3. The Canadian Centenary Series, the largest effort in the twentieth century to write the national history of Canada, was rooted in traditional nation-building theories, especially the "Laurentian" school of Anglo-Canadian history. According to this thesis, the St. Lawrence/Great Lakes system and the commercial classes of Montreal and, later, Toronto, which exploited its linkages to the far-flung reaches of northern North America, played the dominant roles in shaping the character of the future country of Canada. See, for example, Creighton, *The Commercial Empire of the St. Lawrence*.

10 Gillmor and Turgeon, *Canada: A People's History*, *Volume One*, x.

11 Allen, remarks in "Canadian History in Film."

12 "Step by Step: One Story: Many Perspectives," in "Behind the Scenes—About the TV Series," at http://history.cbc.ca/history (accessed December 28, 2007).

13 See the BBC History Homepage, http://www.bbc.co.uk/history/british/launch _tl_british.shtml.

14 *Making History.*

15 Olsen, *Early Voyages and Northern Approaches, 1000–1632.*

16 Cuddon, A *Dictionary of Literary Terms*, 283.

17 Clark, "Engaging the Field."

18 Cuddon, A *Dictionary of Literary Terms*, 225; Abrams, A *Glossary of Literary Terms*, 50.

19 Tillyard, *The English Epic and Its Background*, 5–13.

20 Bakhtin, "Epic and Novel," 13.

21 Dick, "A Growing Necessity," 223–52.

22 Bakhtin, "Epic and Novel," 16–23.

23 Morson and Emerson, *Mikhail Bakhtin*, 419–23.

24 Frye, *Anatomy of Criticism*, 52.

25 Starowicz, "Afterword," 325.
26 Clark, "Engaging the Field."
27 For an elaboration of the nature and role of melodrama in contemporary television programming, see Himmelstein, "Melodrama."
28 Starowicz, "Afterword," 325.
29 Plantinga, *Rhetoric and Representation in Nonfiction Film*, 165.
30 http://history.cbc.ca/history/?MIval=GENcont.html$series_id=4&episode_id=99&chapter_id=1&page_id=7&lang=E
31 For some current definitions and a discussion of the opposing rationales for employing the competing terms "rebellion" and "resistance" with regard to the Northwest conflict of 1885, see "Back to Batoche" an interactive exhibit prepared as part of the Virtual Museum of Métis History and Culture (Saskatoon: Gabriel Dumont Institute, May 2003). http://www.museevirtuel.ca/Exhibitions/Batoche/html/about/index.php.
32 See the discussion in Dick, "Nationalism and Visual Media," 2–18.
33 Gillmor and Turgeon, *Canada: A People's History, Volume One*, 255, 286.
34 Gillmor, Michaud, and Turgeon, *Canada: A People's History, Volume Two*, 318.
35 Dick, "A New History for the New Millennium," 100–03.
36 See the website of Carleton University's graduate seminar in public history, www.carleton.ca/historycollaborative.ca, which in 2001 and 2002 was devoted in part to analyzing aspects of audience response to *Canada: A People's History*.
37 In a book published by the CBC to celebrate the television corporation's first half-century, the author wrote of *Canada: A People's History*: "*History*'s executive producer Mark Starowicz accepts that his fifteen-part series says a great deal about Canada and Canadians in the mid-'90s. 'The world was changing so rapidly,' he says. 'Globalization and open borders meant that the Canada we knew seemed to be slipping away before our eyes. Railways were shutting down. Airlines failing. The Quebec referendum made us wonder if there was going to be a Canada. At the same time the millennium was approaching and there was an idea we were packing for a long, uncertain voyage'" (Cole, *Here's Looking at Us*, 240–41).
38 Dick, "A New History for the New Millennium."
39 Dick, "A New History for the New Millennium," especially 106–09.

References

Abrams, M.H. *A Glossary of Literary Terms*, 4th ed. New York: Holt, Rinehart and Winston, 1981.

Allen, Gene. "The Professionals and the Public: Responses to *Canada: A People's History*." *Histoire Sociale/Social History* 68 (November 2001): 381–91.

———. Remarks in "Canadian History in Film: A Roundtable Discussion." *Canadian Historical Review* 82 (2): 332.

"Back to Batoche." Available at http://www.museevirtuel.ca/Exhibitions/Batoche/html/about/index.php. Accessed February 14, 2008.

Bakhtin, Mikhail. "Epic and Novel." In *The Dialogic Imagination*, edited by Michael Holquist, translated by Caryl Emerson and Michael Holquist. Austin: Texas University Press, 1981, 3–40.

Berger, Carl. *The Writing of Canadian History*. Toronto: Oxford University Press, 1976.

"Canada: A People's History—Merchandise." CBC History Home Page, http://
    history.cbc.ca/history/webdriver?MIval=GENcont.html&series_id=4&episode
    _id=99&chapter_id=1&page_id=1&lang=E. Accessed December 28, 2007.
Canada. Broadcasting Act, 1991, 3(1)(m)(vi).
Clark, Penney. "Engaging the Field: A Conversation with Mark Starowicz." *Cana-
    dian Social Studies* 36 (2). Available at http://www.quasar.ualberta.ca/css/Css
    _36_2/ARengaging_the_field.htm. Accessed December 28, 2007.
Cole, Stephen. *Here's Looking at Us: Celebrating Fifty Years of CBC-TV*. Toronto:
    McClelland & Stewart, 2002.
Creighton, Donald. *The Commercial Empire of the St. Lawrence*. Toronto: Ryer-
    son Press, 1937.
Cuddon, J.A. A *Dictionary of Literary Terms*. Harmondsworth, UK: Penguin Books
    1979.
Dick, Lyle. "A Growing Necessity for Canada: W.L. Morton's Centenary Series
    and the Forms of National History, 1955–1980." *Canadian Historical Review*
    82 (2) (2001): 223–52.
———. "Nationalism and Visual Media in Canada: The Case of Thomas Scott's
    Execution." *Manitoba History* 48 (Winter 2004–05): 2–18.
———. "'A New History for the New Millennium': *Canada: A People's History*."
    Canadian Historical Review 85 (1) (2004): 85–110.
"Docudrama." *The Encyclopedia of Television*. Chicago: The Museum of Broad-
    cast Communications, 2003. Available at www.museum.tv/archives/etv/D/htmlD/
    docudrama/docudrama.htm. Accesssed December 28, 2007.
Frye, Northrop. *Anatomy of Criticism: Four Essays*. Princeton: Princeton Univer-
    sity Press, 1957.
Gillmor, Don and Pierre Turgeon, *Canada: A People's History*, Volume One.
    Toronto: McClelland & Stewart, 2000.
Gillmor, Don, Achille Michaud, and Pierre Turgeon. *Canada: A People's History,
    Volume Two*. Toronto: McClelland & Stewart, 2001.
Himmelstein, Hal. "Melodrama." In *The Encyclopedia of Television*, edited by
    Horace Newcomb. Chicago: Museum of Broadcast Communications, 1997.
    Available at www.museum.tv/archives/etv/M/htmlM/melodrama/melodrama
    .htm. Accessed December 28, 2007.
Morson, Gary Saul and Caryl Emerson. *Mikhail Bakhtin: Creation of a Prosaics*.
    Stanford, CA: Stanford University Press, 1990.
Nichols, Bill. *Representing Reality: Issues and Concepts in Documentary*. Bloom-
    ington: Indiana University Press, 1991.
Olsen, Tryggvi. *Early Voyages and Northern Approaches, 1000–1632*. Toronto:
    McClelland & Stewart, 1962.
Plantinga, Carl. *Rhetoric and Representation in Nonfiction Film*. Cambridge: Cam-
    bridge University Press, 1997.
"Remaking the CBC (2): What Defines Public Broadcasting in the 1990s?" *Globe
    and Mail*, March 23, 1999.

Saunders, Doug. "The CBC: Spotlight on a House Divided." *Globe and Mail*, December 16, 1998.

Starowicz, Mark. "Afterword." In Don Gillmor, Achille Michaud, and Pierre Turgeon, *Canada: A People's History, Volume Two*. Toronto: McClelland & Stewart, 2001.

Starowicz, Mark. *Making History: The Remarkable Story Behind* Canada: A People's History. Toronto: McClelland & Stewart, 2003.

"Step by Step: One Story: Many Perspectives." In "Behind the Scenes—About the TV Series," at http://history.cbc.ca/history. Accessed December 28, 2007.

Tillyard, E.M.W. *The English Epic and Its Background*. London: Chatto and Windus, 1954.

Filmography

Canada: A People's History (CBC, 2000–01)

Making History (CBC, 2000)

JULIE RAK

Canadian Idols?

CBC's *The Greatest Canadian* as Celebrity History

When Tommy Douglas won CBC Television's contest to name "the Greatest Canadian" in November 2004, the real victor was not Douglas but a genre whose development is unique to television: the serial biographical vignette. Popularized by the *Biography* series developed by A&E Television and widely imitated by other networks—including the CBC—the serial biographical vignette presents the life of its subject through interviews with friends and family, the voice of an unseen narrator, and the employment of personal documents of various types, including photographs and film clips.[1] In the case of *The Greatest Canadian* vignettes, something else was added: the programs were about the lives of the "top ten" most significant Canadians in history, and they were narrated by celebrity advocates who sought to prove why their candidate deserved to win.

This formula had already been successfully employed by the BBC in their contest, called *Great Britons*, and it has been used by television networks and newspapers around the world. And the celebrity pitches gave the vignettes a competitive edge that made them look more like episodes from *Canadian Idol*—another Canadian spinoff from a British television show, *Pop Idol*—than like a more traditionally conceived Canadian documentary. The presence of celebrities was also supposed to make the programs more appealing for younger viewers. For example, Tommy Douglas's celebrity advocate was George Stroumboulopoulos, a MuchMusic video host and producer whose profile of Douglas showed rhetorical flair. Between archival footage of Douglas's impassioned speeches and successful debate with Pierre Trudeau, Stroumboulopoulos narrates Douglas's life and achievements as aggressively as possible. A dramatic high point of the vignette is a scene where Stroumboulopoulos blows up an outdoor privy in a farmer's field to show how happy Saskatchewan residents must have been when Douglas helped make indoor plumbing a reality in the province. "Mr. Outhouse: go to hell!" yells Stroumboulopoulos before he hits the detonator. The privy bursts into flames and Stroumboulopoulos says, "Ahh, so good!"[2]

As one of the co-executive producers for *The Greatest Canadian* series, Mark Starowicz, would be the first to point out, episodes like this are not usually part of the solemn, sober CBC that Canadians viewers know and do not necessarily love.[3] This is unabashedly partisan and populist history mixed with celebrity glamour. It is meant to appeal to a far younger segment of the Canadian population than the one that watches other shows, such as *On the Road Again* or *Coronation Street*, on the CBC. As a result, many media pundits decided that *The Greatest Canadian* was not to be taken seriously—and not just because *Hockey Night in Canada* commentator Don Cherry had been voted into the top ten.[4]

But *The Greatest Canadian* deserves more than this kind of dismissal. Its populist format and mixing of showbiz commentary with more documentary-style film techniques are the latest indicators of an important shift in public broadcasting from the use of documentary as a record of events to the use of biography as a form of documentary. In this populist form of biography, celebrity discourse underwrites what history is and history itself becomes the record of individual lives. This approach to history as the record of individual activity has underpinned the popularity of biography since the nineteenth century and contributes to the dominance of celebrity in the contemporary public sphere.

In the case of *The Greatest Canadian*, this mix of celebrity discourse and biography also points to the transnational character of biography itself. In the nineteenth century, anyone could use the category of biography to create a "unique" collection of national lives, called the collective national biography.[5] This popular form of national history survives in the twenty-first century in the serial biographical vignette, a form that can be exported to any nation to create "national lives" and public discussion on television in the format of the top ten genre. The ease with which televised national biography can be adapted from one place to another as an "apparently" nationalist form means that, as David Hogarth has said of documentary more generally, biography has "gone global" and is now part of the circulation of national representations as commodities between national markets.[6] In the vignettes about Tommy Douglas, Don Cherry, and Terry Fox, it is possible to see how the biographical approach to history and the advent of celebrity discourse creates a product that has mass appeal but cannot participate in what I call a televised public sphere.

The "New Grammar" of Documentary

Mark Starowicz strongly believes that shows like *The Greatest Canadian* belong on public television because public television provides public space for national debate. As he said in an address to the Senate Standing Committee on Transport and Communications in 2003, in the case of public television the economic model is different from the commercial model: "Large audiences matter—don't let anyone fool you. But the unit of measure really is one person, one vote. In commercial television, the unit of measure is the number of consumer [sic]. In public television, the unit of measure is the number of citizens, one person, one vote."[7]

The basis for Starowicz's belief that public television is inherently democratic and should act as a public sphere is his contention that public television is for *each individual* Canadian rather than for demographic units. The phrase "one person, one vote" represents a liberal view of national belonging where each citizen has a voice and can participate. This is why his documentary series *Canada: A People's History* enacts the history of Canada through the voices and documents of individuals.

When he was interviewed about *The Greatest Canadian*, Starowicz called the shift to a treatment of individual lives within history an important part of "a new grammar" of documentary television.[8] In Starowicz's version of this "grammar," historical documentary is recast to appeal to younger audiences and to be more populist in its orientation by emphasizing how individuals shape historical events. It is, literally, history about the people for the people.

In keeping with this philosophy, *The Greatest Canadian* was designed as a voting exercise where the CBC acted as an arbiter but did not influence who was selected as the "greatest" Canadian of all time. In April 2004, the CBC asked its viewers to nominate "the Greatest Canadian" for inclusion in the upcoming series. More than 140,000 nominations were received. From these, a list of the top 100 was formed and 50 names from that list were presented on the first show. The top ten nominees had mini-documentaries created about them, each with a celebrity advocate. Series host Wendy Mesley presented forty of the top fifty nominees during the first episode of *The Greatest Canadian* and revealed the top ten at the end of the show. Viewers were asked to vote for their favourites from the top ten list throughout the series. The rest of the episodes featured the top ten nominees, and the last episode was a "roundup" in which all ten advocates appeared to make their final pitch to a live studio audience. Many audience members cheered, just as enthusiastic audiences do during *Canadian Idol*. The top ten nominees were John A. Macdonald,

Figure 1. A publicity shot for *The Greatest Canadian*: George Stroumboulopoulos makes his case for Tommy Douglas as a Canadian rebel. By permission of CBC Television Archives.

Lester B. Pearson, David Suzuki, Don Cherry, Pierre Trudeau, Sir Frederick Banting, Alexander Graham Bell, Wayne Gretzky, Tommy Douglas, and Terry Fox. At the very end, the winner—NDP politician Tommy Douglas—was proclaimed with great fanfare, although it was not a great surprise because Douglas had been the front-runner since the beginning of the contest.

Almost immediately, and to the delight of the CBC executives, *The Greatest Canadian* generated public discussion and controversy. During the first episode, 1.1 million viewers tuned in, which was seen as a good result, although the number of viewers declined for subsequent episodes until the final one, when the numbers approached 1.1 million again in the last half-hour.[9] There were complaints about the fact that there were no women included in the top ten and that the highest-ranked woman was a musician and celebrity, Shania Twain. Radio-Canada did not participate in the voting, so there were only nineteen francophones on the top fifty list. Only one, Pierre Trudeau, made the top ten. The only person of colour in the top ten was David Suzuki, and no Aboriginal people were represented at all. There were other complaints about the presence of Don Cherry, whose achievements seemed less significant than those of the inventors or political figures. And it was noted that one of the people in the top 100 was Hal Anderson, a radio host from Winnipeg who had sponsored a mass voting campaign to get himself included.[10] After Douglas was announced as the winner, media coverage became more respectful and aspects of Douglas's life and achievements were widely reported.[11]

Clearly, the media debates about the series were predicated on a politics of inclusion and exclusion—who was on the list, why were women absent, and so on. Some pundits even pointed to the arbitrariness of list-making itself, even as they groused about who was left off. But what was not debated was how *The Greatest Canadian* was part of a change in thinking about the role of documentary on television, in Canada and elsewhere, even as it participated in a revival of a way to understand history that became part of a populist approach to thinking about the past as the sum of individual lives rather than of social movements or other factors. Although I think that Mark Starowicz is right that a new grammar of documentary is informing productions like *The Greatest Canadian* on the CBC, I would contend that this grammar has little to do with democracy and much to do with an approach to history as a series of biographies, an approach that lends itself well to international export via the politics of its discursive cousin, celebrity.

The understanding of history as biography was pioneered in the work of Wilhelm Dilthey, a nineteenth- and early twentieth-century German philosopher who worked on hermeneutics, the philosophy of history, and phenomenology. Dilthey insisted that it was impossible to understand events without keeping in mind the relationship between what individuals can know about their own experiences and the context given by history. This approach to contexts for knowledge helped prepare the way for classical approaches to sociology.

In his most important work, *The Formation of the Historical World in the Human Sciences*, Dilthey argues that people understand meaning by establishing a relationship, or "nexus," between their understanding of their own lives and the world around them. The relationship between individual experience and the world is always dynamic, or "productive."[12] The beginning of understanding anything about history therefore involves an understanding of the centrality of the individual and his or her "life course" within what Dilthey called the "ocean" of history itself. As he says, "The basic material of life is one with history, and history consists of all life in the most diverse relationships. History is merely life apprehended from the perspective of the whole of humanity conceived as interconnected."[13] The "life-nexus," or the way people understand how their lives are connected to the greater whole, comes into play when biography is used as a "tool" to organize individual perceptions about a life and the social contexts that made that life.

Just as a person must look for connections to find personal meaning, so the biographer must sense how memories and documents provide the same sense of organization. Dilthey calls biography "the fundamental cell of history" because this process mirrors how "history" makes sense of individual lives, just as individual lives must make sense of history.[14] Biography itself is a "nexus" that holds together the meaning of thousands of lives within the course of a single life. Because it can make connections between people and their social environments even as it makes sense of individual motivations, Dilthey is convinced that biography is essential to any understanding of history as a structuring force for whole peoples. "How can anyone deny that biography is especially significant, the great nexus of the historical world?" asks Dilthey for this reason.[15]

Dilthey's thinking about the connections that biography could make between individual lives and history proved to be highly influential during the nineteenth century, when biography began to be understood as a way to understand history and a way to learn from the lives of others in order to better oneself. These ideas about biography can be seen in a highly popular development during this time: the publication of national collections of lives. Fuelled by other developments in psychology that stressed the moral importance of learning from "genius" and new theories about the formation of consciousness from psychoanalysis, collective national biographies like Leslie Stephen's *Dictionary of National Biography*, a compendium of British lives, were widely read and discussed.[16] As Alison Booth has pointed out, collections of "worthy" lives like these functioned for their readers as a kind of reproducible self-help narrative that demonstrated what model citizenship could be.[17]

One of the by-products of these collections was the sense, particularly in the United States, that national history could be understood in terms of what Leigh Gilmore has called "representativeness," where the subject of a biography or autobiography could be seen to represent the character of an entire nation.[18] At a time when industrialization and the growth of international trade were beginning to change how English citizens thought of themselves as subjects of the British Empire as it expanded, or how citizens of the United States could still understand themselves as good Americans during a time of rapid social and economic change, collective national biography served to tell its readers what it meant to have a nationality, even as the idea of what a nation is was altering in the modern era.

The success of *The Greatest Canadian* depends on a similar appeal to national stability at a time when the forces of economic and cultural globalization appear to be calling the terms of national belonging into question. The "new grammar" of documentary that mixes biographies of individual lives with documentary footage is informed by an older approach to history as two stories: the story of the experiences individuals have had within a historical context and the story of *representative* individuals whose lives seem to encapsulate the "character" of a nation. In other words, the grammar of *The Greatest Canadian* makes biography a "nexus," as Dilthey would have it, for a people. In the life of one representative person, an entire nation appears to have a single set of characteristics. As I have argued elsewhere, this is why television series like A&E's *Biography* and the CBC's *Life and Times* and *The Greatest Canadian* treat history as a type of national biography made up of individual lives, since it is in effect impossible to close the narrative gap—the "biography" of a nation—that opens up when the singularity of an individual life is tied to the life of a nation as singularity.[19] The arguments about inclusion and whether "greatness" is a series of innate national qualities, such as Canadian politeness, or a series of achievements are the mark of this narrative gap and of how the repetition of biographies seeks to close it.

The transnational nature of national representativeness in televised biographies makes for a complex dialectic. On the one hand, shows like *The Greatest Canadian* would not seem to lend themselves to export since each program is based on an assumption that identities do not cross political borders and that national character can be ascertained. On the other hand, this assumption has not prevented the BBC's *Great Britons* from being exported to many countries and regions around the world. In addition to *The Greatest Canadian*, adaptations of *Great Britons* have resulted in televised contests in the United States, Germany, the Czech Republic, Australia, South Africa, and the Netherlands. Magazine-based polls were also held in India and Belgium. Currently, a *Greatest Arabs* show is under way, sponsored by the Middle East Broadcasting Center.[20] Although these contests have sometimes resulted in activating national controversies— *Great South Africans* was stopped when a supporter of apartheid and a sports figure involved in a cricket scandal made the top ten; the *Unsere Besten (Our Best)* contest in Germany saw the inclusion of Copernicus, a Polish citizen who was claimed as German during the Nazi period; and *Suuret Suomalaiset (Great Finns)* contained a number of joke entries in the top twenty—what is remarkable is that the format of *Great Britons* has proved to be easy to adapt in many countries. According to Rupert Gavin, then CEO of BBC Worldwide, it is the *format* of the show that makes it so adaptable: "The *Greatest* format is a global concept that truly works on a local level. Giving people the chance to determine the outcome of a series is a fantastic way to fully engage an audience in every country."[21] Gavin's comment shows how the politics of *Great Britons* is portable because it contains what the citizens of modern nations understand: a "nexus" in its condensation of the national on an individual level in its use of biographical conventions, a pattern of voting recognizable to countries that have democratic conventions in place, and the use of celebrities, who are always available in countries or regions that have media networks. The convergence in modernity of these ideas—that the nation is a unique place with unique people, that individuals are unique and make history happen, and that celebrity discourse in mass media now stands in for the older discourse of fame and merit—have meant that this form of televised biographical documentary is transnational. National lives, and the idea of national life, circulate easily in a global economy, and in fact work to support it.

Celebrity and Biography: Exporting National Lives

The Greatest Canadian series referred to something else that is unusual to see in programs produced by the CBC but that is found in the other *Greatest* shows and at times in shows produced by or for A&E's *Biography*: celebrity discourse appears in the context of a historical presentation. As I mentioned, each of the ten biographical vignettes in *The Greatest Canadian* had celebrity advocates, or at least advocates who would probably be recognized as celebrities of a sort by some segment of the Canadian population.[22] In some shows, most notably in the programs about David Suzuki and Wayne Gretzky, the lives and personalities of the advocates seemed to have even greater importance than the life of the person for whom the celebrity was advocating. Beyond the fact that the format of the original *Great Britons* also had celebrity advocates, why would *The Greatest Canadian* feature celebrities, and why did some of them seem to overshadow the lives of the top ten Canadians themselves? Moreover, why *was* Don Cherry, a media celebrity, in the top ten and why was the highest-ranking woman, Shania Twain, a celebrity rather than a historical figure? The answer can be found in an examination of the roots of celebrity discourse itself at the beginning of the modern era in the Western world and the concomitant development of a genre that originally supported it: biography.

The phenomenon of celebrity, Charles L. Ponce de Leon argues, is directly related to the development of modernity in the eighteenth century.

It is an outgrowth of increased social mobility, the advent of liberalism and its advocacy of individual freedom as its central tenet, and the rise of democratic values in Britain and Europe. As print publics came into existence during the eighteenth century, the idea of celebrity—that someone can become famous no matter who he or she is or what he or she has done as long as that person has a presence in print media—developed among middle-class people who wanted to become upwardly mobile. Some of these people, chief among them Benjamin Franklin and Jean Jacques Rousseau, wrote either life narratives about themselves or biographies and memoirs about others as a way to support their positions as public figures. As Ponce de Leon explains, the result of this new social mobility is a new interest in the role of biographer as a historian *and* as a public person who was either a celebrity or someone who could create celebrities:

> With the emergence and steady expansion of the public sphere, virtually any man could be famous—could become a public figure known to a large number of people. It was no longer necessary to be a member of the nobility or aristocracy: nor was it even necessary to be rich, though having money and the social position that came with it was certainly an asset. Those aspiring to fame, moreover, could "author" themselves, creating public personas that rejected aristocratic models of achievement in favor of an emerging democratic model that would steadily evolve in tandem with changes in values ... But the real importance of the public sphere lay not so much in the opportunities that it created to achieve visibility, but rather in the ways in which it led men and women alike to rethink how they presented themselves in public, a process that sparked a new self-consciousness about appearances ... Aiming his work toward the literary marketplace, where readers were as eager to be entertained as they were to know the truth, the modern biographer assumed an important new role within the public sphere as a largely independent, though not unbiased, arbiter of the claims made by public figures. This role would be adopted later by the reporter for the mass-circulation press.[23]

Therefore, modern celebrity was directly supported, and is still supported, by biographical work that was and is carried about by the media when they treat the life of a celebrity as if it can be known intimately by a public. The popular press took up this role and created the celebrity human interest interview, where it is presumed that celebrities are "ordinary" people who can be known by the public, even as they seem to lead extraordinary lives. This creates a paradox where intimacies with the famous are sought but then found to be disappointingly nonexistent, as the glamour of celebrity is removed when too many details are known—

leading to an outcry against celebrity in the reporting of the very press that helps to perpetuate it.[24]

In *The Greatest Canadian*, the discourse of celebrity is used to recast biographical history itself as *celebrity history*. Since celebrity does not have to be attained by merit but can be attained by notoriety or the work of a publicity machine, celebrity in itself is an ambiguous discourse that moves its subjects from a celebration of their merit to a critique of what Joshua Gamson calls "a fame meritocracy" where celebrities, especially in the early days of American cinema, were often described as special people who got a "lucky" break rather than very talented actors.[25] In celebrity history, Dilthey's formulation of biography as the nexus between the individual and his or her social context becomes grafted to celebrity discourse's assumption that the lives of famous people contain some combination of glamour and merit—they are exotic and special—and luck—they are ordinary people whose lives contained a lucky break. The history of a nation is not a history of events but a history of achievements made by ordinary, yet special, persons. Knowing about these people's lives means that a nation can "know" itself in the repetition of the lives of successive, and successful, individuals from the proposed origin of the nation to the present. In celebrity history, merit can be present—and up for debate—but it is not essential.

It *is* essential that the individual be known by others, so notoriety can stand in for merit. In the case of *The Greatest Canadian*, this explains why so much use is made of celebrity advocates and why television personalities like Don Cherry or David Suzuki—who is famous because he is on television, not because he is a scientist—were voted into the top ten list of greatest Canadians of all time. On *The Greatest Canadian*, "greatness" at times signifies the older meaning of "fame" based on merit, but at other times it signifies "greatness" of personality and how it represents what are held to be essential Canadian qualities. The way in which these ideas are held together is via the discourse of celebrity.

Three of the programs in *The Greatest Canadian*—those featuring Tommy Douglas, Terry Fox, and Don Cherry—can serve to illustrate how biographical treatments, celebrity, and national representativeness work together to create this ambiguous sense of what "greatness" means in the series.

What "Greatness" Means: Tommy Douglas, Terry Fox, and Don Cherry

The winner of *The Greatest Canadian* was left-wing politician and former Saskatchewan premier Tommy Douglas. Although he was never elected prime minister, Douglas was one of Canada's most popular politicians during the 1950s. As the leader of the NDP in a minority government, he is credited with ensuring that universal medicare for Canadians, the achievement for which he is best known, was legislated by the Liberal Party in 1961.

Although universal, publicly funded health care has been considered to be at the core of Canadian national identity and values, Douglas did not win *The Greatest Canadian* contest on merit alone. Unlike other contenders, such as Pierre Trudeau or Wayne Gretzky, Douglas's public persona was homespun. As a rural minister who spoke and acted very plainly, his rhetorical style was more suited to grassroots campaign speeches than to the more polished style of televised debate. In other words, Douglas did not look or act like a celebrity. This should have counted against him, since the target demographic of *The Greatest Canadian* was not even born when he was alive and probably did not know who he was. I would argue that Douglas won on the strength of his advocate's understanding of celebrity and on the emphasis the show that featured him placed on the ambiguity of celebrity itself.

At the opening of the Tommy Douglas program, Douglas's advocate, George Stroumboulopoulos, at the time a good-looking host for a Much-Music alternative music show, is sitting in a '50s-era convertible at a drive-in. The film playing on the screen is *Rebel Without a Cause*, starring James Dean. The camera shifts from a scene with Dean to Stroumboulopoulos, who says that James Dean just *looks* like a rebel, but Tommy Douglas really was one. "Granted," Stroumboulopoulos says, "our guy didn't much look the part: kinda geeky, scrawny and not technically cool. But our guy wasn't playing a part: he was living it. His name was Tommy Douglas, and he fought for a better Canada, where no one got left behind."[26] The comparison that Stroumboulopoulos makes is between real heroism and fake heroism during the 1950s, and between false celebrity and true merit. His use of the phrase "our guy" is also meant to show that James Dean is American: American rebels are part of Hollywood, but "we" Canadians have political rebels. Therefore, Tommy Douglas is a real person and a real Canadian. And he is not American or of an American world where celebrity stands in for heroic merit.

With just a few words and images, Stroumboulopoulos establishes a nexus between Douglas as an individual and Douglas as representative of Canadian values in its implicit rejection of celebrity as un-Canadian. Throughout the rest of the program, including the outhouse scene mentioned in the beginning of this chapter, Stroumboulopoulos emphasizes that Douglas lived his life in rebellion against the establishment and that he lived by his principles without caring about appearances. The metonymic symbol for Douglas's efforts is Stroumboulopoulos's use of vintage convertible cars, which he drives along Saskatchewan roads as he narrates, to show how Douglas, as a rebel, is progressive, just as the cars "progress" along the Saskatchewan roads that Douglas's policies helped modernize. In reality, Tommy Douglas was not that rebellious, since he was a political leader and a minister as well. But the metonym of the car always on the move toward the horizon, with its youthful, rebellious driver, communicates that Douglas's values are timeless and that his personality was somehow identified with the car's retro styling, as well as with Stroumboulopoulos himself. The style of the vignette, with its constant shifting between old film footage of Douglas and images of Stroumboulopoulos in contemporary Saskatchewan, make Douglas acquire a kind of anti-celebrity in the rebel posturing of its celebrity host. In its whole-hearted embrace of the contradictions of celebrity discourse and national representativeness, the Tommy Douglas program created an unbeatable formula for victory.

The attention given to Douglas as the winner means that it is easy to overlook the second-place finisher, Terry Fox. But the Terry Fox vignette, narrated by Sook-Yin Lee, a celebrity advocate with popular culture credentials as an alternative musician, host and producer of the CBC Radio new-music show *Definitely Not the Opera*, and actress in the films *Hedwig and the Angry Inch* and *Shortbus*, is interesting in its similar approach to the ambiguities of celebrity discourse and national values.

When he was eighteen, Terry Fox lost a leg to cancer. He garnered national attention in 1979 when he began to run a marathon a day across Canada to raise money for cancer research. As the campaign escalated, and after he was forced to abandon the run when the cancer returned, Fox became a hero for millions of Canadians. Since his death in 1981, a foundation named for him has sponsored fun runs that have raised millions of dollars for cancer research in Canada and around the world.

Unlike Tommy Douglas, Terry Fox was an ordinary person who became famous because he attempted something extraordinary. He was also famous because his run was televised: people across Canada still remember Terry Fox as someone they saw on the nightly news. In the vignette about his life, Sook-Yin Lee argues that Fox is a hero in the classical sense with references to the heroism of Phidippides, the mythic runner who brought the news of the Battle of Marathon before he dropped dead. The parallel to Fox's own run and his death is clear. Lee also emphasizes Fox's celebrity by focusing on the *image* of Fox as unforgettable even though he was ordinary, but then she undercuts this image by saying that Fox himself rejected the trappings of celebrity when he refused corporate endorsements. Lee ends the show with an appeal to Fox as representative: she says that Fox's true greatness lies in his ordinariness, an ordinariness that can convince others to attempt great things. Fox is a hero, Lee says "because of how he's reflected in us" and because he "embodies the most cherished Canadian values: compassion, commitment, perseverance."[27] In the Terry Fox vignette, "greatness" is about the refusal of celebrity and is associated directly with what Lee calls Canadian values. Unlike the Tommy Douglas vignette, the Terry Fox program does not fully embrace the contradictions and irony of celebrity discourse, but it presents merit and ordinariness as dialectical, so that Fox's traits become the values of the Canadian national imaginary.

As I have mentioned, of all the entries in the top ten of *The Greatest Canadian* series, the inclusion of Don Cherry caused the most debate, since many commentators thought that Cherry's position as a media celebrity cheapened the contest. In fact, the presence of Cherry in the top ten highlights the contradictions that are inherent in celebrity history and the idea of national greatness. Unlike Douglas, Cherry cannot be presented as a nation builder, and unlike Fox, he cannot be seen as someone who has attempted great things, since Cherry himself was an unsuccessful hockey player and only a moderately successful hockey coach before he became a television personality. Therefore, Don Cherry's advocate, the professional wrestler Bret "The Hitman" Hart, does not base his appeal on Cherry's merit but on Cherry's representativeness as an "average" guy who embodies national values, even as he is forced to argue that Cherry is on the list because he is not "average" but in fact a celebrity. The tone of the vignette is tongue-in-cheek to account for the ambiguity of celebrity and ordinariness that Hart must negotiate because, unlike Lee or Stroumboulopoulos, Hart cannot resolve the difficulties of the notion of celebrity by showing that Cherry is indeed heroic. At the beginning of the narrative, a voice-over by Hart says that Cherry embodies Canadian values connected to patriotism, hockey, and honesty: "'He loves Canada. He loves hockey. He's good. He's bad. He's unfiltered and uncensored ... he's the heart and soul of this country.'"[28] As Hart speaks these words, a disembodied Don Cherry, pictured as a bouncing head with a cartoon mouth and a puppet body, flits across the screen. Other images, including cartoons of Sikh and Jewish hockey teams, appear to show how universal hockey is. While Hart's narration connects Cherry to national values, the cartoonish nature of Cherry and hockey itself serves to undercut any seriousness in the show.

The reason becomes apparent when Hart attempts to account for Cherry's celebrity status by exposing the very idea of celebrity as something that is performed, even by honest men like Cherry or himself. Stepping out of a cartoon ring into a ringside set, Hart compares the faint ridiculousness of Cherry's persona as an onscreen dandy with Hart's own, also faintly ridiculous persona as a professional wrestler. Hart says: "I understand Don Cherry. We have a lot in common. He's high collars and fancy suits. I'm pink tights. Let's face it: we're both showmen." Hart's words stress that celebrity status is not real and not to be taken seriously. But at the same time, Hart asks that Cherry's patriotism and blunt speech, which is also part of his on-screen persona as a tough hockey coach, be taken seriously because those are the values of "ordinary" Canadians. Cherry and Hart understand these values to be ones shared by conservative English-Canadian working-class men. Cherry himself acknowledged this when he said in an interview that the nomination showed his status as a populist icon for that group. According to Cherry, ordinary people triumphed in the vote for him: "I think the people, the working-man people, made a statement here, that you don't have to be a college graduate to be a good Canadian."[29] Therefore, the Don Cherry vignette deliberately appeals to different national values and a different type of populism than those exemplified in the programs about Tommy Douglas or Terry Fox, although his claim to be a popular "hero" is similar to the ones made for them. Instead of attempting to resolve tensions between celebrity representation on television and "true" heroism or rebellion, the cartoonish nature of the Don Cherry story is meant to highlight how television celebrity is about surface appearances and cannot be regarded as real. But the "admission" that celebrity is not real means that celebrities who admit this can use it as a vehicle to express values that *are* to be taken as real. Hart's case for Cherry comes closest to disregarding the merit discourse in celebrity history and to making an appeal for Don Cherry as a populist ideologue who embodies the contradictions of celebrity without resolving them. Since in the voting, Cherry finished ahead of John A. Macdonald, Alexander Graham Bell, and Wayne Gretzky, this tactic probably was successful.

Conclusion

The shows about Tommy Douglas, Terry Fox, and Don Cherry in *The Greatest Canadian* series indicate that when celebrity history as biography is placed into a nationalist frame, the result is a heightening of the ambiguities of celebrity itself. As each celebrity host deals with the problems of celebrity, where the life of an ordinary person must be made to seem special and representative or must be dismissive of celebrity even when that discourse underlies the structure of advocacy itself, celebrity history reveals itself to be populist, but ultimately not democratic. Mark Starowicz's claim that causing debate about the nature of a top ten list is an inherent sign that the new grammar of television documentary creates a public sphere is an attractive position to take. But the discourses of the national imaginary and celebrity history that have long been part of collective national biographies serve to make *The Greatest Canadian* documentary style a well-worn formula for speaking about national lives. This formula makes certain ways of talking about national history easy to import and export, but, in the end, the formula of individual achievement and "one person, one vote" does not create the debate about the problems of national belonging or national histories beyond the level of debate about who will be the next *Canadian Idol*.

Acknowledgements

I wish to thank the undergraduate students in my course in English 378, Canadian Literature and Culture: Contemporary Contexts, in fall 2005 for helping me think critically about *The Greatest Canadian* series.

Notes

1   For a detailed discussion of serial biography on television, see Rak, "Bio-Power."
2   "Tommy Douglas," *The Greatest Canadian*.
3   "The Greatest Canadian."
4   For a small sample of complaints about the list's arbitrariness, see Deziel, "Great Canadian Exercise in Futility"; Intini, "Greatness Has Been Thrust upon Them"; and Rick Salutin, "Canadians Are the Greatest."
5   See Marcus's discussion of collective national biography in *Auto/biographical Discourses*, 49–61.
6   See Hogarth's introduction in *Documentary Television in Canada*.
7   Starowicz, "Notes for Remarks."
8   "The Greatest Canadian."
9   Dixon, "Solid Ratings for CBC's Greatest Canadian."
10 For a summary of the media discussion, see Doyle, "The Importance of Being Witty."
11 For a sample of the extensive coverage of the results, see "Douglas Named CBC's Greatest Canadian"; Finn, "Was Tommy Douglas Our Greatest Canadian?"; and Esmail, "Take Pride in the Concept." Esmail's article used Douglas's win to discuss the feasibility of medicare, which indicates how seriously the results were regarded.
12 Dilthey, *The Formation of the Historical World*, 258.
13 Dilthey, *The Formation of the Historical World*, 257.
14 Dilthey, *The Formation of the Historical World*, 247.
15 Dilthey, *The Formation of the Historical World*, 248.

16 See Marcus's discussion of the relationship between collective biography and the corresponding ideas in psychology, *Auto/biographical Discourses*, 57–59.

17 See Booth's introduction to *How to Make It as a Woman*.

18 For a discussion of representativeness, see Gilmore, "Represent Yourself."

19 See my discussion of national biography in "Bio-Power," 19–21, and the work of Benedict Anderson on what he calls the biography of the nation.

20 See *"Great Britons* Spin-Offs," at http://en.wikipedia.org/wiki/Greatest_Britons _spin-offs (accessed December 15, 2005).

21 See BBC Worldwide Press Releases, "Canadians Nominate in Record Numbers."

22 The advocates for the top ten greatest Canadians were· Melissa Auf de Mer, a bassist for the band Hole, for David Suzuki; popular historical author Charlotte Grey for John A. Macdonald; former Reform Party MP Deborah Grey for Wayne Gretzky; actor Paul Gross for Lester B. Pearson; professional wrestler Bret "The Hitman" Hart for Don Cherry; Sook-Yin Lee, host of a CBC new-music show, for Terry Fox; journalist and television personality Rex Murphy for Pierre Trudeau; former MuchMusic VJ and current host of CBC's *The Hour* George Stromboulopoulos for Tommy Douglas; CBC host Evan Solomon for Alexander Graham Bell; and actress Mary Walsh for Frederick Banting. See the CBC's *Greatest Canadian* webpage at www.cbc.ca/greatest/advocates for a list and more details about the advocates.

23 See Ponce de Leon, *Self-Exposure*, 16–21.

24 For a discussion of the development of "intimacy" in celebrity reportage, see chapter 1 of Ponce de Leon's *Self-Exposure* and Gamson's "The Assembly Life of Greatness," 259–282. For a discussion of celebrity theory, see Wilson's review of celebrity studies in *Oprah, Celebrity and Formations of Self*, 159–163, and Marshall's argument that "celebrity" is a discursive social formation in *Celebrity and Power*.

25 See Gamson's discussion of the ambiguity of celebrity treatments as a "fault line" between meritocracy and democracy in "The Assembly Life of Greatness," 261–65.

26 "Tommy Douglas," *The Greatest Canadian*.

27 "Terry Fox," *The Greatest Canadian*.

28 "Don Cherry," *The Greatest Canadian*.

29 "I'm Good, But I'm Not the Greatest," interview with Don Cherry, CBC News Online, at www.cbc.ca/story/canada/national/2004/10/22/cherry_greatest041022 .html.

References

BBC Worldwide Press Releases. "Canadians Nominate in Record Numbers in the Hunt to Find the Greatest Canadian." June 16, 2004. Available at www. markstarowicz.com/articles/ BBC_Greatest_Canadian.doc. Accessed December 28, 2007.

Booth, Allison. *How to Make It as a Woman: Collective Biographical History from Victoria to the Present*. Chicago: University of Chicago Press, 2004.

Deziel, Shanda. "Great Canadian Exercise in Futility." *Maclean's*, November 1, 2004: 50.

Dilthey, Wilhelm. *The Formation of the Historical World in the Human Sciences*. Edited and translated by Rudolph A. Makkreel and Frithjof Rodi. Princeton: Princeton University Press, 2002.

Dixon, Guy. "Solid Ratings for CBC's Greatest Canadian." *Globe and Mail*, December 1, 2004. Archived by Friends of Canadian Broadcasting at www.friends.ca/News/Friends_News/archives/articles12010409.asp. Accessed December 29, 2007.

"Douglas Named CBC's Greatest Canadian." *Globe and Mail*, November 29, 2004.

Doyle, John. "The Importance of Being Witty and Snippy (*The Greatest Canadian*)." *Globe and Mail*, November 15, 2004: R2.

Esmail, Hadeem. "Take Pride in the Concept, Not the Execution." *Guelph Mercury*, December 8, 2004: A11.

Finn, Ed. "Was Tommy Douglas Our Greatest Canadian? No One Else Comes Close." *CPCA Monitor*, February 2005: 4.

Gamson, Joshua. "The Assembly Life of Greatness: Celebrity in Twentieth-Century America." In *Popular Culture: Production and Consumption*, edited by C. Lee Harrington and Denise D. Beilby, 259–82. Malden, MA: Blackwell's, 2001.

Gilmore, Leigh. *The Limits of Autobiography: Trauma and Testimony*. Ithaca, NY: Cornell University Press, 2001.

"*Great Britons* Spin-Offs." Available at http://en.wikipedia.org/wiki/Greatest_Britons_spin-offs. Accessed December 15, 2005.

"The Greatest Canadian." *Globe and Mail*, October 16, 2004.

Hogarth, David. *Documentary Television in Canada: From National Public Service to Global Marketplace*. Montreal and Kingston: McGill-Queen's University Press, 2002.

"I'm Good, But I'm Not the Greatest: Don Cherry." CBC News Online, October 22, 2004. Available at www.cbc.ca/story/canada/national/2004/10/22/ cherry_greatest041022.html. Accessed December 28, 2007.

Intini, John. "Greatness Has Been Thrust Upon Them." *Maclean's*, December 13, 2004: 56.

Marcus, Laura. *Auto/biographical Discourses: Theory, Criticism, Practice*. Manchester: Manchester University Press, 1994.

Marshall, P. David. *Celebrity and Power: Fame in Contemporary Culture*. Minneapolis: University of Minnesota Press, 1997.

Ponce de Leon, Charles L. *Self-Exposure: Human-Interest Journalism and the Emergence of Celebrity in America 1890–1940*. Chapel Hill: University of North Carolina Press, 2002.

Rak, Julie. "Bio-Power: CBC Television's *Life and Times* and A&E Network's *Biography*." Special issue edited by Laurie McNeill, "Reconsidering Genre," *Life Writing* 1 (2) (2005): 19–45.

Salutin, Rick. "Canadians Are the Greatest." *Globe and Mail*, October 22, 2004: A19.

Starowicz, Mark. "Notes for Remarks by Mark Starowicz before the Senate Transport and Communications Committee." CBC/Radio-Canada Online Archives, April 28, 2003. Available at www.cbc.radio-canada.ca/speeches/20030428.shtml. Accessed December 28, 2007.

Wilson, Sherryl. *Oprah, Celebrity and Formations of Self*. New York: Palgrave Macmillan, 2003.

Filmography

"Don Cherry," *The Greatest Canadian* (CBC, 2004)
"Terry Fox," *The Greatest Canadian* (CBC, 2004)
"Tommy Douglas," *The Greatest Canadian* (CBC, 2004)

MICHELE BYERS

Canadian Idol and the Myth
of National Identity

Idol: 1. a. An image used as an object of worship. b. A false god. 2. One that is adored, often blindly or excessively. 3. Something visible but without substance.[1]

In 2003, Canadians were captivated by the reality series *Canadian Idol* (*CI*), which brought together millions of viewers every week to name the first "Canadian Idol." In 2004, 2005, and 2006, even more Canadians tuned in to name the nation's second, third, and fourth Idols.

Although one of the foundational myths of Canadianness is its pluralism—the impossibility of reducing it to a single identity—*CI* demonstrates that many Canadian viewers revel in the opportunity to participate in the elevation of one individual to iconic Canadian status. The purpose of this inquiry into *CI* is less about the nation itself than about those identities that are produced as belonging authentically to it within the limits of the nation's ability—that is, the ability of those who can be counted among its citizens—to imagine community.[2] *CI*'s use of the actual, posited as the real, to produce and reproduce mythic ideas about Canadianness places the series squarely within the television hybrid between reality and fiction that this book is about.

In the following pages, I will explore several of the competing discourses that structured and circulated within *CI*. These discourses concern themselves primarily with questions of regional and national identity. Looking across several seasons of *CI*, I ask what particular patterns—patterns of exclusion but also patterns of success—might tell us about how at least some Canadians imagine the nation and its citizens. The purpose of this examination of what is clearly an important phenomenon in Canadian popular culture is not to unearth a truth that is generalizable across all texts or even all seasons of *CI*. Rather, I read *CI* as a productive space in which some of the myths about Canadian identity—historical, national, regional, spatial, classed, racialized, gendered—are put on display and, in a sense, battled over.[3] There is no essential quality that defines Canadians, nor is there some empirical truth to be found in the regional and/or national stereotypes that are at times mobilized by *CI*. In fact, as Kim Sawchuk has noted, the exclusive focus and critique of stereotypes tends to elide the way that multiple discourses about region, nation, space, class, gender, sexuality, and racialized identity participate in the governance of populations through a variety of modalities, including the media.[4] This chapter is thus an attempt to interrogate the way mythic ideas about Canada and Canadians are deeply embedded in the fabric of everyday life and to ask how they circulate in the most visible spaces of our public cultures.

It is important to point out, of course, that *CI* is not a Canadian show per se, in the sense that the original idea did not come from the mind of a Canadian, nor was the original series upon which the ever-expanding franchise is based conceived of here. *CI* is but a single national articulation of the hugely popular and successful *Idol* franchise developed by Simon Fuller, originally as *Pop Idol* in the UK and now with at least thirty-five versions airing globally. Production partner Fremantle Media's website says, "The global number of votes for *Idols* has now exceeded three billion!"[5] What is interesting about *Idol* as an intertextual matrix of texts is how each trades on particular notions of nation and national authenticities while marginalizing—except perhaps in the never to be repeated *World Idol* event of 2003—the franchise's non-national origins. In Canada, it's true that the show airs in the summer months, when most popular series are not running new episodes. But the show's popularity has garnered a lion's share of the audience in many parts of the country—sometimes close to three million viewers, if ratings posted on the CTV website are to be believed—in season after season. And this popularity may be seen to reside in the way it plays by turn into myths about the particularity and the universality of Canadian national identity and in the ways it both consciously models and distances itself from the even more popular *American Idol*.

The competition's explicit purpose, to select a star, is connected to an implicit purpose, to select a representative Canadian. The necessity, and the difficulty, of doing this can be seen in the way that Canadianness, or perhaps more specifically local and/or regional affiliation, is made integral to the way both the series' episodes and the star identities of the contestants are constructed. For example, Jenny Gear's identity as a Newfoundlander, not a Canadian, was a point returned to again and again over the course of the first season. Her pride in her "home" is paralleled by the pride her local and/or regional supporters voiced throughout the competition, at times in interviews on camera, as they asserted their intention to vote for their local talent and to push for her to win the national competition. In Nova Scotia, where I live, the plight of first-season contestants Richie Wilcox and Gary Beals was a regular feature on the local news, where viewers were encouraged to watch and vote as often as possible for "our" potential idols. Although we cannot know for sure what motivates viewers in their voting choices, the results of *CI* across the first four seasons suggest that determining Canadianness often takes precedence over star quality because of the regional loyalties of at least part of the voting audience. This is also suggested by the show's promotion and mobilization of mythic fictions of regional identity, as embodied by contestants like Jenny, Richie, Gary, and others. Similar fictions of national identity were also mobilized, including the normative "Joe Canada" influence of the show's presenter, Ben Mulroney, and to a lesser extent his sidekick, John Dore, and even the judges.[6]

The show itself consists of a singing competition in which the judges—formerly minor figures in Canadian music but now celebrities—choose thirty contestants from across Canada and then, in the weeks that follow, voice their opinions on the singers' abilities from a performance hall in Toronto. Later, the viewing audience is invited to phone in to vote for the singer they would like to see remain in the competition. A key split in the text occurs when the judges voice opinions but no longer actually decide who remains in the competition. While the judges appear to be neutral and their own regional, local, or community ties are often virtually invisible on the show, the audience's provincial affiliations seem to influence voting patterns. While voter breakdowns are not available to the public, it is interesting to note that what tends to emerge as the competition nears its final episodes is a vision of Idolness—that is, of *Canadian* Idolness—that is non-urban. Racialized and ethnic identities appear to be mediated through this primary category, as well as through gender and possibly class. That is, racialized and ethnic urban identities, as well as urbanness more generally, become less and less visible as the competition progressed in all of the first four years of broadcast. Racialized identities that are non-urban and feminine are somewhat more visible in the later stages of the competition.[7] Certain identities—Aboriginal, poor, recent immigrant or refugee (among them many of the nation's poorest citizens), religious but not Christian, and non-English- or French-speaking, for example—are not present at all.[8]

Regional Identity on *Canadian Idol*

Mythic contradictions between national and regional identity are built into *CI*. The early episodes, shot during the audition period, are regional; some late episodes, filmed after the final ten contestants have been chosen, include video segments given over to an exploration of contestants' lives "behind the scenes." A lot of this attention is lavished on contestants who live outside Canada's major cities—the majority of the top ten every season thus far. Newfoundland, for example, received a great deal of coverage during the first season of *CI*; co-host John Dore visited singer Jonathan King's rustic Newfoundland home and, later in the show, kissed a cod at a local pub. The exoticization of Newfoundland may also help explain the success of jazz singer Jenny Gear discussed previously. This evocation of regionalism overflows with familiar, culturally dichotomous stereotypes about good ole white boys and girls from rural regions and stylish, sophisticated, multicultural urbanites. Musical choices often reflect this split, although breaking with the judges' expectations and what they implicitly suggest about identity can pay off. Jenny Gear, for example, seemed to be more fascinating to the judges as a rural Newfoundlander who was singing jazz than as a "good" singer. The jazz stylings of other, often urban singers did not necessarily elicit the same enthusiasm.

The regional composition of the show is telling in other ways. Canada's three largest cities make up fully one-third of the country's population, mid-sized cities another third, and small towns the final third. Of the top thirty contestants on *CI*'s first season, twenty-two were from metropolitan Canada; nine of these from the three major centers, including seven from Toronto. In the final eleven, five were from non-urban Canada and none of the other six were from the major centers.[9] Among the top thirty, 44 per cent of the contestants were not white, while in the final eleven, only 27 per cent of the contestants were not white.[10] A similar pattern could be seen in season two. Of the top thirty contestants, nine were from the three major centres, eighteen hailed from the largest ten urban centres, and of these only ten came from non-metropolitan Canada. But of the final ten contestants, only one came from a top ten centre, Vancouver, and three came from non-urban Canada. Among the top thirty in 2004, fully half were not white, while in the top ten, all but two contestants, or 80 per cent, were white.[11] Scattered throughout all four seasons were a small number of francophones, as well as a few contestants whose whiteness was complicated by their ethnic heritage.[12] The link between racialization and location, or urbanness and otherness, is thus evident on the show.

It is useful to think about mediated identity as being produced in the relationship between spaces, audiences, and media texts. Canadian cultural theorist Jody Berland writes, "The production of texts cannot be conceived of outside of the production of diverse and exacting spaces ... occupants of spaces ... who, by being *there*, help to produce definite meanings and effects."[13] Texts produce spaces, are produced by and within spaces, and are made meaningful by audiences occupying particular spaces.

What exactly are the identities produced through the spatial and textual relationships on *CI*? How might viewers make sense of them? And how might these spatially inflected identities be read as a narrative that both asserts and resists the meta-myths of Canadian national identity, which are both fictions and realities?[14]

The narrative and mythic threads that are woven together to make televised images of Canadian spaces legible are produced in languages that it is assumed viewers occupying various spaces will have particular relationships to or ways of reading, in this case of reading *CI* and its participants. So, for example, a "character" like Kalan Porter is linked to the semi-rural landscape of southern Alberta, with its own mythic links to the West, whiteness, family values, religiosity, innocence, youth, and so on. Kalan Porter *is* a person who hails from Medicine Hat and may embody many of these traits, but he is also a character constructed within the mediated production of *CI*, with particular identity markers highlighted, in much the same way that characters on other more traditionally "fictional" television series are produced, to make his character as legible, meaningful, and appealing as possible to a broad national audience.

CI draws extensively on this mythic language, usually by using a shorthand for particular—often regional and spatial, but also racialized, gendered, and classed—Canadian identities shared among viewers across the nation who, like television viewers more globally, might have no firsthand—and thus only mythic—knowledge of people living in regions other than their own. As Aniko Bodroghkozy remarks in her reading of *Street Legal*, Canadian television texts tend to engage with the question "Where is here?" but to do so means asking that question from a multiplicity of regional positions, each of which will give a different answer. In the case of *Street Legal*, which took place in urban Toronto, the series allowed for the "pleasures of national self-recognition" and at the same time encouraged critiques of the centre from the regional "hinterland[s]."[15] *CI*, conversely, is not rooted in a single location but imagines itself to take place in "the nation," and so creates a constantly evolving and mobile space from which audiences can interrogate the questions "Where is here?" and

"Who belongs (t)here?" Using media texts as a way of mapping the nation has a long history in this country, but it is also clearly meaningful on a wider global scale.[16] And that is very likely one of the reasons why the *Idol* franchise has been successfully replicated in so many countries.

Canadian Identity on *Canadian Idol*

As the first season of *CI* wound towards its end, there was a shift away from the regional in the narrative focus. The contestants, while still often visibly connected to their local sites of emergence, were in a sense reframed as national markers. The audience was reminded again and again that their (our) choices would determine who the next Canadian Idol would be, and the importance of each vote in favour of a particular contestant was confirmed ("Your vote counts!"). The reasons for the voting patterns that emerged, and the more particular characteristics of the voting patterns— who actually voted for which contestant according to various demographic categories—are not available for scrutiny. However, what can be seen across the first four seasons of *CI* is a narrowing of the spectrum of identities among the contestants as each season progressed. As I discussed in the introduction, this was seen primarily through the exclusion of urban and non-white participants. While most of the top ten competitors every season were white, those few contestants who were not white were often of mixed-race parentage. They were also not from major Canadian urban centres, nor were they recent immigrants or refugees.[17] That is, within the multiple and contested discourses circulating within *CI*, there appears to be a relationship between nation and the refusal of certain forms of otherness associated in large part with urbanism.[18] We can see this in the departures of Toya Alexis, Mikey Bustos, Jermain Maxwell, Quinsha Wint, Davika Mathur, Danian Vickers, Alisha Nauth, and others.

Ryan Malcolm, a moderately talented, moderately attractive, and altogether bland young white man from Kingston, Ontario, wins the 2003 competition. Kalan Porter, an eighteen-year-old blond, blue-eyed, dimple-cheeked, Christian, family-oriented young man from Medicine Hat, Alberta, wins in 2004. In 2005, the winner is Melissa O'Neil, a seventeen-year-old high school student from Calgary whose father is white (Irish and French) and mother Chinese. And in 2006, it is Eva Avila, a nineteen-year-old postal clerk and beauty consultant from Gatineau with a French Canadian mother and Peruvian father. Melissa was almost voted out twice in the early episodes of the top ten—Rex Goudie was favoured to win in 2006. In season four, Tyler Lewis, who finished third, and Chad Doucette, fourth—two white men from small towns in Saskatchewan and

Nova Scotia, respectively—were the judges' picks for the final two. In the first season, the runner-up was Gary Beals, a black Nova Scotian from East Preston; in season two, it was Theresa Sokyrka, a Ukrainian woman from Saskatoon. In both years, the judges' pick for winner was the third-place contestant: Billy Klippert and Jacob Hoggard, two white men from out West, Alberta and BC, who have gone on to have some professional success. In years three and four, the runners-up were both white men from Newfoundland, Rex Goudie and Craig Sharpe.

Is there any pattern here at all? Perhaps not, except, as I have been arguing, for what is absent or what has been excluded—that is, visible social difference—and what appears in its place—that is, a vision of difference that might be read as gentler and easier to assimilate or already assimilated into the Canadian multicultural myth. Rhoda Howard suggests that most Canadians are "schooled in tolerance and multiculturalism" yet still grudgingly accede that "their vision of a typical Canadian" is "a blue-eyed, white-skinned Anglo-Saxon."[19] Herein lies a paradox of Canadianism, caught between the iconic figures of multiculturalism and the *pure laine* white Anglo and French cultures of settlement. At the same time that state-sanctioned multiculturalism has resisted a "common national culture or shared national identity and set of traditions," it has not displaced the myth of origins played out by protagonists whose particular identities are often still considered most unproblematically Canadian.[20] The further a *CI* contestant travels from this set of markers, urban and racialized, but also related to religion, gender, class, and linguistic competency, the less likely she or he is to move forward in the competition.

Media texts produce images of Canadianness, and in so doing participate in the establishment of a commonsense understanding of what a Canadian *is*—or *isn't*. This is not to suggest that all viewers buy into these images, but that the media reiterate discourses of privilege that already structure the everyday worlds that we live in. *CI* draws on mythological notions about nation and national identity in Canada, and although much of the series is lighthearted, playful, and kitschy, it nonetheless participates in the consolidation and recirculation of these familiar myths. Writing about the second round of *CI* in *Maclean's*, Shanda Deziel suggests that one of the best things about *Idol* 2004 was "Canadian Humility": "Unlike its American sibling, the more folksy *Canadian Idol* doesn't take itself too seriously … What the show lacks in musical integrity, it makes up for with heart."[21] If "folksy" may be defined as "modest," "traditional," and "unpretentious," then, according to Deziel, *CI* bears out another myth about Canadianness: that Canadians are unpretentious and thus they look not for cold talent but for heart, the ability to represent the nation.[22]

Clearly, such an essentializing notion of Canadianness does little to further our understanding of identity, but it does demonstrate that these types of mythologies are constantly in circulation in the public spaces of Canadian mass culture and as such are performative. That is, in their reiteration across various spaces within the public sphere, notions of who and what is Canadian are reinforced and made to matter.[23]

The *CI* series sets in motion the production of spaces in which the Canadian public can choose among its best and brightest young unknowns to crown an Idol. Only certain performers are able to access a discourse that positions them as natural extensions of the Canadian landscape, authentic owners of Canadianness.[24] Others connect to their Canadian roots in more fragmented and complex ways. While state-sanctioned discourses present non-hierarchical multiculturalism as an incontestable truth, some Canadians are seen to be simply Canadian, while others must balance their Canadianness with an at least perceived assortment of other identities that keep them at arm's length from a truly rooted—and largely mythic—Canadianness. Writing about the second season of *CI*, Shanda Deziel lamented Canada's—that is, Canadians'—lack of "soul," a euphemism for an urban, non-white sound. The three members of the 2004 top thirty addressed in Deziel's article were all voted off before the top ten, all three are black, two from Toronto and one from Montreal. Contestant Liz Titian is quoted as saying the 2004 top ten lacked "black style, people singing R&B. The talents, voices and styles are too similar."[25] This sameness, however, appears to have resonated with large segments of the viewing and voting audience.

By the time only the final three contestants of the first season of *CI* were left, all singers hailing from major Canadian cities had been eliminated. The three remaining were young men from mid-sized Canadian cities—Billy from Calgary, Gary from Halifax, and Ryan from Kingston—two were white, and one was black Nova Scotian.[26] In the second season of *CI*, the final three contestants were from mid-sized or small Canadian cities: Jacob from Abbotsford, Teresa from Saskatoon, and Kalan from Medicine Hat. In 2004, all the contestants were white, although this time one was a woman. In 2005, all the contestants were from mid-sized cities or small towns—Aaron from St. Thomas, Ontario; Rex from Burlington, Newfoundland; and Melissa from Calgary—one finalist was not white and one was a woman. And the very same patterns emerged in 2006, with Tyler from Rockglen, Saskatchewan; Craig from Upper Island Cove, Newfoundland; and Eva from Gatineau, Quebec. In 2004 and 2005, the winners were both young women of mixed-race parentage. In each year, urban Canadian identities, with their suggestion of specific and often less recuperable forms of racialized, ethnic, linguistic, and religious differences, and sexual orientations, were displaced from the televisual frame.

Voting Canadian Idol

Media images are ideological, invested in what can be represented as authentic in a given context.[27] Although these images can be contested, they are important purveyors of the discourses that construct identity, difference, and nation in Canada and legitimize and render certain identities legible, visible, and authentic while others are marginalized, if seen at all. *CI* is a specific type of reality TV in which audiences appear to be granted some control over the outcome of the narrative. In this case, the control involves the seeming investment of viewers with the authority to define both Canadianness and Idolness through what Jeffrey Jones has called a "televised participatory democracy" or what Douglas Rushkoff, in another context, called "MTV's nod to democracy."[28] Again, we are talking about mythic structures—voting for an Idol, or for a national leader, for that matter, does not in itself constitute, at least not necessarily, either an act of resistance or an act of hegemony. The audience can only intervene within the limited set of discursive formations they have access to. That is, they are bound within the limits of both the text and the historical, social, and cultural relations of power that form the context in which they live and within which the text is both produced and consumed.

Writing in *Harper's* magazine, Francine Prose acknowledges, "*American Idol*, the talent show that asks fans to vote for their favorite contestants by telephone, received 110 million calls during its first season, 15.5 during the final show alone."[29] CTV has also consistently reported high ratings for *CI* among Canadian viewers. In his article on talk television, Jeffrey Jones describes the increasing adoption by political talk shows of what he calls "the people's voice in action," or "vox pop," wherein part of a program's structure is a "rewarding [of] the viewer as an 'engaged' citizen as he or she help[s] construct the programming." Further, "The variety of ways in which programs intentionally recognize and flatter their audiences ha[s] greatly increased."[30]

The producers of the critical PBS documentary *The Merchants of Cool: A Report on the Creators and Makers of Popular Culture for Teenagers* use the MTV call-in video show *Total Request Live* as an example of this process at work. *TRL* was developed during a period when MTV's "coolness" factor was lagging, and the idea behind its development was to reassert the network's authenticity as a voice of American youth culture by creating a fantasy of viewer control. However, as Ann Powers, music critic for the *New York Times,* points out in the documentary, this itself is part of the myth: "I mean, I guess you could say that *Total Request Live* is democratic in the way that, you know, this year's [2000] election was democratic. The candidates, the field of candidates, is very small. And there are organizations behind them, not unlike the Democratic and Republican parties, who are deciding which candidates get promoted. So, in other words, you can't just be, you know, Joe Fabulous who's releasing your little indie record and get on *Total Request Live.*"[31]

Reality series like *CI* work in a similar way, engaging the audience in what appears to be a straightforward participatory process. The myth they enact in this process is that every person who presents him- or herself before the *CI* judges has an equal chance of becoming the next Idol. This reaffirms the fantasy that all Canadians are equal and elides the way issues of urbanness, region, racialization, ethnicity, gender, language, ability, sexual orientation, religion, and age come into play in determining the appropriate head to wear the *Idol* crown. The series cannot exist outside of relations of power—viewers and text alike come into being in a context constructed by these discourses.

The phantasm of the active audience appears to create a space of resistance, in that it pits the judges against viewers who, at a certain point, can—and do—reject the judges' authority. Here is the space where the audience seems able to refuse the traditional televisual order, where the experts and producers appear to have all the power. But this resistance is limited. As is the case with *TRL,* the choices made on *CI* are made within a set of constraints: for example, a huge number of potential choices have already been eliminated by the time the audience gets a chance to vote. But in a more complicated way, resistance is also limited by the discursive space in which Canadianness itself is defined. The fact that the four seasons of *CI* evidence a similar pattern of exclusion of the urban—and the multiplicity of identities that are collapsed within its confines—in favor of more mythic, and arguably safer, images of Canadianness attests to these limits.

Conclusion

In *CI,* we can see some of the great myths through which many ideas about Canadian identities are brought into being. We see which identities circulate most comfortably within the discourses of nationhood mobilized by the series. The choice of winner appears to be inflected not only by our conception of talent and appreciation for song, but also by our connection to region and our understanding of Canadianness along such axes as gender, racialization, and location (urbanness). *CI* produces an ambivalent televisual space within which mythic notions of Canadianness are reinscribed and contested, within certain limits. While the first four Canadian Idols crowned seem at first glance quite different, a closer look at the road from top thirty to last man or woman standing reveals a distinct pattern. Year after year, what is excluded from the competition is the urban, and with it all the identities that we associate with contemporary urbanness, especially racialized populations, the poor, immigrants, and refugees, as well as queer and trans populations.[32]

The fact that the *Idol* franchise has been so successfully reproduced, although not without ambivalence and contestation, in so many national contexts suggests something about the labour that such series perform in producing nationalist fictions. There is something paradoxical about the global reach of *Idol* as a universal meta-narrative that is also about the particularities of national identity, but it's something that seems well suited to the neo-liberal/conservative moment in which it has bloomed. Katherine Meizel, an American doctoral student who is writing her dissertation on *American Idol*, calls the US version of the series a "civil religion," one that produces "denuded … 'safe' aspects of African-American and popular culture," and argues that the show is rife with idealized "Southern archetypes" that are as pervasive among *American Idol* winners as they are among politicians. Meizel sees these patterns, yet also notes the idiosyncratic nature of her own voting patterns, which she studied as part of the thesis work—in 2006, she voted for the Jewish contestant because she's Jewish; in 2007, she voted for the woman who she felt rejected stereotypical notions of racialized and ethnicized gender identity by refusing to straighten her curly hair.[33]

What Meizel observes reiterates my reading of *CI* as a text in which national identities are performed in contradictory although largely hegemonic ways. At the same time, like Meizel, I am conscious of seeking out, as I suspect many viewers do, my own favourite contestants based on the unique identities they put on display and the proximity I feel they have to my own shifting sense of self, whether on the basis of ethnicity, gender, sexual orientation, region, or style. Thus, it may be that part of the global appeal of these series lies in the possibility—usually, if not always, deferred—of the disruption of the very nationalist ideals they call into being and have thus far seemed destined to reiterate.

Television texts cannot be understood outside of the spaces within which they are produced, nor can cultural identities be thought of as being articulated entirely outside of these spaces. Neither texts nor identities can be understood outside of their contexts of production, contexts which are framed by the discursive limits through which concepts like national identity or Canadianness have been constituted. There are, potentially, possibilities for resistance. The discourses circulating in and around *CI* potentially contest but also shore up mythic notions about Canada as a nation and about Canadians, the people who live and seek to belong within its borders. While the relationships between and within the texts, spaces, discourses, and identities produced and disseminated in and through television texts like *CI* are complex, contradictory, and shifting, we must continually try to tease out the possible ways that they help or hinder us— and, increasingly, a globalized community of viewers—understand and at times misunderstand the landscapes and identities in which we live.

Acknowledgements

Early drafts of this paper were presented at the Second Annual Canadian Association of Cultural Studies Conference in Hamilton in 2004 and the Standing Conference on Organizational Symbolism in Halifax in 2004. Thanks also to Antje Rauwerda, who co-wrote the original conference proposals.

Notes

1   At www.dictionary.com (accessed January 7, 2008).
2   Anderson, *Imagined Communities*; Higson, "The Limiting Imagination of National Cinema"; Wagman, "Wheat, Barley, Hops, Citizenship." I am indebted here to Andrew Higson's critique of the by now ubiquitous—and too often uncritical—use of Benedict Anderson's description of national "imagined communities" and to Ira Wagman's article on the Molson "I am Canadian!" ads, which directed me to Higson. Higson argues that Anderson "seems unable to acknowledge the cultural difference and diversity that invariably marks both the inhabitants of a particular nation-state and the members of more geographically dispersed 'national communities'" (Wagman, "Wheat, Barley, Hops, Citizenship," 78).
3   That is, taking a cue from Barthes (1973), not untruths but commonsense understandings of the world shared by many people, understandings that are rarely unpacked to reveal how they are rooted in historical matrices of power.
4   Sawchuk, "Feminist Media Studies."
5   At www.fremantlemedia.com/our-programmes/view/Global+Hit+Formats/view programme/Idols (accessed January 7, 2008).
6   The idea or category that I call Joe Canada or Joe Canadian is actually quite flexible. It is, in a sense, a mythic category of white, largely ex-urban (both outside of the urban but also transcending it) masculinity through which complexly signifying identities such as location, ethnicity, class, occupation, and religion are collapsed into a mythic signifier. The judges have much more complex identities—as racialized, gendered, or ethnicized minorities—that are almost never activated within the discourses that circulate on the show, except in the most essentialist ways; for example, the suggestion that Sass Jordan is "nice" because she is a woman.

7 I use "urban" here to refer not to all cities but to the major metropolitan centres of Canada: Vancouver, Toronto, and Montreal. According to 2006 data at www .statcan.ca, the metropolitan areas of Canada include, in descending order, Toronto, Montreal, Vancouver, Ottawa–Gatineau, Calgary, Edmonton, Quebec City, Winnipeg, Hamilton, London, Kitchener–Waterloo, Saint-Catharines–Niagara, Halifax, Oshawa, Victoria, Windsor, Saskatoon, Regina, Sherbrooke, St. John's (NL), Barrie, Kelowna, Abbotsford, Sudbury, Kingston, Saguenay, Trois-Rivières, Guelph, Moncton, Brantford, Thunder Bay, Saint John (NB), and Peterborough. However, the bottom sixteen metropolitan areas have populations of less than 200,000, while the bottom twenty-four have less than 500,000.

8 There are very few Canadians of Asian, South Asian, Arabic, Middle Eastern, Latin, or African descent represented in the series. Whether this reflects the lack of participation of these groups in the *CI* competition is not clear. However, it is worth noting that this invisibility mirrors the relative invisibility of these groups, with notable exceptions, in Canadian television more generally.

9 Although one contestant is from Etobicoke, Ontario, a town of 348,000 that is now part of the Greater Toronto Area, and another is from Weston, Ontario, a town of 120,000 that is now also part of the GTA.

10 I recognize how problematic the use of the terms "white" and "non-white" are. When possible, I have tried to be more specific in designating the racial and/or ethnic affiliation of the *CI* contestants. Although making this particular linguistic choice runs the risk of recreating a binary with whiteness as the prioritized term against which all others are judged and found wanting, I believe that it is necessary to mark this split as it plays out on the television screen. Unlike American television, which is seen as explicitly segregated, breaking along a black/white binary, Canadian television is produced through the mythic discourses of Canadian multiculturalism that fantasize this nation as "colour blind and race neutral" (Fleras, "Racialising Culture/Culturalising Race," 431). My desire here is thus to mark the way that the body as a racialized site of Canadian politics and social power emerges in opposition to this myth.

11 Similar patterns are evident in the later seasons as well. In season three, only five contestants hailed from Canada's largest cities, although two more came from Mississauga and eleven from mid-sized cities. In the final ten, no contestant came from the top three and five came from smaller metropolitan areas. In season four, this pattern was even more pronounced. Among the top twenty-two, only one hailed from a top three city, while eight came from smaller cities. In season three, among the top thirty, seven contestants and two among the top ten were not white. In season four, five of the top twenty-two and two of the top ten were not white.

12 Theorized by some as being "off-white." See, for example, Gilman, *The Jew's Body*.

13 Berland, "Angels Dancing," 39, emphasis in the original.

14 In a February 2007 article in the *Globe and Mail*, Marina Jiménez explores "cracks in the mosaic" of Canadian multiculturalism. Talking to young second-generation Canadians who are "visible minorities," Jiménez identifies a growing dissatisfaction with the gap between the myth of multiculturalism and inclusivity, and the feelings of exclusion, inequality, and racism these young people encounter in their everyday lives. She quotes Tarek Fatah, the co-founder of the Muslim Canadian Congress, as saying, "Multiculturalism is the single biggest con job done on racial minorities."

15 Bodroghkozy, "As Canadian as Possible," 539. The same is true of more recent series such as *Little Mosque on the Prairie*, where the disconnect between the urban

(Toronto) imam and the small-town Muslim community in the Prairies that he is brought in to serve is played for as many laughs as the Muslim community's disconnect from the rest of the small-town residents.

16 Hogarth, *Documentary Television in Canada*. Although *CI* is multiply located, physically in the first episodes and via its contestants in later ones, the exclusion of urban contestants year after year might indicate that something is at work here that is not so dissimilar to the "hinterland" critique described by Bodroghkozy in "As Canadian as Possible."

17 Mahtani, "Interrogating the Hyphen-Nation." As Mahtani points out, the way mixed-race Canadians are "read" is complex and contradictory, and often relates to the origins of their parents and their physical appearance. Also see Hill, *Black Berry, Sweet Juice*.

18 Jiménez reports that "visible minorities made up 13.4 percent of the population [in Canada] and nearly half of big cities such as Toronto" (Jiménez, "Ethnic Enclaves").

19 Howard, "Being Canadian," 139.

20 Jiménez, "Ethnic Enclaves." As Mahtani describes in "Interrogating the Hyphen-Nation," the further one travels from this image of Canadianness, the less one's assertion of Canadian identity is accepted uncritically, hence the more one is expected to explain one's origins. This is true of many Canadians who may be second, third, or fourth generation but are not white.

21 Deziel, "Sweet Success."

22 At www.dictionary.com (accessed January 7, 2008).

23 Butler, *Bodies That Matter*.

24 David Young argues that CARAS (the Canadian Academy of Recording Arts and Sciences) has dealt with the criticism that it has discriminated against Canadian minority groups by "attempting to secure Anglo cultural hegemony through consent." As examples, he gives the creation of new awards aimed specifically at excluded groups, the inclusion of members of excluded groups on an advisory council, to provide legitimacy for exclusion, and the expansion of opportunities for excluded groups, perhaps not as winners but as showcased performers (Young, "Ethno-Racial Minorities and the Juno Awards," p. 200). These strategies can be seen—or imagined—in *CI* as well.

25 Deziel, "Canada, Where's Your Soul?"

26 Gary Beals, who comes from Atlantic Canada, presents a version of non-white masculinity that is distanced from a truly urban black masculinity. Further, Beals's identity was complicated by a tendency among many viewers to read him as occupying a queer subject position.

27 Hall, "Racist Ideologies and the Media."

28 Jones, "Vox Populi"; Rushkoff, "The Merchants of Cool."

29 Prose, "*American Idol*," 59. Maybe in the future we should allow federal, provincial, and municipal voters to vote by phone after watching speeches made by political candidates on TV.

30 Jones, "Vox Populi," 20, 26.

31 *Frontline*, "The Merchants of Cool."

32 Although certainly not only the urban, as Aboriginal identities, for example, often and mistakenly imagined as only rural, are absent as well. The North is also largely absent from *CI*. While there have been examples of feminized masculinity on *CI*, queer and trans identities have been very marginal on the show.

33 Kingston, "Get a Ph.D. in 'American Idol.'"

References

Anderson, Benedict. *Imagined Communities*. London: Verso, 1991.

Barthes, Roland. *Mythologies*. London: Paladin, 1973.

Berland, Jody. "Angels Dancing: Cultural Technologies and the Production of Space." In *Cultural Studies*, edited by Lawrence Grossberg, Cary Nelson, and Paula Treichler, 38–50. London: Routledge, 1992.

Bodroghkozy, Aniko. "As Canadian as Possible … Anglo-Canadian Popular Culture and the American Other." In *Hop on Pop: The Politics and Pleasures of Popular Culture*, edited by Henry Jenkins, Tara McLean, and Jane Shattuc, 566–89. Durham, NC: Duke University Press, 2003.

Brydon, Diana. "Introduction: Reading Postcoloniality, Reading Canada." *Essays on Canadian Writing* 56 (1995): 1–19.

Butler, Judith. *Bodies That Matter: On the Discursive Limits of Sex*. London: Routledge, 1993.

Day, Richard. "Identity, Diversity and the Mosaic Metaphor: The National Jewel as the Canadian Thing." *Topia: Canadian Journal of Cultural Studies* 2 (1998): 42–66.

Deziel, Shanda. "Sweet Success." *Maclean's*, September 27, 2004, 44–45.

———. "Canada, Where's Your Soul?" *Maclean's*, August 2, 2004, 90.

Fleras, Augie. "Racialising Culture/Culturalising Race: Multicultural Racism in a Multicultural Canada." In *Racism Eh? A Critical Inter-Disciplinary Anthology of Race and Racism in Canada*, edited by Camille A. Nelson and Charmaine A. Nelson, 429–443. Concord, ON: Captus Press, 2004.

Gatehouse, Jonathon. "And the Winner is … Ben Mulroney." *Maclean's*, September 15, 2003: 20–26.

Gilman, Sander. *The Jew's Body*. New York: Routledge 1991.

Gittings, Christopher E. *Canadian National Cinema*. New York: Routledge, 2002.

Hall, Stuart. "Racist Ideologies and the Media." In *Media Studies: A Reader*, edited by Paul Marris and Sue Thornham, 160–68. Edinburgh: Edinburgh University Press, 1996.

Hay, Carla. "The Tube: 'World Idol' Names Norwegian No. 1." *Billboard*, January 24, 2004. EBSCO search primer 2005.

Higson, Andrew. "The Limiting Imagination of National Cinema." In *Cinema and Nation*, edited by Mette Hjort and Scott MacKenzie, 63–74. London: Routledge, 2000.

Hill, Lawrence. *Black Berry, Sweet Juice: On Being Black and White in Canada*. Toronto: Perennial Canada, 2001.

Hogarth, David. *Documentary Television in Canada*. Montreal and Kingston: McGill-Queen's University Press, 2003.

Howard, Rhoda. "Being Canadian: Citizenship in Canada." *Citizenship Studies* 2 (1): 133–52.

Jiménz, Marina. "Do Ethnic Enclaves Impede Integration?" *Globe and Mail*, February 8, 2007: A8.

Jones, Jeffrey. "Vox Populi as Cable Programming Strategy." *Journal of Popular Film & Television* 31 (1): 18–28.

Kingston, Anne. "Get a Ph.D. in 'American Idol.'" *Maclean's*, June 4, 2007. Available at www.macleans.ca/article.jsp?content=20070604_106064_106064& source=srch. Accessed January 8, 2008.

Lopez, Ana M. "Are All Latins from Manhattan? Hollywood, Ethnography, and Cultural Colonialism." In *Unspeakable Images: Ethnicity and the Modern Cinema*, edited by Lester D. Friedman, 404–24. Champaign: University of Illinois Press, 1991.

Mahtani, Minelle. "Interrogating the Hyphen-Nation: Canadian Multicultural Policy and 'Mixed Race' Identities." *Social Identities* 8 (1): 67–90.

Noble, Jean. "Bound and Invested: Lesbian Desire and Hollywood Ethnography." *CineAction* 45 (1998): 30–40.

Prose, Francine. "Voting Democracy off the Island." *Harper's*, March 2004: 58–64.

Sawchuk, Kim. "To What Extent Have Feminist Media Studies in Canada Taken Broadcast Policy Intervention as a Programmatic Goal? What Trade-offs Would Doing So Involve?" Paper presented at Converging in Parallel: Linking Communications Research and Policy in Emerging Canadian Scholarship, Montreal, November 2006: 42–44.

Wagman, Ira. "Wheat, Barley, Hops, Citizenship: Molson's 'I Am [Canadian]' Campaign and the Defense of Canadian National Identity through Advertising." *The Velvet Light Trap* 50 (2002): 77–89.

Young, David. "Ethno-Racial Minorities and the Juno Awards," *Canadian Journal of Sociology* 31 (2) (2006): 183–210.

Filmography

American Idol (Fremantle Media North America/Fox, 2002–)

Canadian Idol (Insight Production/CTV, 2003–)

Street Legal (CBC, 1987–94)

Frontline, "The Merchants of Cool: A Report on the Creators and Makers of Popular Culture for Teenagers" (PBS, 2001)

DEREK FOSTER

Hockey Dreams
Making the Cut

Hockey programming, from *Hockey Night in Canada* to instructional videos, has always been a prominent feature of Canadian television. In recent years a "pseudo-real" style of hockey-themed programming has appeared, epitomized by the CBC show *Making the Cut*, a thirteen-part series broadcast in 2004 that documented the quest of thousands of Canadians who "auditioned" for the show in an attempt to win a tryout with a Canadian National Hockey League team.

Making the Cut presented the viewer with "actuality" and thus distinguished itself from other pseudo-real hockey representations that tend to retell well-known hockey tales through reconstructions. *Making the Cut* did not re-create real people with the goal of communicating their story and their characters. Rather, real hockey hopefuls had their every action documented as they experienced the thrills and the hardships of competing for a coveted spot on an NHL team roster. Of course, *Making the Cut* is not the same as NHL hockey. Nor does watching the two forms of televised hockey constitute the same sort of experience. But while there may be some aspects of the professional game with which the average viewer has a difficult time identifying, such as the skill level, the salary level, and the pros' lifestyle, the NHL experience is arguably a paradigmatic example of Canadian dreams come to fruition. Indeed, *Making the Cut* is based on this mythos. Before I analyze the show, it is necessary to provide some background on the hockey–TV relationship.

In the minds of many, NHL hockey is "real" hockey. This is not to suggest that all other forms of hockey on television are necessarily fictive. There is nothing "pseudo-real" about amateur hockey tournaments, from the junior level to the Olympics, televised or not. In fact, "real" hockey that is presented "as is" and that is perceived to be dramatic because of the nature of the game and the competition is quite distinct from other forms of hockey programming that either attempt to represent some aspect of that "real" game or that use "real" hockey as a backdrop for dramatic and comedic storylines. The latter iterations can be termed "pseudo-real" in that they depend, to varying degrees, on a connection to the "real" game of hockey but are very obviously something separate from it.

Forms of television programming that incorporate or simulate "real" hockey are consistently featured on Canadian TV screens. Apart from the CBC's regular attempts to reinvigorate its cultural capital with depictions of the sport, one need "merely flick through the sports-specialty channels in the upper reaches of your cable and satellite landscapes (the NHL Network, ESPN Classic Sports, Leafs TV, etc.), not to mention the mainstream offerings on TSN, Sportsnet and The Score, and you quickly will see countless excellent specials about hockey and its heroes."[1] These programs frequently straddle reality and fiction, and operate as a site of identity formation for Canadians. Ultimately, through a focus on *Making the Cut*, I will show that the significance of this programming lies less in its contribution to Canadian identity and more in its constitution of the ideal of NHL hockey within the Canadian consciousness.

Hockey-based Programming and Its Centrality to Canadian Broadcasting

By the early 1960s, "*Hockey Night in Canada* became the CBC's most popular television show, drawing audiences as large as 3.5 million English Canadians and 2 million French Canadians."[2] In 2003, *Hockey Night in Canada* was CBC's highest-rated show and ranked nationally between fifteenth and twentieth each week.[3] Today, hockey and television seem to go hand in hand in Canada. While there might be other cultural forms and popular pursuits that similarly engage Canadian audiences, hockey remains both a popular and frequent source of entertainment on Canadian television. It is a central preoccupation of both television producers and viewers. Hockey, specifically *Hockey Night in Canada*, is seen as integral to Canadian identity, and it has certainly been integral to Canada's public broadcaster. It is profitable for the network, with a widespread and devoted audience and enthusiastic sponsors and advertisers. Some suggested the CBC stood to lose between $20 and $50 million of advertising and sponsorship revenue during the 2004–05 NHL strike.[4] And it satisfies the CRTC's Canadian expression mandate.

Indeed, the NHL is central to the CBC's continued health. Ian Morrison, head of the Friends of Canadian Broadcasting, noted, "NHL hockey accounts for about 15 per cent of the CBC's audience, 25 per cent of its air time and 40 per cent of its ad revenue."[5] With aggressive lobbying for NHL broadcasting rights that are up for renewal in 2008, CTV and its sports cable channel, TSN, created the possibility that NHL hockey could move from its longtime home on Canada's public broadcaster to private networks or that the bidding war that would ensue could increase the rights fees to such a degree that NHL hockey would no longer be a cash cow for the CBC. In the fall of 2006, CBC president Robert Rabinovitch opined that it was "distinctly possible" that the CBC would lose the right to broadcast NHL hockey. Were this to happen, he noted, the CBC would "have to seriously re-evaluate almost everything about English television."[6] This "doomsday" scenario did not come to pass. As some had speculated, the CBC won rights to broadcast NHL games until 2014 and paid more for the privilege of NHL programming but did not lose the brand altogether. CTV and TSN gained more Canadian programming, and the NHL maintained the brand's value for future negotiations.[7]

Regardless of the eventual outcome, it is important to note how much collective hand-wringing accompanied the anticipated loss of the NHL from the public broadcaster. One sports report summarized the situation: "Like the Montreal Forum and Maple Leaf Gardens, nothing lasts forever and the CBC must now consider a future without Canada's national pastime—a future that poses many questions about the network's own health and welfare."[8] Here, as in so many other sources, the loss of NHL hockey was conflated with the loss of Canada's national pastime. Yet not all hockey-themed programming would disappear from the CBC with the loss of professional hockey.

In fact, maybe as a sign of things to come, other hockey-based content seems to be increasingly popular fare on the CBC. Among other shows, *Making the Cut*, like *Hockey Night in Canada*, is attractive to a public broadcaster that is charged with telling Canadian stories to Canadians. Upon its debut, the executive director of network programming at the CBC, Slawko Klymkiw, reported that the series "reinforces CBC's commitment to Canadian hockey."[9] But even with other hockey programs, such as *The Tournament*, there may be reason to doubt this commitment. As a result of the 2004–05 NHL labour dispute, the CBC cancelled *Hockey Day in Canada*. This five-year old, day-long celebration of the sport was built around an NHL triple-header involving the six Canadian teams, including hours of features and clips of hockey at the grassroots level, and was based in a small community; the installment for 2004 took place at Shaunavon, Saskatchewan. The cancellation of this telecast event suggests that it ought to have been called "NHL Day in Canada."[10] Similarly,

Making the Cut did not depict hockey in small-town Canada; its entire premise is built around the dream of playing in the NHL. What, then, was the commitment of Canadian audiences to this series, designed originally as an adjunct to *Hockey Night in Canada*—a supplement to NHL action or a substitute for it?

Overall, the series averaged 457,000 viewers an episode, which was in line with the CBC's top shows but 30 per cent below expectations.[11] An article archived on the website of the National Hockey League Fans' Association reports one potential explanation for the show's relative success: "Many hockey fans believe CBC's *Making the Cut* is the logical substitute for *Hockey Night in Canada* during the NHL lockout."[12] Yet instead of replacing one form of hockey with another, CBC introduced *Movie Night in Canada*, which at its peak attracted 1.1 million viewers. By comparison, CBC reports that *Hockey Night in Canada* consistently draws a typical audience of 1.2 million people on Saturday nights.[13] And even though *Making the Cut*'s debut featured narrator Scott Oake declaring, "It's fine to sing and dance, but in this country, the real idols wear skates," CTV's reality hit, *Canadian Idol*, generated average audiences of more than two million viewers per episode when it first hit the airwaves in summer 2003.[14]

Other hockey-based programming also attracted smaller audiences than expected. CBC's two-night broadcast of *Canada Russia '72* in 2006 attracted an average audience of 793,000, well below what many anticipated would be more than a million.[15] Audiences for another hockey-based production, the 2006 CBC production of *Kraft Hockeyville*, were difficult to calculate since ratings are calculated based on viewers in major television markets whereas the show was geared toward smaller communities. Thus, even though some reports suggest viewership dropped below 100,000, the show was enough of a hit to justify a second installment in 2007.[16]

An even more pronounced shock was the audience response to the marquee production *Hockey: A People's History*. Heavily promoted in 2006, the ten-part series "dug up fascinating stories from our national game and evocatively brought them to life."[17] At a time when Richard Stursberg, executive vice-president of English TV at the network, declared one million viewers the benchmark for a successful primetime CBC show, *Hockey: A People's History* fell woefully short. "Just slightly more than 500,000 viewers tuned in to watch the series in mid-September. On the third night, when the show was up against the popular American reality show *Amazing Race*, it lost more than 200,000 viewers."[18] On September 24, it "drew just 390,000 viewers ... Nine times as many Canadians (2.7 million) watched *Desperate Housewives* that night at the same hour on CTV."[19] This performance contributed to the subsequent directive to make fewer miniseries and concentrate on long-running programs to generate larger audiences.[20] In part, this was due to scheduling. Most of the series was shown before the NHL broadcast season began. With no natural CBC synergy, "At least one major sponsor that had signed on early to *Hockey: A People's History* requested a discount from the network when it learned of its programming strategy."[21]

One should not look at these figures and automatically assume that Canadian audiences prefer pop culture over hockey. The executive producer of *Making the Cut* admitted his series "was body-checked by the prolonged hockey lockout. 'Our show is about the dream of playing in the NHL ... Apparently that dream's not true at this particular time.'"[22] To be sure, as soon as the labour dispute ended, "Canadian hockey fans' euphoria at having their game back ... saw CBC ratings soar to their highest level in more than a decade and TSN's set an all-time record." Subsequent ratings reflected the NHL's popularity as having returned to nearly pre-lockout levels: "The NHL is still far and away the country's top television sports draw."[23]

The Fact and the Fiction of TV-based Hockey

Of course, while all of these hockey-based productions depend on the NHL for some of their appeal, they also help constitute and reproduce the mythic nature of NHL competition. It is worthwhile, then, to ask why *Making the Cut* attracted far fewer people than *Hockey Night in Canada*. Though the content is ostensibly similar, one telling reason may be format. *Making the Cut* is a reality show based on sports, or, conversely, a form of sports programming with an injection of actuality. "Reality TV" is a cumbersome misnomer, for, as James Friedman notes, "Television cannot bring 'reality' to viewers; it can only provide a representation of an event."[24] Similarly, reality TV has been described as "an unabashedly commercial genre united less by aesthetic rules or certainties than by the fusion of popular entertainment with a self-conscious claim to the discourse of the real."[25]

In a sense, then, just as with *Hockey Night in Canada*, *Making the Cut* was programming designed to entertain viewers with "authentic" personalities, real situations, and a narrative that distinguished it from fictional television. "Although originally promoted as a reality TV series, *Making the Cut* ... is more of a documentary that, if nothing else, celebrates this country's love of hockey and the pursuit of the Canadian dream: to play in the National Hockey League"[26] And it is consistent with the CBC's attempt

Figure 1. The "look" of hockey, reality-TV style. Image courtesy of Network Entertainment Inc. (2006)

to do something different, appear less staid, and conduct "constructive observational documentary."[27] While not a documentary per se, it aspired toward a realistic depiction of hockey and the quest to fulfill hockey dreams—a particularly resonant quest in the landscape of the Canadian imaginary. It is documentary insofar as its primary interest is in referentiality, the power of the series to "indicate about the world through sounds and images" rather than in accurately depicting a sense of proximity to everyday life.[28] Seemingly reticent with the label "reality show," *Making the Cut*'s creators termed it a "hockeymentary."[29] Following the Griersonian vision whereby documentaries ought to involve "the creative treatment of actuality," the term "hockeymentary" seems to sum up the conflation of fiction and fact, of drama and actuality involved in *Making the Cut*.[30]

In this spirit, we might refer to Mavis Gallant, who, writing in the late 1940s, observed, "It was neither factual programming nor its fiction counterpart that epitomized 'culture on the air,' but rather a hybrid of the two."[31] Thus, we can see *Making the Cut* and its representation of Canadian culture via its creative retelling of the hockey dream as a prime example of "dramality." Attributed to Mark Burnett, creator of *Survivor*, this label refers to the convergence of drama and reality where drama is engendered by real events. Whether one prefers the label "docutainment" or

Figure 2. Smash-mouth hockey—the reality of the game. Image courtesy of Network Entertainment Inc. (2006)

"the entertaining real," *Making the Cut* seems consistent with television's "postdocumentary context" insofar as it commingles performance with naturalism.[32] Thus, *Making the Cut* is also consistent with the docudrama, "Canada's oldest and most critically acclaimed documentary form ... the dramatization of real-life events."[33]

The label "docudrama" is an interesting one. As Derek Paget points out, docudrama may be used (a) to retell events from national or international histories, either reviewing or celebrating these events, (b) to re-present the careers of significant national figures, and (c) to portray issues of concern to national or international communities. Increasingly, in recent times, it has also aimed (d) to focus on "ordinary citizens" who have been thrust into the news because of some special experience.[34]

All of these approaches have been used in the telling of hockey stories. Examples include *Canada Russia '72*, the celebration of what many suggest is a pivotal moment in Canada's cultural history; *Gross Misconduct*, the sensational, sad, true-life story of what can happen to hockey stars after retirement, focused on the life of Brian Spencer; *Net Worth*, which documents the quest to unionize the NHL; and *Waking Up Wally*, which focuses on the recent life of the father of hockey's most celebrated player. Notably, the promotional material for *Making the Cut* positioned it as "an unprecedented national event and televised docudrama."[35] The show's executive producer acknowledged the balancing act between fiction and documenting of action: "We're looking to extract as much drama as we can out of those situations ... In a way we're as much a docu-drama as we are a reality genre ... Our players don't move on because our fans vote for them in a popularity contest. Our players move on because in the hockey world they have what it takes."[36]

Injections of the "Real": NHL-branded Hockey

Ultimately, when it comes to docudramas, there should be a principle of "relative transferability" wherein the essential elements of a prior event in the real world are recognizable in subsequent dramatizations of that event.[37] With *Waking Up Wally* or *Canada Russia '72*, *Net Worth*, or even *Gross Misconduct*, the events are often well known. In this capacity, like all docudramas, they mine subject matter "that is usually already familiar or accepted as widely known to its audience."[38] *Making the Cut* also has this quality—as do most "reality" shows. These other docudramas are based on events transferred from real life: the struggle to recover from medical trauma, the struggle for international hockey supremacy, the struggle to unionize, or the struggle to deal with post-NHL life and a player's personal demons. All of these occur against the backdrop of hockey. With *Making the Cut*, on the other hand, the essential element of the real world that must be recognizable in its dramatic documenting is the playing of hockey. The prior text that must "show through" so that *Making the Cut*'s narrative is as compelling and authentic as the game of NHL hockey itself.

Most docudramas rely on "unwritten rules of casting (where a broad resemblance to the real-world original is an advantage)."[39] Quebec actor Roy Dupuis, who played Montreal Canadiens star Maurice "Rocket" Richard three times—in a *Heritage Minute* spot, a TV miniseries, and most recently as the title character in the film *The Rocket*, released earlier in Quebec as *Maurice Richard*—said, "I never wanted to do an imitation of him ... I wanted to get the essence of this man, the energy."[40] This was the goal of *Making the Cut*, too—it was not designed as a simulacrum of the NHL game but an embodiment of it. Indeed, hockey-themed productions presume viewers' familiarity with the game and its most popular players. With *Waking Up Wally*, the actor cast to play Wayne Gretzky "needed extensive skating lessons and practice just to get to the point where he can fake being the Great One on-camera."[41] Similarly, *Canada Russia '72* needed to cast actors who were believable as hockey icons. Both productions also required locations that were convincing replicas of the originals. For instance, in the Walter Gretzky story, Edmonton stands in for New York

City and for Brantford, Ontario—birthplace of number 99, the "Great One." "Rexall Place was tricked up with various signage and rink boards to replicate exact moments in time and NHL arenas in other cities. On certain days, the arena represented Maple Leaf Gardens, the old Northlands Coliseum, the Great Western Forum and even Madison Square Garden."[42] For similar cost-cutting reasons, production of *Canada Russia '72* featured the Aitken Centre at the University of New Brunswick in Fredericton as the old Luzhniki Ice Palace and Harbour Station in Saint John doubled as the Vancouver Coliseum.[43]

Other hockey-themed productions seek to reinforce their link to the NHL through cameos of established hockey stars. The 2005 installment of *The Tournament* added "gravitas" with the appearance of former NHL superstar Phil Esposito. Similarly, Showcase Network's *Rent-A-Goalie* (2006) has featured NHL old-timers such as Tiger Williams. *Net Worth* was a 1995 CBC production that told of the exploitation of NHL players in the 1950s and the quest for organized players' rights. The reality of an NHL player's average salary today is far removed from the story in *Net Worth*. Hence, the film ends with a postscript to textually remind the viewer of the tragedies that befell a number of players and reinforce that the events dramatically portrayed actually occurred. Captions at the end of *Net Worth* were used to ground its production in reality and situate its events historically. *Gross Misconduct* used another tactic: it intercut documentary material of NHL games into its story, grafting the real onto its dramatized reconstruction as an important way of authenticating its narrative. Instead of disrupting its retelling, this use of actual footage of hockey games from the period in question served to contextualize the story in a way that actors arguably could not. *Canada Russia '72* also integrated archival material of the actual event into its retelling. The sound of Foster Hewitt's original colour commentary automatically transports the viewer to that era and adds authenticity to the project, as does grainy black and white footage of then Prime Minister Pierre Trudeau at the actual games. Even *Hockey: A People's History*, which was either a miniseries or a multi-episode documentary, employed dramatizations to tell part of the story of hockey in Canada, especially its early years.

Deviations from "the Real": Dramatizing Hockey

Making the Cut continues in this tradition of "routineness in the exchanges of real and fake … that is rarely mentioned."[44] The premise of the "real" surrounded *Making the Cut*. Most importantly, the production of the show hinged upon the authenticity of the training camp. To get the NHL's six

Canadian teams to agree to open up training camp spots for the show's participants, the process needed to be overseen by credible hockey people. Yet the "fake"—or the fictionalization of this drama—was also necessary to create credible "televisual drama." With *Making the Cut*, the spectacle of hockey competition was intended to be drama enough. The drama of the hockey tryout process, with its merciless whittling down to the final winners, is intended to be captivating enough without the casting of the slacker, the redneck, the introvert, or other such stereotypes upon which "reality" shows frequently depend. Yet NHL games, the standard of real hockey against which *Making the Cut* is measured, do not feature microphones attached to players or hand-held camera operators on the ice who become part of the action. *Making the Cut*, through the use of such technologies, created on-ice spectacle quite distinct from "real" hockey. Through the pre-recording of action, *Making the Cut* created a vast excess of material to be edited out to maintain an audience's attention. Also, non-game action was intercut with game play to create iconic images, such as a close-up of the Bell Canada *Making the Cut* logo on a puck and slow-motion video of a quick hockey stop, dramatically depicting an ice-level, first-person view of a blanket of ice shards. Ultimately, through the conventions of popular television, *Making the Cut* dramatized the "reality" of an NHL tryout camp and grafted fiction onto documentation while still preserving the authenticity of the project.

The quest for success at the highest level of professional hockey provides the theme for *Making the Cut*, but the hockey hopefuls are arguably not even the most important players. Some have suggested that "the format itself is the primary actor in a reality game show."[45] Thus, even though its producers sought as authentic an environment as possible in which to watch talent emerge, much like the inhospitable regions of *Survivor* or the "observational containment field" of *Big Brother*, *Making the Cut* manufactured drama in seclusion and heightened competition. During their time at the training camp, all of the participants were required to cut themselves off from the outside world, with the exception of rare and fully supervised phone calls and emails. The constructed "atmosphere" of the real was reinforced by the absence of a live audience for the spectacle of the game play. This is ironic, since much of the drama in live NHL games comes from the crowd, whose activity is a necessary adjunct to the action on the ice. Yet *Making the Cut* is akin in this manner to "television drama, 'audience-less' at the moment of its performance for the recording agents ... remade for transmission in post-production."[46] *Making the Cut* (re)presented the public adulation that is a significant part of the staging of the game only in the final episode, with its staging of the *Making the Cut* "draft" in a stadium amid hockey fans.

Making the Cut–style hockey also differed from NHL hockey in its adoption of different rules. Most notable among these was the "no fighting" rule. Fighting is an important element of hockey's machismo, which Bruce Dowbiggin highlights as a contradiction at the heart of Canadian identity when he compares this principle of mutual deterrence in the game of hockey with arguments made by the gun lobby in the United States. He notes how Canadians largely reject this idea "when they see the cost of that liberty expressed in lost lives. Change those guns into sticks, though, and Canadians staunchly uphold the Don Cherry Code of Mutually Assured Destruction."[47] Many see the elimination of fighting as a necessary condition for the game to gain greater exposure in the United States. Thus, the non-inclusion of fighting in *Making the Cut* only undercuts the myth of an organic, unchanging, traditional, "Canadian" game that is somehow intrinsically "ours." But *Making the Cut*, with its absence of fighting, seems somehow less realistic in its representation of professional hockey—even less Canadian.

Hockey on TV as a Reflection of Canadian Culture

Perhaps more important than a list of differences between *Making the Cut* and the NHL brand of hockey is the manner in which *Making the Cut* elevated NHL hockey. *Making the Cut*'s opening-episode narration begins: "In cities and towns across the nation, there are Canadians who share a dream, the dream of playing in the NHL ... Hockey laces Canada together. It's truly embedded in the social fabric of the country." Yet instead of focusing on the dream, it focused on the competition and arguably reinforced the idolatry of the prize rather than simply documenting the journey. But the lure of the dream depends, in part, on the prize. "Hockey stars have articulated the dreams of generations of young Canadian men about stepping out from the familiarity and rootedness of hometown lives towards the beckoning bright lights and brighter opportunities of new careers."[48] *Making the Cut* reproduced this narrative, even down to its gender exclusion. Even though the series depicted women trying out at the earliest stages, it ultimately reinforces the idea that women do not fit in with this traditional story of hockey. The hockey pinnacle for females is still at the amateur level, and this is reinforced when one female competitor makes the cut to 1,000 players but is not part of the next round of 120 players. She is nonetheless told that her name would be forwarded to the Canadian National Team. While other TV movies, such as *The Game of*

Her Life, depicting the road to the first-ever women's Olympic hockey tournament, *Manon Rhéaume: Woman Behind the Mask*, and *Chasing the Dream: Women's International Hockey*, promote hockey as a game at which anyone can excel, *Making the Cut* reifies success at the pro level as a male privilege.

Other points about the racial, ethnic, and regional diversity of *Making the Cut* are salient: The final sixty-eight players came from fifty-three different cities and towns from across Canada, with each province represented. This parallels Team Canada at the 2006 World Junior Hockey Championship, which featured "kids from seven of ten provinces and a variety of social and ethnic backgrounds."[49] Like Canada's population, the majority of players on *Making the Cut* came from Ontario and very few hailed from the Maritimes. In this capacity, the series' "regional diversity" also reflects that of the "real" game of hockey on Canadian television. For instance, *Hockey Night in Canada* could more accurately be called Hockey Night in Toronto, as other Canadian teams have taken a back seat to viewer-rich Southern Ontario and its legion of Leafs lovers, who help swell ratings on both CBC and TSN.[50]

In a similar vein, just as minority groups are becoming slightly more visible in the NHL, CBC's hockey-based reality series featured a sprinkling of Aboriginal players and Canadians of African descent, including one who described himself as an "ethnic Canadian." The DVD of *Making the Cut* featured a blurb from the *Globe and Mail*'s TV critic, John Doyle, proclaiming that the series was "the perfect expression of who we are," but its diversity did not always translate into tension-free ethnic relations. This was particularly notable in the attitudes of players from Canada's "two solitudes." After a slashing penalty, one player hurled the following insult: "That's a [bleep] French move, isn't it? Straight from Quebec." Similarly, racism and the political and social struggles of French Canadians is the real subject of 2006 Maurice Richard hockey biopic *The Rocket*. Not just a historical artifact, it can be an unwelcome component of the contemporary game, too. NHL player Sean Avery played a bit role in the movie as a Richard foe and described a hit by Denis Gauthier: "[It] was typical of most French guys in our league with a visor on, running around and playing tough and not backing anything up."[51] Just like Don Cherry's sometimes outrageous and even offensive statements, the pseudo-real presentation of hockey on *Making the Cut* fits the mould of the real game.

Interestingly, the quest to play in the NHL, and its blurring of the real and the fictional, mirrors the marketing put out by the NHL itself in late 2005. To remind consumers that the sport had returned from its 301-day lockout, the NHL created ads around a twenty-seven-year-old former college player from Minnesota who never made it to pro hockey, much less the NHL. Instead of focusing on its marketable stars of the game, NHL Enterprises president Ed Horne declared, "The campaign is supposed to symbolize every NHL player."[52] Though these ads featured a samurai theme, they did not feature any NHL players. Here, the reality of the game is obscured with models chosen to invoke it, just as "contestants" on *Making the Cut* are meant to metonymically represent the spirit of the (professional) game as they engage in competitions modelled after it.

Hockey on the CBC and NHL-style Competition

In its contribution to hockey—and Canadian—culture, *Making the Cut* also naturalizes the notion of NHL hockey as the only hockey that counts. It celebrates the spirit of the game even as it further focuses on the big-league rinks and teams instead of encouraging participation at the community level. In this sense, it is akin to *The Tournament*, a six-part "mockumentary" that aired on the CBC in the 2004–05 season. This show achieved much of its (comic) potential through the drama inherent in competition for a cherished prize. *The Tournament* followed the fictional Briarside Warriors, a team of ten- to twelve-year-olds, in its quest to win the 2005 Chateauguay Atom Invitational Tournament, but the real focus of the series was the behaviour of crazed hockey parents.

Both *The Tournament* and *Making the Cut* operate in the shadow of the professionalization of hockey, a game whose ultimate codes for success are far removed from backyard rinks and pickup games on rivers and ponds. The narrative of *Making the Cut* implies that being given the chance to play at the pro level is all that counts. The "second chance" that is offered to players assumes that their current circumstances are not good enough. As the series depicts it, success at the NHL level demands a constant dedication and application that promotes hockey success and not necessarily well-rounded personalities. After all, "The myths of 'making it' only have their evocative power in contrast to parallel myths that embrace the ever-present possibility of failure, even tragedy."[53] Thus, Canadian audiences can come to expect other docudramas, such as *Gross Misconduct*, that document the falls from grace of some players after success at the NHL is achieved. *Making the Cut*, therefore, only represents one side of the human drama.

It should also be noted that the dream of NHL success was never ultimately realized for the six players who "made the cut" on the final episode. After the NHL lockout had ended, the six finalists showed up to rookie camps with their respective NHL clubs. Ultimately, each was demoted.

Some were sent for American Hockey League tryouts with affiliated teams, while others were bound for the less prestigious East Coast Hockey League. At the end of the series, it was announced that twenty-five of sixty-eight players had signed pro contracts, either in North America or Europe. But players signed on for the NHL experience, and at least in the mythological Canadian imagination, any other professional hockey dreams surely paled in comparison.

One final point remains to be made about the portrayal of hockey in *Making the Cut*'s "reality" format. Identification with contestants is an essential aspect of some reality shows.[54] A major reason for the hype surrounding *Making the Cut* was the expectation that Canadians inherently identified with the subject matter of the show. I suggest that viewers of *Making the Cut* were asked to identify with professional players in the NHL, and those who aspired to become NHL players, rather than with the game itself.

The problem with this strategy is that such players are being paid to play a game that is rhetorically positioned as somehow an organic part of who we are. This is, ironically, a major reason why *Making the Cut* did not have as much affinity with *Hockey Night in Canada* as its producers would have liked. Professional athletes "play" the game, albeit for high salaries. Yet *Making the Cut* exposes audiences to the work that underlies the play metaphor. It highlights the high degree of labour and discipline, and the workout regimes, training programs, and coaching surveillance to which all "players" are subjected. This "behind the scenes" privilege was touted as one of the main draws of *Making the Cut*, but it could also disarticulate the dream from the myth of innocence and joy involved in playing a game for a living. The text of *Making the Cut* did not merely vividly portray the hard work involved in success at the highest level, but it also occurred against the meta-text of a hockey stoppage in which the sport seemed to be a game played by a small number of affluent men. With the business side of hockey taking front stage on an everyday basis, the romance of fulfilling hockey dreams seemed more than ever an illusion instead of a reality kept alive by the successes of a fortunate few.

Perhaps to help counteract this perception, the NHL partnered with the CBC and Kraft Canada to present a new reality show with a sports theme in February 2006. Rather than searching for the best potential NHL players, *Kraft Hockeyville* searched for the Canadian community that best embodied the spirit of hockey and hometown pride. Interestingly, the judges included Mike Bossy and Glenn Anderson, two NHL Hall of Famers, and actor Gabriel Hogan, whose clearest link to hockey was his portrayal of Ken Dryden in *Canada Russia '72*.[55] With one of the prizes being the opportunity to play host to a National Hockey League exhibition game, NHL commissioner Gary Bettman admitted that the show ought to promote hockey awareness in Canada.[56] More than *Making the Cut*, this exercise emphasized the CBC's connection with hockey writ large, including links to the grassroots and amateur levels and not exclusively the NHL.

Making the Cut: Reality TV for Public and Private Broadcasters

When the CBC cancelled three prominent series including *The Tournament* in February 2006, it announced that it would revamp its thin drama schedule with more "fast-paced," "escapist," and "positive and redemptive" programming.[57] Ironically, *Making the Cut* seemed to fit this description. Though its costs were high, its theme, its series format, and its hybrid combination of reality and dramatic licence made it attractive. Unlike *Waking Up Wally* or *Canada Russia '72*, a movie of the week and a miniseries that do not encourage ongoing viewing, it is the kind of "exciting reality program" that can build audiences and fits the new agenda of "the broadcaster's expanded and 'critically important' factual-entertainment programming."[58]

Making the Cut reinforces the idea that the game of hockey is a metaphor and a great stage for Canadians to tell themselves about what it means to be Canadian. It is important to note, though, that networks other than the national broadcaster also find pseudo-real hockey programming attractive. In 2006, a second season of *Making the Cut* appeared, this time on Global TV. In some ways, it suffered from the same lacklustre ratings that have dogged other examples of pseudo-real hockey programming described above. Like the original *Making the Cut*, which suffered from the lack of NHL hockey on the CBC during the 2004–05 season, the second season of *Making the Cut* on Global was originally tied to the network's NFL Sunday programming. After drawing poor afternoon ratings, the series was relaunched in an evening slot in January 2007.[59]

Called *Making the Cut—Last Man Standing*, the show featured the same second-chance narrative and the possibility of cracking the NHL as a prize. Thus, it appears as though the concept was given a second chance, too. However, some important format changes altered the overall message of the series. As the title change indicates, this time the series would result in only one winner. Instead of announcing six winners and inviting these players to NHL training camps, the goal was to assess who was the best. The series website set the tone: "Time will be short. The pace will be brutal, and the cuts ruthless. One by one the pretenders will be eliminated. Like any great competition, *Making the Cut—Last Man Standing* is designed to crown a single champion."[60]

With a $250,000 endorsement contract and representation from a top NHL agent as the ultimate prize, the second season appeared to be much more consistent with other competition-based reality TV shows. Promotional material for the series trumpeted it as a "real life drama."[61] NHL central scouting was even more involved in the second season of the show. Instead of depending on tryouts across the country, information was gathered at the NHL central scouting draft combine, and thirty-six of the top players who were not selected at the NHL entry draft were whittled down for inclusion on the series.[62] Watching the show, viewers also cannot fail to notice that fighting is now permitted as part of this hockey trial, discarding a major rule that defined season one of *Making the Cut* and distanced its representation of hockey from the "real" game at the NHL level. Thus, when the media advisory for season two claims that viewers will be transported "inside the competitive world of a pressure-packed, high-stakes hockey training camp, bringing home the hockey passion that fuels millions of Canadians from coast to coast," we are to understand that the empirical realism of the series will imbue it with an emotional realism.[63] One may not agree with the NHL scout who claims, "The atmosphere is as realistic a hockey environment as you can get."[64] But it is important to heed David Morley's observation that "realism need not be of an empirical kind. The stories can be recognized as realistic at an emotional level, rather than at a literal or denotative level."[65]

Coda: The Persistent Fascination of Hockey

Whether measuring it against the NHL standard or assessing it on its own merits, *Making the Cut*, like other pseudo-real hockey programming, can present one version of the stereotypically "Canadian" game and, in so doing, bespeak Canadian realities and reflect Canadian dreams. Just as the game of hockey is frequently posited as a device that helps Canadians make sense of their cultural life and times, *Making the Cut* is a representation of the game that naturalizes the NHL as the apex of hockey in Canada. In the end, it is possible to assert that "hockey's enduring link to the idea of 'Canadianness'" is minimized next to the idea of Canadians' linkage of the NHL and hockey.[66] *Making the Cut* does not define Canadiana per se, nor does it define or reflect all that there is about Canadian hockey. Instead of asking whether its representation of (pro) hockey is accurate, we should ask what it says about Canadian TV's preoccupation with hockey. All pseudo-real representations of hockey on television are between reality and fiction. And insofar as much of this programming continues to represent the NHL as "real" hockey, we must ask whether it is the game of hockey that occupies a significant place in the popular imagination, or merely hockey stars. Admittedly, a player need not be an NHL All-Star to be a hockey star. Cassie Campbell and other success stories in women's hockey demonstrate this point. But *Making the Cut* did not significantly contribute to a sense of "who we are" for Canadian viewers as much as it further buttressed a particular view of what we, as Canadians, celebrate.

Notes

1 Harris, "Hockey Night on CBC."
2 Gruneau and Whitson, *Hockey Night in Canada*, 105.
3 Hutsul, "Flicks, Not Sticks."
4 Houston, "Gloom and Doom at *Hockey Night in Canada*"; MacDonald, "Movie Night Scores for CBC."
5 Goodman, "CBC-TV Head Denies Network."
6 Brioux, "Game Over."
7 Houston, "CBC Takes Early Lead"; Zelkovich, "Canada Buoys Sinking NHL."
8 Burns, "'Hockey Night' Power Play."
9 Rip, "Making the Cut."
10 Houston, "*Hockey Day in Canada* Cancelled."
11 Zelkovich, "Six Players Get a Shot at the NHL."
12 Brown, "For TV Viewers."
13 MacDonald, "Movie Night Scores for CBC."
14 Bracken, "Slow Start for CBC's *Making The Cut*."
15 Houston, "Truth & Rumours."
16 Brioux, "Game Over."
17 Dillon, "CBC in Ratings Tailspin."
18 Canadian Press, "Few Canadians Watching Home-Grown Television."
19 Brioux, "Game Over."
20 Goodman, "Success Abroad, Online Viewing."
21 Dillon, "CBC in Ratings Tailspin."
22 Brioux, "T.O. Native in Final Cut."
23 Zelkovich, "Hockey Ratings Take a Tumble."
24 Friedman, "Introduction," 5.
25 Murray and Ouellette, "Introduction," 2.
26 Zelkovich, "CBC's *Making the Cut*."
27 Gill, "Reality Bites Canada."
28 Corner, *Television Form and Public Address*, 86.
29 Summerfield, "Beyond the 30-Second Spot," 26.
30 Paget, *No Other Way to Tell It*, 102.
31 Hogarth, *Documentary Television in Canada*, 29
32 Kleinhans and Morris, "Court TV," 159; Murray and Ouellette, "Introduction," 4; Corner, "Performing the Real," 6–7.
33 Hogarth, *Documentary Television in Canada*, 86.

34 Paget, *No Other Way to Tell It*, 61.
35 Doyle, "If You Like Reality TV."
36 Cook, "CBC Reality Show Hits the Ice."
37 Paget, *No Other Way to Tell It*, 205.
38 Paget, *No Other Way to Tell It*, 62.
39 Paget, *No Other Way to Tell It*, 75.
40 Howell, "Dupuis Guardian of the Rocket's Secrets."
41 Tilley, "Telling Walter's Story."
42 Floren, "Walter Gretzky's Inspirational Comeback Story."
43 Arsenault, "Team Spirit and More"; Richer, "Filming Underway on CBC Hockey Drama."
44 Paget, *No Other Way to Tell It*, 75–76.
45 Brenton and Cohen, *Shooting People*, 54.
46 Paget, *No Other Way to Tell It*, 33.
47 Dowbiggin, *The Stick*, 166.
48 Gruneau and Whitson, *Hockey Night in Canada*, 131.
49 Cox, "Juniors Win Our Hearts."
50 Zelkovich, "Leaf Car Wreck."
51 Woolsey, "Movie Goes Beyond the Game."
52 Westhead, "After the Lockout, a Rich Ad Campaign."
53 Gruneau and Whitson, *Hockey Night in Canada*, 141.
54 Brenton and Cohen, *Shooting People*, 52.
55 In an interesting case of intertextuality, Gabriel Hogan also portrayed Lance "the Boil," the best goalie-for-rent in *Rent-A-Goalie*. Both this series and the miniseries *Canada Russia '72* were directed by T.W. Peacocke. See the *Rent-A-Goalie* cast and crew page at www.showcase.ca/rentagoalie/downloads/RAG_cast_post_premiere_bios.pdf.
56 Houston, "*Hockeyville*."
57 Whyte, "CBC Taps American to Craft New Shows."
58 Gill, "CBC-TV's New Number Chase."
59 Zelkovich, "Sportsnet Wants to Rock You."
60 At http://makingthecut.ca/about.html (accessed January 9, 2008).
61 "*Making the Cut* Returns."
62 Pridham, "*Making the Cut*."
63 "*Making the Cut* Returns"
64 Pridham, "Making the Cut."
65 Morley, "Changing Paradigms in Audience Studies," 31.
66 Gruneau and Whitson, *Hockey Night in Canada*, 7.

References

Arsenault, Tim. "Team Spirit and More." *Halifax Chronicle Herald*, April 10, 2006. Available at www.1972summitseries.com/canadarussia72movie0019.html. Accessed January 9, 2008.

Bracken, Laura. "Slow Start for CBC's *Making the Cut*." *Playback*, October 11, 2004. Available at www.playbackmag.com/articles/magazine/20041011/cut.html. Accessed January 9, 2008.

Brenton, Sam and Reuben Cohen. *Shooting People: Adventures in Reality TV*. London: Verso, 2003.

Brioux, Bill. "Game Over for the CBC." *Toronto Sun*, October 5, 2006. Available at http://jam.canoe.ca/Television/TV_Shows/H/Hockey_Night_in_Canada/ 2006/10/05/1956531.html. Accessed January 9, 2008.

———. "T.O. Native in Final Cut of Hockey Saga." *Toronto Sun*, December 14, 2004. Available at http://jam.canoe.ca/Television/TV_Shows/M/Making_The _Cut/2004/12/14/782196.html. Accessed January 9, 2008.

Brown, Dan. "For TV Viewers, What Replaces *Hockey Night in Canada?*" CBC News Online, October 20, 2004. Available at www.nhlfa.com/news/nr10 _20_04.asp. Accessed January 9, 2008.

Burns, Howard. "'Hockey Night' Power Play Bad News for CBC." *The Hollywood Reporter*, November 14, 2006. Available at https://secure.vnuemedia.com/ hr/content_display/features/columns/nosebleeds/e3i98c4a037e0b2cf439 2cb185bb8423981. Accessed January 9, 2008.

Canadian Press. "Few Canadians Watching Home-Grown Television." October 2, 2006. Available at www.ctv.ca/servlet/ArticleNews/story/CTVNews/20061002/ canadians_television_061002?s_name=&no_ads. Accessed January 9, 2008.

Cook, Jon. "CBC Reality Show Hits the Ice." At http://jam.canoe.ca/Television/ TV_Shows /M/Making_The_Cut/2004/06/07/733808.html. Accessed January 9, 2008.

Corner, John. "Performing the Real: Documentary Diversions." *Television and New Media* 3 (3): 255–69.

———. *Television Form and Public Address*. London: Edward Arnold, 1995.

Cox, Damien. "Juniors Win Our Hearts." *Toronto Star*, January 6, 2006: R2.

Dillon, Mark. "CBC in Ratings Tailspin." *Playback Magazine*, October 30, 2006. Available at www.publicairwaves.ca/index.php?page=1784. Accessed January 9, 2008.

Dowbiggin, Bruce. *The Stick: A History, a Celebration, an Elegy*. Toronto: Macfarlane Walter & Ross, 2001.

Doyle, John. "If You Like Reality TV, You'll Love Next Year's Lineups." *Globe and Mail*, May 11, 2004. Available at www.friends.ca/print/News/Friends_News/ archives/articles05110404.asp. Accessed January 9, 2008.

Floren, Erik. "Walter Gretzky's Inspirational Comeback Story." *Edmonton Sun*, November 6, 2005. Available at http://jam.canoe.ca/Television/2005/11/06/ 1294935.html. Accessed January 9, 2008.

Friedman, James. "Introduction." In *Reality Squared: Televisual Discourse on the Real*, edited by James Friedman, 1–22. New Brunswick, NJ: Rutgers University Press, 2002.

Gill, Alexandra. "CBC-TV's New Number Chase." *Globe and Mail*, May 17, 2006: R3.

———. "Reality Bites Canada." *Globe and Mail*, May 22, 2004. Available at www .friends.ca/News/Friends_News/archives/articles05220401.asp. Accessed April 25, 2008.

Goodman, Lee-Anne. "CBC-TV Head Denies Network Is 'Beleaguered,' But Ad Revenues to Stay Soft." Canadian Press, January 30, 2007. Available at www.cbc .ca/cp/entertainment /070130/e013077A.html. Accessed January 9, 2008.

————. "Success Abroad, Online Viewing, CBC Troubles Dominated Canadian TV in '06," *Canadian Press*, December 21, 2006. Available at www.cbc.ca/cp/media/061221/X122104AU.html. Accessed January 9, 2008.

Gruneau, Richard and David Whitson. *Hockey Night in Canada: Sport, Identities and Cultural Politics.* Toronto: Garamond Press, 1993.

Harris, Bill. "Hockey Night on CBC." *Toronto Sun*, September 17, 2006. Available at http://jam.canoe.ca/Television/2006/09/17/1852317.html. Accessed January 9, 2008.

Hogarth, David. *Documentary Television in Canada: From National Public Service to Global Marketplace.* Montreal and Kingston: McGill-Queen's University Press, 2002.

Houston, William. "CBC Takes Early Lead in Battle for NHL TV Rights." *Globe and Mail*, December 7, 2006. Available at www.cbcwatch.ca/?q=node/view/2135. Accessed January 9, 2008.

————. "Truth & Rumours." *Globe and Mail*, April 12, 2006: R9.

————. "Hockeyville." *Globe and Mail*, February 3, 2006: R7.

————. "*Hockey Day in Canada* Cancelled by CBC." *Globe and Mail*, January 12, 2005. Available at www.friends.ca/News/Friends_News/archives/articles 01120501.asp. Accessed January 9, 2008.

————. "Gloom and Doom at *Hockey Night in Canada*." *Globe and Mail*, June 3, 2005. Available at www.cbcwatch.ca/?q=node/view/1125/1338. Accessed January 9, 2008.

Howell, Peter. "Dupuis Guardian of the Rocket's Secrets." *Toronto Star*, April 21, 2006: D3.

Hutsul, Christopher. "Flicks, Not Sticks, on CBC." *Toronto Star*, September 23, 2004. Available at www.publicairwaves.ca/index.php?page=787. Accessed January 9, 2008.

Kleinhans. Chuck and Rick Morris. "Court TV: The Evolution of a Reality Format." In *Reality TV: Remaking Television Culture*, edited by Susan Murray and Laurie Ouellette, 157–177. New York: New York University Press, 2004.

MacDonald, Gayle. "Movie Night Scores for CBC." *Globe and Mail*, November 10, 2004. Available at www.publicairwaves.ca/index.php?page=838. Accessed January 9, 2008.

"*Making the Cut* Returns as Mike Keenan & Company Deliver Last Man Standing." At www.greatervernonmultiplex.ca/news/media_release_060913.pdf. Accessed January 9, 2008.

Morley, David. "Changing Paradigms in Audience Studies." In *Remote Control: Television, Audiences, and Cultural Power*, edited by Ellen Seiter, Hans Borchers, Gabriele Kreutzer, and Eva-Maria Warth, 16–43. London: Routledge, 1989.

Murray, Susan and Laurie Ouellette. "Introduction." In *Reality TV: Remaking Television Culture*, edited by Susan Murray and Laurie Ouellette, 1–17. New York: New York University Press, 2004.

Paget, Derek. *No Other Way to Tell It: Dramadoc/Docudrama on Television.* Manchester: Manchester University Press, 1998.

Pridham, Brandon. *"Making the Cut."* Blog Central, August 22, 2006. Available at www.nhl.com/blogcentral/css_aug.html. Accessed January 9, 2008.

Richer, Shawna. "Filming Underway on CBC Hockey Drama." *Globe and Mail*, May 17, 2005. Available at www.publicairwaves.ca/index.php?page=1027. Accessed January 9, 2008.

Rip, Zachary. *"Making The Cut:* Reality Show Debuts on CBC." *Sheridan Sun*, September 28, 2004. Available at www-acad.sheridanc.on.ca/sun/sept_28_2004/sports_sportstelevision.html. Accessed January 9, 2008.

Summerfield, Patti. "Beyond the 30-Second Spot." *Strategy Magazine*, September 2004.

Tilley, Steve "Telling Walter's Story." *Edmonton Sun*, February 2, 2005. Available at www.canoe.ca/NewsStand/EdmontonSun/Entertainment/2005/02/02/917710-sun.html. Accessed January 9, 2008.

Westhead, Rick. "After the Lockout, a Rich Ad Campaign." *Toronto Star*, September 22, 2005: D1.

Whyte, Murray. "CBC Taps American to Craft New Shows." *Toronto Star*, March 30, 2006: D3.

Woolsey, Garth. "Movie Goes Beyond the Game." *Toronto Star*, April 21, 2006.

Zelkovich, Chris. "Canada Buoys Sinking NHL Ratings." *Toronto Star*, February 9, 2007. Available at www.thestar.com/Sports/article/179976. Accessed January 9, 2008.

———. "Sportsnet Wants to Rock You in Your Living Room." *Toronto Star*, January 19, 2007. Available at www.thestar.com/article/172794. Accessed January 9, 2008.

———. "Hockey Ratings Take a Tumble," *Toronto Star*, November 30, 2006. Available at www.cbcwatch.ca/?q=node/view/2131/15996. Accessed January 9, 2008.

———. "Leaf Car Wreck Could Sideswipe the CBC." *Toronto Star*, March 31, 2006.

———. "Six Players Get a Shot at the NHL," *Toronto Star*, December 15, 2004.

———. "CBC's *Making the Cut.*" *Toronto Star*, September 21, 2004.

Filmography

The Amazing Race (Jerry Bruckheimer/CBS, 2001–)
Big Brother (Endemol Entertainment/CBS, 2000–)
Canada Russia '72 (Dream Street Pictures, 2006)
Canadian Idol (Insight Production/CTV, 2003–)
Chasing the Dream: Women's International Hockey (Take 3 Productions, 2002)
Desperate Housewives (Cherry Alley Productions/Touchstone Television, 2004–)
The Game of Her Life (National Film Board of Canada, 1997), dir. Lyn Wright
Gross Misconduct (CBC, 1993), dir. Atom Egoyan
Hockey: A People's History (CBC, 2006), dir. Peter John Ingles
Hockey Night in Canada (CBC, 1952–)

Kraft Hockeyville (CBC, 2006–)

Making the Cut (Network Productions MTC, 2004)

Making the Cut—Last Man Standing (Network Pictures MTC Two, 2006)

Manon Rhéaume: Woman behind the Mask (National Film Board of Canada, 2000),
     dir. Wendy Hill-Tout

Maurice "Rocket" Richard (Historica Foundation, 1997)

Net Worth (Morningstar Entertainment/CBC, 1995), dir. Jerry Ciccoritti

Rent-A-Goalie (Alliance Atlantis/Showcase, 2006)

The Rocket (Cinémaginaire, 2005), dir. Charles Binamé

Survivor (Mark Burnett Productions/CBS, 2000–)

The Tournament (Adjacent 2 Entertainment, 2005–06)

Waking Up Wally: The Walter Gretzky Story (Accent Entertainment, 2005), dir.
     Dean Bennett

ZOË DRUICK

Laughing at Authority or Authorized Laughter?

Canadian News Parodies

I n Canada, a nation with a television system closely bound to both American politics and American popular culture, news has fulfilled a particularly prominent role in the media landscape. As most Canadian news promotion emphasizes, Canadian news gives not only a view of Canada but, perhaps more importantly, a Canadian perspective on world affairs, inflecting, to use Mary Jane Miller's term, not only the genre of news but also perspectives on the American foreign policy that dominates its content.[1] The imagined Canadian nation is thus well accustomed to the idea of a peripheral perspective on disruptive, disastrous world affairs from the relative safety of the margins of both geopolitics and media-scape.

It is often noted that Canada has achieved some measure of success in sketch comedy in general and news parody in particular, and given television's nation-building role in this country, it seems like no coincidence. In this chapter, I argue that Canadian news parody has proved popular with comedians and audiences alike precisely because it lampoons a sober official discourse with close ties to nation building on the one hand and American television on the other. The topic of news parody also raises larger questions about the meaning and transformation of televisual texts and genres. I consider the history of news parody as a spinoff of sketch comedy and look at how this genre developed in Canada in shows such as *SCTV*, *CODCO*, *This Hour Has 22 Minutes*, *Royal Canadian Air Farce*, *Double Exposure*, and *The Rick Mercer Report*.[2]

But, first, the news. Since the 1970s, the news has come under attack by media scholars for being a ritualistic exercise in presenting a limited view of reality filtered through the values that organize the rhythms of the visual journalism workplace.[3] The emphasis on binaries—for and against—the almost exclusive reliance on elites, the insistence on concision, and the integrating and ultimately reassuring presence of the news anchor, a trusted "supersubject," to use Margaret Morse's term, not to mention the close, even incestuous relationship between government and news reporting, are just some of the characteristics of television news highlighted by scholars.[4] Rather than distortions of the "real world," these parameters are intrinsic to the materialization of a cultural discourse about the world known as the news.

As all-news channels proliferate, news has sustained itself as one of the most iconic forms of television. Although assigned a privileged relationship to reality and politics, news and current affairs programming has long been affected by the storytelling conventions of entertainment programming—when it comes to televisual strategies, reality and fiction are not necessarily very far apart.[5] Today, along with a proliferation of news parodies, there have appeared a variety of hybrid genres of infotainment, including tabloid news, as well as more legitimate forms of the so-called new news.[6] Emerging in the 1990s, the new news displays a heavy reliance on visuals and a low emphasis on editorial content, much like a tabloid newspaper, and is seen to be targeted at a youth market accustomed to music videos and video games.[7]

In this chapter, I explore some of the ways in which humour is used in news parodies to bring about a rethinking of news as discourse, a topic imbricated with the theory of texts, or genre. Genre is most often defined in television studies as a basis for the industry's categorization of shows—a categorization used by producers and audiences alike.[8] According to this perspective, the television industry organizes audiences according to generic preference as a way of delivering coherent markets to advertisers. This analysis is no less pertinent for news. As news genres multiply, so do the divisions in the news audience.

News as Genre

Although the theory of genres as taxonomy has abundant uses in media studies, I propose that a Bakhtinian notion of genre is more effective for talking about the ongoing process of genre hybridization that is such an essential aspect of television.[9] For Mikhail Bakhtin, a twentieth-century Russian literary theorist, genre represents not just a type of speech but also an essential site of creative expression. According to Bakhtin, all utterances are inevitably responses to previous utterances, a phenomenon that implicates all speech, and therefore all culture and individual psychology, both of which are mediated by signs, in social relations of power.[10] Bakhtin uses the concept of genre, or what he calls "speech genre," to think about expression as a site of social and historical struggle, neither the purview of a dominating system nor a realm of unconstrained creative freedom.[11] As in the dominant notion of genre as taxonomy, speech genres also provide the shared reference points for speakers, listeners, and, by implication, industries involved in the production of media products. This expanded and socially embedded concept of genre introduces a social and historical layer of mediation to all signification. For Bakhtin, "dialogism" is another word for the many voices—social, institutional and individual—involved in genres. Each utterance, wrote Bakhtin, "is filled with dialogic overtones."[12] These two key concepts, dialogism, or the connection of each utterance to a linguistically mediated social field, and genre as the particular weave of time and space produced by the rules organizing cultural expression, were further elaborated by Julia Kristeva with her development of the concept of "intertextuality."[13]

Humour is a pointed example of dialogism. According to Jerry Palmer, some of the key work of humour is the creative juxtaposition of unlikely terms—repetition that includes difference—not unlike a good metaphor or a parody, and in this sense, humour is a telling example of a multi-voiced discourse.[14] Some of the key work of humour is to make the predictable unpredictable, to defamiliarize the everyday.[15] In news parodies, exactly such an operation occurs: the predictable text signalled by the iconic news set and the stentorian voice and serious demeanour of the anchor is made strange by replacing one of the terms of the news speech genre. If the prevailing news scenario combines a sober-looking person with serious discourse to produce a trusted news source, news mockery needs to replace at least one term to subvert the expectation of the speech genre: silly person delivering serious news; silly person delivering silly news; serious person delivering silly news. Arguably, this mockery implies a dialogue between audience, authority, and comic utterance.

Some clarification should be given on the terms "parody" and "satire." Parody is a double-voiced discourse and as such addresses a sophisticated reader or viewer expected to decode multiple texts in dialogic relation. Parody is, then, by nature a self-reflexive textual manoeuvre. Satire, by contrast, is a commentary not on a text but on the social world. Where parody is a discourse on texts, satire is a discourse on things.[16] Be that as it may, "Satirists choose to use parodies of the most familiar of texts as the vehicle for their satire in order to add to the initial impact and to reinforce the ironic contrast."[17] As a result, satires often use texts as metonyms of the aspects of the social world most deserving of comment. It follows that the objective to satirize the political process, or public discourse on national or international affairs, would choose to parody the vehicle of the news (a similar move has appeared in documentary with the advent of the "mockumentary").[18] As a reality-based speech genre most closely associated with the performance of official positions on topics of social and political import, the news makes a legitimate target for satiric parody.

To deliver the news, the anchor must occupy, in terms of speech, dress, and demeanour, "a zero-degree of deviation from the norm."[19] The anchor's ability to utter legitimate discourse is therefore a tempting starting place for disrupting the chain of normative utterances associated with news. Palmer argues that humour is the process of disturbing "normal usage," of "constructing absurd actants" of statement and/or utterance.[20] In the best cases, this construction can spark in the audience a critical reassessment—or confirmation—of some alternative vision of reality. "The butt of the absurd," writes Palmer, "is always, inherently, a feature of the real social world in some form or other."[21] Because parody has a parasitic relation to previous texts, its power is often described as limited. "Parody's transgressions ultimately remain authorized—authorized by the very norm it seeks to subvert," writes Linda Hutcheon. "Even in mocking, parody reinforces; in formal terms, it inscribes the mocked conventions onto itself. Thereby guaranteeing their continued existence."[22] Yet the dialogism of all absurdity against an implicit norm presumes a tacitly critical position.

Of course, humour need not be political. In Freud's terms, joke-work is similar to dream-work. Both deal with transgressions of taboos and the play of the unconscious through doubled meanings and a non-logical both/and—what Kristeva calls a double- or dia-logic.[23] For this reason, Palmer argues, much humour, like the unconscious mind itself, is childish, in the sense of playing with rather than by the rules. "What the childish mind demands, what the pleasure principle demands, is the play of the signifier, and this play of the signifier is repressed by the reality principle just as are the other primary processes. Thus the focal point in this process, the point at which subversion occurs in all forms of comic utterance, is the relation of denotation."[24] Humour in all its forms, then, uses surprise to mobilize an absurd logic that contravenes normal logic and asserts instead a playful logic of subversive reversal where each statement is pregnant with its opposite.

News as genre, in the Bakhtinian sense, invites a reading of news parody as an intertext that calls upon the audience both to reflect on the production of television news and, potentially, to question the authority of the news as the official television discourse of the "real."[25] However, there are many ways, with a variety of effects, to engage with the news genre. For example, the double-voiced discourse about the news can become a commentary on television itself. Alternatively, the use of the news idiom can be an attempt to displace the "real" news by a parodic version. In the case of a successful news parody, not only will the parodic text demonstrate its own implausibility, but by troubling the equation between form and content, it will also imply the tenuousness of all news discourse as a genre with limited ability to represent or explain the world. As we will see, however, most news parody doesn't go much further than bringing about a surprising, and preferably silly, end to the news syllogism.

Sketch Comedy and the Parodic Newscast

The beginnings of such reversals and absurdities in television about television date from the late 1960s and early 1970s. In his analysis of the preponderance of parody in 1970s American cinema, John G. Cawelti attributed this phenomenon to what he described as the "tendency of genres to exhaust themselves, to our growing historical awareness of modern popular culture, and finally, to the decline of the underlying mythology on which traditional genres have been based."[26] He noted that genres have life cycles, from articulation and discovery to conscious self-awareness on the part of creators and audiences to a moment when conventions become tired and predictable, when "parodic and satiric treatments proliferate and new genres gradually arise."[27] By the 1970s, many classic popular forms were, according to Cawelti, exhausted. Cawelti's prescient analysis of the increasing preponderance of self-reflexive, double-voiced media, not to mention the connection between the exhaustion both of genres and of their founding mythologies, adds an important dimension to the notion of genre put forward by Bakhtin.

British youth-oriented, anarchic sketch comedy shows such as *That Was the Week That Was*, or *TW3* (BBC, 1962–63), *The Two Ronnies* (BBC-1, 1971–87), and especially *Monty Python's Flying Circus* (BBC, 1969–74) satirized social mores and parodied dominant cultural forms. As media about mass culture, they represented some of the first examples of widespread televisual self-reflexivity. One of the targets of this genre was television itself as a sign of all that was authoritative, over-rehearsed, and serious. In the US, with notable exceptions such as *Rowan and Martin's Laugh In* (George Schlatter–Ed Friendly Productions/Romart, NBC, 1968–73), sketch comedy was overshadowed by a strong industry system that favoured building situation comedies around stand-up comedians. Late-night celebrity talk shows, beginning with *The Tonight Show* (NBC,

1954–), were genres for commenting on and participating in popular culture, and not only became more self-reflexive over time but also served as one of the templates for television itself: people chatting in front of a studio audience on a set resembling a living room.

In terms of the mocking of news, *Saturday Night Live* (NBC, 1975), produced by Canadian Lorne Michaels, and *SCTV*, which ran on two Canadian networks (Global, 1978–89; CBC, 1980–81) before being picked up to run after *Saturday Night Live* by NBC (1981–83), both featured a range of self-parodying skits about television and popular culture.[28] *SCTV* was built around the antics and products of the television station in the fictional town of Melonville. Unlike *SNL*, which broadcast from New York City and strove to achieve quintessential downtown comedy, *SCTV* mocked its Canadian provenance by making fun of small-town television.

SCTV's newscasters were Earl Camembert and Floyd Robertson, loosely based on Earl Cameron, affectionately known as Mr. CBC News for anchoring the flagship CBC show *The National* from 1959 to 1966, and Lloyd Robertson, a CBC journalist who moved to CTV to anchor its national news in 1976 and is still the anchor there.[29] On the *SCTV* news sketch, Camembert, played by Eugene Levy, and Robertson, played by Joe Flaherty, were often distracted from their roles as local and national newscasters, respectively, by their interpersonal relationship and underlying rivalry. In one sketch from 1981, Robertson, returning from an absence prompted by an attempt to control his drinking, reports disinterestedly on a massive May Day parade in Melonville. Using footage obviously taken from postwar Soviet newsreels, the appearance of this event in North America is ludicrous—impossible. By contrast to Robertson's disengagement, Camembert wants to discuss how shocking it is that this many communists are active in town, but Robertson ignores him. The encounter underscores the falsity of most banter between anchors. Here, Camembert is expressing true shock, rather than the banal chat we expect from newscasters. Robertson's refusal to respond highlights the degree to which this "dialogue" is usually inauthentic.

A second, almost incidental comment on the news is made in this sketch by the reversal of expectations. The Soviet May Day Parade was an annual event. Where most planned state events like this would be precisely the kind of thing that the news would be called upon to report, Camembert's shock at the overrunning of Melonville by communists ruptures the collusion between news and the state that we are used to and thus has the potential to defamiliarize the news. Despite the improbability of a May Day parade in North America, the news is recast as a genre in which personal emotions and relationships figure more prominently than

Figure 1. Eugene Levy as Earl Camembert and Joe Flaherty as Floyd Robinson, *SCTV*'s newsreaders in 1998. Image courtesy of The Second City Entertainment Inc./CBC Still Photo Collection.

reference to external events. Robertson's refusal, as he battles his inner demons, to banter with the eternally sunny Camembert is the emotional core of the sketch.

Chronologically speaking, the next important sketch comedy show on Canadian television was *CODCO* (Salter Street Films/CBC, 1988–93), built around the antics of a theatre group from Newfoundland. The troupe's work was originally based on its members' background in live performance but increasingly came to utilize and lampoon the conventions of television itself. Typical, perhaps, of Canadian culture formed in the 1970s and 1980s, the target of many *CODCO* satirical sketches was American image politics and media. Routines about Ronald Reagan's failing intelligence, American celebrity-watching shows such as *Entertainment Tonight*, and parodies of *Dynasty* were common fare. Sketches about Canadian culture, by contrast, tended to be located in the St. John's context, with particular emphasis on scathing satires of the church—the most extreme of which, "Pleasant Irish Priests in Conversation," was censored by the CBC and led to the indignant resignation of founding member Andy Jones—and small-town rebels. Although "House of Budgell" was ostensibly a parody of soaps like *EastEnders*, the target of its humour was at times no more cutting than a subtle rumination on the vagaries of aging.

CODCO included an ongoing parody of US news, generically titled "American News," in which the complicity of news with dominant ideologies was emphasized. In one piece on terrorism in the Middle East, newscaster Dawn Day, played with impeccable superficiality by Tommy Sexton, parodies both the inscription of gendered roles in newscasting and American insularity: "Dan, when is it going to end, this bizarre, frightening behaviour ... these acts of terrorism for no apparent reason that we as Americans can comprehend?"[30] By inhabiting and exaggerating the noncritical and jingoistic aspect of American news, the comedians were able to highlight the complicity of news with dominant ideologies.

Cast member Greg Malone developed an imitation of Barbara Frum, at the time a very well-known Canadian news media personality. Her show, *The Journal* (CBC, 1982–92), a current affairs show that aired after *The National*, was renamed *The Jugular*, and Malone encapsulated her characteristically unsympathetic interviewing style with the catch phrase "Are you bitter?" which was asked of everyone who appeared on the show, including, absurdly, a weather system (September 14, 1989). Much of the humour in *CODCO*, as well as in *Monty Python* and *Kids in the Hall* (CBC, 1988–94), for that matter, came from male cross-dressing such as this. So not only her catch phrase, but also her big hair and shoulder pads were part of the creation of Frum as an absurd actant.

One of the troupe's most biting news parodies appears on the video *CODCO Uncensored* (1995). Titled "News Breakdown," the sketch builds up the usual expectation for news, a serious set and a serious topic, presented by a sober-looking anchor; the subversion occurs with the mode of expression. The sketch consists of Malone dressed as a well-coiffed male anchor seated behind a desk in front of a map of the world, the most basic set-up of the news genre. He gives a report of a typical topic for the news, a recent summit on AIDS in Africa. However, with a straight face, Malone describes the conference, "Blaming Africa for AIDS," in a racist doggerel that ostensibly unearths the unspeakable subtexts of colonialism, economic exploitation, and anal sex subtending the AIDS crisis. The American delegation is quoted as saying: "It's all your fault. It's all your fault. Nah nah nah nah nah nah. You're black, you're black, take your dirty bugs back. You're screwing green monkeys and giving it to our junkies. We give you all our foreign aid, and all we gets back is AIDS, AIDS, AIDS."

This combination of implausible speech and a news context makes for the shocking difference necessary for humour and parody. Rather than focus on sending up Canadian news personalities, the piece succeeds in being a satire of north–south relations that teeters on the edge of offen-

Figure 2. Greg Malone as Barbara Frum and Tommy Sexton as a hapless guest on *The Jugular*, CODCO's parody of the CBC current affairs show *The Journal*, in 1986. Image courtesy of Halifax Film Co./CBC Still Photo Collection/Bruce Macaulay.

siveness. Malone's phrase "all we *gets back* is AIDS, AIDS, AIDS" also signals the show's Newfoundland origins, which further distances it from official mainstream Canadian diction. "In order to produce laughter," writes Palmer, "[comedy] must be genuinely surprising, and preferably a little shocking: the contradiction of discursively defused expectations must be as sharp as it possibly can be. But if the shock is too great, it risks either (or both) giving offense or creating embarrassment."[31] With sketches such as this, I believe that *CODCO* treaded the line between humour and offence more dangerously than any other Canadian comedy show.

In 1993, *CODCO* cast members Mary Walsh and Cathy Jones were joined by Greg Thomey and Rick Mercer to create *This Hour Has 22 Minutes* (Salter Street Films/CBC, 1993–). Unlike earlier sketch comedies such as *SNL*, *SCTV*, and even *CODCO*, which incorporated the occasional news parody into an overall variety format taken from their evolution as stage shows, *This Hour* made television its focus and integrated a wide array of sketches into an overall news format. This reversal has a number of significant implications. First and foremost is the indication of an entrenched self-reflexivity relying on television itself as a source.[32] This reliance is signalled in the title of the show, which makes direct reference to an earlier CBC show, *This Hour Has Seven Days* (CBC, 1963–66), as well as indicating the number of content minutes in a typical half-hour television show.[33]

The performers appear at different points throughout the show, including at the beginning and the end, at a highly iconic news desk, to the accompaniment of percussive "news" music. The camera work, zooming in from the audience to the "news" presenters, connects the conventions of TV news with other studio set genres, such as the variety show and the late-night talk show. The show ultimately undercuts the news by combining a highly conventionalized reporting style, in which an anchor is framed in medium close-up behind a desk with a number of monitors behind him or her and next to a video insert, with humorous juxtapositions in order to make a comment on either a major current event, the absurdity of some minor news footage, or something completely unrelated to news. In any of the three cases, the show's format allows for the dialogic connection between unlikely or surprising elements. In one sketch from 1997, a story that starts off talking about finance minister Paul Martin's austerity cuts and comparing the Canadian economy to that of Australia ends up showing a group of Australian consumers stripped of their clothes—the result of austerity measures. The story doesn't go where political reporting usually goes. Instead, we are presented with a surprise ending, nudity that would never be shown on the news, which has the ancillary effect of destabilizing the news by showing how conventional its stories usually are.

In a trope borrowed from investigative journalism and stalkarazzi tabloid reporting, as the 1990s wore on the 22 *Minutes* trademark became the ambushing of politicians in media scrums by outlandish fake journalists, such as Marg, Princess Warrior, a bespectacled, middle-aged version of Xena played by Mary Walsh, and Marg Delahunty, her dowdy auntie counterpart. In these ambushes, 22 *Minutes* became part of the spectacle of television news production in Canada, drawing attention to its reliance on media routines and the good behaviour of "real" journalists. Marg's excessive behaviour, which often included planting kisses on the cheeks of provincial leaders and telling them how cute and lovable they were, allowed her to skewer their political and economic policies in an era of expanding neo-liberalism.

As the show became more and more well known through the 1990s, however, the ambushes diminished and politicians became cooperative participants on the show, goofing around with the cast in a variety of situations. Prime Minister Jean Chrétien shared a burger at Wendy's with Rick Mercer, shared golf tips with Marg Delahunty, and sprayed breath fresh-

Figure 3. The original cast of *This Hour Has 22 Minutes*, Mary Walsh, Greg Thomey, Cathy Jones, and Rick Mercer, in 1995. Image courtesy of Halifax Film Co./CBC Still Photo Collection.

ener at Greg Thomey after the Vancouver APEC Conference pepper spray controversy. Although these examples served to highlight issues in the news, they played mostly on personality and the show was accused of providing promotion rather than satire of the Canadian media and political establishment.[34] Still, many saw the show as an important social commentary, and through the 1990s, its ratings remained high, approximately 2.5 million per week for the show and its rebroadcasts.[35]

More recently, *This Hour* has spun off into an occasional series, *Talking to Americans* (2001)—which drew 2.7 million, the highest audience for a TV comedy broadcast on the CBC—and *The Rick Mercer Report* (2004–). *Rick Mercer* continues the same mix of commentary on news coverage and bantering with public figures seen in *This Hour* but adds a new commitment to cross-Canada road pieces where Mercer spends time with ordinary folks, such as university students and soldiers, as well as public figures, in different parts of Canada.[36] Doing away with the team of anchors, Mercer, a white man, has greater potential to parody the singular, monologic news host or pundit. However, he tends not to send himself up so much as to use the news desk as a platform to make fun of politicians.

Following on the success of *This Hour*, the CBC moved two shows from radio to television in the 1990s, both of which have been huge hits: *Royal Canadian Air Farce* (CBC, 1993–) and *Double Exposure* (CBC, 1994–6; CTV/Comedy Network, 1997–). At the peak of its popularity, *Air Farce*, a sketch comedy show with an emphasis on political satire that makes regular use of news as a motif, was drawing up to 2.5 million viewers per week.[37] The emphasis of the news sketches is usually, as in *SCTV*, the inappropriate language, class, or emotional expressions of the anchors, including relationships between the presenters—in short, the subversion of the news genre. Recent examples have included presenters reading the news from a trailer park, wearing rain gear and speaking in Newfoundland accents, and a male news reader making direct sexist attacks on a female presenter (*Royal Canadian Air Farce*, 4x4, 2003). In each of these examples, a surprising substitution is made in the news syntagm, but arguably these differences serve to reinforce the rightness of the "real" news by contrast.

Air Farce has also been home to a long-running gag about Peter Mansbridge, *The National*'s anchor, that pokes fun at the self-important attitude of the new Mr. CBC News, as well as his physical features, such as pursed lips and bald head. This sketch is more or less along the lines of *Air Farce*'s political satires, which usually consist of broad imitations of well-known Canadian politicians, especially the prime minister and the leaders of the other political parties. As with all double-voiced discourses, it is hard to know the degree to which this mimicry destabilizes the authority of the original or merely provides a relief valve for authorized laughing at authority. This ambiguity became especially marked as politicians such as Jean Charest, Preston Manning, Joe Clark, Deborah Gray, Mike Harris, Jean Chrétien, and Sheila Copps began to appear regularly on the show's annual New Year's Eve specials.[38]

Double Exposure, which is composed by dubbing in silly soundtracks over video images of news events, particularly the pseudo-events of the news

Figure 4. Roger Abbott as CBC newsreader Peter Mansbridge. Image courtesy of Air Farce Productions Inc.

conference or the ceremonial meeting of leaders, as well as the imitation of politicians, news readers, and other public figures, raises a similar question of effectivity. In satirizing the official culture of politics and news through the addition of usually puerile countertexts about sex and other material equally inappropriate for the public sphere, the show laughs at official culture without establishing any kind of sophisticated critique.

The Newsroom (CBC, 1996–97, 2002, 2004–05), one of only a few successful situation comedies in Canadian television history, deserves mention for its self-reflexive parodic satire of Canadian news media. Written by, directed, and starring Ken Finkleman, the show is a behind-the-scenes satire of the people who produce and read the news. Using the CBC building in Toronto as its set and constantly referencing the Canadian media elite, as well as featuring cameos by Canadian pundits such as Linda McQuaig and Naomi Klein, the show travesties the sobriety assumed to be part of the news production process, highlighting the ratings-grabbing choices behind the decisions to air particularly sensationalist stories. In a newsroom composed of a particularly disaffected group of producers, a vain and superficial newsreader, and, running it all, a dangerously myopic and self-obsessed producer whose main concerns are the prestige of his parking spot, the flavour of his muffins, and his ability to seduce young women, the show takes cruel pleasure in demonstrating the mundane concerns of the people behind television's most important contribution to democracy.

Conclusions: The Sorry State of Canadian Satire

I've addressed the Canadian aspect of these popular and increasingly omnipresent comedies about news and, by extension, self-reflexive humour about television. By way of conclusion, I want to also consider them in relation to two related non-Canadian shows, the BBC's *Spitting Image* (1984–92) and Comedy Central's *The Daily Show* (1996–). In a recent article on *Spitting Image*, Ulrike H. Meinhof and Jonathan Smith point out that the show was equally a satire of British politics and a parody of British television. "*Spitting Image*'s entertainment value surely derived from the way it pointed up and made play with the things we already half-knew about television itself, and about the ways in which, perhaps increasingly, television programmes are conceived and watched."[39] Using life-size latex puppets to caricature well-known public figures, the show achieved mimetic status of both humans and television genres. By substituting the infinitely malleable puppet signifier for the human referent, the show was able to highlight the semiotic aspect of television, where images of people and events in the world stand in for—represent—those specific people and events while simultaneously representing general categories. The puppets allowed for the burlesque of human life. Placed in recognizable television formats, they also made a stinging critique of television and our reliance on it for knowledge about the public sphere.

Jason Mittell notes a similar process at work in animated series such as *The Simpsons*. "Through parodic conventions such as caricature and hyperexaggeration that are typical of animation, *The Simpsons* forces us to question the codes of realism associated with live-action systems of representation."[40] It bears noting that both *The Simpsons* (20th Century Fox Film, 1989–) and *Family Guy* (20th Century Fox Film, 1999–) at times contain outrageous parodies of news that use the properties of animation to exceed what is possible in sketches with actors and arguably to import an intensely defamiliarizing experience to the news. As shows organized around the fictional worlds of their characters, however, their news parodies, no matter how intertextual, tend to be about lampooning the pomposity of the news readers and the news itself rather than about commenting on particular real-world news stories.

When *The Daily Show* (Comedy Central, 1996–) was hosted by Craig Kilborn (1996–9), it ran along lines similar to *Double Exposure*'s juvenile commentary on figures of authority or political scandals. Since it has been hosted by Jon Stewart (1999–), however, it has surpassed any previous news parody show. Currently, a million people watch *The Daily Show* on a regular basis and there has been a great deal of discussion about how it has filled the role of news for disaffected young people who no longer either watch the news or participate in the democratic process, such as it is.[41]

As with other news parodies, *The Daily Show* features a comedian—stand-up, not sketch—performing a dialogue between the genres of news and comedy. Unlike most other news parodies, however, *The Daily Show* is sufficiently timely, coming at the end of each day and even competing with 11 p.m. newscasts, to actually provide a specific rather than general rereading of the news. Stewart takes on a newscaster persona, sitting on a set in front of a live studio audience and relating to "field reporters" and experts through monitors even when they're in the studio and commenting ironically on news clips. As with *SCTV* and *Air Farce*, Stewart expresses emotional stakes inappropriate in the news genre, but unlike those shows, his comments are made in the spirit of deflating the real news' parasitic relationship with the government.

Jon Stewart also regularly features interviews on the show, which brings it closer to late-night talk show than parodic newscast. Politicians, writers, and pundits are regularly featured in this section of the show. In these pieces, Stewart's own liberal-left position is often clearly expressed, unlike the diffuse anti-authority or anti-everything position of much Canadian news comedy. Stewart's show does what news never does explicitly and most news parodies obscure: he takes a position, albeit mainly through the parodic satire of official news discourse. Stewart's following among the young, then, may well have to do not only with his parody of the news but also his political views, which are those that young voters and viewers are often sympathetic with.

In this increasing emphasis on comedic forms such as news parody rather than traditional forms of documentary or other sober attempts to intervene in public discourse, a popular left-wing politics, epitomized in the US by the practical-jokey style of someone like Michael Moore, has found a way to sidle onto mainstream TV. These cultural producers have heeded advice given by scholars such as Robert Stam that the left need not lecture to be heard: "An austere, super-egoish left that addresses its audience in moralistic terms—while advertising and mass culture speak to its deepest desires and fantasies—is theoretically and pragmatically handicapped."[42] Nevertheless, despite the fact that this dialogic form of humour does have the potential to introduce a different sort of logic into public discourse, restricting political opposition to the double-voiced or intertextual discourse of parody may well lead to a political and cultural dead end.

Even so, by contrast to the scathing mimesis of *Spitting Image* and the serious left-wing parody of Stewart's show, Canadian news parody has been quite timid. From the character-based skits of *SCTV* to the panparodic character of *This Hour* and its spinoffs, the equal-time parody of *Air Farce*, the facile mimicry of *Double Exposure*, and the cringe-worthy though hilarious navel gazing of *The Newsroom*, Canadian humour in the realm of news parody has actually been a fairly soft touch. The one show that did seem to pack a satirical punch was *CODCO*, which made power the unrelenting target of all its humour. But with the departure of Greg Malone and Andy Jones from TV projects in the early '90s and the untimely death of Tommy Sexton in 1994, the legacy was muted in *This Hour*.

Where the target of *CODCO*'s humour was often the media and politics in America and everyday life in Canada, *This Hour*, *Talking to Americans*, and *The Rick Mercer Report* tend to lampoon Canadian politics and media, as well as the everyday life, or at least everyday opinions, of Americans. Paradoxically, this shift has taken the edge off the satire. The change seems to have occurred as the *CODCO* troupe and its breakaway groups moved from their marginal position in Newfoundland toward Ontario, the centre of both Canadian media and Canadian politics. In *On Location*, Serra Tinic argues that, because of their position on the margins of Canada, the creators of *This Hour* are able to construct a "counter-narrative" of the nation, a site of resistance to both central Canada and the United States.[43] Although the show's Newfoundland accent allows for subversive expressions, literal and figurative, unavailable to non-regional Canadians, the extent of the show's ultimate challenge to the national narrative is certainly debatable.

The preponderance of news comedies on the CBC in the 1990s may also point to specific policy and cultural contexts during this period. As the CBC was faced with massive cutbacks and the threat of privatization, the corporation and its supporters fought back by emphasizing the role of the public broadcaster as the voice of the nation. Many nationalist programs were made during this period, including *Canada: A People's History* and the *Heritage Minutes*, discussed elsewhere in this book, and a Canadian-ization of the corporation was undertaken. It bears consideration, then, that the creation of spaces for authorized dissent occurred at the very moment that legitimacy was being shored up by the broadcaster for its authorita-tive newscasts and other nation-building programming.

By that token, the presence of such shows on the public broadcaster also most likely muted their satire, as the CBC was then and continues to be under scrutiny for any sign of promoting the party in power.[44] The safest route for comics reliant on public funds is to apply the satire thinly and evenly across the political spectrum. Arguably, the less the comic news shows can be seen to take a particular position, the more they paradoxi-cally reinforce the similar tropes of balance and objectivity upheld by the sober news. The non-subversive aspect of *This Hour* and *Air Farce* in par-ticular was underscored when the CBC began airing the shows in rerun on Newsworld in 1996. Baton Broadcasting, which had just been awarded a licence for a comedy channel, contested this move, claiming that the shows did not belong on a news channel. The CBC argued that they operated like political cartoons and therefore had a place alongside the news. Said Slawko Klimkiw, head of Newsworld at the time, "We think a network like ours needs a place where people can sit back and laugh from time to time at the events that transpire around us."[45] But the regulatory body, the Canadian Radio-television and Telecommunications Commission, sided with the private broadcaster and disagreed, finding that the shows were not adequately related to politics to qualify as satire.[46]

The context of news comedy production in Canada, and the debates the shows have spawned, help highlight the role of genre as regulated social text and a site of a creative dialogue constrained by rules and, at times, industry and policy frameworks as well. Although intelligent and often highly amusing, these shows risk restricting political opposition to the double-voiced or intertextual discourse of parody, a parasitic rela-tionship that ultimately reinforces the primacy and authority of news even while it brings authorized discourse into question. However, although news parody may provide nothing more than a safety valve for author-ized laughter, its widespread presence, in the Canadian context and else-where, is at the very least an indication of an ongoing struggle over official forms of knowledge. Self-reflexive comedy such as news parody has become a particularly typical televisual form, which may well signal the exhaustion of the news and widespread disillusionment with its founding mythology about democratic deliberation and the promise of the elec-tronic public sphere. This disillusionment deserves attention and can teach us something about the role of dialogic cultural forms, of which television is currently one of the most important, for negotiating both culture and politics.

Acknowledgements

I would like to thank Roy Harris of CBC Archives (Toronto) and Tyana Grundig of CBC Library (Toronto). My thanks also to Anil Narine, Cassandra Savage, and Benjamin Woo for invaluable research assistance.

Notes

1   Miller, "Inflecting the Formula."
2   *The Kids in the Hall* (CBC, 1988–94), one of Canada's most successful sketch comedy shows, avoided news parody altogether.
3   Tumber, "Introduction."
4   Morse, "The Television News Personality."
5   Hogarth, *Documentary Television in Canada.*
6   Barkin, *American Television News*; Glynn, *Tabloid Culture.*
7   Glynn, *Tabloid Culture.*
8   Creeber, *The Television Genre Book*; Feuer, "Genre Study and Television"; Mittell, *Television and Genre*; Neale, *Genre and Hollywood.*
9   See, for example, Grant, *Film Genre Reader III.*
10 Volosinov, *Marxism and the Philosophy of Language.*
11 Bakhtin, "The Problem of Speech Genres."
12 Bakhtin, "The Problem of Speech Genres," 92.
13 Although "intertextuality" is widely used to refer to the practice of quotation, its meaning as a translation of "dialogism" is much broader, encompassing the concept of speech genre outlined above. For more on the history of the use of the dialogic and intertextuality concept in media studies, see Zoë Druick, "Dialogic Absurdity: TV News Parody as a Critique of Genre," in *Television and New Media* (forthcoming).
14 Palmer, *The Logic of the Absurd*, 61; Hutcheon, *A Theory of Parody*, 33.
15 Palmer, *The Logic of the Absurd*, 46.
16 Dane, "Parody and Satire."
17 Hutcheon, *A Theory of Parody*, 57.
18 See Roscoe and Hight, *Faking It.*
19 Morse, "The Television News Personality," 57.
20 Palmer, *The Logic of the Absurd*, 218, 90.
21 Palmer, *The Logic of the Absurd*, 90.
22 Hutcheon, *A Theory of Parody*, 75.
23 Allen, *Intertextuality*, 44; Freud, *Jokes and Their Relation to the Unconcscious*; Kristeva, *The Kristeva Reader*, 42.
24 Palmer, *The Logic of the Absurd*, 221.
25 This gloss on genre connects it with another Bakhtinian concept, that of carnival (Bakhtin, *Rabelais and His World*). Space constraints force me to sideline that discussion in this context.
26 Cawelti, "*Chinatown* and Generic Transformation," 260.

27 Cawelti, "*Chinatown* and Generic Transformation," 260.
28 Although it is outside the parameters of this paper, I would note that one of the original writers for *Saturday Night Live* was Rosie Shuster, at the time Lorne Michaels's wife. Shuster was the daughter of Frank Shuster, one half of the earliest successful sketch comedy team in Canada, Wayne and Shuster (Durden-Smith, "Breaking Up America," 17).
29 Eugene Levy's parody was even mentioned in Cameron's obituary ("Mr. CBC News").
30 Cited in Peters, "From Salt Cod to Cod Filets," 15.
31 Palmer, *The Logic of the Absurd*, 140.
32 The show is produced by Geoff D'Eon, who took the job after working as executive producer of CBC Halifax's television news.
33 *This Hour Has Seven Days* (CBC, 1963–66) was a public affairs show in the form of a variety show. It combined filmed sequences with studio interviews, editorials from the hosts, skits, and even musical synopses of the week's events. The show had a satirical edge and courted controversy, and it was brought to a well-publicized end in 1966 when CBC management fired its young hosts, Patrick Watson and Laurier LaPierre.
34 Cobb, "Willing Victims." In one complex example, during the 2004 federal election, NDP candidate Ed Broadbent used a rap video produced by *This Hour* to promote his campaign (Pilieci, "Broadbent Gets Rapped").
35 In 2000, the *This Hour* team successfully inspired over one million people to sign an online petition supporting the idea of a referendum to force Stockwell Day to change his name to Doris. This gag petition came in the wake of the newly formed Canadian Alliance's attempt to install a model of direct democracy based on referenda supported by 3 per cent of the population, in order to bypass Parliament and the Supreme Court on contentious issues such as abortion and gun control ("Rick Mercer's Referendum"). The success of the absurd petition effectively put the issue to rest (Riley, "*This Hour Has 22 Minutes* Becomes Effective Opposition").
36 D. Grant Black has characterized Rick Mercer as the "Wayne Ronstad of comedy" (Black, "More Offence, Please").
37 Kellogg, "Year of the Farce."
38 Turbide and Ajello, "The Air Farce Is Flying High"; Canadian Press, "Old PMs Yuk It Up"; Honey, "Did You Hear the One about the *Air Farce?*"
39 Meinhof and Smith, "*Spitting Image*," 60.
40 Mittell, "Cartoon Realism," 24.
41 McKain, "Not Necessarily Not the News"; Feldman, "The News about Comedy."
42 Stam, *Subversive Pleasures*, 238.
43 Tinic, *On Location*, 155, 151.
44 Rebecca Addelman has argued in an article in *The Walrus* that this can be attributed to a chilly climate produced by the omnipresent threat of litigation.
45 Atherton, "Newsworld Is Going for Laughs."
46 Zerbisias, "*Farce* and *This Hour* Ordered Off."

References

Addelman, Rebecca. "The Last Laugh: Why Canadian Satire Can't Measure Up to *Stewart* and *Colbert*." *The Walrus*, May 2007: 34–36.
Allen, Graham. *Intertextuality*. London: Routledge, 2000.

Atherton, Tony. "Newsworld Is Going for Laughs." *Calgary Herald*, June 3, 1996: C10.

Bakhtin, Mikhail M. *Rabelais and His World*. Bloomington: Indiana University Press, 1984.

Bakhtin, Mikhail M. "The Problem of Speech Genres." In *Speech Genres and Other Late Essays*, 60–102. Austin: University of Texas Press, 1986.

Barkin, Steve M. *American Television News: The Media Marketplace and the Public Interest*. Armonk, NY: M.E. Sharpe, 2003.

Black, D. Grant. "More Offence, Please." *Globe and Mail*, October 6, 2007: D15.

Canadian Press. "Old PMs Yuk It Up on New Year's Eve." *Calgary Herald*, December 30, 1998: C1.

Cawelti, John G. "*Chinatown* and Generic Transformation in Recent American Films." In *Film Genre Reader III*, edited by Barry Keith Grant, 243–261. Austin: University of Texas Press, 2003.

Cobb, Chris. "Willing Victims: Politicians Seem Eager to Be Mocked on *This Hour Has 22 Minutes*." *Halifax Daily News*, December 10, 1996: 35.

Coulter, Diane. "Yuk Yuk Canuck: Rick Mercer Takes a Poke at Our American Neighbours' Cultural Myopia." *St. John's Telegram*, June 30, 2001: E1.

Creeber, Glen, ed. *The Television Genre Book*. London: British Film Institute, 2000.

Dane, Joseph A. "Parody and Satire: A Theoretical Model." *Genre* 13 (1980): 145–59.

Druick, Zoë. "Dialogic Absurdity: TV News Parody as a Critique of Genre." *Television and New Media* 10 (3) (forthcoming).

Durden-Smith, Jo. "Breaking Up America: How One Honorary and Six Real Canadians Create a Weekly Panic called *Saturday Night Live*." *The Canadian*, May 29, 1976: 16–18.

Feldman, Lauren. "The News about Comedy: Young Audiences, *The Daily Show* and Evolving Notions of Journalism." Paper presented at the annual meeting of the International Communication Association, New York, 2005: 1–29. www.allacademic.com/meta/p13125_index.html. Accessed February 12, 2008.

Feuer, Jane. "Genre Study and Television." In *Channels of Discourse Reassembled: Television and Contemporary Criticism*, 2nd ed., edited by Robert C. Allen, 138–60. Chapel Hill: University of North Carolina Press, 1992.

Fiske, John. *Television Culture*. London: Routledge, 1987.

Freud, Sigmund. *Jokes and Their Relation to the Unconscious*, Pelican Freud Library, Vol. 6. Translated by James Strachey. Harmondsworth, UK: Penguin, 1976.

Glynn, Kevin. *Tabloid Culture: Trash Taste, Popular Power, and the Transformation of American Television*. Durham, NC: Duke University Press, 2000.

Grant, Barry Keith, ed. *Film Genre Reader III*. Austin: University of Texas Press, 2003.

Hogarth, David. *Documentary Television in Canada: From National Public Service to Global Marketplace*. Montreal and Kingston: McGill-Queen's University Press, 2002.

Honey, Kim. "Did You Hear the One about the *Air Farce* on CBC?" *Globe and Mail*, January 1, 2002: A1, A4.

Hutcheon, Linda. *A Theory of Parody: The Teachings of Twentieth-Century Art Forms*. Urbana: University of Illinois Press, 1985.

———. "The Politics of Postmodern Parody." In *Intertextuality*, edited by Heinrich F. Plett, 225–36. Berlin: Walter de Gruyter, 1991.

Kellogg, Alan. "Year of the Farce: Pure Canadian Comedy Team Is at the Top of Its Form." *Edmonton Journal*, May 16, 1997: D10.

Kristeva, Julia. *The Kristeva Reader*, edited by T. Moi. New York: Columbia University Press, 1986.

McKay, John. "Canadian Comics Weighing in on Tuesday's U.S. Presidential Election." Canadian Press News Wire, October 29, 2004. Available at http://proquest.umi.com/pqdweb?did+731907121&Fmt=3&clientld=3667&RQT=309&VName+PQD. Accessed January 10, 2008.

McKain, Aaron. "Not Necessarily Not the News: Gatekeeping, Remediation, and *The Daily Show*." *The Journal of American Culture* 28 (4): 415–30.

Meinhof, Ulrike H. and Jonathan Smith. "*Spitting Image*: TV Genre and Intertextuality." In *Intertextuality and the Media: From Genre to Everyday Life*, edited by Ulrike H. Meinhof and Jonathan Smith, 43–60. Manchester: Manchester University Press, 2000.

Miller, Mary Jane. "Inflecting the Formula: The First Seasons of *Street Legal* and *L.A. Law*." In *The Beaver Bites Back? American Popular Culture in Canada*, edited by David H. Flaherty and Frank E. Manning, 104–22. Montreal and Kingston: McGill-Queen's University Press, 1993.

Mittell, Jason. "Cartoon Realism: Genre Mixing and the Cultural Life of *The Simpsons*." *The Velvet Light Trap* 47 (Spring 2001): 15–28.

Mittell, Jason. *Television and Genre: From Cop Shows to Cartoons in American Culture*. New York: Routledge, 2004.

Morse, Margaret. "The Television News Personality and Credibility: Reflections on the News in Transition." In *Studies in Entertainment: Critical Approaches to Mass Culture*, edited by Tania Modleski, 55–79. Bloomington: Indiana University Press, 1986.

"Mr. CBC News Set the Tone for a Generation." *Edmonton Journal*, January 15, 2005: E9.

Neale, Stephen. *Genre and Hollywood*. London: Routledge, 2000.

Palmer, Jerry. *The Logic of the Absurd: On Film and Television Comedy*. London: British Film Institute, 1987.

Peters, Helen. "From Salt Cod to Cod Filets." *Canadian Theatre Review* 64 (Fall 1990): 13–17.

Pilieci, Vito. "Broadbent Gets Rapped in Final Debate." *Ottawa Citizen*, June 25, 2004: B3.

"Rick Mercer's Referendum: Hundreds of Thousands of Canadians Log on to the Internet to Support: Direct Democracy Demand Comes Back at Stockwell Day." *Halifax Daily News*, November 17, 2000: 47.

Riley, Susan. "*This Hour Has 22 Minutes* Becomes Effective Opposition." *StarPhoenix* (Saskatoon), March 1, 1997: C1.

Roscoe, Jane and Craig Hight. *Faking It: Mock-documentary and the Subversion of Factuality*. Manchester: Manchester University Press, 2001.

Stam, Robert. *Subversive Pleasures*. Baltimore: Johns Hopkins University Press, 1989.

Tinic, Serra. *On Location: Canada's Television Industry in a Global Market*. Toronto: University of Toronto Press, 2005.

Tumber, Howard. "Introduction." In *News: A Reader*, edited by Howard Tumber, xv–xix. Oxford: Oxford University Press, 1999.

Turbide, Diane and Robin Ajello. "The Air Farce Is Flying High." *Maclean's*, February 26, 1997: 52–4.

Volosinov, V.N. *Marxism and the Philosophy of Language*. New York: Semina Press, 1973.

Zerbisias, Antonia. "*Farce* and *This Hour* Ordered Off CBC Newsworld." *Toronto Star*, March 7, 1997: D14.

Filmography

CODCO: Uncensored (Salter Street Films, 1995)

This Hour Has 22 Minutes, Best of 1994–5; Best of 1996–7 (Salter Street Films)

Royal Canadian Air Farce, 4x4 (Air Farce Productions/CBC, 2003)

SCTV: Network 90, Vol. 1 (NBC, 1981)

Whose Child Am I?

The Quebec Referendum and
Languages of Affect and the Body

You cut the umbilical cord of a baby, it's a kind of separation, but one that brings new life.
—Quebec sovereigntist, interviewed on *The National*, October 23, 1995

It's like taking a part a piece of your heart—it's a piece of my country. I don't want to see it hurt.
—Canadian nationalist, interviewed on *The National*, October 27, 1995

O n October 30, 1995, residents of Quebec went to the polls for the second time to decide whether their province should separate from Canada to become a sovereign country.[1] In the lead-up to this event, Canadian national media made a concerted effort to uphold a very particular narrative of an undivided nation. My examination of two years of CBC news programming about the referendum—news coverage, news documentaries, and special programs—reveals a recurring language of affect, punctuated with words like "vulnerability," "tragedy," "anger," "hurt," "pain," and "healing." Generally, it was not just people who were described as having these feelings, but also the country itself, with the nation becoming corporeal. I will argue in this chapter that CBC news coverage of the referendum debate constituted an affective supertext that, with its narrative of heterosexual romance, operated in a fashion reminiscent of the emotion-laden dramatic serial, making use of many of the feminine codes of melodrama.[2]

Melodrama, which emerged from early nineteenth-century French theatre, has been theorized as a genre that, with its dualistic forces of good and evil, could stand in for the sacred in the modern age.[3] Peter Brooks has pointed out that melodrama was and perhaps remains more than a literary or theatrical genre: it was a way of being in the world, or what he called "the central fact of the modern sensibility."[4] Melodrama has been recuperated by feminist theory as a way to theorize, as Suzanna Walters puts it, "the relationship between gender and genre, between the construction of sexual difference and the specific signifying practices of a particular type of representation."[5] The soap opera, then, with its waves of emotion and its audiences' affective responses, becomes another way to think about melodrama as a cultural force that makes central the feminized themes of family, excess, romance, and hysteria and also produces nodes of community and collective affect among its audiences.[6]

The narrative of the Quebec referendum, while at times mimicking the soap opera, also relied heavily on the paradigm of a body in both psychic and physical pain. A variety of bodily metaphors—from birth to death by cancer—were discursively utilized, but it was the troubled heterosexual couple that became the overriding metaphor of Quebec's relationship to Canada. Kim Sawchuk writes of Quebec separatism, "The language of pain … not only humanized the [national] body, but it gave it an age, a gender, and a life in a traditional heterosexual family structure."[7] Melodrama, then, is constitutive of what Nowell-Smith has called "a set of psychic determinations which take shape around the family." It was "the ideal genre for this particular family drama."[8]

My study of the Quebec referendum will differ from that of Sawchuk and others by using affect theory—an examination of visceral, embodied, and pre-discursive feeling that has only recently appeared on the radar of cultural and media studies.[9] For the purposes of this chapter, affect theory is a useful tool with which to rethink the relation of television and audiences. Affect displays itself on and through the body—gestures, expressions, sounds—and these displays are always in relation to what other people are doing with their bodies. As Gay Hawkins points out, echoing Brooks, with affect theory it is not so much about having individual feelings or drives and more about acknowledging the ways in which we feel in and with the world.[10] This notion of affect as *relational* is particularly useful in analyzing moments of simultaneity like the televised reportage of the Quebec referendum. But affect theory also functions as a kind of corrective to theories of melodrama, moving beyond the primary text to audiences, bodies, and communities. Departing from psychoanalytic theory's more fixed notion of spectator as sutured by text, affect theory allows for different viewer responses to infect and transform one another, as well as for the potential for new subjectivities to emerge from this process.

News as Drama

News reportage has often been described as a dramatic and even melodramatic form. If the news, in this formulation, becomes a national drama, its structure and placement evoke the television serial. Nick Browne argues that the serial is television's "paradigmatic form." He writes that it "orders and regulates television programming—from daily news and talk shows through the typical weekly sequencing of primetime entertainment programs."[11] Historically, the serial was a way of doing away with sponsor-financed drama anthologies like CBC's *General Motors Presents* (1954–61), replaced by the more profitable system of selling advertising spots, which also gave networks more institutional and creative autonomy.[12]

Browne's point is that the text of the serial is a result of negotiation between advertiser, network, and audience.[13] CBC news is not, I will argue, immune to these tropes, negotiating as it does between the axes of commercial interest and national identity. Writes Browne, "It is one of the traditional commitments of network programming to try and secure a loyal flow of audience attention through the primetime hours, warding off potential defections through strategies of continuity."[14] Like any other genre of television, news programming is never a discrete unit. Rather, it exists as one of a series of texts whose unity is designed to attract an audience for the longest period possible. In other words, news coverage is also commodified via a serial structure—even, I would argue, under the aegis of a public network.

The serial nature of CBC's coverage of the Quebec referendum also served to narrativize national sentiment in the form of the romance genre via a heavily coded language of body and emotion. Indeed, romance and nationalism frequently work together.[15] In the case of the Quebec referendum, I will argue that melodramatic affect became a way of organizing bodies and minds at an extremely unstable moment in Canadian history. Thus, national sentiment, embodied on English-language television in a kind of melodramatic battle between the good of federation and the evil of separation—the good of Chrétien, the evil of Parizeau—then became *narratively* mobilized as a means of managing Quebec on behalf of English Canada.

Early Days

The coverage of the referendum debate began in earnest in February 1995, nine months before the actual referendum itself, mimicking another bodily process: pregnancy. The gestation of the televisual debate began with

Carnevale in Quebec City. Over footage of snow and dancing ice skaters, a voice-over said that the rumblings of the upcoming debate seemed at this point "somewhat faint" (*Sunday Report*, February 1995). Subsequent interviews with the usual suspects—doughnut shop denizens, seniors, and the inhabitants of main-street Quebec—confirmed that while people's identification with or against sovereignty is "from the heart ... it's still too early to get excited" (*CBC News*, February 5, 1995). This foreshadowing of a slowly rising tide of emotion is characteristic of melodramatic narratives. As Robin R. Warhol has pointed out in her study of soap opera, such narratives allow for a limited range of emotional affect to rise and fall in a regular pattern, resulting in an open-ended seriality that "keeps the pattern of affect constantly moving."[16]

The referendum discourse in Quebec triggered a parallel nationalist discourse in Canadian news media. The nine-month lead-up to the referendum was punctuated with flashbacks to an older, more patriotic past. On February 5, the anniversary of the current Canadian flag, there was a special episode of *The National* in which images of flag-waving children, a flag cake, and the designer of the flag—conveniently, a Québécois by birth—were pointedly intercut with sovereigntist billboards in Montreal. "Ironically," said host Pamela Wallin, with no sense of irony at all, "the Canadian flag has emerged as the principle symbol of the campaign to keep Quebec in the country." Paul Henderson, the iconic hockey player who had scored the winning goal in the Canada–Russia hockey finals, was moved to say: "We need to become flag wavers. I think it would bring us together" (*The Magazine*, February 15, 1995).

Many scholars have noted the relationship between sentiment and national identity, and the state's role in managing emotion to induce patriotism. Kaja Silverman, for example, writes that a material relation to the nation-state—citizenship rights, health care, geographical relation—is invested in an imaginary relation to the nation. This relation is, she argues, underpinned by affect: it is a *hope*, or a *nostalgia*, rather than a reality.[17]

However, questions of race and gender produced disequilibrium within this narrative early on, providing regular crises true to melodramatic form. The Quebec referendum debate leaned heavily on what British intellectuals have dubbed the "new racism," in which national culture and its enactments of patriotism are implicitly white. Keohane has described the project of Quebec separatism as being similar to that of right-wing, often racist projects like those of the Reform Party and the Heritage Front: "These projects seek to solve the problem of the diversity and multiplicity of Canadian identities by categorically identifying and demarcating a singular centre and systematically excluding elements that do not fit that category."[18]

In a foreshadowing of the race scandal that was to become the Parti Québécois' downfall, Lucien Bouchard, Quebec premier and leader of the referendum campaign, appeared on CBC saying: "Do you think it makes sense to have so few children in Quebec? We are one of the white races that has the fewest children" (*CBC Special Report*, October 17, 1995). Astonishingly, the CBC completely ignored the racial implications of this remark, allowing critiques of sexism but not racism to surface. Bouchard was later shown on television reconciling with a feminist leader of the Yes (sovereigntist) campaign. As often happens when race relations are an issue on Canadian television, it was women, and "women's issues," that became the bearers of discourse on inequality, obscuring the race issue yet again.[19]

Race came up again on CBC television, if briefly, when the Cree of Quebec held their own referendum, one week before the official one. That referendum resulted in an overwhelming No vote—a fact that was buried in larger stories about the economic uncertainties of separation, making literal Prasenjit Duara's notion of the "hidden other" that works productively to destabilize the nation at the same time that its otherness is crucial to the *relational* identity of nationalism.[20] Hiddenness and unspeakability are also characteristic of the melodramatic mode. If, in melodrama, taboos are broken at all, the information comes too late and cannot, like the Cree referendum or Parizeau's revealing post-referendum utterances, be made use of.[21]

Seriality, Soaps, and Melodrama

The titles of CBC "special reports," magazine shows, and mini-documentaries, as well as the music and lead-ins that went with them, also evoked notions of soap opera–style seriality. Indeed, television theorist Glen Creeber's description of seriality could well describe CBC's referendum coverage: "Like the soap opera, the series reoccurs regularly throughout the schedule, weaving in and out of the domestic space ... Simply in terms of hours alone the series can produce a breadth of vision, a narrative scope and can capture the audience's involvement in a way equalled by few contemporary media."[22]

If the etymology of "melodrama" is the Latin *melos* (music) and "drama"—a genre in which music marks moments of excessive affect—then the violin strains accompanying the introductory programs about the referendum, overlaid with sound bites of different political actors in the debate, intercut with Parliament's Peace Tower splitting in two, presented the emotional terms of the family romance that was about to unfold.[23]

Peter Brooks develops the relation of music and narrative further: "The emotional drama needs the desemanticized language of music, its evocation of the 'ineffable,' its tones and registers ... called upon to invest plot with some of the inexorability and necessity that in pre-modern literature derived from the substratum of myth."[24] Melodramatic music, so characteristic of the soap opera, signals passion, pleasure in excess, and the operatic registers of emotional expressivity. Within the soap's narrative structure, it is the family that provides the raison d'etre of such music-accompanied affect.

In Freudian terms, the "family romance" is an imaginary scenario about paternity where a child asks, "Whose child am I?"[25] Questions of paternity are prevalent in the plots of Western melodrama, and most especially in soap opera. This sets the stage for the enactment of bourgeois familial concerns: property, inheritance, lineage, and crises of masculinity. In melodrama, the family is a kind of fortress constantly prone to infidelity, alcoholism, and other social tragedies. Separation—of husband from wife, child from father—is the great evil of melodrama, the wellspring of all tragedy, and the antithesis of community and family, which is always melodrama's unfulfilled desire. Women, usually charged with the responsibility of holding the fortress together, were later to become a predominant theme in the referendum's own family romance.

Federalist politicians repeatedly used the spectre of family dissolution as an emotive hook. In an eleventh-hour address to the nation, Prime Minister Jean Chrétien was pictured in his office between two sets of photos: one of his wife on the left and a grouping of family snapshots on the right. In the middle, visually holding the two ends of the family together, was Chrétien. Leaning forward slightly and speaking in a low, intimate voice, he asked, "Do you really think that you and your family will have a quality of life and a better future in a separate Quebec?" In the same news program, New Brunswick premier Frank McKenna was reported as saying, "It's a time for all Canadians ... to show their affection for their brothers and sisters in Quebec." (*The National,* October 25, 1995). Subsequent television coverage echoed this trope, as when CBC reporter Hanna Gartner blurted out on referendum night, "Clearly, we are a dysfunctional family."

A spring 1995 poll conducted by the CBC presented a 60:40 split between those who opposed and those who supported Quebec's separation. Subsequent polls revealed that women in Quebec formed the largest number of undecided voters. Suddenly, the province of Quebec had a gender: female. As CBC's Mark Kelley reported: "The province is ready to decide—but *she* can't. *She*'s not alone. Ten per cent of Quebec women—

twice that of men—can't decide either" (*The National*, special report, September 16, 1995, emphasis added). The gendered corporeality of the campaign had begun in earnest.

Gendered and Racialized Corporeality

Eight months into CBC coverage of the referendum debate, anxiety was at its height—as might be expected, presumably, in the month before birth. This produced a kind of uncanniness: news coverage began to mimic actual plays and TV shows; love stories and romantic tragedies were narrated again and again. A special report on the female vote was titled *The Women*, as though it were a play. In it, the first of many Anglo–French Canadian romances was featured in a round table of women voters hosted by Hanna Gartner. One woman said, "I fell in love with a Quebecker and then with Quebec," while another wife, a francophone married to an anglophone, declared her intention to vote No.[26]

Not long after this feature, Gartner introduced an even more pointedly narrativized news documentary called *All in the Family*, an intertextual reference to the 1970s TV series of the same name about a bigoted blue-collar worker, Archie Bunker, and his dysfunctional family. The CBC documentary, about a biracial white and South Asian family on different sides of the debate, began with Gartner's voice-over: "All in the family: the father's voting Yes, the mother's voting No, and the daughter has to make up her mind. The story of one woman caught between the two solitudes at home."[27] The American *All in the Family* repeatedly expressed anxieties concerning miscegenation via the marriage of Archie's blonde daughter, Gloria, to Polish-American Mike, whom Archie referred to alternatively as "Polak" or "meathead." Similarly, the CBC-TV documentary serial evoked not the two solitudes of French and English but those of French and allophone, and fears—expressed earlier by Bouchard—about the declining numbers of white Quebeckers.

Francine Pelletier, a well-known journalist, hosted the three-episode program. And when she mentioned the long-running Québécois TV series *La Famille Plouffe*, she made yet another intertextual reference to television seriality. In the clip that followed, Monsieur Plouffe was shown as saying, "I'm beginning to get tired of Canada." Running from 1954 to 1959, this hugely popular—in Quebec—program attempted to bridge the English–French cultural divide by, as Ira Levin writes, "providing English-speaking audiences with a French-Canadian family they could care about, in a limited sort of way."[28] In the CBC documentary, Monsieur Gauthier, a sovereigntist, stood in for Plouffe *père*, while, according to Pelletier, "Mama

Gauthier is a new Canadian and just as fervent a federalist." Cut to Madame Gauthier, who says, "When I see all the problems all over the world, I think Canada is the best country in the world."[29] Archie to Mme Gauthier's Edith, Monsieur Gauthier says, in French, "We want complete control of our economy, of our culture ... we want to be sovereign master in our own home." The Gauthier's daughter, twenty-four-year-old, mixed-race Natasha, is, like Gloria Bunker, caught in between her parents' affective modes. She is, as Pelletier reports with pointedly affective language, "neither in love with Canada nor with a sovereign Quebec." Pelletier painfully extends the narrative of heterosexual romance, turning the Gauthier couple into a convenient, if racially and emotively overdetermined, metaphor for Quebec:

> PELLETIER (to Madame Gauthier): But you're not about to divorce are you?
> MADAME GAUTHIER: No, we've been married twenty-six years.
> PELLETIER: ... You'll still be sleeping with your husband after the referendum.
> GAUTHIER: *Yes!*

Natasha seems confident, hip, politicized. Her strong sense of herself as a Québécoise represents both excess and lack. As a woman of colour, she lacks the ability to reproduce the white race in Quebec; as a self-determined allophone Québécoise, she exceeds the sovereigntist expectations of allophones in Quebec.

While people of colour and immigrants were presented on English-language television as tangential to the referendum's outcome—in effect as sitcoms to the referendum's drama—their significance was enormous, both in terms of votes and in the ways in which Quebec politicians' fear of otherness became vocalized. In the final weeks of the referendum debate, racism was to become visible in Quebec as never before—to use Prasenjit Duara's terms, *productively destabilizing* the sovereigntist agenda.[30]

"Quebec On T'Aime": The Final Week

A kind of hysteria pervaded the last week of the referendum. The word "danger" was used repeatedly by reporters and anchors, especially with regard to the vulnerable national economy. The language of romance was presented as an affective solution to this political and economic crisis.

In an extended CBC newscast on September 27, 1995, the word "emotion" was used a dozen times in one hour, and an improbable lexicon of intimate words such as "hurt," "desperation," and "love" came up repeatedly. CBC reporter Paul Adams leads into a story about a No rally in Montreal with the following words: "For many of the thousands who came here from outside Quebec, it was an *emotional* journey" (*The National*, September 27, 1995). Cut to a middle-aged white woman attending the rally, flanked by federalists of all ages. She says, for all the world like a spurned lover, "It's like taking a part a piece of your heart—it's a piece of my country. I don't want to see it hurt." Cut again, to an enormous Canadian flag floating on a sea of people chanting "Can*ada*! Can*ada*!" in French, no less, with the accent on the last syllable. Cut to some young men with a homemade sign saying "*Quebec on t'aime*—BC" (Quebec, we love you—BC). Never had patriotism been taken up so ardently by this post-1970s generation of white Anglos: nationalism was suddenly a corporeal matter of life, death, and breath. Marvin and Ingle write: "As the referendum for Quebec independence approached, a newspaper headline proclaimed, 'Canada holds its breath as Quebec votes.' … Ritual is creative; it seeks the unity of form and substance, which is embodiment. Thus, media are ritually driven to offer the illusion of bodily presence restored."[31]

As the language of the body increased to almost comedic heights, PQ leader Lucien Bouchard's body became more visually prominent. Bouchard has walked with a cane and a slight limp since he lost a leg in an attack of flesh-eating disease. His disability, usually tactfully ignored, was mentioned repeatedly in the last days of the referendum campaign. One CBC description went as follows: "Because of his charisma, because of his brush with death last year, Lucien Bouchard has been elevated into the status of a living martyr." Accompanying this voice-over was a waist-down shot of Bouchard's limping legs and his cane (*The National*, September 27). But it was on October 29 and 30, referendum eve and night, respectively, that metaphors of ill bodies took over the utterances of sovereigntists and federalists alike.

Referendum Night

KEN DRYDEN: I haven't been feeling very good this week. It's like I have a hole in my stomach and it won't go away … I want one Canada for me because I hate the hole I feel. Maybe you feel that hole too.

PETER MANSBRIDGE (as Yes vote edges up to 58.9%): There are a lot of nervous stomachs in a lot of different parts of the country and a lot of different parts of this province. (*The National*, October 30)

Candlelight vigils. Rallies for the No side across the country. Another squabbling couple ("She's for No, he's for Oui!"). And a divorced couple,

Peter Mansbridge and Wendy Mesley, anchoring the special October 29 and 30 coverage of the referendum.

The lead-in to CBC's October 30 special news program looked quite a bit like the trailer for a low-budget film. As the hands of a clock appeared over a Canadian flag, Mansbridge's voice introduced the lead-in: "Thirty minutes before the ballot counting begins. We know the stakes. We've heard the voices of the politicians." Over a shot of Quebec flags, Parizeau's voice was heard saying, "I think we'll have a country pretty soon." A man waving the Canadian flag, then a dissolve to a fleur-de-lys in the top half of a horizontal split screen, a No rally in the bottom half. Chrétien in voice-over, "We have every reason to be extremely proud to be Canadian." More voices and images, and then the sequence ends with the clock superimposed against a Canadian and a Quebec flag, and Mansbridge's voice: "In thirty minutes we hear the voice of the people. Will it be Yes or No?"[32]

As voting began in Northern Quebec, a vertical line appeared on the bottom half of the screen: blue for Yes on one side, red for No on the other. The first poll to be counted was Ungava, where the split was 50.5 per cent Yes, 49.5 per cent No. That almost equally divided red and blue line was hardly to change all night.

PETER MANSBRIDGE: Nervous? A little bit edgy? Well you are not alone. The Yes side, the No side, all Quebeckers and all Canadians are nervous.

As the evening wore on, newscasters worked hard to fill airtime, which made for plenty of slippage and peculiar utterances.[33]

HANNA GARTNER: I'm watching your blood pressure go up, Brian Tobin!
TOBIN: I'm feeling not cocky but confident.
GARTNER: Earlier, you were about to lose your dinner! (CBC round-table discussion, October 30, 1995)

Michel Foucault described the body as a capillary of power; power flows into individual bodies, affecting gesture, posture, and utterance.[34] In these terms, the language of the demasculinized, romantic, pathological body—Quebec—flows back into the economic power relations of Canadian nationalism. This heterosexualized and feminized, and occasionally disabled, subaltern body is the one that the discourse of nationalism serves to preserve—but in a benevolent colonial fashion.

Brian Massumi speaks of "a complex flow of collective desire" in which certain bodies stand in for certain images.[35] These are something different from unknowing Cartesian bodies.[36] These bodies know, to paraphrase social critic Himani Bannerji, the dark side of the nation. Some of them know it intimately; others know it from afar.

That night, Parizeau said, famously and bitterly, in a televised concession speech, "We were beaten by money and the ethnic vote" (*The National*,
September 30 1995).

The Racialized Other

PETER MANSBRIDGE: Good evening. Canada is still here tonight—but just
barely. (*The National*, October 30 1995)

Bannerji argues that certain racist moments, like Bouchard's and Parizeau's
awkward utterances, are usually individualized (e.g., the "bad apples" of
the Somalia affair) and are used by English Canada to obscure its own
racist project.[37] The discursive legacy of the Quebec referendum debate has
not been a more critical approach to the ideology of nationhood. It was,
I would argue, quite the opposite: an increase in racially overdetermined
ideas of the nation, underpinned by melodramatic calls to patriotic excess
and the moral binaries of the genre.

Reporter Tom Kennedy had this to say about Parizeau's comment, over
footage of Parizeau chanting, "*Vive le Québec*," followed by a shot of a
young woman of colour looking dismayed: "If anyone expected healing
words after such a divisive campaign, they didn't get it. Jacques Parizeau
took aim right away at Quebec's minorities, who voted massively to stay
in Canada. 'We were beaten,' he said, 'by money and the ethnic vote'"
(*The National*, October 30, 1995).

People of colour, formerly bit players in the televised referendum serial,
were recuperated back into the drama. Natasha Gauthier, the No-voting
mixed-race daughter of the present-day Plouffes, was pulled into the CBC
studios and asked her opinion of Parizeau's comment. "It made my hair
stand on end," she said, "I think it was a very unastute thing for him to
say" (*The National*, October 31, 1995). In one of the most insightful com-
mentaries in weeks, Gauthier *fille* went on to say, "We'll have to see what
the backlash does to the allophone and the anglophone communities, especially since Parizeau has singled them out." She recounted a conversation
at a Yes party where someone said that if the No side won, there should
be a law passed like one in Belgium where immigrants can't vote until the
third generation. Marvelled Gauthier: "He actually said that. People were
going, 'Yeah, yeah, that's a good idea.' So you can't say that what Parizeau
said was out of the blue and that it didn't reflect what Quebeckers feel!"

In the days after referendum night, pain diminished to hurt—hurt
being, as Sawchuk has pointed out, an indication that someone is responsible for the pain.[38] On October 31, CBC's *The National* reported that

Parizeau had resigned. Commented Mansbridge, "In defeat, he had said words that *hurt*." On November 13, 1995, when it became clear that Parizeau would not apologize, Mansbridge reported, "The Parti Québécois tried to reach out to the people the premier may have hurt." This somewhat less painful affect referred to racism rather than separation.

National Time

> We are "national" when we vote, watch the six o'clock news, follow the national sport, observe, while barely noticing, the repeated iconographies of landscape and history in TV commercials. (Eley and Suny, *Becoming National*)[39]

According to implicit assumptions in CBC coverage, Quebeckers and Canadians did have one thing very much in common: a shared belief in the viability of nationhood. That this is a contested notion, both academically and historically, was never broached. Not once did I see anyone on CBC-TV questioning the *idea* of sovereignty, be it that of Quebec or of Canada. Indeed, it seemed that affect was utilized in almost identical ways on both sides as a way of naturalizing the imagined community of nation and providing it with unquestionable stature. Sawchuk also argues that federalists and sovereigntists had much in common: "Both sides understood their own position as real, but temporarily delegitimated, and the position of the other as inherently false or 'manifestly fictitious.' Both deploy the image of the human body 'to substantiate' or to lend an air of 'reality' to a shaky ideology."[40] This ideological doubling brought these national bodies back together in a paradoxical manner. Tom Lutz, like Steve Neale, posits that melodrama insists upon both the imagined powerlessness and the imagined agency of the viewer: "The resolution of melodrama is always in important ways 'too late' for the characters ... Our mourning for lost possibility and our demand for continued possibility combine to elicit tears."[41]

CBC responded to melodrama's demand for a continuous narrative for as long as it possibly could. A serial approach to the dilemma of a divided country continued well into the 1996 season. A March 1996 serial titled *Remaking Canada* aired over several weeks and utilized some of the strategies of reality TV: "Twenty-five Canadians have seventy-two hours to remake Canada ... Tomorrow at 10." But by the end of 1996, the referendum debate had more or less faded from view in national media, thus fulfilling the imperative of serial melodrama. This fading away can also be seen as a kind of legitimation. As Roger Silverstone argues, "The gradual withdrawal of the reporting of the event into the regular news programs is, once again, evidence of its incorporation into the familiar and hopeful, distancing and denying structures of the daily schedule."[42] The event of the Quebec referendum, integrated back into the television routine, changed in meaning, then, from a traumatic rupture in the fabric of nationhood to historic proof of the nation's cohesiveness. Neil Bissoondath, a federalist South Asian Canadian writer who frequently appears as a CBC commentator, said during an interview: "I got for the first time for a long time the idea that Canadians were beginning to discover the possibilities of their own power. For the first time in my memory there was a huge and massive gathering of what we like to call ordinary Canadians all coming together to save their country, for the first time taking the agenda away from the politicians ... so there's hope" (*The National*, November 2, 1995).

Bissoondath is referring to September's No rally in Montreal. What Bissoondath fails to mention is that this rally was funded, produced, and staged by the federal Liberal Party. While Bissoondath here perpetuates a kind of fantasy narrative of a unifying nationalist community, Keohane asserts that it is, rather, antagonism—in this case, the antagonism of competing political parties—that continually reconstitutes the notion of Canadian unity.[43]

Conclusions

As I have attempted to demonstrate, during the news coverage of the Quebec referendum, the affective modes of melodrama created a serial rooted in the ideology of the family, bodily metaphors, and national time. Ann Cvetkovich suggests, as have others, such as Lauren Berlant and Lawrence Grossberg, that affect, with its passionate feelings located in the body, often stands in for social problems.[44] The racialized nature of both sides of the Quebec referendum, and the largely unmentionable white supremacist project of separatist leaders Bouchard and Parizeau, produced a provocative and unsettling emotional landscape, one in which hurt, pain, and disease were repetitively and traumatically evoked. But as Berlant proposes, "The authenticity of overwhelming pain that can be textually performed and shared is disseminated as a prophylactic against the reproduction of a shocking and numbing mass violence."[45] Perhaps, then, it was melodrama itself, in its constant deferral of an authentic struggle to do with race and nation, that "saved" the country from separation. Racialized modes of nationalism became the way in which English and French Canada were conjoined—it's one thing that they have in common. Canada was at risk of disappearing ("barely there") without its other: Quebec. But the final, almost-tied outcome ensured that the open-ended seriality of Canada–Quebec relations, as seen on TV, would endure.

Notes

1   The first referendum was in 1980, but the 1995 referendum was only the latest step in a history of Québécois nationalism that dates back to the origins of a Canadian federation in the mid-nineteenth century. An emerging separatist movement in the 1960s led to the formation of the Parti Québécois, a party pledged to separatism, which came to power in 1976. For further analysis of Quebec nationalism, see Keating, "Canada and Quebec."

2   Brooks, *The Melodramatic Imagination*; Gripsrud, *The Dynasty Years*.

3   Creeber makes some important distinctions between the series (e.g., *ER, Law and Order*), which is designed to run indefinitely, and the serial, which has a limited number of episodes and a discernible narrative arc. He argues that it is the *serial*, such as the 1970s American serials *Roots* (1977) and *Holocaust* (1978), more than the series, that provides a site for somewhat more complex exploration of race and identity on TV. I would argue that these are nominally less official versions of history, but, like the Quebec referendum, their framing within the genre of the serial allows rich analytical opportunities.

4   Brooks, *The Melodramatic Imagination*, 21.

5   Walters, *Material Girls*, 79.

6   Warhol, *Having a Good Cry*.

7   Sawchuk, "Wounded States," 97.

8   Nowell-Smith, "Minnelli and Melodrama," 192.

9   For more on this topic, see Cvetkovich, *An Archive of Feeling;* Munt, *Queer Attachments*; and Shaviro, *Passion and Excess.*

10   Hawkins, "Documentary Affect."

11   Browne, "The Political Economy of the Television (Super) Text," 72–73.

12   Browne, "The Political Economy of the Television (Super) Text," 73.

13   Creeber also notes that seriality is so prevalent that television advertising now frequently mimics the serial.

14   Browne, "The Political Economy of the Television (Super) Text," 77.

15   For further theorization of the connection between romanticism and nationalism, see Nairn, *Faces of Nationalism.*

16   Warhol, *Having a Good Cry*, 117.

17   Silverman, *Male Subjectivity at the Margins*, 22.

18   Keohane, *Symptoms of Canada*, 7.

19   It has been suggested, in an informal discussion with former NAC president Sunera Thobani, as well as by others, that francophone feminists actively participated in obscuring the race issue in Quebec. For further feminist analysis of the racialized nature of Quebec sovereignty, see Bannerji, *The Dark Side of the Nation.*

20   Duara, "Historicizing National Identity."

21   Cvetkovich, *An Archive of Feeling.*

22   Creeber, "Taking Our Lives Seriously," 441.

23   Nowell-Smith, "Minnelli and Melodrama."

24   Brooks, *The Melodramatic Imagination*, 14.

25   Freud, "Mourning and Melancholia."

26   Certainly, these kinds of domestic splits did exist. A Canadian independent film, *Just Watch Me*, depicted a real-life couple, an Anglo and a francophone, based in Quebec. As the referendum approaches, they begin to review their options. They have decided to move if the Yes vote wins, because they want their children to have easy access to the English-speaking side of their family. A heart-wrenching sequence of interviews with each partner, rapidly intercut, reveals the depth of

each person's attachment to her or his part of the country. The Yes vote loses, but they end up moving to English Canada anyway, not wanting to live in such a divided environment.

27 This is another intertextual reference, to Hugh MacLennan's 1945 novel, *Two Solitudes.*

28 Kentner and Levin, *TV North,* 136. Levin also notes that an American spinoff of *Les Plouffes, Viva Valdez,* transformed the working-class, Quebec City–based Plouffes into a Latino family living in a Los Angeles barrio.

29 Such a testimonial is standard for CBC immigrant narratives. As Sedef Arat-Koc has pointed out, gratefulness is usually the only legitimate stance for immigrants (Sedef Arat- Koc, "Tolerated Citizens or Imperial Subjects").

30 Duara, "Historicizing National Identity."

31 Marvin and Ingle, *Blood Sacrifice,* 142–143.

32 I must admit, in the interests of full disclosure, that when reviewing archival footage of referendum night, I was no detached observer, even eight years after the fact. Like the audience for a melodrama whose genre I knew well, my heart was in my throat—to use another bodily metaphor. I knew how the story would end but I *still* wiped away a tear when the vote reached 50:50, and then again when the No side won by the slimmest of margins: 50.6 per cent. Like anyone returning to the site of a trauma, I wasn't crying for the lost object, I was crying for myself, for the memory of the emotions felt at the original scene.

33 According to J.L. Austin in *How to Do Things with Words,* language is as much a mode of action as it is a mode of information. The meaning of the word is less important than the production of the word. Certain performative utterances, including those of newscasters, do not so much state a fact as perform an action, one that sutures them into normalcy. So one might ask of these newscasters and reporters, what do they mean by their speech, rather than, what does this or that word mean? The repetition of certain words or gestures generates performativity: the meeting of certain social conventions, the reproduction of normalcy.

34 Foucault, *Discipline and Punish.*

35 Sawchuk, "Wounded States," 103.

36 For a compelling Foucauldian analysis of the Cartesian subject, see McWhorter, *Bodies and Pleasures.*

37 Bannerji, *The Dark Side of the Nation.*

38 Sawchuk, "Wounded States," 104.

39 Eley and Suny, *Becoming National,* 29.

40 Sawchuk, "Wounded States," 99.

41 Lutz, "Men's Tears," 200–01.

42 Silverstone, *Television and Everyday Life,* 17.

43 Keohane, *Symptoms of Canada,* 8.

44 Cvetkovich, *An Archive of Feeling,* 156.

45 Berlant, "Poor Eliza," 657.

References

Arat-Koc, Sedef. "Tolerated Citizens or Imperial Subjects? Muslim Canadians and Multicultural Citizenship in Canada, Post 9/11." Paper presented at the annual Canadian Sociology and Anthropology Association meeting, Dalhousie University, Halifax, June 2003.

Austin, J.L. *How to Do Things With Words*. Cambridge: Harvard University Press, 1962.

Bannerji, Himani. *The Dark Side of the Nation: Essays on Multiculturalism, Nation and Gender*. Toronto: Canadian Scholars Press, 2000.

Berlant, Lauren. "Poor Eliza." *American Literature* 70 (3): 635–68.

Brooks, Peter. *The Melodramatic Imagination: Balzac, Henry James and the Mode of Excess*. New Haven, CT: Yale University Press, 1976.

Browne, Nick, "The Political Economy of the Television (Super) Text." In *American Television*, edited by Nick Browne, 69–80. Chur, Switzerland: Harwood, 1994.

Caruth, Cathy. *Trauma: Explorations in Memory*. Baltimore: Johns Hopkins University Press, 1995.

Creeber, Glen. "'Taking Our Lives Seriously': Intimacy, Continuity and Memory in the Television Drama Serial." *Media, Culture & Society* 23: 439–55.

Cvetkovich, Ann. *An Archive of Feeling: Trauma Sexuality and Lesbian Public Cultures*, Durham, NC: Duke University Press, 2003.

Duara, Prasenjit. "Historicizing National Identity, or Who Imagines What and When." In *Becoming National*, edited by Geoff Eley and Ronald Suny, 151–78. London: Oxford University Press, 1996.

Dumm, Thomas. "Telefear: Watching War News." In *The Politics of Everyday Fear*, edited by Brian Massumi, 307–21. Minneapolis: University of Minnesota Press, 1993.

Eley, Geoff and Ronald Suny. *Becoming National: A Reader*. Oxford: Oxford University Press, 1996.

Elsaesser, Thomas. "Tales of Sound and Fury: Observations on the Family Melodrama." In *Movies and Methods Volume II*, edited by Bill Nichols, 165–89. Berkeley: University of California Press, 1985.

Foucault, Michel. *Discipline and Punish: The Birth of the Prison*. London: Vintage, 1977.

Freud, Sigmund. "Mourning and Melancholia." In *Standard Edition of the Complete Works of Sigmund Freud*, Vol. 14, translated by James Strachey, 243–58. London: Hogarth, 1957.

Gripsrud, Jostein. *The Dynasty Years: Hollywood Television and Critical Media Studies*. London: Routledge, 1995.

Grossberg, Lawrence. *We Gotta Get Out of This Place: Popular Conservatism and Postmodern Culture*. New York: Routledge, 1992.

Hawkins, Gay. "Documentary Affect: Filming Rubbish." *Australian Humanities Review*, September 2002. Available at www.lib.latrobe.edu.au/AHR/archive/Issue-September-2002/hawkins.html. Accessed January 10, 2008.

Keating, Micheal. "Canada and Quebec: Two Nationalisms in the Global Age." In *The Ethnicity Reader*, edited by Montserrat Guberneau and John Rex, 170–86. Cambridge: Polity, 1997.

Keohane, Kieran. *Symptoms of Canada: An Essay on Canadian Identity*. Toronto: University of Toronto Press, 1997.

Kentner, Peter and Martin Levin. *TV North: Everything You Wanted to Know about Canadian Television*. Vancouver: Whitecap, 2001.

Lutz, Tom. "Men's Tears and the Roles of Melodrama." In *Boys Don't Cry: Rethinking Narratives of Masculinity and Emotion in the U.S.*, edited by Milette Shamir and Jennifer Travis, 182–204. New York: Columbia University Press, 2002.

MacLennan, Hugh. *Two Solitudes*. Toronto: Macmillan, 1951.

Marvin, Carolyn and David W. Ingle. *Blood Sacrifice and the Nation: Totem Rituals and the American Flag*. Cambridge: Cambridge University Press, 1999.

McLuhan, Marshall. *Understanding Media: The Extensions of Man*. New York: McGraw-Hill, 1964.

McWhorter, Ladelle. *Bodies and Pleasures: Foucault and the Politics of Sexual Normalization*. Bloomington: Indiana University Press, 1999.

Munt, Sally. *Queer Attachments: The Cultural Politics of Shame*. Aldershot, England: Ashgate, 2008.

Nairn, Tom. *Faces of Nationalism: Janus Revisited*. London: Verso, 1997.

Nowell-Smith, Geoffrey. "Minnelli and Melodrama." In *Movies and Methods Volume II* edited by Bill Nichols, 190–94. Berkeley: University of California Press, 1976.

Sawchuk, Kim. "Wounded States: Sovereignty, Separation and the Quebec Referendum." In *When Pain Strikes*, edited by Bill Burns, Kim Sawchuk, and Cathy Busby, 96–115. Minneapolis: University of Minnesota Press, 1999.

Shaviro, Steven. *Passion and Excess: Blanchot, Bataille, and Literary Theory*. Tallahassee: Florida State University Press, 1990.

Silverman, Kaja. *Male Subjectivity at the Margins*. New York: Routledge, 1992.

Silverstone, Roger. *Television and Everyday Life*. New York: Routledge, 1994.

Walters, Suzanna. *Material Girls: Making Sense of Feminist Cultural Theory*. Berkeley: University of California Press, 1995.

Warhol, Robin R. *Having a Good Cry: Effeminate Feelings and Pop Culture Forms*. Columbus: Ohio State University Press, 2003.

Filmography

All in the Family (CBC, 1995)

CBC News (1995)

General Motors Presents (CBC, 1954–61)

Just Watch Me: Trudeau and the Seventies Generation (National Film Board of Canada, 2000), dir. Catherine Annau

The Magazine (CBC, 1995)

The National (CBC, 1995)

Remaking Canada (CBC, 1996)

Special Report (CBC, 1995)

Sunday Report (CBC, 1995)

The Women (CBC, 1995)

PART TWO

Making Citizens

Public Broadcasting/
National Television
CBC and the Challenges
of Historical Miniseries

I n a mixed televisual universe such as Canada's, public broadcasting seems to be endowed with a sacred trust: the guardianship of the nation's history. Any attempt to dramatize Canada's past is met with an intensity of scrutiny that challenges the old adage that Canadian history is boring. Costly and high-profile productions such as historical miniseries, because they deal with an aspect of Canada's past, participate in the court of public opinion by demonstrating the Canadian Broadcasting Corporation's nation-building function. What is placed under the microscope is the public broadcaster's raison d'être as a purveyor of the Canadian reality and the fictions mobilized in aid of this reality. This situation is informed by the unique challenges of the Canadian broadcasting system—in particular, proximity to the United States and competition with its television industry—as well as the shifting ideological winds when it comes to Canadian cultural funding by the government of the day.

The CBC's commitment to historical programming for a domestic audience demonstrates that Canadian mythmaking continues to be an essential feature of the public broadcaster's policy mandate to "contribute to shared national consciousness and identity."[1] Indeed, Serra Tinic has documented a growing emphasis at the CBC on creating a monolithic mode of national address that speaks to an official culture rather than to multiple points of address, which emphasize interregional communication rooted in the lived experience of place. While I agree that interregional communication must be emphasized anew, my chapter poses the importance of recasting national citizenship within the public broadcasting context.

Recent historical miniseries such as *Trudeau* (2002) and *Shattered City: The Halifax Explosion* (2003), as well as documentary-based forays such as *Canada: A People's History* (2000–01) and *The Greatest Canadian*

(2004), do bear out Tinic's claim. The intention of such programs is to ameliorate a collective memory deficit, producing feelings of solidarity, rootedness, and shared purpose—in other words, a sense of citizenship. For this reason, historical reconstruction has a tradition at the CBC and is part of the corporation's efforts to distinguish its services as a *Canadian* public broadcaster from those of its private sector competitors, who fill their schedules with American imports. But referring to the CBC as a public broadcaster is to some degree misleading. Although the institution is publicly funded, the CBC also seeks advertising revenue to top up its annual budget. The CBC represents a mixed model, which has consequences for the history we get and the mode of address deployed.

Using the 1979 historical miniseries *Riel* as a case study, I will examine the challenges faced by a mixed-model public broadcaster in using a mediated approach to nation building. One reason for choosing the 1979 production of *Riel* is that it foretells the increasing privatization of the CBC throughout the 1980s and '90s. Following recommendations in the 1982 *Report of the Federal Cultural Policy Review Committee*, public funding was shifted away from the public sector and its cultural institutions and into the private sector and its cultural industries. Over this period, the CBC changed its role from an in-house producer of Canadian programming to a commissioner of out-of-house productions. Presaging this shift, *Riel* was co-produced with an independent, Green River Pictures, in part to show that the corporation could work on the private sector's terms. As a text, *Riel* is a negotiation of pressures resulting from this partnership and from other institutional strains that shaped its version of Canadian history.

Barbara Selznick has shown that since the 1990s, historical miniseries have increasingly become an exercise in global storytelling, offering multiple locales and transnational stars in stories of movement and migration, because they are co-produced internationally. Except for *Random Passage* (2002), a story about migration and settlement made with Irish co-producers, the CBC has been bucking this trend, adhering to nationalist deployments of the historical miniseries made popular in the United States in the late 1970s and throughout the '80s. As a late-'70s production made on the cusp of a neo-liberal shift in public policy, *Riel* speaks to this context and also heralds pressures with far-reaching impact on the CBC's institutional mode of address.

Studying these pressures and their outcomes helps to identify the goals emphasized during production and to assess their meaningfulness vis-à-vis public broadcasting. Along these lines, the CBC's contemporary investments in historical miniseries such as *Prairie Giant: The Tommy Douglas Story*

(2006) and *October Crisis* (2006) participate in the corporation's nation-building mandate through an emphasis on the creation of a national historical consciousness. The purpose of this chapter is to formulate a means by which to evaluate the English-language broadcaster's past and recent investments in portraying Canadian history in order to examine the type of engagement encouraged. The various goals these productions are meant to serve show the intermingling of nationalist, market, and public policy objectives. How such discourses play out, both in the making of historical miniseries and in the negotiation of their modes of address, form the basis of my case study and offer strategies for future analysis.

In the Canadian context, questions of historical representation within media and their relationship to national institutional contexts have received little scholarly attention. At the same time, historical reconstruction has generated a substantial amount of literature among scholars studying the British, French, and American contexts, thanks to the popularity of costume dramas, historical films, and literary adaptations in the 1980s and '90s.[2] Among the concerns expressed is a moral panic about the apparent susceptibility of audiences to the referential power of the image—its appearance as a document of the past rather than a representation or version of it.[3] Problems of definition and boundary arise as the lines between fact and fiction, information and interpretation are blurred. The reenactment or reconstruction of the recent or distant past for film and television raises questions and anxieties about the form and aesthetics of historical representation, as well as the politics and function of public memory.

Discussing docudrama, Alan Rosenthal identifies two traditions of historical representation rooted in specific national institutional contexts: the "reconstructive political and social investigation" of British public service docudrama and the "entertainment biographies and sensational scandals" of commercially driven American network docudrama. Going one step further, Derek Paget borrows the term "dramadoc" to apply to the British approach and "docudrama" to apply to the American to distinguish between the two and acknowledge the impact of institutional histories and practices on form, content, and mode of address.[4] Can a Canadian approach to historical representation be distinguished, and if so, what contextual factors might account for it and for the resulting mode of address?

One of the difficulties faced by anyone attempting to reconstruct the past for television is the expectation of both historical accuracy—that is, the facts pertaining to a certain time period or significant event—and historical fidelity—that is, adherence to a particular version of history. When well-publicized controversies erupt around a production, the attacks can use the language of names, dates, and places to criticize the perceived lack of historical accuracy. Such criticism, however, usually masks the true cause of discord: the presentation of a version of history that, for whatever reason, is not agreeable. As Rosenthal notes, "Many critics attack docudrama as a *form*, when what really disturbs them are the *opinions* being expressed."[5] Television is a medium for interpreting reality, whether contemporary or in the past, and opinion is a constant element. But finding ways to judge between interpretations, to assess and evaluate versions of the past, is an important task that must show sensitivity to the particularities of television as a medium and an institution without losing sight of its power to move, inform, and persuade.

The challenges of historical representation are compounded at the CBC by the corporation's precarious position as a publicly funded cultural institution mandated to unite the nation in a cohesive identity and as a mixed-model broadcaster directed to compete with other televisual offerings for the entertainment audience that advertisers demand. In this situation, it would not be surprising for the CBC to encounter difficulties when dealing with stories about the past that might disunite the nation with a version of history that is potentially discordant and that opens the already vulnerable institution to further attack. The scrutiny with which these productions are met unmasks the reality that former differences and past hurts form the very basis of contemporary struggles in Canadian politics and society.

The Case of *Riel* (1979)

The historical miniseries *Riel*, as well as the controversy surrounding its production and reception, is a good case in point. For one thing, Louis Riel, the Métis man who played a prominent role in the Red River (1870) and Northwest (1885) resistances, is a much-storied figure in Canadian culture.[6] On the CBC alone, he has been the subject of a televised play (1961), an opera (1969), a miniseries (1979), and a hotly contested retrial (2002) in which Canadians were invited to vote over the Internet on Riel's innocence or guilt.

The retrial was merely a more recent reminder that Riel continues to be a cultural barometer by which to gauge tensions in Canadian society and politics. Mavor Moore, who created an opera about Riel, sums up his cultural significance to Canada: "Why does Louis Riel matter nowadays? Less because of what he actually was or did ... than because societies everywhere always need someone to personify their wishes, fears, hopes, guilts,

Figure 1. Raymond Cloutier stars as the title character in the historical mini-series *Riel*, produced in 1979 by the CBC and Green River Pictures. Image courtesy of CBC.

dreams and nightmares. The man once known as Louis Riel has become a screen upon which we project, as Canadians did in 1885, the outlines of our psyche."[7] In a recent book on the subject, Albert Braz traces the changing representations of Riel from a traitor against Canada who was madly obsessed with securing French Catholicism in the West to a father of Canadian Confederation who was also a visionary precursor to modern-day bilingualism and multiculturalism.[8] These representations, concludes Braz, "are important not so much because of what they tell us about Riel but because of what they reveal about Euro-Canada, the dominant sector of Canadian society that for over a century has been able to create essentially the Riel it wishes—or needs—to see."[9] The figure of Riel in the 1979 production speaks to a vision of Canada that is consonant with the wishes and anxieties of the moment.

The $2.2-million miniseries aired on the CBC in two parts, split inopportunely by a hockey playoff scheduled for Monday night, at 8:30 p.m. on Sunday, April 15, and Tuesday, April 17. It features Raymond Cloutier and Roger Blay, actors familiar to French Canadian viewers, in the roles of Riel and Gabriel Dumont, respectively. They are supported by a cast of Canadians noteworthy for their Hollywood careers, including most prominently Christopher Plummer as Prime Minister John A. Macdonald, with Leslie Nielsen and William Shatner in supporting roles. A week earlier, the CBC had aired *The Other Side of Riel* (1979), a half-hour documentary on the making of the drama, which includes behind-the-scenes footage and interviews emphasizing the production's epic quality and entertainment value, as well as the historical significance to Canada of the events portrayed. This promo aired opportunely on Sunday, April 8, at 7 p.m. as a lead-in to the 51st Academy Awards, in a timeslot usually reserved for the popular *Beachcombers* series.

The CBC's promotional strategy for *Riel* was intensive and was even commented upon by the media.[10] Promos included television and radio spots on the CBC, full-page newspaper advertisements nationwide, press releases detailing the production, and—four days before the broadcast—a gala premiere at Rideau Hall, the Governor General's residence in Ottawa. *Riel* seemed to be modelled as an American movie blockbuster, with a novelization and soundtrack touted for their cross-marketing potential, and a great deal of attention was paid to saturation and the creation of a unified look and message.[11] An educational component was built into the promotion, too, with a pamphlet, *Riel: An Experiment in Learning with Entertainment*, produced in association with the Canadian Association for Adult Education. More than 200,000 copies were distributed to roughly 4,000 educational and community organizations along with a poster advertising the production.[12] The pamphlet's purpose was to "encourage you and others to discuss with family and friends the meaning of Canada's past to its future," and it provided historical information, a chronology of key dates, and discussion questions.

The CBC tracked column inches devoted to advance publicity on the production and was methodical in contacting the press about doing stories.[13] However, the main tactic was to "confidently and aggressively ride over" the mass media in communicating about *Riel* with "credible controlled messages" that were positive, as a counterweight to the perceived negativism directed against the CBC by pundits.[14] The control over messaging included no advance press screenings, which was atypical of a CBC drama. *Riel* and its promotion was an attempt "to build public confidence in the national broadcasting service."[15] That confidence may have been shaken by the CBC's previous dramatic venture of *Riel*'s magnitude, the period miniseries *The Whiteoaks of Jalna* (1972), adapted from the novels of Mazo de la Roche and widely perceived as a failure. *Riel* was likely intended to turn the tide and was billed by the corporation as "the most ambitious single dramatic film ever undertaken by the CBC."[16] *TV Guide* stated that the miniseries was being touted as "an all-purpose Canadian *Roots*," setting as the standard the highly successful 1977 American television miniseries that dramatized author Alex Haley's family history, from the enslavement of his ancestor, Kunta Kinte, to the liberation of Kinte's descendants.[17]

Riel attracted more than 4.5 million Canadian viewers, along with detractors and supporters who voiced their opinions in letters to the editor or in newspaper columns.[18] The drama generated sufficient controversy to become a media event. According to a CBC-commissioned report that included tracking the print media surrounding *Riel*, more than three-quarters of coverage was positive or neutral, with regional perceptions apparently playing "a limited role."[19] However, the authors did note that "columnists favored the program in Saskatchewan and Manitoba far more than their Ottawa and Toronto counterparts, while much Ontario support came from letters to the editor. In Quebec, response was encouraging, particularly from the French-language press."[20]

The less favourable response from Ontario is instructive in establishing the context for this case, as well as its significance. That context includes, first, the upcoming 1979 federal election, which would see the defeat of the Trudeau Liberals and the formation of a short-lived minority Conservative government led by Joe Clark, and, second, the issue of Quebec separatism, which was gaining momentum throughout the 1970s. The latter issue reared its head early during the production in advance publicity about the actors portraying Riel and Dumont. During the making of the film, both Cloutier and Blay were vocal in their support of Quebec's sovereignty and the allegorical connections they saw between the past they were dramatizing and the current political situation in Canada vis-à-vis Quebec and national unity.[21] Even without knowledge of Cloutier's and Blay's political views, the parallels between the past of the film and the present of Canada were already part of the popular consciousness and influenced the interpretation of Canadian history found in the production.[22] As the *Toronto Sun*'s Bob Blackburn aptly noted at the time, "Given the fact that the hanging of the Métis rebel leader in Regina in 1885 is generally credited with having started the Quebec nationalist movement which in 1979 threatens to split this country asunder, and the fact that Prime Minister Trudeau is winding up to fight a federal election campaign with national unity as his foremost issue, it seems pretty safe to hang that 'controversial' label on the movie, even without having seen it."[23] The question of national unity and the looming federal election contributed to reading the film as an allegory for modern-day Canada, as did the on-screen treatment of the Métis resistance as lessons in French–English and provincial–federal relations.[24]

The dramatization achieves this reading in its situating of Riel as a pawn in a power struggle between the Quebec bishop Ignace Bourget and Prime Minister Macdonald over settling the Canadian West. While events unfold on the Prairies, the film cuts to Montreal and Ottawa to give Bourget's and Macdonald's perspectives. In the *Calgary Herald*, reviewer Bill Musselwhite remarks that these historical figures "too often take the stage to comment, with 20–20 hindsight, not on the 19th century but the 20th century."[25] Indeed, at one point, the two are shown in a conversation—one that never occurred—over their conflicting ideas about the Canadian West and ultimately about the future composition of Canada as a nation. The emphasis on their points of view stresses the contemporary reading of these historical events as symbolizing French–English relations to the detriment of offering any meaningful consideration of the Métis struggle.

One of the ways the French–English theme is accorded so much significance is by not portraying the Métis as a people with their own culture, history, and traditions. In fact, the Métis are not portrayed at all as a community that included men, women, children, and families along with farmers, merchants, and buffalo hunters.

Before the resistances, land had become an issue for the Métis because they could no longer rely on the buffalo hunt and were increasingly turning to agriculture, using the river lot system, with its long narrow plots that front the water's edge. As well, the Métis had already awakened to a sense of their ethnic, national, and cultural potential long before Riel entered the equation. The film rejects this understanding and offers a simplistic rendering of the Métis as a tragic band of noble but savage hooligans with no buffalo to hunt and prone to bouts of whooping and hollering more suited to a typical Hollywood Western.[26] Métis women are largely absent from the scene and, when present, silent. Because *Riel* does not show the Métis as a community, there is no opportunity to reflect on their struggle as a

Figure 2. Jean-Louis Roux as Quebec bishop Ignace Bourget and Christopher Plummer as Prime Minister John A. Macdonald in the 1979 historical miniseries *Riel*, enacting a meeting that never took place between the historical figures. Image courtesy of CBC.

people. The reliance upon the vocabulary of the American Western makes it easy to subsume the conflict within the overarching French–English thematic and to offer justification for the coming of the Canadians as carriers of culture, order, and civility. As in the American historical dramas *Gone with the Wind* (1939) and *Roots* (1977), to which *Riel* has been disparagingly compared, the story of the racialized other is there to service the story of white normativity.[27]

In addition, the film's emphasis on the spiritual and educated Riel as a mediating figure caught between the French world of Catholicism and faith and the English world of law and reason further establishes the narrative stakes. The full-page advertisement for the series aptly summarizes these: "A Prime Minister had a vision of a Confederation joined from sea-to-sea by a railroad, with the West secured. A Quebec bishop had a vision of a Catholic New France west of the Ontario border. A Métis leader had a vision of a western nation within or without the new Canada. Three visions in conflict, an explosion that became one of the most turbulent episodes in Canadian history."[28] In the poster, as in the film, preeminence is given to reading past historical events as a clash between the French and the English, with Riel's hanging for treason "the spark which set off the modern Quebec separatist movement."[29] As the screen Macdonald prophetically notes, "Symbols have a habit of living for a long time."

The text of the poster also frames Riel's vision for his people as choosing between sovereign status within Confederation or separate from it, obviously referring to Quebec and the "sovereignty association" question prominent in political debates of the 1970s. The film shores up such a reading through the Macdonald character. When Riel forms a provisional government at Fort Garry, Macdonald exclaims, "God man! This means separation!" Writing about *Riel* a few months after the broadcast, art historian Kenneth Coutts-Smith observed that Red River "can hardly 'separate' from a confederation to which it does not yet belong."[30] Later, after the Métis leader is put on trial for treason and the nation awaits his fate, Macdonald ponders the implication for French–English relations in Canada and asks, "Must every issue large or small, provincial or federal, become the test of the very identity of this country?" Then, in a direct address to the modern Canadian viewer, he expresses his hope "that we will mature and that future generations will be spared such a destructive spectacle."

At the same time, the CBC's promotion was not geared to address the ongoing relevance of these historical events for the contemporary Canadian viewer. Anxiety permeates the publicity with the sense that the perception of relevance might interfere with the experience of entertainment, jeopardizing *Riel*'s success as an epic televisual offering. Certainly executive producer Stan Colbert and co-producer John Trent were publicly insistent that the drama did not contain any intentional political connotations.[31] The miniseries' reception in the Ontario press gives credence to these anxieties among the producers. Generally, the attacks on *Riel* did not invite any genuine engagement with the contemporary resonance of its subject matter but, rather, seemed aimed at suppressing a reading of the Métis resistances that would open old historical wounds at a critical point in Canada's debate about its future. The drama's more favourable, or at least apparently non-controversial, reception in Quebec suggests that *Riel* presents a version of events on the Canadian prairie that largely squared with current French Canadian perceptions.

Unlike the CBC's publicity strategy, the educational material authorized by the corporation did ask viewers to draw contemporary political parallels.[32] The educational aspect occurred outside the CBC's main communications around the historical miniseries, which was billed first and foremost as an "entertainment epic."[33] *Riel*'s producers were clear on this, however contrary to the views of the screenwriter and the actors playing Riel and Dumont.[34] The CBC's communication strategy emphasized the entertainment value of the production, in part as a way to attract as many viewers as possible. In seeking to generate a large audience, the CBC was likely responding to the pressure to satisfy its main corporate sponsor for the *Riel* broadcast—General Motors of Canada. The CBC's documented objectives were "(i) To deliver the largest television audience possible," and "(ii) To present *Riel* to the Canadian people as a great piece of entertainment of epic proportions."[35] Meanwhile, the CBC saw the educational program as appealing to a "special-interest audience," in particular educators and young people.[36] The main target was the general audience of television entertainment.

While the CBC's explicit strategy was to "ride over" the media, an implicit or unstated goal appears alongside, and that is to control readings of the film to avoid possible conflict over the version of history presented. The emphasis on entertainment as the dominant reading strategy was an exercise in issue management that belied anxieties about potential criticisms of *Riel* for its interpretation of historical events. The repeated suggestion was that *Riel* was to be understood as drama rather than document and that, as such, liberties would be taken in the interpretation to enhance the story's dramatic and epic quality. The drama's contemporary relevance or politically charged quality was constructed as a function of reception and not of the text itself and was offered to "special-interest" viewers outside the general audience. In this way, the CBC adopted an apolitical definition of entertainment as innocuous diversion on a historical subject of intense contemporary interest.

Institutional factors play a role in the type of historical drama practised and in the resulting mode of address—one that strives toward the vocabulary of American entertainment with general-interest texts while keeping an eye toward the British model of public service in the reception by special interests. This approach has been demonstrated recently in *Shattered City: The Halifax Explosion* and *Canada: A People's History*, for which the CBC offered extratextual materials directed primarily at educators and students. While extratextual goals around engaging the citizenry are commendable, more study is needed to assess their overall impact and intent. For instance, do these materials encourage critical thinking about the past, opening spaces for what cultural theorist George Lipsitz calls "counter-memory," which involves "[looking] to the past for hidden histories excluded from the dominant narratives"?[37] Or, conversely, do extratextual elements engage in mythmaking about Canada, offering universals that marginalize or exclude disagreement and difference?

In this respect, *Riel*'s fleeting self-consciousness hints at the possibility of creating history-based dramas that openly refer to the ongoing signifi- cance of past struggles to the present and future of Canadian politics and society. To suggest such contemporary resonance, however, need not be an exercise in postmodernist or anti-illusionist practices, but could be woven into dialogue, as with *Riel*, to present a conventional narrative style, if that is the expectation. However, postmodernist or anti-illusionist tech- niques are now a regular and integrated part of television fare, to the degree that they are widely regarded as entertaining and whimsical rather than subversive or disruptive of pleasure. Increasingly, television seems to be the medium in which to engage with playful subversions of narrative and genre, reality and fiction. It is a wonder, therefore, that the CBC's recent forays into history-based programming do not make use of such techniques, not only to engage with the meaning of past events for Cana- dians today but also to prompt questions about the form of historical rep- resentation.[38] After all, the topicality of historical events is an opportunity to acknowledge the role that interpretation plays in their dramatization. Only those stories from the past that still resonate in contemporary times are told and retold, and they are made to resonate through a process of interpretation that adapts the significance of past events to the needs of the current moment. Indeed, we can only tell stories about the past from our own points of view, and these are always contemporary and shaded by processes of selection, compression, symbolization, and arrangement.[39] As an unresolved story, Louis Riel has become a much-storied figure in Canadian culture, and his story has accordingly been adapted at various times to meet the changing concerns and anxieties of Canadian society.

So what are we to make of his 1979 incarnation? Although historical reenactment necessarily involves a *re*telling, there still must be ways to judge between interpretations.

Historian Robert A. Rosenstone offers a useful way to judge between interpretations of history that is sensitive to the unique limits and possi- bilities of visual media. For Rosenstone, doing history on film always involves "fiction," but not in a negative sense:

> At the outset, we must accept that film cannot be seen as a window onto the past ... This means that it is necessary for us to learn to judge the ways in which, through invention, film summarizes vast amounts of data or symbolizes complexities that otherwise could not be shown. We must rec- ognize that film will always include images that are at once invented and true; true in that they impart an overall meaning of the past that can be verified, documented and reasonably argued.[40]

Rosenstone goes on to explain that "the ongoing discourse of history" provides the means by which to judge the overall veracity of the meaning imparted. Once a film enters discourse, it must be evaluated according to its engagement with existing knowledge and debate about the past, like any other work of history.[41] While understanding that invention is necessarily a part of the filmic representation of history, Rosenstone argues that any invention must still be assessed according to whether it breaches the discourse of history. He refers to "false invention" as a violation of what is known or debated about the past. False invention ignores the discourse of history, while "true invention" engages it.[42]

Does *Riel* bestow a meaning to the past that can be validated, therefore constituting a true invention, or does it offer a false one that cannot be adequately supported within the discourse of history? And what are the implications for a cultural institution such as the CBC and its specific goals?

The significance placed on differences of point of view between the French and the English over events in the Canadian West is a distillation of what we know to be true—that opposing attitudes about Riel and the Métis resistances sharply divided Quebec from the rest of Canada. However, in synthesizing the conflict to make it understandable for the contemporary viewer and manageable for the purposes of television entertainment, *Riel* does simplify and generalize, resulting in a loss of historical specificity that aids in creating a unifying Canadian myth. The drama ignores the role of Protestant radicals, such as the Orangemen, in fomenting English opposition to the possibility of a French Catholic stronghold on the Prairies, and it ignores the role of non-Métis Catholics in Red River and Batoche who fought alongside their Métis comrades. That being said, it is not false to offer an interpretation of these historical events as a test of French–English relations in Canada, because that is one way in which they were truly experienced and in which they continue to be understood.

The discord in the Ontario press over the film's interpretation results from the volatility of the political times in which the program aired and the fear of revisiting past hurts at a critical juncture in Canadian politics. But too few writers commented on the film's treatment of the Métis. Although *Riel*'s generalized view of the French–English conflict can be regarded as a true invention, it nonetheless comes at the expense of a false one—a version of the Métis people not verifiable within the discourse of Canadian history. In the formula of the entertainment biopic, the film individualizes the Métis resistances through the focus on Louis Riel and his conflicts with Bourget and Macdonald, and also romanticizes his individual suffering as a necessary sacrifice to the building of Canada.[43] The meaning imparted to the Métis's political struggle falsely begins and ends with Louis Riel.

Rosenstone's theory of invention is useful for understanding the strategies that historical films employ in constructing screen versions of the past. At the same time, closer analysis of historical dramas such as *Riel* can indicate the interdependence of true and false inventions, showing how these can exist within the same representation and can even depend on each other, leading to the creation of myth. As Canadian historian Daniel Francis notes:

> Myths idealize. They select particular events and institutions which seem to embody important cultural values and elevate them to the status of legend. In Canadian history that would be the Mounties, to take an example, or the transcontinental railway, or the North. Conversely, myths demonize. They vilify, or at least marginalize, anyone who seems to be frustrating the main cultural project—Indians, for example, or communists, or Quebec separatists. Myths organize the past into a coherent story, the story of Canada, which simplifies the complex ebb and flow of events and weaves together disparate threads of experience. Myths are echoes of the past, resonating in the present.[44]

In ignoring the historical significance of the Métis as a community and in absenting the religious antagonism between Protestants and Catholics in Canada at the time of the resistances, *Riel* participates in the myth of Canada as a secular society with two founding nations, French and English. Canada is also presented as a land *of* and *for* immigrants through the film's recuperation of Louis Riel on behalf of a modern multicultural Canada. This recuperation gives the historical miniseries the same thematic trajectory of immigration that structures *Canada: A People's History*, assessed by Lyle Dick in this volume. Coutts-Smith importantly observes that the class dimension to the Métis's fight against land appropriation and property speculation is suppressed in favour of what he terms "admirable but meaningless" liberal sentiments about identity and culture.[45] Indeed, in his closing argument at his trial for treason, the screen Riel expresses his vision of "a place where the oppressed of the world could come, people who need this land." His dream for Canada is presumably the same for the contemporary Canadian viewer, versed in official multicultural policy.

The real Riel, however, was interested in providing refuge primarily to dispossessed Catholics fleeing oppression in Protestant-dominated countries, particularly the United States. This Riel might have balked at seeing his screen version tell the dying Thomas Scott—an anti-French, anti-Catholic Mason executed by the provisional government at Red River—that they would be brothers in heaven. Here, the specifics of the Métis resistances are glossed over in favour of vague generalities that support cherished Canadian ideals suited to the context of the 1979 production. Loss of historical specificity comes at the expense of portraying forces of disagreement and difference in all their complexity. Instead, these are subsumed under a centripetal myth of Canada as a multicultural nation founded by two cultures.

Conclusion

Mythmaking is a central function of historical miniseries, and *Riel* is no exception. As national allegories, historical miniseries enact and reenact stories that are seen as foundational to the culture at large or as somehow expressing the essential qualities upon which a collectivity's destiny is based. As Francis states: "With repetition [myths] come to form the mainstream memory of the culture, our national dreams, the master narrative which explains the culture to itself and seems to express its overriding purpose. This is the story of Canada, we say, the story which contains our ideals, which gives our experience continuity and purpose. This is who we are."[46]

But is it a public broadcaster's role to participate in the fabrication of national mythologies? Historical miniseries from *Riel* to *Prairie Giant* invite Canadians to experience the nation's past without controversy or debate, in the hope that this process will contribute to social cohesion and the apprehension of a shared national identity. The production of *Riel* was poised on the brink of dramatic changes to the Canadian televisual landscape. The aims and pressures this production experienced in the making of a Canadian past for television are instructive in assessing the CBC's contemporary forays into the nation's history. As a mixed model, the CBC experiences commercial pressures to entertain and draw large audiences to satisfy sponsors. The corporation is also obliged to distinguish itself from private broadcasters to justify public funding and to look visibly Canadian as the way to achieve this. *Riel* and the CBC's more recent historical representations adopt citizenship as the domain of extratextual materials that encourage public debate among "special interests" about the relevance of past events to the present and future of Canada. However, as a consequence of policy priorities and the CBC's mixed model, such debate and engagement are not the domain of programming that must compete for the entertainment audience.

The CBC's rescheduling of *Prairie Giant* to March 2006 so it would not air during the federal election in January is an example of the kind of risk aversion that this political-economic context encourages. *Prairie Giant* is a two-part miniseries about Tommy Douglas, the first leader of the federal New Democrats and credited as the father of Canada's health care system. The fear of the perception of relevance and of encouraging public debate about the future of Canada during a particularly volatile election that resulted in the second minority government in a row seems to have led to the decision to delay the broadcast until after the election. In the end, the avoidance of divisive political meanings in the pursuit of entertainment satisfies both the CBC's cultural-nationalist goals around unity and the competitive practicalities of its industry context. The goals of the nation are at one with those of the market.

Yet a tension still exists between the drive to offer unifying myths of nationhood as uncontroversial entertainment and the desire to encourage critical thinking about the past in keeping with the civic virtues of debate and deliberation. In *Entertaining the Citizen: When Politics and Popular Culture Converge*, Liesbet van Zoonen suggests that entertainment can be used to close the gap between citizens and politics and evoke civic virtues in an era of ever-decreasing democratic engagement, exemplified in low voter turnouts. She maintains that it is pointless to nostalgically and puritanically call for an imaginary time before television when political communication was somehow untainted. According to van Zoonen, the reality is that citizenship competes for our spare time with other identities and other diversions, and must therefore harness popular means of political communication if civic participation is to be experienced as fun, entertaining, and pleasurable. She therefore sees entertainment as a relevant resource for citizen engagement. Her contention is that citizens must not only be engaged at a rational level but at an affective one, too, in stories that make the performance of citizenship possible through the invitation of empathy, investment, enthusiasm, and commitment.[47]

Van Zoonen recognizes the rational and the affective dimensions of citizenship, reminding us that emotion and reason have always interacted in the making of citizens. Entertainment and citizenship need not be mutually exclusive, and as David Hogarth demonstrates in this volume and elsewhere, these imperatives have informed the CBC's programming since its inception. The CBC has always been in the position of entertaining its citizenry with Canadian content. In this position, the terms of debate seem to hang on a definition of national television. Writing of the British context, John Caughie questions the notion of national television. He asks whether the purpose of a national public broadcaster is to act as *"repre-*

sentation of the nation, capturing the images around which the complexity of the nation can identify itself as a unit" or as *"representative* of the nation, offering channels for different voices capturing its diversity and reflecting the fault lines which disunite the culture into differences and complexities." He suggests that the former creates "an imaginary and marketable identity often implicit in the desire for a unified National Culture," which obscures "what is local, awkward and complex within the nation."[48]

National television as representation of the nation seems to sit squarely within the unifying realm of myth, while national television as representative of the nation resists mythmaking in favour of disruption and dialogue. But such resistance to national mythology need not be a factor in disunity when citizen engagement over the past, present, and future of Canadian society is an ideal toward which we can strive.

Notes

1   CRTC.
2   This list is by no means exhaustive, but for some examples, see Cartmell and Whelehan, *Adaptations*, on literary adaptation; Higson, *English Heritage, English Cinema*, on costume drama; and Rosenstone, *Visions of the Past*, on the historical film. For Canadian examples, see my work on the period television series *Road to Avonlea* (1990–96), adapted from the novels of L.M. Montgomery; and Jeanette Sloniowski, "Popularizing History: *The Valour and the Horror.*"
3   Eitzen, "Against the Ivory Tower."
4   Rosenthal, *Why Docudrama?* 4. In the scholarly literature and in industry parlance, "docudrama" is an umbrella category that can apply to a range of productions, from disease-of-the-week movies to sweeping historical epics. Paget, *No Other Way to Tell It.*
5   Rosenthal, *Why Docudrama?* 9.
6   Refer to chapter 3, note 31. See also Maurice Charland, "Newsworld, Riel, and the Métis: Recognition and the Limits to Reconciliation."
7   Moore, "Haunted by Riel," 414.
8   See also *Rielisms.*
9   Braz, *The False Traitor*, 204.
10 Matrix, "The Promotion of *Riel*," 32.
11 In an internal CBC memo dated September 6, 1979, William E. Wilkerson, director of communication and public affairs at the time, noted "the importance of an integrated public communication effort" in public awareness of *Riel.* Wilkerson was commenting on a forty-nine-page report, "The Promotion of *Riel*: A Case History," commissioned by the CBC from Matrix Communication of Toronto to assess the promotional strategy adopted for the production, as well as public and press response. Documents such as this report, as well as memos, press releases, educational and promotional materials, and newspaper clippings, were found in the Riel File at the CBC Library in Toronto during research conducted in December 2004.
12 Noted in a CBC release dated April 5, 1979, and titled "CBC *Riel* Film Sparks Educational Experiment" (Riel File). The CBC and CAAE produced this pamphlet in haste in the month before the airdate because an educational booklet due from

NC Press, a private sector educational publisher, was so far behind schedule that it was not expected to be distributed in time for the broadcast (Matrix, "The Promotion of *Riel*," 22–25).

13 Internal CBC correspondence from Babs Pitt, associate director in the department of communication and public affairs, "Aide Memoire: *Riel* Update," dated March 16, 1979 (Riel File). One report documented 2,666¼ column inches devoted to advance print on *Riel* in the spring and summer of 1978 (Riel File).

14 Matrix, "The Promotion of *Riel*," 10–11.

15 Matrix, "The Promotion of *Riel*," 27.

16 "*Riel*—CBC-TV Drama Production Announced by John H. Kennedy," dated March 13, 1978 (Riel File).

17 Donaldson, "Louis Riel Signals Rebellion: A CBC TV-Movie Reminds Canadians of What Once Went Wrong in the West" (Riel File).

18 Most famously, historians Michael Bliss ("*Riel* Was Unreal") and Desmond Morton ("*Riel* TV Massively Distorted"). Other examples include the *Toronto Star*'s Dennis Braithwaite ("Don't Count on Viewing *Riel*"), the *Globe and Mail*'s Ray Conlogue ("*Riel* Attacked"), the *Calgary Herald*'s Bill Musselwhite ("Radio and Television"), and the *Toronto Sun*'s Peter Worthington ("CBC's Version of History"). Audience figures come from A.C. Nielsen of Canada, as noted in a CBC release dated May 2, 1979, and titled "*Riel* Part I Pulls Record Audience—Over 4.5 Million on English and French TV" (Riel File). The English-language broadcast drew more than 3.5 million viewers, while the French-dubbed version attracted more than 1.1 million. On the second night, English viewers dropped to just over 3 million, while the French audience increased to more than 1.5 million. Noted in a CBC release, dated May 9, 1979, and titled "*Riel*'s Record TV Audience Holds Up for Second Night" (Riel File).

19 Matrix, "The Promotion of *Riel*," 31. The report's authors analyzed fifty-eight press clippings from newspapers and magazines in Ontario, Quebec, Manitoba, Saskatchewan, and the Maritimes. It is not indicated why Alberta and British Columbia were excluded, but my guess is the smaller French presence in those provinces, comparatively speaking, and the lack of an obvious connection to the Métis resistances.

20 Coutts-Smith claims that "the French press more or less ignored the occasion" ("CBC's *Riel*," 235).

21 A particularly negative article came from the *Globe and Mail*'s Blaik Kirby, whose inflammatory piece, "Separatist Team Treads History's Path," inspired a *Leader-Post* editorial, taking Blay to task for portraying Dumont as a separatist ("Rebel Misinterpreted"). The separatist connection was also mentioned by the *Toronto Star*'s Bruce Kirkland ("Actor with a Mission") and *TV Guide*'s Gordon Donaldson ("Louis Riel Signals Rebellion").

22 Certainly screenwriter Roy Moore was aware of the current significance, stating in a *TV Guide* article: "It's such a political script ... There are so many ways of looking at the man, and it's a hot issue among modern-day separatists." In the same article, he noted that "Riel's persona was and still is a reflection of Canada" (Donaldson, "Louis Riel Signals Rebellion"; see also Musselwhite, "Radio and Television"). This awareness was also very much a part of the novelization, according to its authors, Dennis Adair and Janet Rosenstock.

23 Blackburn, "Unveiling the *Riel* Reality."

24 The *Toronto Star*'s Dennis Braithwaite ("Don't Count on Viewing *Riel*") suggested that the view of Canadian history presented in *Riel* was so unfavourable to the fed-

eral government that the broadcast was in jeopardy of ever airing. In a follow-up piece, Bruce Kirkland wrote about speculation that the film "might be postponed until after the impending election or dumped altogether because the CBC is afraid the spectre of Riel's ghost would stir up the disunity debate just when Prime Minister Trudeau was trying to calm French–English animosities and win a new mandate for his beleaguered government," while the CBC dismissed any claims that its broadcast of *Riel* was under threat ("Actor with a Mission").

25 Musselwhite, "Radio and Television."

26 In a letter to the CBC, Harry Daniels, then president of the Native Council of Canada, objected to the film on the grounds that it did not acknowledge the Métis's contributions to the development of Canada and implied that the Métis were "buffalo hunters who only found a cause with the arrival of the literate Riel" (Coutts-Smith, "CBC's *Riel*," 231)—a point that current Métis critics still justifiably make (see *Rielisms*).

27 Blackadar, "*Riel* Sold like *Gone With the Wind*"; Coutts-Smith, "CBC's *Riel*," 228–36.

28 Riel File.

29 Musselwhite, "Radio and Television."

30 Coutts-Smith, "CBC's *Riel*," 232–33.

31 Donaldson, "Louis Riel Signals Rebellion"; Kirkland, "Election"; Riches, "*Riel*'s New Aim."

32 Along with the pamphlet mentioned earlier, the CBC also authorized an 8½-by-11-inch, twenty-page booklet, belatedly produced by NC Press (Riel File). It included stills from the production, along with historical information describing the events and the individuals dramatized. Photographs of the actors in character appear alongside those of the real people they portray. The booklet also features a chronology detailing the two resistances, maps of the Red River Settlement (1870) and military operations in the Northwest (1885), and a copy of the "List of Rights" (1869). This document was drafted by Riel and his provisional government and eventually led to the creation of the province of Manitoba. The booklet's accompanying "Suggested Activities and Topics for Discussion" include Question 6: "After nearly one hundred years, Riel and the Métis uprising still arouse controversy and excite intense interest. What relevance do they have to current discussions on national unity?" The pamphlet produced in association with CAAE was even more pointed than the NC Press booklet in asking about "the legacy of Riel" in "our attempts to chart the future of Confederation" and in the "fundamental questions about ourselves as a nation" that his legacy raised. Specific questions focused on majority rule and minority rights, and self-determination and regional differences within a sovereign state. The pamphlet was apparently well received (Matrix, "The Promotion of *Riel*," 24–25).

33 Noted in the copy for the full-page newspaper advertisement that publicized the *Riel* broadcast (Riel File). Moreover, a CBC release distributed a month before the broadcast insistently frames *Riel* as entertainment: "a film that is compelling, very exciting and, above all, entertaining"; "we set out to entertain"; "*Riel* is entertainment"; and "we wanted to do a major entertainment." These expressions are ascribed to John H. Kennedy, head of TV drama for the CBC's English network at the time, in a CBC release, "*Riel* Proves Canada's Past Very Exciting, Says Drama Head," dated March 15, 1979 (Riel File).

34 Donaldson, "Louis Riel Signals Rebellion"; Powers, "Louis Riel Movie"; Riches, "*Riel*'s New Aim."

35 Matrix, "The Promotion of *Riel*," 12.
36 Matrix, "The Promotion of *Riel*," 24.
37 Lipsitz, *Time Passages*, 213.
38 Compare Paget, *No Other Way to Tell It*; Higashi, "*Walker* and *Mississippi Burning*."
39 Rosenstone, *Visions of the Past*.
40 Rosenstone, *Visions of the Past*, 70–71.
41 Rosenstone, *Visions of the Past*, 72.
42 Rosenstone, *Visions of the Past*, 72.
43 Compare Coutts-Smith, "CBC's *Riel*," 229.
44 Francis, *National Dreams*, 11.
45 Coutts-Smith, "CBC's *Riel*," 235.
46 Francis, *National Dreams*, 10.
47 van Zoonen, *Entertaining the Citizen*, 16–17, 66.
48 Caughie, "The Logic of Convergence," 223.

References

Adair, Dennis and Janet Rosenstock. "Our *Riel* Is Not Anti-Anglo." *Toronto Star*, April 15, 1979. Riel File.

"Back to Batoche." The Virtual Museum of Métis History and Culture. http://www.museevirtuel.ca/Exhibitions/Batoche/html/about/index.php. Accessed February 18, 2008.

Blackadar, Bruce. "*Riel* Sold Like *Gone With the Wind*." *Daily Star*, April 12, 1979. Riel File.

Blackburn, Bob. "Unveiling the *Riel* Reality." *Toronto Sun*, March 25, 1979. Riel File.

Bliss, Michael. "*Riel* Was Unreal, Historian Says." *Daily Star*, April 18, 1979. Riel File.

Braithwaite, Dennis. "Don't Count on Viewing *Riel*." *Daily Star*, January 5, 1979. Riel File.

———. "CBC Trapped into Reshaping History." *Toronto Star*, April 17, 1979. Riel File.

Braz, Albert. *The False Traitor: Louis Riel in Canadian Culture*. Toronto: University of Toronto Press, 2003.

Canada. *Report of the Federal Cultural Policy Review Committee*. Ottawa: Minister of Supply and Services Canada, 1982.

———. Broadcasting Act, 1991. Available at www.crtc.gc.ca/eng/legal/broad.htm. Accessed January 10, 2008.

Cartmell, Deborah and Imelda Whelehan, eds. *Adaptations: From Text to Screen, Screen to Text*. New York: Routledge, 1999.

Caughie, John. "The Logic of Convergence." In *Big Picture, Small Screen: The Relations Between Film and Television*, edited by John Hill and Martin McLoone, 215–23. Luton, UK: Luton University Press, 1996.

Charland, Maurice. "Newsworld, Riel, and the Métis: Recognition and the Limits to Reconciliation." *Canadian Journal of Communication* 32.1 (2007): 9–27.

Collins, Richard. *Culture, Communication and National Identity: The Case of Canadian Television*. Toronto: University of Toronto Press, 1990.

Conlogue, Ray. "*Riel* Attacked with Guts and Honesty." *Globe and Mail*, April 14, 1979. Riel File.

Coutts-Smith, Kenneth. "CBC's *Riel:* Who Gains from This Rewriting of History? Certainly Not 1 Million Métis." *Centrefold* 3 (5): 228–36.

Donaldson, Gordon. "Louis Riel Signals Rebellion: A CBC TV-Movie Reminds Canadians of What Once Went Wrong in the West." *TV Guide*, Canadian edition, July 1–7, 1978. Riel File.

Eitzen, Dirk. "Against the Ivory Tower: An Apologia for Popular Historical Documentaries." In *New Challenges for Documentary*, edited by Alan Rosenthal and John Corner, 409–18. Manchester: Manchester University Press, 2005.

Francis, Daniel. *National Dreams: Myth, Memory and Canadian History*. Vancouver: Arsenal Pulp Press, 1997.

Higashi, Sumiko. "*Walker* and *Mississippi Burning*: Postmodernism versus Illusionist Narrative." In *Revisioning History: Film and the Construction of a New Past*, edited by Robert A. Rosenstone, 188–201. Princeton, NJ: Princeton University Press, 1995.

Higson, Andrew. *English Heritage, English Cinema: Costume Drama Since 1980*. Oxford: Oxford University Press, 2003.

Hogarth, David. *Documentary Television in Canada: From National Public Service to Global Marketplace*. Montreal and Kingston: McGill-Queen's University Press, 2002.

Kirkland, Bruce. "Actor with a Mission to Play Quebec's Hamlet." *Toronto Star*, April 8, 1978. Riel File.

———. "Election Gets in a *Riel* Tangle." *Daily Star*, January 11, 1979. Riel File.

Kirby, Blaik. "Separatist Team Treads History's Path." *Globe and Mail*, June 13, 1978. Riel File.

Kotsopoulos, P.A. "'Our Avonlea': Imagining Community in an Imaginary Past." In *Pop Can: Popular Culture in Canada*, edited by Lynne van Luven and Priscilla Walton, 98–105. Toronto: Prentice-Hall, 1999.

———. "Avonlea as Main Street, USA? Genre, Adaptation and the Making of a Borderless Romance." *Essays on Canadian Writing* 76 (2002): 170–94.

———. "The Nostalgic Appeal of a Popular Place: Female Fans Interpreting *Road to Avonlea*." *Canadian Children's Literature* 113/114 (2004): 73–97.

———. "L.M. Montgomery on Television: Romance, Industry and the Adaptation Process." In *Canadian Cultural Poesis: Essays on Canadian Culture*, edited by Sheila Petty and Garry Sherbert, 271–87. Waterloo, ON: Wilfrid Laurier University Press, 2006.

Lipsitz, George. *Time Passages: Collective Memory and American Popular Culture*. Minneapolis: University of Minnesota Press, 1990.

Matrix Communication. "The Promotion of *Riel*: A Case History." Commissioned by the Canadian Broadcasting Corporation, August 1979. Riel File.

Moore, Mavor. "Haunted by Riel." In *Images of Louis Riel in Canadian Culture*, edited by Ramon Hathorn and Patrick Holland, 411–16. Queenston, ON: Edwin Mellen Press, 1992.

Morton, Desmond. *"Riel* TV Massively Distorted." *Globe and Mail*, April 24, 1979. Riel File.

Musselwhite, Bill. "Radio and Television." *Calgary Herald*, April 14, 1979. Riel File.

Paget, Derek. *No Other Way to Tell It: Dramadoc/Docudrama on Television*. Manchester: Manchester University Press, 1998.

Powers, Ned. "Louis Riel Movie Transforms History into Entertainment." *StarPhoenix* (Saskatoon), March 23, 1979. Riel File.

"Rebel Misinterpreted." *Leader-Post* (Regina), June 13, 1978. Riel File.

Riches, Hester. *"Riel'*s New Aim: To Entertain." *Globe and Mail*, April 14, 1979. Riel File.

Riel File. CBC Library, Toronto. Accessed December 2004.

Rielisms. Catalogue of an exhibition held at the Winnipeg Art Gallery, January 13 to March 18, 2001, and the Dunlop Art Gallery, May 12 to July 8, 2001.

Rosenthal, Alan, ed. *Why Docudrama? Fact-fiction on Film and Television*. Carbondale: Southern Illinois University Press, 1999.

Rosenstone, Robert A. *Visions of the Past: The Challenge of Film to Our Idea of History*. Cambridge, MA: Harvard University Press, 1995.

Selznick, Barbara. "World-Class Budgets and Big-Name Casts: The Miniseries and International Coproductions." In *Contracting Out Hollywood: Runaway Productions and Foreign Location Shooting*, edited by Greg Elmer and Mike Gasher, 157–75. Lanham, MD: Rowman & Littlefield, 2005.

Sloniowski, Jeanette. "Popularizing History: *The Valour and the Horror*." In *Slippery Pastimes: Reading the Popular in Canadian Culture*, edited by Joan Nicks and Jeanette Sloniowski, 159–74. Waterloo, ON: Wilfrid Laurier University Press, 2002.

Tinic, Serra. *On Location: Canada's Television Industry in a Global Market*. Toronto: University of Toronto Press, 2005.

van Zoonen, Liesbet. *Entertaining the Citizen: When Politics and Popular Culture Converge*. Lanham, MD: Rowman & Littlefield, 2005.

Worthington, Peter. "CBC's Version of History." *Toronto Sun*, April 19, 1979: B11.

Filmography

Riel (CBC/Green River Pictures, 1979)

KATARZYNA RUKSZTO

History as Edutainment

Heritage Minutes and the Uses
of Educational Television

I t has been over fifteen years since the *Heritage Minutes* debuted on Canadian television networks with the first production, *The Underground Railroad*, in 1991, paving the way for the series that has since become embedded in the landscape of Canadian mass media. Originally created by the CRB Foundation Heritage Project, an organization helmed by businessman Charles Bronfman that was mandated to "enhance Canadianism," the series is highly visible on television networks and cinema screens, and is now heard on radio. Some *Minutes* have been translated into comics and distributed through fast food outlets, and all are available on the Internet. In addition, the CRB Foundation Heritage Project, and now the Historica Foundation, which took over much of the Heritage Project's materials and activities, have developed a wide variety of teaching materials and activities for history classrooms and online learning.* The *Heritage Minutes* straddle the line between classroom and broader education, and are admired by some as leading the way in popularizing Canadian history.

The impetus behind the creation of the *Minutes* is manifold. Certainly the debates about the role of mass media in education influenced the particular direction of the CRB Foundation Heritage Project. The *Heritage Minutes* can be viewed as answering the call of the 1975 *Report of the Commission on Canadian Studies* (the *Symons Report*) to harness electronic media for the purpose of exciting Canadians about their history. But the project was also driven by specific political interests. In many interviews,

---

* The Minutes are now called *Historica Minutes*. Despite the name change, I will refer to the series as *Heritage Minutes* to signify the continuity between the goals of the CRB Foundation Heritage Project and Historica. The name also clearly signifies the centrality of the heritage discourse within the series.

Charles Bronfman expressed his frustration with the sovereigntist movement in Quebec as divisive and contrary to both national and provincial
interests. Here is Bronfman on national identity: "In a country like Canada,
there has to be a national purpose. And if there is no national purpose, then
there isn't any country, or any reason to have a country. I don't think we
can say that our national purpose is to have a health-care system. We have
to have something more that binds us together. And I believe we do. I
believe that Canadian society is unique."[1]

From their inception, the *Heritage Minutes* were promoted as a non-
partisan effort to foster this nationalist vision. They were on air during
the tumultuous 1990s, including the 1995 Quebec referendum. Perhaps
it is no surprise that some were skeptical of the Heritage Project's non-
partisan claim. In the late 1990s, Quebec journalist Normand Lester
revealed that the *Minutes* were funded in part by hidden federal grants.[2]
This information was entered in 2004 into the testimony at the Gomery
Inquiry into the federal sponsorship program.[3] Thus, the *Heritage Minutes* are but one of the latest examples in the long history of federal government activities promoting a sense of belonging and national identity
among citizens.[4]

The *Heritage Minutes* can be seen as successfully applying ideas from
the debates about media and education to the political agenda of national
unity. For the creators of the *Heritage Minutes*, educational television can
turn indifference and lack of knowledge into patriotism and individuals into
citizens by producing a pan-Canadian history that celebrates collective
accomplishments and is anchored by the already familiar values of tolerance, diversity, and pioneering. And this address to the nation is delivered
through the emotional and persuasive techniques of television production. This chapter will address the effectiveness of the *Heritage Minutes*
as a form of public citizenship education, in the context of the critiques
of heritage discourses and the ongoing public discussion about national
identity and the politics of belonging in Canada.

Citizenship, National Cohesion, and Heritage

It is commonly accepted by political scientists and artists alike that "[Cana-
dian] citizenship is now diffuse, multiple, and ever-shifting."[5] What it
means to be Canadian, to belong as citizens, is discussed on the pages of
academic journals and daily newspapers, in conference rooms, and on the
streets. Pressing issues of the day—racial profiling by police, the Maher Arar
inquiry, the reanimation of separatist parties in Quebec, Aboriginal treaty
rulings, and so on—relentlessly force Canadians to think about the mean-

ing of Canadian citizenship and national identity. To many, this is a time of shifting power relations, of changing the symbolic order in the Canadian imaginary, of contesting for greater inclusion and representation of minoritized groups. Rather than causing excitement, however, these changes signify to some a time of national crisis. The challenges to the dominant political and symbolic order are seen as nothing less than a threat to social cohesion, common values, and culture.

Much of the recent literature on Canadian citizenship has been devoted to imagining national belonging in the new political terrain of minority rights, communitarian theories of identity, and the broad critiques of liberal democratic citizenship. The latter has been assessed as too individualist, as unable to cope with the pluralist nature of Canadian society and collective identity claims.[6] New theories of citizenship range from Will Kymlicka's multicultural citizenship model, which recognizes minority rights within the liberal democratic tradition, to Charles Taylor's "politics of recognition" of minority claims within what he calls the "multinational society," to more radical rethinking of belonging, often exemplified in grassroots political campaigns such as the No One Is Illegal campaign for the rights of undocumented workers.[7] While previous approaches accept the model of multiculturalism produced by state policy as a starting point for a discussion of Canadian citizenship, No One Is Illegal, not least by its name, calls into question Canadian immigration policies and others that determine economic and social belonging in Canada.

The contentious debate over the meaning of Canadian identity and belonging has been felt in all areas of political and social life in Canada. The panic over the future of Canadian identity is conspicuous in Jack Granatstein's blockbuster polemic *Who Killed Canadian History?* (1998), in the growth of new history foundations, and in the federal government's now infamous sponsorship program to strengthen federalism. The *Heritage Minutes* were born from such concerns. Marrying the goals of the heritage industry with the tradition of citizenship education and the insights of media education, the *Minutes* promote national cohesion by selling populist ideas—and imagined populations—in a familiar commercial form to the nation.

Located at the intersection of popular culture and education, the pedagogical potential of television anchors and frames the series. However, the pedagogical aspect of the series is informed by the politics of heritage. Much of the scholarship on the heritage industry presents heritage as a site of contestation between those who support heritage discourses as a tool of preserving and representing national identity, and those who charge heritage discourses with representing a colonialist national identity. For instance, Robert Hewison argues that heritage as an industry and a discourse of nostalgia is a misguided response to the drastic economic dislocation of working people, the shifts in cultural politics resulting from globalization, and the growing civil unrest that followed the dismantling of the welfare state.[8] For "people's history" proponents like Raphael Samuel, on the other hand, heritage can democratize national history by incorporating the perspectives of ordinary people.[9] The creators of the *Heritage Minutes* are influenced by the latter perspective on the potential of heritage. In *Minute by Minute* (1998), a promotional documentary about the *Heritage Minutes*, producer Michael Levine states that the CRB Foundation Heritage Project differs from most heritage activities. The project, he believes, is "an inclusionary foundation [that wants] everybody in the country to understand that they have a part and a stake in the country."

This perspective is in line with the official mandate of Canadian Heritage. Less embroiled in the politics of defensive protection of "tradition" than its British counterpart, the heritage industry in Canada largely presents itself as a partner in fostering the principles of acceptance, tolerance, and national pride that are the official goals of Canadian multiculturalism. In short, the task of the heritage discourse is to develop a sense of shared citizenship in the context of diverse Canada.

Heritage practitioners like the makers of the *Minutes* understand that heritage can create dissonance. One group's inheritance may become the source of another group's exclusion or disinheritance.[10] The notion of inheritance projects a past "in common" while simultaneously implying that it is restricted to particular groups.[11] The sense of disinheritance, dispossession, or exclusion created by the discourse of national heritage results from the contradiction between heritage notions of belonging and the fact that modern nation-states are structured by profound differences and inequalities along regional, class, gender, race, citizenship, and other lines. The creators of the *Minutes* do recognize that Canadians are divided on the basis of regional, linguistic, ideological, and other differences. But they refuse to believe that such differences negate the possibility of sharing a common archive of stories. The *Heritage Minutes* are meant to be a collective expression of Canadian identity and history, based on the respectful acceptance of diverse ways of becoming Canadian. Thus, the varying historical experiences and demographic diversity of the Canadian population are incorporated to some extent into the framework of an overall nationalist address mode of the *Minutes*. This representational focus on pluralism and historical differences is an attempt at citizenship education that addresses rather than ignores the contemporary tensions of belonging.

Heritage Minutes as Citizenship Education

Inevitably, the debate over the meaning of Canadian citizenship includes in its scope a discussion of educating for citizenship. As Kymlicka puts it, "A basic task of schooling is to prepare each new generation for their responsibilities as citizens."[12] Accomplishing this task is difficult in the context of changing ideas about ways of belonging to the nation. For instance, the assimilationist model of citizenship education has, since the 1980s, given way to multicultural education. More recently, preparing students for the economic market was the top priority of the educational agenda of the 1990s.[13] Some argue that active citizenship must be fostered by developing critical analytical skills among young people; others worry that such a critical approach will not develop a sense of national feeling among young Canadians.[14] Added to these shifting priorities is the increasing concern among some educators that traditional schooling must compete with young people's interest in mass media and other forms of entertainment.

Kymlicka argues that the emphasis on history in citizenship education is particularly important in modern multicultural societies that need to produce a sense of shared membership among citizens divided by ethnicity, language, and culture: "In multination states ... citizenship education typically has a dual function—it promotes a national identity within each constituent national group, defined by a common language and history, but it also seeks to promote some sort of transnational identity which can bind together the various national groups within the state."[15] Kymlicka argues that this does not mean that history should be sanitized or inaccurate. What is important is that history teaching promote "an emotional identification" with the historical stories, so that students can collectively feel both pride and shame about their shared past.[16] A sense of historical identification with the past may in fact be one of the few means to achieve social unity in a diverse society.[17]

At first glance, the *Heritage Minutes* reflect the above understanding of the role of history in citizenship education. Thomas Axworthy explains that the goal of the CRB Foundation Heritage Project was "to tell our wonderful stories, which we don't know because we speak different languages and we live apart."[18] The project's founders seem aware that Canadians have different historical experiences, different memories, different stories to tell. Rather than a problem, this diversity is seen to enrich Canada as a whole. The *Heritage Minutes* are a televisual representation of the official formula of multiculturalism as "unity out of difference." The *Minutes* are meant to stimulate Canadians' interest in and engagement with "our" history.

This engagement, however, is channelled in a particular direction. Kymlicka's proposal of history as citizenship education encouraged a non-sanitized, non-heroic telling of history. According to him, to become active citizens committed to a just society, students must learn about the historical injustices as part of their burdensome past, theirs to rectify. The *Heritage Minutes*, however, are about the development of national identification through sharing stories in a decidedly celebratory form. The fact that the *Minutes* were partly funded by the Liberal sponsorship money simply underscores the fact that the implicit purpose of the *Minutes* is to foster national unity and social cohesion. Together, the *Minutes* construct a national narrative meant to bind all Canadians. Yet, ironically, the nationalist address seems to borrow from the critical stream of media education.

The creators of the *Heritage Minutes* proclaim quite passionately that today's pedagogies must reflect the reality of media-savvy youth: "Today's generations connect more readily with the visual than with the written or spoken word. Our mass media feed the public's hunger for a meaningful understanding of the past and for coherent explanations of present-day phenomena. The CRB Foundation hopes to influence popular culture, not academic discourse. We put our money into film and television, not the university presses. We must never confuse education with schooling."[19] This awareness of learning in the world outside the school seems to be influenced by media educators' calls to integrate different forms of media and media literacy into educational strategies. Opposing those who warn against the negative influence of mass media—the spectres of violent youth, moral decline, ignorance and political apathy, and growing consumerism, to name a few frequently cited threats—there are others who believe that our media-saturated landscape requires ever-greater engagement with media as a form of educational strategy.[20] Television in particular is often blamed for young people's lack of interest in and ignorance of history, and their supposedly diminishing civic pride.[21] In response, media educators argue that what is needed is enhanced media literacy that would enable media users to develop critical skills with which to not only navigate media messages but also use and produce media texts.

Officially, these were the goals of the CRB Foundation Heritage Project, and they continue to be endorsed by the Historica Foundation. The *Minutes* are meant to inspire Canadians to learn more about Canadian history. Historica's website is interactive and invites students, teachers, and all other interested Canadians to engage in their own quest for historical knowledge. The school-based Heritage Fairs are designed to enable students to produce their own heritage minutes, all the while learning to be media literate. But the goal of media literacy is undermined by the nationalist project of the foundation. Despite the claims of promoting media literacy, the *Heritage Minutes* reflect a much more traditional approach to media as educational aids "to make learning more palatable."[22] The idea that traditional teaching needs to be supplemented by more exciting forms is easily discernible on Historica's website, where games, lesson plans for using the *Minutes* in the classroom, and other activities are encouraged as means to make learning more fun and interesting.

The *Heritage Minutes* link public history programming and the formal education system, producing educational programming delivered within the commercial space of the television and movie industries. As a form of educational television, the *Heritage Minutes* transform the home and the movie theatre into "virtual classrooms."[23] But what do they teach?

Televising Ideal Citizens and an Ideal Canada

The content of the *Heritage Minutes* leaves an observer doubtful of their potential to inspire critical thinking. Firmly infused in the heritage discourse of national celebration, the *Minutes* induce Canadians to participate in an act of commemoration akin to attending traditional sites of collective memory, such as museums. In fact, the *Heritage Minutes* are symptomatic of the "electronification of memory."[24] Certainly, in Canada, television has become a common form through which representations of the past are experienced by citizens—witness the popularity of the historical series *Canada: A People's History*, discussed elsewhere in this volume. The pedagogical intent of much of this programming resembles the mandate of the modern museum—to integrate diverse, and divided, populations.[25] Just as the museum's attempt at democracy was accomplished by striving for maximum entertainment value via blockbuster exhibitions, so television history also blurs the boundaries between truth and fiction, education and entertainment. In place of information or engagement with difficult knowledge, the *Heritage Minutes* offer viewers the opportunity to emotionally connect to other Canadians through these stories. As Patrick Watson explains in *Minute by Minute*, the greatest challenge for the makers of the *Minutes* was "to avoid the temptation to be too informative and to concentrate on the dramatic."

This strategy makes sense in the context of the nationalist agenda of the *Minutes*. Media studies show that while viewers may not recall details of information gleaned from the media, they are influenced by the overall perspectives presented in the media.[26] Thus, the focus on "the dramatic" makes sense if the goal is to strengthen citizens' attachment to their nation. The text aims at the viewers' emotions by humanizing the protagonists, by heightening the narrative drama through sound, lighting, and other techniques, and by drawing on relatable themes of belonging, community, acceptance, success, and dignity. The *Minutes* are meant to excite Canadians about their past, noting that Canada produced heroes and successes. But, even more, viewers are asked to identify with the pain and triumph of the protagonists, to feel their dilemmas and successes, to see these stories as part of the viewers' own collective history. The details of the stories are less important than the common national identification they signify.

Almost all of the *Heritage Minutes* follow the same storytelling formula. The narratives are linear, with a central conflict resolved at the end and summarized by the narrator. The *Minutes* elevate individuals, events, objects, legends, and geographical sites to the status of national symbols. Many of the stories centre around an underdog—for example, the creator of Superman is initially ridiculed; Jennie Trout is mocked by her male colleagues as she contends for her right to be in medical school—eliciting viewer's sympathy for the unlikely hero. The narrator reassures the viewer that the hero eventually succeeds. Many of the *Minutes* use already known, clichéd images and themes to further link the viewer to the story—the wilderness, the canoe, "natives," Canadian/American difference. Finally, the *Minutes* address viewers openly, calling to them—us—as participants in this larger story, through the caption "a part of our heritage." This implied intimate link between the viewer and the narrative encourages the viewer's participation in the national story. With each *Minute*, viewers are reminded that these stories belong to all Canadians. Using all of these techniques, the *Heritage Minutes* send a uniform message: that Canadians are marked by creativity, strength, unity, and, above all, tolerance. In short, the *Minutes* are to serve as an emotional glue that binds Canadians despite their diversity. These stories tell us who we are as Canadians and help explain what we have become as a nation.

A number of the *Minutes* establish French and English presence in Canada as foundational. This foundational presence provides opportunities to tell the story of English–French relations as the beginning of the Canadian ethic of cultural cooperation. *Baldwin and Lafontaine* celebrates the cooperation between the two politicians in their quest for electoral reform in the British colonies of Upper and Lower Canada. The drama is primarily produced through contrasts: lightness and darkness, chaos and order. The vignette opens to a dark night, with mobs of angry men on the street on "election night in Quebec, 1841." The danger is palpable—shouts, fists, and angry faces flitting across the screen. A fight breaks up as one group blocks another from voting. Lafontaine admonishes the crowd against violence. Next we see Lafontaine gazing out of the darkness into the daylight outside his window, lost in thought, calm and rational. A letter is delivered from Baldwin, who wants Lafontaine to run in Ontario. The next scene contrasts with the previous two—Lafontaine meets Baldwin at the Toronto docks. It is an airy, sunny, bright day. The docks are busy with merchants and others, suggesting the future prosperity of this union. "Mr. Lafontaine, think of the history we'll make when a French Canadian runs and wins in York," Baldwin says. Lafontaine wins the seat, and the narrator tells viewers, "Together, Robert Baldwin and Louis Lafontaine would forge the basis of responsible government in Canada."

This story accomplishes a number of things. It reinforces the already familiar idea of the two founding nations. Rather than telling a story of conflict, it foreshadows the political event of Confederation as peaceful and cooperative. The parallel histories of English and French settlers are brought together, and the conquered French are incorporated as equals in the national story.

Founded by the French and English, Canada is also multicultural. True to the official discourse of multiculturalism, the French and English foundation—with Aboriginal peoples often in the background—is supplemented by *Minutes* representing other ethnic groups as nation builders. *Nitro* and *Soddie* exemplify the ways in which diversity is celebrated while at the same time conflict is disavowed.

Nitro presents a moment in the life of a Chinese railway worker in the late 1800s. The vignette opens to a construction site and a makeshift camp. The image evokes dirt and heat—the brightness of a scorching sun, sweaty, grungy faces. A white supervisor is looking for a volunteer to set a nitroglycerine charge in a mountain tunnel: "Who wants to earn some danger pay? Buy fare for the wife?" A young man volunteers, face beaming with hope for the promised family reunion. The man descends into the darkness of the tunnel. Sombre music echoes the fear and sense of danger as he disappears. Next the scene explodes with fire and smoke. "Damn, that's the third one we lost this week," a second white supervisor casually notes. The young man suddenly emerges, and the faces of his co-workers change from despair to happy disbelief.

In this *Minute*, the narrator is visible. He is the worker himself, now an old man, who tells children sitting at his knee, "They say there is one Chinese man for every mile of the track." This ending underscores the truthfulness of the story and makes explicit the link between the sacrifices of the early immigrants and later generations of Chinese Canadians.

Nitro pays homage to the Chinese railway workers for their heroism and hard work, celebrating their survival while honouring those who died. The systemic discrimination that the Chinese endured during this period is replaced in this story with an admission of individual prejudice, as seen in the figure of the callous white supervisor.

Soddie is another story of immigrant survival and success, this time depicting Ukrainian settlers building their home from the prairie soil they farmed. The *Minute* has a dreamy quality to it, and quiet music is heard in the background of images depicting the labour and joy of the immigrant couple as they build their first home. Two peasants, a man and a woman, get off a buggy in the middle of a vast Alberta field. The land seems to stretch on forever, with nothing in sight. The scene shifts to the couple. They work the land in solitude, building their home out of sod. The drama is in the natural rhythms of work: seasonal changes marked by alternating rains and scorching sun; muddy, sweaty faces. At times, the camera captures movements in slow motion—the straining muscles of horse's legs, the grimaces and smiles of a hard day's work. The struggle with the environment ends triumphantly, the finished house finally built, as the narrator explains, "from the same earth that would grow their bread."

These two *Minutes* typify the treatment of immigration in heritage discourses. They feature different immigrant communities, but their specific difference and particular histories are eclipsed by the narrative function they serve as stories of immigrant integration. In each story, there is the climax of struggle, even a hint of mistreatment in the case of *Nitro*, but the message of both *Minutes* is of immigrants' contribution to national settlement. The *Minutes* don't tell us much about the citizenship status of these groups in the periods depicted, but they do reinforce the idea of pioneer ingenuity and spirit that, according to the dominant nationalist discourse, marks all Canadians.

In addition, these stories of immigrants' struggle and survival may also be compelling because they reference current experiences of hardship. Many can identify with the hardships represented in the above *Minutes* in a general way by relating these stories to the difficulties some groups experience in contemporary Canada. The eventual success and survival of the early Chinese and Ukrainian immigrants may give hope that difficulties currently experienced by immigrant groups will also be resolved. Multiculturalism is affirmed as a positive approach to diversity because immigrant groups become integrated into the larger Canadian family. Immigrants are positioned in the *Minutes* as symbols of Canada's evolving progressive attitudes, allowing viewers moments of reflection on the difficulties and value of achieving the vision of multicultural Canada. Commemorating the past hardships of some Canadians is an experience that can be shared by *all* Canadians.

While the above two *Minutes* dramatize cultural difference and racial and ethnic conflict, the *Minutes* depicting black subjects positively erase them. All three—*The Underground Railroad, Jackie Robinson*, and *Maurice Ruddick*—affirm Canadian tolerance in contrast to American racism.

Maurice Ruddick, a first-person account of the 1958 mining disaster in Springhill, Nova Scotia, is the only story with a black Canadian as its subject. The scene opens to a man standing in the darkness of the mine. He takes off his hard hat and begins to walk toward the camera, telling his story. The camera zooms in on his face as he recalls the horror and camaraderie that are part of working in a mine. His face is alive with memory, his gaze piercing. He tells us that after the disaster, the survivors were given free vacations in the United States, but American segregation laws prohibited Ruddick from going. His comrades were ready to abandon their trips in solidarity. Soft music plays behind his final words: "Seventy four died in that bump, but that was life around the Springhill Mines. Closed now, so much death ... but my, didn't we sing those hymns—together."

This is another story of survival, of a miner's life, full of quiet dignity and daily danger, as well as camaraderie and equality. It is difficult not to be moved by the trauma of the story and the sheer poise of the protagonist, both made emotionally powerful by the intimate, as if face-to-face, delivery. The authoritative appeal of the figure of Ruddick, as a black miner speaking from personal experience, makes the message all the more compelling. The message is clear: as opposed to the racism in the United States, Canada's race relations have been harmonious, positive. *Maurice Ruddick* is quite a spectacular example of the outright erasure of the Canadian history of discrimination. The story is set in the 1950s, a period of segregation and discrimination against black communities. In fact, the infamous pathologizing and eventual bulldozing of Africville, the well-known Halifax black community, was yet to happen.

As these examples show, as a series the *Heritage Minutes* produce an idealized Canada that reflects most of the dominant discourses and policies of Canadian citizenship. Canada is multicultural within a bilingual framework, blessed by ethnic and racial harmony and cooperation, social conflicts are minimized or disavowed, and the national story is marked by equality and inclusion of different groups of Canadians. Viewers are to note the diversity of these stories, but also their similarities. The satisfaction of achievement, of struggle and triumph, of community building, is ours to share. As historical arguments for Canada, the *Heritage Minutes* certainly attempt to represent the *spirit* of the nation.

History as Edutainment

The purported ignorance of history among Canadians is frequently mentioned as the original impetus for the *Heritage Minutes*. In particular, the lack of interest in Canadian history among children and youth has been identified as worrisome and in need of reversal.[27] This lack has been attributed partly to the uninspiring ways in which history is traditionally taught in schools. The *Heritage Minutes* were produced to show the way history can be made relevant, exciting, and useful in promoting active citizenship.

The format and content of the *Minutes* is shaped by the assumptions of the makers of the series about audiences, in particular Canadian youth. The series is very much influenced by the alarm raised by some political analysts that political engagement is declining, most acutely among the current generation of young people. The argument is that young people feel disaffected with politics, are seduced and pacified by consumerism and mass media, and are generally ignorant of political processes and issues. In addition, the preponderance of media means that traditional methods of education and culture cannot compete for the attention of youth.[28] Ironically, it is television and other forms of mass media that are increasingly seen as the necessary pedagogical tools in the efforts to shape the future generation of citizens.[29]

The *Minutes* take their lead from this approach. The focus on the dramatic rather than the informational is clearly guided by the perceived need to balance the educational requirements of the series with the need to entertain presumably easily bored audiences. The sixty-second format speaks as much to the programming requirements of television as to the attention span and scanning patterns of television viewers. The *Minutes* borrow heavily from the common representational forms and themes familiar to consumers of popular culture, and especially the forms and themes in youth-oriented programs. For example, the heavy emphasis on discoveries, inventions, and adventures reflects the assumptions about "boys' interests" that form much of children's programming.[30] One of the criticisms of traditional history teaching is that it has been dry and boring, focusing on official figures who are difficult for modern youth to identify with. So the *Minutes* focus on lesser-known Canadians and ordinary people, and use humour in many of the stories. Often, ordinary Canadians come alive through a direct emotional appeal to the viewers, using such techniques as the direct gaze, close-ups, and music.

In all this, the *Minutes* create or presume a particular public while foreclosing others. Michael Warner states that a public "exists by virtue of being addressed."[31] In other words, a public is made real through texts and discourses that speak to it. And such is the case with the publics of the *Heritage Minutes*. While the exact number of viewers of the *Minutes* can never really be known, and they certainly can include non-Canadians and various groups of Canadians who may all view and relate to the *Minutes* in different ways, the *Minutes* presume a particular imagined public as its desired audience. The hope is that members of this audience will find themselves in the heritage discourse, will accept belonging to the public that is being addressed. This sense of belonging to the public is guided by the discourse's references, topics, and language.[32]

The primary public imagined by the *Heritage Minutes* is young and well versed in mass media culture. Hence the modes of address are from television, advertising, and film. This public is imagined as familiar with the discourse of multiculturalism but ignorant of the actual histories of diverse groups in Canada. So the themes are diversity, tolerance, and national unity. This imagined public is positioned in the series as a collective pupil, the authority of the *Minutes* as educational materials underlined by the authoritative voice of the narrator summarizing each vignette. But the function of the *Minutes* stretches beyond educating the public—they are also attempts to enlist members of this public into active citizenship. The *Minutes* call on the viewers to see themselves as part of the national story, to become conscious of their membership in the national community.

The problem with public address is that as it speaks to the imagined public, it excludes or forecloses others—those viewers who know history, who reject the heritage discourse, who interpret the stories in unintended ways, who read media messages critically, or who find themselves missing from rather than included in the national story. After all, as Warner points out, discourses addressed to a public circulate in a concrete world.[33] The discourse of heritage addressed to Canadian youth in the *Heritage Minutes* circulates in the context of Canadian politics, unequal relations, and different perspectives about Canada. The address of the *Minutes* does not take account of the possibility that some members of the youth audience sought by the *Minutes* are unlikely to recognize themselves as members of the imagined public. Perhaps herein lies the unintended lesson of the *Heritage Minutes*: that the very conditions posing a challenge to a nationalist agenda—diverse perspectives, critical awareness, media literacy—are the prerequisites of active citizenship in contemporary Canada.

Notes

1 Milner, "'So Drained I Had Nothing Left.'"
2 For details on Lester's investigation, see Conlogue, "Introduction."
3 For the testimony by Robert-Guy Scully to the commission, see the transcript for Monday, December 13, 2004 (Canada, Transcript 49).
4 On the history of federal departments' changing activities in the area of citizenship education, see Russell, "Bridging the Boundaries."
5 Hébert and Wilkinson, "The Citizenship Debates," 3.
6 Hébert and Wilkinson, "The Citizenship Debates," 10.
7 Kymlicka, *Multicultural Citizenship*; Taylor, *Multiculturalism*. No One Is Illegal is an international network of locally based chapters committed to the rights of all migrants. Chapters in Canada oppose national border controls such as the immigration policies and state practices of deportation, racial profiling, and the use of security certificates.
8 Hewison, *The Heritage Industry*.
9 Samuel, "Resurrectionism."
10 Tunbridge and Ashworth, *Dissonant Heritage*.
11 Corner and Harvey, *Enterprise and Heritage*, 49.
12 Kymlicka, *Politics in the Vernacular*, 293.
13 Hébert and Wilkinson, "The Citizenship Debates," 26.
14 For an overview of the current issues in citizenship education as identified by the Citizenship Education Research Network, see Hébert and Pagé, "Citizenship Education."
15 Kymlicka, *Politics in the Vernacular*, 314.
16 Kymlicka, *Politics in the Vernacular*, 315.
17 Kymlicka, *Politics in the Vernacular*, 315.
18 *Minute by Minute*.
19 Axworthy, "Memory Matters!"
20 For a sense of the scope and direction of media education in Canada, see the special issue titled "Media Education," *Orbit* 35 (2), 2005.
21 Buckingham, *The Making of Citizens*, 4.
22 See "Using the Minutes to Think Critically" in the Lesson Plans link on Historica's website, www.histori.ca; de Castell and Jenson, "Videogames and Digital Game Play," 18.
23 Goldfarb, *Visual Pedagogy*, 12.
24 Urry, "How Societies Remember the Past," 63.
25 Goldfarb, *Visual Pedagogy*, 146.
26 Buckingham, *The Making of Citizens*, 15.
27 Granatstein, *Who Killed Canadian History?*
28 For a discussion of key texts expressing these positions, see Chapter 1 in Buckingham, *The Making of Citizens*.
29 I thank Professor Kari Dehli for elaborating on this point in an earlier review of my research.
30 Buckingham, *The Making of Citizens*, 41.
31 Michael Warner, "Publics and Counterpublics," 50.
32 Michael Warner, "Publics and Counterpublics," 75.
33 Michael Warner, "Publics and Counterpublics," 81.

References

Axworthy, Thomas. "Memory Matters!" Presentation to the Winnipeg Canadian Club, 1997.

Buckingham, David. *The Making of Citizens: Young People, News and Politics.* London: Routledge, 2000.

Canada. *Commission of Inquiry into the Sponsorship Program and Advertising Activities* (The Gomery Report), December 13, 2004. Transcript 49. Available at www.gomery.ca/documents/transcripts/en/2005/01/200511152625.pdf. Accessed January 10, 2008.

Conlogue, Ray. "Introduction." In Norman Lester, *The Black Book of English Canada.* Toronto: McClelland & Stewart, 2002.

Corner, J. and Harvey, S., eds. *Enterprise and Heritage: Crosscurrents of National Culture.* London: Routledge, 1991.

de Castell, Susan and Jennifer Jenson. "Videogames and Digital Game Play—The New Field of Educational Game Studies." *Orbit* 35 (2): 17–19.

Goldfarb, Brian. *Visual Pedagogy: Media Cultures in and beyond the Classroom.* Durham, NC: Duke University Press, 2002.

Granatstein, Jack. *Who Killed Canadian History?* Toronto: HarperCollins Canada, 1998.

Hébert, Yvonne and Michel Pagé. "Citizenship Education: What Research for the Future?" In *Citizenship in Transformation in Canada*, edited by Yvonne M. Hébert, 228–48. Toronto: University of Toronto Press, 2002.

Hébert Yvonne and Lori Wilkinson. "The Citizenship Debates: Conceptual, Policy, Experiential, and Educational Issues." In *Citizenship in Transformation in Canada*, edited by Yvonne M. Hébert, 3–36. Toronto: University of Toronto Press, 2002.

Hewison, Robert. *The Heritage Industry: Britain in a Climate of Decline.* London: Methuen, 1987.

Kymlicka, Will. *Multicultural Citizenship: A Liberal Theory of Minority Rights.* Toronto: Oxford University Press, 1995.

———. *Politics in the Vernacular: Nationalism, Multiculturalism and Citizenship.* Oxford: Oxford University Press, 2001.

Milner, Brian. "'So Drained I Had Nothing Left': Two Years after Moving to New York, Charles Bronfman Says He Had His Reasons." *Globe and Mail*, January 26, 1999: A21.

Russell, Roberta. "Bridging the Boundaries for a More Inclusive Citizenship." In *Citizenship in Transformation in Canada*, edited by Yvonne M. Hébert, 134–49. Toronto: University of Toronto Press, 2002.

Samuel, Raphael. "Resurrectionism." In *Representing the Nation: A Reader*, edited by David Boswell and Jessica Evans, 162–84. London: Routledge, 1999.

Symons, T.H.B. *To Know Ourselves: The Report of the Commission on Canadian Studies.* Ottawa: Association of Universities and Colleges of Canada, 1975.

Taylor, Charles. *Multiculturalism and the "Politics of Recognition."* An essay with commentary by Amy Gutman, edited by Steven C. Rockefeller, Michael Walzer, and Susan Wolf. Princeton, NJ: Princeton University Press, 1992.

Tunbridge, J.E. and G.J. Ashworth. *Dissonant Heritage: The Management of the Past as a Resource in Conflict.* New York: John Wiley, 1996.

Urry, John. "How Societies Remember the Past." In *Theorizing Museums*, edited by Sharon Macdonald and Gordon Fyfe, 45–68. Oxford: Blackwell, 1996.

Warner, Michael. "Publics and Counterpublics." *Public Culture* 14 (1): 49–89.

Filmography

Heritage Minutes (Historica Foundation, 2001)
Minute by Minute: The Making of a Canadian Mythology (Corvideocom, 1998)

MICHELE BYERS

Education and Entertainment

The Many Reals of *Degrassi*

One of the most successful franchises in Canadian television history, *Degrassi*, in all its incarnations, has attracted audiences with a unique blend of "slice of life" authenticity and educational content that is often heralded as speaking to rather than for young people.[1] This "authenticity of a distinctly Canadian voice" is precisely what authors Peter S. Grant and Chris Wood worry will be lost if the Canadian government abandons the "tool kit" it has historically provided to Canadian media producers.[2] *Degrassi Talks* (*DT*), a six-part documentary series about youth issues that aired in 1992 after the finale of the original *Degrassi* series and was funded by Health and Welfare Canada, exemplifies the widespread and institutionalized nature of the "official recognition and support" of the series' edutainment project, but also the relationship between Canadian dramatic television and documentary form.[3] *Degrassi*, popular at home, in the US, and abroad, is the pivotal example Grant and Wood use to anchor their argument. The most well-known *Degrassi* series are fictional; that is, scripted and played by actors. But the series have always made claims—or had claims made for them—about their authenticity that seem to root them in an ambiguous space between fictional programming and documentary style. In what follows, I explore the interplay of realisms that have informed and continue to inform the *Degrassi* series, and how these have contributed to the popularity of the franchise and its meaning for viewers for more than two decades.

In a sense, "between fiction and reality" is an organizing theme of *Degrassi*, and this has been true since its earliest days as an emergent, grassroots voice in the tiny TV market for teens in the mid-1980s. The first series were attempts to create a pedagogically rich terrain within the televisual realm, and, as perhaps an unforeseeable consequence, they developed a complex intertextual universe—a *Degrassi*verse—whose popular deployment and reception around the world was rooted in a unique way of telling stories that could not be easily reduced to a binary of reality/fiction. This can be read through the intertextual matrices of the *Degrassi* texts in several ways. First, a hallmark of all the series has been a frequent but not always successful attempt to speak openly and honestly about youth experience, and to create characters and situations that many viewers cannot only identify with but are reminiscent of the people they encounter in their everyday lives.[4] Second, the series' creators have used and continue to use their viewers' intertextual knowledge of the *Degrassi* universe as entry points for the documentation of "real" experiences of Canadian young people. Whether in the way episodes of *DT* focus on social issues linked to the classic series' (*Degrassi Junior High* and *Degrassi High*, which I will call *Degrassi Classic*, or *DC*) narratives and characters or the deployment of discourses about youth circulating in the press and the community at a particular moment, *Degrassi* refuses any easy demarcation between fictional and documentary narratives within its wider intertextual world.[5] Third, *Degrassi*'s historical importance has to be understood in relation to changing technologies and their impact on the production of Canadian televisual texts over time. That is, while intertextually tied to one another, the series exist within different temporal frames that invite different types of understanding and analysis from viewers in terms of, for example, the way each series is coded as authentic. Thus, *DC* is more closely linked to discourses of authenticity vis-à-vis its visual difference from—and the most recent spin-off, *Degrassi: The Next Generation* (*TNG*), vis-à-vis its visual resemblance to—American television. In other words, part of *DC*'s authenticity, as this value has come to be constituted intertextually within the public sphere, comes from its deployment of codes that are read as systemically different from those that are identified with mainstream representations of youth culture produced in the United States. *TNG*'s authenticity, by contrast, appears to stem from the text's lack of articulatable visual differences from and its ease in circulating within the mainstream global and US teen TV markets.[6]

In a sense, the *Degrassi* series are messy texts, or "textually messy," in that they continually refuse an easy location within generic boundaries.[7] This may be underscored stylistically by *DT*'s use of clips from the *DC* series that blur the line between fiction and reality. The power of *DT* is drawn intertextually; that is, from the authenticity already won by the characters—here presented as their actor alter egos—on the other *Degrassi* series, which owes its power to its own intertextual insistence that these texts are as close to the lived experiences of real teens as fictional TV can get.

The persistent reiteration of the unique way the series grappled with provocative, youth-centred narratives and cast actual teens in teen roles conferred upon them a sense of authenticity not easily transferred to other popular youth series. By examining the intertextual linkages that continue to sustain the franchise, the rest of this chapter will explore the way realism and fiction were and are woven into the fabric of *Degrassi* in challenging and inventive ways.

More Real Than Thou: The World of *Degrassi Classic*

In discussions with students and friends about *DC*, on websites devoted to the series, and in articles written by and about its fans, one central issue emerges: the "realness" of the shows' characters and stories, particularly those narratives that address issues that had never directly been broached on (youth) television before but are dramatic representations of issues that many teens deal with every day.[8] Cult filmmaker Kevin Smith, for example, has long admitted his fascination with the Canadian phenomenon—so much so that he appeared in episodes of seasons four and five of *TNG*. In *TV Guide*, he wrote: "These were ordinary-looking ... kids like *I* had been in high school ... dealing with *real* problems—not that 90210 kinda TV problem-crap ... I could *identify* with these kids ... These non-glamorous, unpolished, awkward, age-appropriate-for-the-roles actors made me believe that I was a kindred spirit to the characters they played."[9]

Part of this sense of authenticity comes from the groundbreaking portrayal of issues—particularly taboo subjects like abortion—innovations in structure—resistance to closure, focus on teens' point of view, marginalization of adult–teen relationships in favor of the peer group—and casting age-appropriate, non-professional actors, without the "manufactured eventfulness" associated with belaboured attempts of series on their way out to recapture their audiences. In her essay about *Ellen*'s "coming out" episode, Anna McCarthy notes that these last-gasp "media events" are significant in that they represent moments of rupture in which politically taboo subjects "are allowed to enter the world of prime-time light entertainment."[10] On *Degrassi*, by contrast, political discourse was an outgrowth of the original series' grassroots origin and acted as a kind of a priori element in the series' stream of signification. Viewers recognize when they are being manipulated by the introduction of stylistic or thematic elements that radically break with a series' historical formations or that will not follow through after the "very special" event. With *Degrassi*, while audiences might indeed feel manipulated by certain narratives that seem especially inclined to a pedagogical or lesson-learned model of discourse, such special events are not special at all; rather, they are part of the everyday diegetic realities of the series in each of its incarnations.

While certainly not the exclusive domain of teen or youth series, the "special event" episode focusing on taboo topics is a hallmark of the genre. As Rhonda Wilcox notes in her work on *Buffy the Vampire Slayer*, *Buffy* creator Joss Whedon explicitly distanced himself from other teen fare in his refusal to ever produce this type of "very special episode."[11] Wilcox's argument—and Whedon's—hinges on *Buffy*'s refusal of "unmediated presentation" of social issues in favour of symbolic monstrosity made flesh in the form of vampires and demons. As with *Buffy*, however, where monsters are both events and mundane parts of the everyday landscape the series' teens must navigate on their road to adulthood, so on *Degrassi* social and political issues are central to the discursive fabric of the whole franchise. *DC*—much like *Ellen* but in a very different televisual context—represented a series of firsts that helped to create a shift in the textual and ritual organization of teen TV—although this is often erased in popular histories of the development of the genre[12]—and also created a kind of intertextual meta-language for the franchise as an industry within Canadian television. This language is represented as "realism" or "authenticity" in various streams of signification within which *Degrassi* can be read as part of a "'public archive' of TV memories … [that] make[s] important contributions to a sense of history and nationhood" for Canadian and global viewing audiences.[13]

The idea of quality, which is at times conflated with realism or truth-telling in the study of television, is also relevant here. As the critical reception of series life *Buffy* and *Star Trek* demonstrate, however, realism in these circumstances is connected to a sense of authenticity, innovation, and/or consistency within the diegetic universe of a particular television series as much as it is to an explicit continuity between what is represented on television and what happens in everyday life. While "quality" is contested across a variety of sites, both spatial and temporal, the "quality" discourse is one that circulates meaningfully among television scholars, producers, and the viewing public. Drawing on Jane Feuer's seminal work on MTM Enterprises and the production of quality TV in the 1970s and 1980s, Betsy Williams notes that textual, technical, and economic changes going on in television production at that time were central factors: the growth of independent production houses, the fragmentation of the previously monolithic network audience and the resulting move to "narrowcasting," the growing focus on privileged demographic groups, and the development of discourses of "self-reflexivity and liberal humanism" in tel-

Figure 1. *Degrassi Jr. High* group shot (l–r): Joey Jeremiah (Pat Mastroianni), Lucy Fernandez (Anais Granofsky), Arthur Kobalewsky (Duncan Waugh), Stephanie Kaye (Nicole Stoffman), Yick Yu (Siluck Saysanasy), Scooter Webster (Christopher Charlesworth), Christine "Spike" Nelson (Amanda Stepto), and Caitlyn Ryan (Stacie Mistysyn). Courtesy of Playing With Time.

evision narratives.[14] *DC* shares some of the "quality" features described by Williams, but its national production context, among other things, mark it as different. While *DC* was produced by Playing With Time, a small production company run by Linda Schuyler and Kit Hood, the series were funded by the CBC, PBS, and, like all Canadian television, through a variety of tax and government incentives. *DC* existed outside of the American network system, of course, but the most significant area of the "quality" discourse that can be associated with the series is in its textual innovation and narrative labours in youth social justice and edutainment.[15]

Despite associations of "quality," teen TV has often been thought of as "TV for *other* people," in this case teens.[16] In the introduction to *Teen TV*, Glyn Davis and Kay Dickinson note, "Television plays a pivotal role in the way that teenagers are managed: what they are allowed to do, what is forbidden and what they are encouraged to become."[17] Thus, part of what is seen as quality in relation to *Degrassi* as a franchise is the way the series are seen to produce narratives about Canadian youth that provide authentic spaces in which young people are invited to participate in managing themselves, in renegotiating traditionally forbidden zones, and in expanding and reimagining their future possibilities. To speak of quality television is thus not to designate a quality of the television text any more than it is to refer to potential readings produced by particular audiences in various contexts.[18] As Mark Jancovich and James Lyons note, the meaning of quality television has an important place in national discourses outside the United States, where there has long been concern that television will be the forerunner of a complete entrenchment of Americanization abroad.[19]

While those authors locate this concern in the 1980s and 1990s in Britain, in Canada these fears have been articulated for as long as television itself has existed.[20] Local quality programming, coming out of specific—and mythically unified—nationalist and also often public broadcasting contexts, with their tendency to take a paternalistic and elite view of broadcasting, was imagined "as a weapon to keep seductive American mass culture on the other side of the border."[21] As Paul Rixon points out in the British context, however, "Such discourses seem to suggest that there is some form of essential national television culture, one constituted by indigenous productions that American programs are endangering." He notes that American programming has actually had a much more complex and shifting role in global television culture, including the way it has been scheduled in various national contexts, the manner in which it has influenced international televisual productions, and in its provision of new "experiences" for producers and viewers internationally.[22] In the Canadian context, we have to remember that homegrown productions exist side by side with American shows in the lineup. Canadian series may have their own sensibilities, and these may have national, regional, and cultural resonances, but they are also deeply influenced by television being produced outside of Canada, primarily in the US but presumably in other contexts, such as the UK, as well. And series like *Degrassi* have equally marked their American counterparts, even though this may be much harder to see.

DC emerged at a time when the "quality" discourse was becoming an important indicator of the changes occurring in American television programming, of technological innovation, and of policy. The series was innovative in several ways and contributed to changes in teen TV, including adding variations to "quality" discourses that now circulate within the genre. Perhaps most significantly, *DC* laboured under the sign of realism in a way that blurred the line between fiction and documentary, fantasy and ethnography. An original series produced at a grassroots level for public television at a time when few options existed in the teen TV landscape, *Degrassi* as a franchise has come to stand for a unique way of weaving together fiction and reality, producing a complex intertextual map through which the televisual production of character and narrative has come to stand in for the very real landscape of the nation.

Degrassi Talks: "Real Kids Talking to Real Kids, from the Heart"

In her work on the cinematic production of racialized and ethnic identities, Ana Lopez has argued that Hollywood cinema has an ethnographic function. Rather than being merely a purveyor of simplified stereotypes, it is a "co-producer." It "creates [ethnicities] and provides its audience with an experience of them," demonstrating "Hollywood's power as ethnographer, as creator, and translator of otherness."[23] Television, as produced in Hollywood and elsewhere, has a similar function, one that we might think of not only as ethnographic but also as documentarian. In Canada, as David Hogarth has so aptly argued, the relationship between television and documentary form stretches back to the medium's earliest days. Not only was documentary important as a formal structure, drawing as it did on the incredible power of Grierson's National Film Board, but documentary has come to be seen as "Canada's most substantial contribution to televisual form, and television's most substantial contribution to a Canadian sense of place." To make the link between the documentary and the ethnographic more explicit, Hogarth points out that Canadian television's aesthetics, criticism, and policy all have deep documentarian roots. He notes that many documentary film producers who also worked in television brought with them a sort of "found object" approach to production—location shooting, an "'as found' look"—and an objective to "not make a show but to find one."[24]

In many ways, the *DC* series operates along these lines, working closely with the people in the community in which it was filmed and filming in that community on location rather than using professional actors and filming on the backlot sets that are the norm on *TNG*. How the new series continues in this "found" tradition, however, is in the sense that the show's ideas are found, discovered less in the imagination of the writers

Figure 2. *Degrassi Talks* group photo (l–r): Back: Caitlyn Ryan (Stacie Mistysyn), Kathleen Mead (Rebecca Haines), Derek "Wheels" Wheeler (Neil Hope), and Christine "Spike" Nelson (Amanda Stepto). Front: Yick Yu (Siluck Saysanasy) and Joey Jeremiah (Pat Mastroianni). Courtesy of Playing With Time.

and producers than in the experiences of Canadian youth and then honed to create compelling dramatic television.

Lopez's and Hogarth's ideas provide meaningful entry points to understanding the discursive shifts between the different valences of realism produced in the *Degrassi* franchise. While *DT* is closer to a social scientific understanding of ethnography, *DC*, like the Hollywood films Lopez describes, co-produces a particular yet multiple form of otherness: adolescence. *DC* acts like a window into the lives of seemingly real teens, and at the same time helps to produce a discourse about the realities of adolescent social life in urban Canada in the mid- to late 1980s. *DT*, created through a complex set of intertextual linkages with *DC*, invites us into the lives of real Canadian teenagers through narrative tropes developed in the earlier *Degrassi* texts. It is important that *DT* uses the familiarity of the young people being interviewed and the audience watching at home with the earlier series for at least two reasons. First, the popularity of the actors assures an audience. Second, the sense of authenticity created by the classic series provides legitimacy for the actors to ask intimate questions and to act as interpreters of the interview data for the audience. The actors often begin their interviews or moments of directly addressing the camera and the home audience by referencing the experiences of their onscreen characters—sometimes with the inclusion of clips from appropriate episodes from the *DC* series—particularly those that are germane to the topic of a particular episode. Thus, Amanda Stepto discusses Spike's experience with pregnancy and childrearing as a way into dialogues with a variety of young women who have been pregnant. Neil Hope not only brings his character's experience with alcohol to bear on his interviews and on-camera discussions, but also shares his own lived experiences.

DT, like other "road trip" narratives to which it is intertextually linked, displays a desire to map the nation by giving voice to many people from across the country. In the opening sequence of *DT*, we see the cast and crew travelling by various means across Canada, the camera panning to signposts of different regional locations, regional sites where the cast will stop and talk to local teens about the social issues that make up the focus of the series. This factor marks the series' documentary and nationalist project as being quite different from that of *DC*, which, although espousing universality, was clearly located in urban Toronto.

This desire to visually map the nation is a significant part of a nationalist project that has been important since the earliest days of Canadian film and television.[25] *DT* fits into the documentary paradigm described by Hogarth because it showcases the nation, bringing voices together across vast distances, allowing them a great deal of freedom to express different points of view and providing the audience with the pleasure of seeing and hearing these differences. While it never received the level of recognition that *DC* did, as an example of documentary television *DT* did continue the Canadian tradition of "represent[ing] the country in televisual form."[26]

I would suggest that *DT* was successful in this because it could also draw intertextually on dramatic tropes established by *DC*. As such, its documentary endeavour drew legitimacy from the perceived authenticity and realism of the *DC* characters and narratives. By blurring the lines between the slice of life that the series provided and the stories told by the teens interviewed on *DT*, these series also created, in the ambivalent space between fact and fiction, a discursive shift in the way that teens could be represented on television.

The Next Generation: "If Your Life Was a TV Show, This Would Be It"

The above quote was the tagline that The N—the American cable channel that airs *Degrassi*—ran for *TNG* during its first two seasons. The third-season tag was "100% Intense"; the fourth, "It Goes There." While the first comes closest to expressing the sentiments about *Degrassi*'s relationship to a sense of realism or authenticity that I have been discussing, the latest also signals an intertextual link to the new series' progenitor: a desire to go into the so-called "real" life issues of teens: school shootings, sex bracelets, mental illness, and abortion—"television's most persistent taboo."[27] This last statement, taken from the title of an article that ran in the July 18, 2004, issue of the *New York Times*, has continually given me pause. Abortion is not television's most persistent taboo; abortion is *American* television's most persistent taboo. This is clear if we consider *Degrassi* intertextually. Abortion narratives form one node that explicitly links the franchise's textual articulations across time (history) and space (network affiliation) in the production of what might be thought of as truthful fictions—although the abortion stories told on *DT* are assumed to be more declarative forms of truth.

The N's decision not to air the 2003 *TNG* abortion story arc caused an outcry among American youth and brought the issue into sharp relief in the press. Significantly, the *New York Times* article highlighted the fact that many American television producers feel that this is a topic they simply cannot and will not touch. But this is not true in Canada. In fact, Rebecca Eckler, in a piece about Shelley Scarrow, who scripted the abortion episodes, notes, "As a study in contrasts, when the episode aired in Canada this winter, there was nary a blip on the censorship radar."[28] In an interview with Mary Jane Miller at least a decade earlier, actor and writer Nada Harcourt notes that both PBS and the BBC reedited or refused to purchase episodes of the *DC* series because of their content. In the same volume, Miller notes that Harcourt and Ivan Fecan, past director of programming at the CBC, attribute this to the ability of Canadian television "to speak more honestly to our audience," allowing for a "richness and complexity" that suggests a greater authenticity or link to some external real.[29] The intertextual conflation of Canadian television with realism is explicitly articulated by Venay Menon in an article about *TNG* in the *Toronto Star*: "Unlike other teen dramas—except perhaps Degrassi's previous 1980s incarnations ...—*Degrassi: The Next Generation* takes on hot-button issues ... When you combine this with the cast—relatively cute but decidedly less photogenic than the flawless specimens showcased on *The*

Figure 3. Cast of *Degrassi: The Next Generation*, Season 6. Courtesy of Epitome Pictures Inc.

O.C. or *One Tree Hill*—the show resonates with a realism often simulated on American television but never fully realized."[30] What each of these voices seems to cry out for is a recognition of *Degrassi*'s difference, in which realism labours in very specific ways to produce not only characters and narratives but also the broader social and national landscape—Canadianness—in ways that appear more authentic than those produced in other (con)texts.

It is here, however, that the intertextual reading of the *Degrassi* franchise as a meta-text breaks down for some long-term viewers. Unlike earlier *Degrassi* series, it is *TNG*'s similarity to other, notably American, texts that is important to its popularity. Discussing a *TNG* focus group run in the United States, Stephen Stohn, executive vice-president of Epitome Pictures, relates:

> They asked the kids [in Raleigh, North Carolina, and Denver, Colorado], all of them, where the show was shot and they pretty much all agreed that it was shot in California ... or they thought it was shot in Florida. They knew it wasn't in their state, but they absolutely, one hundred percent identified with the characters ... The school wasn't like their school, maybe it was a little bit safer than their school, but it was certainly where they wanted to be and it could be their school, and I think that's true whether you're in Raleigh, North Carolina, or St. John's, Newfoundland.[31]

This convergence may be attributable to technological changes in television production that have facilitated the creation of products that "look" American and to the learning curve nations like Canada have followed in adopting production and narrative strategies from their American counterparts.[32] At the same time, an increasingly global marketplace has also focused the tension between universal needs and Canadian sensibilities.[33] If *TNG* looks more like what we see on American television today, it is marked as different by its intertextual link to the earlier series in the *Degrassi* franchise, which involves taking risks—perhaps not in the Canadian context, but certainly in the global context—in the types of narratives you tell and how you tell them.

Conclusion

Hogarth argues that because of the documentary influence in Canadian television, television critics "have generally judged fact and fiction programs alike for the 'purity' of their reflections of Canadian life, for the 'importance' of the issues they have dealt with, and for the merit of the groups they have represented—that is, for their documentary as opposed to dramatic value."[34] *Degrassi* has never focused on the documentary to the exclusion of the dramatic. Linda Schuyler has long maintained that *Degrassi* has always been about finding a balance between education and entertainment. The earlier series' greater association with realism and authenticity is in part attributable to their being read through documentary or ethnographic discourses that were perhaps more germane to their grassroots origins. This is especially true of *DT*, but is really an intertextual through line across which all the series of the franchise are linked. For *DC*, this is articulated in terms of its presentation of young, average-looking teens who live in average homes, wear average-bordering-on-horrible clothes, have average concerns, and do average things in their average lives, but this same structure is read into *TNG* even if its characters are more likely to live in homes that bear the markers of upper-middle classness, to be more conventionally attractive and more fashionably dressed, and to live lives more marked by the unconventional and dramatic.

  DC, *TNG*, and a plethora of teen series produced in Canada, the United States, and elsewhere cover social issues that are relevant to teens and that are somewhat universal and certainly intertextual: parental conflict, school failure, puberty and dating, work, concerns about the future, body image, and so on. But the way in which these and other stories are told is different, and the difference depends on national borders in the sense that different televisual traditions animate their production and different political climates and socio-cultural groups have the power to exert influence over the production and dissemination of media products.

The narrative authenticity of the *Degrassi* series, something that has been consistently commented on throughout the franchise's long history, is rooted in the types of stories it has chosen to tell and the way it has told them, as well as the characters through which they have been told. Elsewhere, David Hogarth provides an excellent discussion of Canadian television documentary in the global context. He addresses the concerns expressed from a variety of quarters that the global market will result in the dissolution of national and cultural specificity by asking, in part, what the specific "places" are that these works are supposed to represent, both in terms of actual spaces and the multiple socio-cultural and historical realities lived within them.[35] *Degrassi*'s longstanding valuation within the Canadian context is rooted at least in part in its ability to compete globally, but also in its creation of an intertextual web that appears to tell stories that are at once highly particular and broadly universal, which is likely related to its refusal of a documentary/dramatic split. Documentary and dramatic fiction, despite their potential overlap, do have different narrative properties. In the case of *Degrassi*, the presence of properties belonging to both televisual forms has reinforced the authenticity or realism of the whole franchise—realism or authenticity that is, in a sense, its meta-fiction.

Clearly, the stories *Degrassi* tells resonate with audiences outside of Canada, and these stories are not unique to Canadian teens. But national context does affect what types of stories can be told on television. Abortion is the most high-profile of these issues, although there are others, including drug use and parental child abuse, that create problems and set limits for producers in different national contexts. The abortion theme has run through all three of the *Degrassi* series I have discussed in this chapter, and it is a real issue for teens around the world. It is not only the intertextual ability of *Degrassi* to tell abortion stories that makes it seem authentic, but the way that it is read against the impossibility of telling these stories, or of telling them in a complex way and without discomfort as part of ongoing narratives rather than one-off or special events—that is, through the experiences of central rather than secondary characters or guest stars—from the perspective of the teen herself rather than that of the adults around her, without "thwarted" narratives where the pregnancy storyline is dispatched before it needs to be resolved, and without one-sided moralizing or ambivalent rhetoric and imagery, which has traditionally been how abortion has been narrated on television, especially television produced for and about teens.[36]

Televisual realism and/or authenticity is not rooted in one area of the medium's production, aesthetic, narrative, or reception but may be associated with any or all of these elements. *Degrassi* began as a grassroots project and morphed into a juggernaut. It is a complex, intertextual universe—not just a TV show or series of TV shows—that for more than two decades has brought reality and fiction together in unprecedented, ambivalent, and hardly unproblematic ways. *Degrassi* as a franchise is a kind of tapestry in whose designs one can find reiterations of televisual fantasy and productive renderings of the very real social, cultural, and historical landscapes of the nation.

Notes

1 *The Kids of Degrassi Street* was actually the first series of the *Degrassi* franchise. It began airing in the late 1970s and ran until the mid-1980s. Although some of the young actors involved in that series were also involved with the later and more widely known *Degrassi* series, in the context of this chapter I consider the *Degrassi* franchise as originating with the classic *Degrassi* texts: *Degrassi Junior High* and *Degrassi High*.

2 Grant and Wood, *Blockbusters and Trade Wars*.

3 Nicks, "Degrassi"; Hogarth, *Documentary Television in Canada*.

4 Certainly not all viewers and/or critics share this view. From my own anecdotal evidence, I have often heard critiques of various *Degrassi* series for their exclusion of the experiences of many Canadian youths, including rural youth, gay youth, Aboriginal youth, and so on. As well, not everyone agrees on the "realism" of the *Degrassi* texts or on their relative value. See, for example, Nicks, "*Straight Up.*" Possibly, the extremely high visibility and popularity of the franchise both nationally and internationally has led to its being positioned as both *the* quintessential Canadian TV product and the final word on youth/teen TV.

5 Peter McLaren's *Cries from the Corridor* (1980), a bestseller about teaching in Toronto's Jane–Finch housing projects in the 1970s, may have been an influence here, for example. In terms of *DT*, the collapsing of character and actor, fiction and truth is quite explicit in the use of Amanda Stepto, whose character, Spike, became pregnant and had a child at fourteen, as the featured player in the *DT* episode about sex; Neil Hope, whose character, Wheels, lost his parents to a drunk driver and in turn became a drunk driver, in the episode about alcohol; and Rebecca Haines, whose character, Kathleen, was beaten by her boyfriend, in the episode that deals with abuse.

6 Certainly, on a narrative level, both series display a difference from their US counterparts in terms of national limits of representability. We might speak here also of blurring the line between fiction and reality.

7 Caldwell, *Televisuality*, cited in Nicks, "*Straight Up,*" 15.

8 A comparison is often made between the *DC* series and the American teen soap *Beverly Hills, 90210* (Fox, 1990–2000), although even the series' producers have time and again noted the odiousness of these comparisons. See also note 4 regarding the importance of recognizing that not all viewers have found *Degrassi* to represent authentic versions of youth culture in Canada.

9 Smith, "High Times," 20, emphases in the original.

10 McCarthy, "'Must See' Queer TV," 88.

11 Wilcox, "There Will Never Be a 'Very Special' *Buffy.*"
12 McCarthy, "Must See,' Queer TV," 89. The teen series is recognized as a part
   of television drama in *The Television Genre Book*, edited by Glen Creeber. No
   mention is made of the *Degrassi* series, despite an acknowledgement that teen-
   focused series have been a staple since the 1980s. See Mosley, "The Teen Series,"
   41–43.
13 Jancovich and Lyons, "Introduction," 7.
14 Williams, "North to the Future," 142.
15 The concept of television as something that labours is drawn from Herman Gray's
   important book, *Race Matters*.
16 Brundson, "Life-Styling Britain," 88; emphasis added.
17 Davis and Dickinson, "Introduction," 10.
18 Hills, "*Dawson's Creek*," 64.
19 Jancovich and Lyons, "Introduction."
20 See, for example, Lipset, *Continental Divide*; Rutherford, *When Television Was
   Young*; Flaherty and Manning, *The Beaver Bites Back?*; and Nicks and Sloniowski,
   Slippery Pastimes.
21 Bodroghkozy, "As Canadian as Possible," 566.
22 Rixon, "The Changing Face of American Television," 50, 59.
23 Lopez, "Are All Latins from Manhattan?" 405–06.
24 Hogarth, *Documentary Television in Canada*, 4–5; Wise, "On the Air," cited in
   Hogarth, 5.
25 Gittings, *Canadian National Cinema*.
26 Hogarth, *Documentary Television*, 106–07.
27 Aurthur, "Television's Most Persistent Taboo," *New York Times*, 1. www.nytimes
   .com. Accessed July 22, 2004. The N has often recut or requested alternate end-
   ings for episodes to make them more palatable for American audiences.
28 Eckler, "Confessions of a Teen Drama Queen," *National Post*, TO3.
29 Miller, *Rewind and Search*, 251, 335–36.
30 Menon, "Degrassi daring dazzles U.S.," *Toronto Star*.
31 Personal interview, May 28, 2002.
32 See Rixon, "The Changing Face of American Television," on the British context.
33 Tinic, *On Location*, 108.
34 Hogarth, *Documentary Television in Canada*, 5–6.
35 Hogarth, *Documentary Television in Canada*, 117–18.
36 Fisch, "Abortions in TV Land."

References

Aurthur, Kate. Television's Most Persistent Taboo." *New York Times*, July 18,
   2004: 1. Available at www.nytimes.com. Accessed July 22, 2004.
Byers, Michele, ed. *Growing Up Degrassi: Television, Identity and Youth Cultures*.
   Toronto: Sumach Press, 2005.
———. "Race In/Out of the Classroom: *Degrassi (Junior High)* as Multicultural
   Context." In *Racism Eh? A Critical Inter-Disciplinary Anthology of Race in
   the Canadian Context*, edited by Charmaine Nelson and Camille Nelson,
   298–315. Concord, ON: Captus Press, 2004.

Bodroghkozy, Aniko. "As Canadian as Possible … : Anglo-Canadian Popular Culture and the American Other." In *Hop on Pop: The Politics and Pleasures of Popular Culture*, edited by Henry Jenkins, Tara McPherson, and Jane Shattuc, 566–89. Durham, NC: Duke University Press, 2003.

Brundson, Charlotte. "Life-Styling Britain: The 8–9 Slot on British Television." In *Television after TV: Essays on a Medium in Transition*, edited by Lynn Spigel and Jan Olsson, 75–92. Durham, NC: Duke University Press, 2004.

Caldwell, John Thornton. *Televisuality: Style, Crisis, and Authority in American Television*. New Brunswick, NJ: Rutgers University Press, 1995.

Creeber, Glen, ed. *The Television Genre Book*. London: British Film Institute, 2002.

Davis, Glyn and Kay Dickinson. "Introduction." In *Teen TV: Genre, Consumption and Identity*, edited by Glyn Davis and Kay Dickinson, 1–13. London: British Film Institute, 2004.

Eckler, Rebecca. "Confessions of a Teen Drama Queen." *National Post*, July 24, 2004: TO3.

Flaherty, David and Frank Manning, eds. *The Beaver Bites Back? American Popular Culture in Canada*. Kingston and Montreal: McGill-Queen's University Press, 1993.

Fisch, Audrey. "Abortions in TV Land." At http://dir.salon.com/story/mwt/feature/2000/03/08tv_abortion/. Accessed March 8, 2000.

Gittings, Christopher. *Canadian National Cinema*. London: Routledge, 2002.

Grant, Peter S. and Chris Wood. *Blockbusters and Trade Wars: Popular Culture in a Globalized World*. Vancouver: Douglas & McIntyre, 2004.

Gray, Herman. *Race Matters: Television and the Struggle for "Blackness."* Minneapolis: University of Minnesota Press, 1995.

Hills, Matt. "*Dawson's Creek*: 'Quality Teen TV' and 'Mainstream Cult'?" In *Teen TV: Genre, Consumption and Identity*, edited by Glyn Davis and Kay Dickinson, 54–67. London: British Film Institute, 2004.

Hogarth, David. *Documentary Television in Canada: From National Public Service to Global Marketplace*. Montreal and Kingston: McGill-Queen's University Press, 2002.

Jancovich, Mark and James Lyons. "Introduction." In *Quality Popular Television*, edited by Mark Jancovich and James Lyons, 11–31. London: British Film Institute, 2003.

Lipset, Seymour. *Continental Divide: The Values and Institutions of the United States and Canada*. London: Routledge, 1990.

Lopez, Ana M. "Are All Latins from Manhattan? Hollywood, Ethnography, and Cultural Colonialism." In *Unspeakable Images: Ethnicity and the American Cinema*, edited by Lester D. Friedman, 404–24. Chicago: University of Illinois Press, 1991.

McCarthy, Anna. "'Must See' Queer TV: History and Serial Form in *Ellen*." In *Quality Popular Television*, edited by Mark Jancovich and James Lyons, 88–102. London: British Film Institute, 2003.

McLaren, Peter. *Cries from the Corridor*. Toronto: Methuen, 1980.

Menon, Venay. "Degrassi Daring Dazzles U.S." *Toronto Star*, October 12, 2004. Available at http://www.friendscb.org/News/Friends_News/archives/articles 10130401.asp.

Miller, Mary Jane. *Rewind and Search: Conversations with the Makers and Decision-Makers of CBC Television Drama*. Montreal and Kingston: McGill-Queen's University Press, 1996.

Moseley, Rachel. "The Teen Series." In *The Television Genre Book*, edited by Glen Creeber, 41–43. London: British Film Institute, 2002.

Nicks, Joan. "Degrassi." Available at www.museum.tv/archives/etv/D/htmlD/degrassi/ degrassi.htm. Accessed January 10, 2008.

———. *"Straight Up* and Youth Television: Navigating Dreams Without Nationhood." In *Slippery Pastimes: Reading the Popular in Canadian Culture*, edited by Joan Nicks and Jeanette Sloniowski, 141–57. Waterloo, ON: Wilfrid Laurier University Press, 2002.

Nicks, Joan and Jeannette Sloniowski, eds. *Slippery Pastimes: Reading the Popular in Canadian Culture*. Waterloo, ON: Wilfrid Laurier University Press, 2002.

Rixon, Paul. "The Changing Face of American Television Programmes on British Screens." In *Quality Popular Television*, edited by Mark Jancovich and James Lyons, 48–61. London: British Film Institute, 2003.

Rutherford, Paul. *When Television Was Young: Prime Time Canada, 1952–1967*. Toronto: University of Toronto Press, 2000.

Smith, Kevin. "High Times." *TV Guide*, January 29–February 4, 2005: 17–20.

Stohn, Stephen. Personal Interview. Toronto, May 28, 2002.

Tinic, Serra. *On Location: Canada's Television Industry in a Global Market*. Toronto: University of Toronto Press, 2005.

Wilcox, Rhona. "There Will Never Be a 'Very Special' *Buffy*": *Buffy* and the Monsters of Teen Life." *Slayage* 2, March 2001. At http://slayageonline.com/essays/ slayage2/wilcox.htm.

Williams, Betsy. ""North to the Future": *Northern Exposure* and Quality Television." In *Television: The Critical View*, 5th ed., edited by Horace Newcomb, 141–54. Oxford: Oxford University Press, 1994.

Wise, Penelope. "On the Air." *Canadian Forum* 17 (1952).

Filmography

Beverly Hills, 90210 (Spelling Television/Torand Productions, 1990–2000)

Buffy the Vampire Slayer (20th Century Fox Television/Mutant Enemy/Kuzui Enterprises/Sandollar Television, 1997–2003)

Dawson's Creek (1998–2004: Outerbank Entertainment/Columbia TriStar Television, 2001–2002; Granville/Procter & Gamble/Sony Pictures Television, 2002–03)

Degrassi Junior High (Playing With Time, 1987–89)

Degrassi High (Playing With Time, 1989–91)

Degrassi Talks (Playing With Time, 1992)
Degrassi: The Next Generation (Alliance Atlantis /CTV/Epitome Pictures, 2001–)
Ellen (Black-Marlens/Touchstone Television, 1994–98)
Northern Exposure (Universal TV/Cine-Nevada Productions, 1990–95)
The O.C. (Wonderland Sound and Vision/Warner Bros. Television/College Hill
    Pictures/Hypnotic (Season 1), 2003–)

MARY JANE MILLER

Haunting Public Discourse

The Representation of Residential
Schools in CBC Television Drama

I think this issue has ended up becoming a kind of flash point and a metaphor
for the relationship between the Indigenous peoples of this land and the recent
arrivals, Canadians of European descent.   —Rick Harp, APTN[1]

In the late 1980s and through the 1990s, residential schools and their
aftermath began to haunt our public discourse.[2] That this issue also
entered the imaginative world of Canadians was due in part to the
widely circulated and often repeated two-hour 1989 CBC Television movie,
Where the Spirit Lives. This was followed in 1992 to 1997 by the CBC series
North of 60, in which the specific language the Dene children learn in
school is the focus of an episode and the impact of residential schools on
the residents of Lynx River, NWT, is an ongoing issue for all of the Dene
characters.

Questions about the education of First Nations people outside of their
own traditions first became visible in Canadian television fiction much
earlier with the award-winning one-hour film *The Education of Phyllistine*
(1964) and the ninety-minute special *Sister Balonika* (1969), both written
by Paul St. Pierre and produced and directed by Philip Keately. To my
knowledge, however, when the CBC finally got down to producing television series, in the 1970s and most of the 1980s Canadian TV drama was
largely silent on the subject, although *For the Record*'s contemporary docudramas (1977–85) and other specials created a climate in which *Where
the Spirit Lives* could be broadcast in 1989.[3] I have already published a
paper on *Where the Spirit Lives*, so I use that drama primarily as context
in this article.[4]

Unlike the three drama specials, *North of 60* (1992–97) was a series
of ninety episodes. It could spend six television seasons exploring the

aftermath of residential schools in the lives of the Dene of Lynx River as a major motif. Many television and film documentaries, as well as theatre works, by First Nations people have also brought those horrors home. Statements in the early 1990s by public figures like playwright and novelist Tomson Highway and Phil Fontaine, grand chief (for the second time in 2005) of the Assembly of First Nations brought media coverage on television and radio and in newspapers.[5]

The scholarly work and even the first-hand accounts I have read, and the few conversations with leaders and elders I have had about residential schools, point to the complexities of the issue. They are not uniformly negative. J.R. Miller's lengthy study not only documents the abuses but also points to the failure of many schools to assimilate the students, to the fact that many children continued to speak their language at school without too many problems, that some parents demanded residential schools, and that some schools were not far from where the parents lived.[6] *Sister Balonika* and *North of 60* both present the complexities of the residential schools while, in the specific case of *North of 60*, not minimizing the long-lasting damage people continue to live with. The issues are usefully summarized in this advertisement for four days of workshops on "Healing the hurt and the shame" in the First Nations national monthly newspaper, *Windspeaker*, in April 2001: "loss of language and destruction of culture; mistrust of leadership and authority; lack of initiative and entrepreneurial spirit; personal rage, shame and dysfunction; political infighting and undermining; weak or broken bonds of love, trust and sharing; the physical and sexual abuse of children, women and other vulnerable people; dependency thinking; chronic addictions; inter-generational abuse; interpersonal violence; spiritual and cultural shame; suicide."

Broadcast Context and Overview

Just as the discourse on how and even whether to educate First Nations children in contemporary skills has changed from *Phyllistine* to *North of 60*, so too has the programming context. In the 1960s, *Phyllistine* and *Balonika* were presented as dramas on the commercial-free anthology *Festival*. *Festival* audiences had learned to expect everything from the French avant-garde dramatists to Ibsen, Pinter, Brecht, and Arthur Miller, as well as poetry, concerts, comedies, and opera. If they didn't like that week's presentation, they had a maximum of four or five channels to turn to—and in many areas of Canada, only one. The source of the one-hour film called *The Education of Phyllistine* was a two-part program on the intermittently broadcast, half-hour-long *Cariboo Country*, an anti-heroic contemporary anthology conceived in part as a Canadian response to the American TV Westerns dominating the air in the mid-1960s. These two episodes were knit together with three additional scenes for *Festival*.[7] *Phyllistine* won the Vancouver Film Festival award and the Canadian Film Award in 1964. The ninety-minute film *Sister Balonika* was specifically made for *Festival*.[8] *Festival*'s audience was eclectic, fairly well educated or self-educated, mostly middle-class, and in 1965 overwhelmingly white. They were also a little more willing to try new things than the average audience may have been.

Where the Spirit Lives was broadcast when cable had begun to fragment audiences. As a series, *North of 60* covered a period when satellite, increased cable coverage, the rise of the PC and video games, and the advent of DVD were creating ever-smaller audiences for most television drama— and yet its audiences averaged 1 to 1.2 million.[9] With its concentration on a small Dene settlement and its focus on Michelle Kenidi, the Dene RCMP constable, the series was planned just after the Oka Crisis and was also a response to a change in the Broadcasting Act in 1991, which states in sub-section 3(o) that the CBC specifically will provide "programming that reflects the aboriginal cultures of Canada ... as resources become available for that purpose." Note also that all of these programs were made by the CBC. Neither CTV nor Global, when it came along, would have made dramas like these in the 1960s, 1970s, or 1980s—in fact, CTV and Global did very little Canadian drama in the 1980s—and certainly would not have invested in a series set in a remote reserve featuring a mostly Dene cast of characters. Since the 1980s, ratings had become a major factor in decisions made at the CBC, but the corporation took a chance on it. *Where the Spirit Lives* and the *North of 60* series and its five movies were all dubbed into French and sold to other television networks worldwide—from the United Arab Emirates to Belgium and Finland. *North of 60* has been in continuous reruns since 2000. *Spirit* was broadcast on PBS in the United States and used by teachers in Ontario schools.

The Education of Phyllistine centres on Phyllistine, a desperately poor child roughly ten years old who lives with Ol' Antoine.[10] The school in Namko is short one student and may close, so Phyllistine is asked to be the tenth. In this film, a prologue to and context for the issues of residential schools, integration without any understanding of Indigenous people's values is shown not to work. This film, *How to Break a Quarterhorse*, and *Sister Balonika*, as well as several episodes in the *Cariboo Country* anthology, pointed to issues of segregation in our own country, where some young people were volunteering in Mississippi Freedom Marches and the rest, along with their parents and grandparents, were being self-righteous about the Canadian record on racism. *Cariboo Country* was a subversive reminder of, or even a corrective to that self-satisfied view. *Phyllistine* added three additional scenes to the two original parts, according to the *CBC Times* for February 13, 1965, and this is the version that survives in the National Archives and was rebroadcast in the CBC retrospective *Rearview Mirror* in the mid-1980s.

Sister Balonika, a ninety-minute special also made for *Festival*, in 1969, seems to offer progress. Although First Nations children from all over the NWT are shovelled into a new residential school staffed by nuns with minimal resources, Sister Balonika is a nun from a Cowichan First Nation who immediately finds a rapport with the children, even though she does not speak their languages. The culture clashes between the nuns and the children are sketched with a deft hand and sometimes comic tone, but the film ends in tragedy. When Balonika fails to keep matches out of the hands of a boy with brain damage, the school burns down, lives are lost, and Balonika has a mental breakdown.

Both programs were filmed on location in black and white. Both evoke the beauty and harshness of the landscapes and the weather. Both used elements of documentary style, including hand-held cameras, deceptively artless composition, no exegetic music, and many non-professional actors. Ironically, some of the children who appeared in *Balonika* came from residential schools. *Where the Spirit Lives* and *North of 60* were made in colour, had high production values, and were also structured by the ads contained in almost all CBC television drama since the early 1980s. *North of 60* was shot in Alberta using permanent sets, with good production values and variable but often imaginative direction, and had the support of interactive websites, good publicity campaigns, and a reasonable amount of attention from newspaper and periodical critics.[11] According to Philip Keately, *Cariboo* and *The Education of Phylllistine* had the informal advice of Chief Dan George and other First Nations actors he used. *Sister Balonika* depended on the experiences of writer Paul St. Pierre, who had spent a lot of time in the Chilcotin. Issues of cultural appropriation dogged *Where the Spirit Lives*. *North of 60* had Dene consultants for every episode and the five movies that followed the series. It also has a sophisticated, many layered, and reliable fan site designed and maintained by Patty Winter, an American working in California.[12]

North of 60 showed the relationships among the members of the Lynx River band: the protagonist Michelle, an RCMP constable; her brother Peter, the band chief; their complex antagonist, Albert Golo, a bootlegger and occasionally band chief; elders Elsie and Joe; Teevee, the punk kid who grows up on the show into band chief; Sarah, the white nurse who has two Dene children by Albert; Albert's son; and, in succession, Michelle's two white and one "urban Indian" RCMP partners. The series (1992–97) and the (unprecedented in Canada) five two-hour *North of 60 Mysteries* (1999–2005) look at many issues in Lynx River: alcoholism; resource management of oil, diamonds, and hydro; anti-fur lobbies; the traditional Dene ways in conflict with new choices and inevitable changes; lack of housing; bored and unemployed youth; racism in urban media and urban policing; and, as a running thread, the adults' struggle to overcome the inheritance of residential schooling. Unlike television drama specials and made-for-TV movies, series television is able to look at an issue from many angles over months and years. *North of 60* was the first series to focus on First Nations people and was widely envied in other Aboriginal communities, particularly in the United States.

All the programs I am considering use major white characters as bridging figures to draw the viewer into the difficult subject matter—rancher Ken Larsen in *Phyllistine*, Sister Superior in *Sister Balonika*, Kathleen Gwillimbury in *Where the Spirit Lives*, and arguably, in *North of 60's* first year, at least Eric, the handsome white cop, and Sarah, the nurse. *The Education of Phyllistine* is framed by Larsen's narration. He is a successful white rancher who never figures out the subtext of the story he tells. As Larsen drives up in his old truck in the first scene, the viewer hears his voice-over, with an opening line rich in irony: "If it wasn't for me, Phyllistine wouldn't have got an education and neither would anyone else in Namko."[13] His speculations about Phyllistine's motivations and her character, and even about her protector, Ol' Antoine, a Chilcotin he has known for years, are mostly wrong, as the audience, with more information and fewer preconceptions, soon learns. The viewer also has to do more work, becoming aware of the nuances, the subtext that fills the pauses, the silences left for the viewer to fill in. In *Sister Balonika*, the older and tired Sister Superior is not really a sympathetic figure—"Our hope is in organization"—as the rigid antagonist to Sister Veronica/Balonika, a Cowichan who is young, lively, and sings and plays her guitar with the children. In *Where the Spirit Lives*, Kathleen, who is also new to the residential school life, is Komi's one sympathetic teacher. Yet she eventually betrays her by agreeing to Reverend Buckley's lie that Komi's parents are dead and then helping with an adoption plan for Komi—who belongs to the Kainai, of the Blood, or Blackfoot, Nation—that would leave her younger brother still trapped in the school. In *North of 60*, many characters provide various takes on the clash of white and Dene culture: handsome but sensitive

Eric Olssen, Michelle's first white RCMP partner (for two seasons); her second partner, the antagonistic and brutal Brian Fletcher (for two and a half seasons); and, for the full run, opportunistic band manager Harris and cynical, often hostile store owner Gerry. Most important is Sarah Birkett, the nurse whose privileged background contrasts sharply with Michelle's but who at one point ends up homeless and pregnant. All of them are wounded in some way, and all of them heal in Lynx River. Harris marries Lois Tenia and settles down. Gerry has a platonic love affair with Rosie Deela and mellows slightly. Sarah finds a partner from the oil field. But it is Michelle's decisions, the way she leads her life as a recovering alcoholic and survivor of the worst physical abuse, as well as the lovelessness of her residential school and her hard-won eradication of the lessons of self-hatred ground into her for many years, which put her at times in the role of the healer and exemplar to Eric and sometimes to her friend Sarah.

The focus of the residential school narrative has changed over the four decades. In the programming under discussion, the values of the First Nations (Chilcotin, Cowichan, Kainai, and Dene) directly clash with the expectations of the teachers or overwhelm them, even when a character is Aboriginal. In none of the programs do the teachers really understand the children or, in the case of *North of 60*, the adults they become. In *Phyllistine*, the adults are usually in the foreground with Phyllistine the silent observer who acts at key moments. In *Balonika*, the children share the screen with Sister Balonika. The child and then young woman Komi takes over in *Where the Spirit Lives*. Finally, the adults enduring the aftermath of residential schools are the primary focus of *North of 60*.

The Education of Phyllistine

Phyllistine enters the story when Larsen, told to ask her by Ol' Antoine—whose relationship to her is never explained but who looks after her—reluctantly enters the sparsely furnished cabin and asks whether she wants to go and live with him and go to school. The camera takes her point of view as he continues in Chinook Jargon, a language used only for trade. When he says "one year" in English, she understands and nods. "You've been in school some, I guess. Very long?" She says no. What is "long" to her and to him? We find out later she has been in school for several years. "You want to go to school?" No response. "What do you say, old dry-as-dust?" to Ol' Antoine, who looks at her and says nothing. When Larsen asks if she will pack her stuff and go with him, Phyllistine nods without a word. In this culture, it is her decision. Meanwhile, Ol' Antoine, looking away, says with a touch of bitterness, "She's got all her stuff," referring to the clothes she is wearing.

As they head for his truck, Larsen explains wryly to Phyllistine that her last name will now be Larsen for a while: "That will get tongues wagging in the Namko country." He gives her a little money and an old school reader with a picture of King George V, which dates it. Politely, she thanks him. In voice-over, Larsen says: "She was sure quiet, even for an Indian kid. I don't even remember how we got rid of her back to Ol' Antoine. That's how quiet she was." During school, the well-meant but ineffectual attempts of Miss Melcher, who is in her first year as a teacher, to communicate with Phyllistine while "normal" activities continue are intercut with several shots of the opaque but alert face of Phyllistine, whose mind and feelings are as closed to the viewer as they are to the rancher and the teacher.

Then the school inspector discovers that she has read the old reader, which is much more difficult than *Fun with Dick and Jane*. He asks which pieces in it she likes. "All, I guess," she replies. He prompts her, "What about the Assyrians?" and then he begins Byron's galloping lines, "The Assyrians came down like wolves on the fold and ... " Phyllistine picks up, " And his cohorts were gleaming in purple and gold." "Very good," he says. He prompts her again with a fragment of Macaulay's " Lays of Ancient Rome"—better known as "Horatius at the Bridge"—"Lars Porsena of Clusium ... " She stumbles on "Tarquin," but gets to "By the nine gods he swore ... " In answer to his questions, she also knows quite well what the Tiber is. Together, the inspector and Phyllistine tell the rest of the class the whole heroic tale. He finishes, "Do you remember what he said?" Phyllistine replies without inflection, "And how can man die better / Than facing fearful odds / For the ashes of his fathers / And the temples of his gods?" The poem is a relic from the height of Victorian imperialism. Yet it somehow seems apt in the mouth of a child whose people have lost much of what they had. The inspector finishes the sequence with, "Ah, Phyllistine, you and I are lucky, we still believe in heroes." When he asks the teacher about Phyllistine, she says she is "a perfectly well behaved child, just a little ... " Inspector: "Passive?" "Yes, passive." The inspector tells the teacher to put Phyllistine into grade five because it is "better to fail grade five than grade one," but not to make her participate. He then points out that "it's tragic to be an Indian child with only white heroes." (Post-colonialism had not been invented yet). Miss Melcher [earnestly]: "Why is it tragic to be an Indian?" His oblique response suggests that he holds out little hope for her ability to teach Phyllistine: "Young lady, I am three years from retirement and Ken Larsen is about to take me down to the river to cast for steelhead. Do you understand that? Go see Dick, go see Jane, go see the school inspector catch the big steelhead fish."

Now that the inspector has reported ten students, Larsen's task is done, but Miss Melcher continues to try. She relentlessly pursues Ol' Antoine, who has taken Phyllistine out of school for the autumn fishing. The teacher is oblivious to the value of what the girl can learn from the old man, but she also asks him to talk to the class about his people's "legends." Eventually, Phyllistine composes and reads a story about a deer, a story of loss and hope that neither adult understands. Other incidents show that Miss Melcher has no idea of the poverty on the reserve.

In the film's climax, Ol' Antoine comes late to the Hallowe'en party with Phyllistine, her hair neatly braided, wearing a dress for the first time. Beaming, Miss Melcher announces to the children and the trustees that "it is a great honour to present a certificate to the most promising student," and she asks Phyllistine to come forward. Phyllistine looks at Ol' Antoine. He nods, so reluctantly she walks up the aisle from the back. Clearly, being singled out in this fashion goes against her own sense of what is appropriate. Then Larsen's daughter, Margaret, says loudly, though without particular malice, "That's my old dress. My mum gave it to her." The two girls look at one another. Margaret is ashamed and looks down. Phyllistine walks back down the aisle and out the door as the parents and kids watch. With one look at the teacher, Ol' Antoine also leaves.

Miss Melcher and Larsen walk out onto the schoolhouse steps. When Ol' Antoine reaches Phyllistine, her eyes and face are shut. He touches her shoulder and the two of them fill the frame. Phyllistine's final words to him are devastating: "Leave me alone. You nothing but a dirty Siwash, same like me."[14] His hand drops. In long shot, she walks out of the frame. As the camera follows Phyllistine down the road, the viewer hears hear Larsen's last lines as a voice-over to the shot of her retreating back: "She never came back, of course, but then who would have thought she would hang tough as long as she did? Poor Phyllistine. I felt kinda bad about the whole business."[15]

The title of the film asks the viewer to think about just what Phyllistine did learn. From Ol' Antoine, she learned fishing skills, traditional stories, patience, and independence. Following the traditions of her people, she was allowed to make her own decisions. She learned both British and American colonialism and sexism from her reading texts, racism from the other students, alienation from the uncomprehending teacher, and self-hatred from the school and the society it represented. The story and characters are fictional but prescient. The dilemma of how to "educate" First Nations children is one that starts to appear on the horizon of the dominant society a few years later. Jean Chrétien's 1969 white paper promoted the abolition of the "separate legal status of Indians" and thus, many First Nations people and others felt, full assimilation.[16] It failed. Residential schools, which still emphasized assimilation and were run by the government and the churches, continued for many years. It should be noted that Inuit children in small remote settlements such as Bathurst Inlet continue to go to school more than a hundred miles away in Cambridge Bay. It should also be noted that the attempt to integrate First Nations children into existing, largely white schools too often creates the same problems experienced by Phyllistine.

Sister Balonika

Sister Balonika presented for the first time to a Canadian television audience how a residential school functioned. The *CBC Times* for March 22–28, 1969, reports that the film is based on two real events, a tragic school fire and a conversation Paul St. Pierre had with "an Indian nun of a French Canadian order." It is also contemporary, and thus set in a transitional time when some schools in the Yukon were being integrated and a few were being built closer to the small communities of what are "probably Carrier and Northern Cree." Note that those peoples are not named in the film itself, nor is their language, Loucheux. The *CBC Times* also notes in its preview that Sister Balonika "questions *everything*. And although she has an enormous pride in her heritage, she will not allow herself to be trapped within the disciplines of being either a nun or an Indian." It identifies her as Cowichan and calls her "a free spirit, fiercely proud of her Indian blood." The phrase "free spirit," also used in the promotional materials and reviews, comes from the 1960s and connotes both admiration and distrust. It should be remembered that the film is made when "do your own thing" was a watchword among the young. In May 1969, *Performing Arts in Canada*, based in part on this article in the *CBC Times*, reviewed the drama, which "covers a subject which, while not exclusively Canadian, nevertheless does, at the moment, present a very acute Canadian problem."[17] The qualifications in that sentence suggest how uncomfortable the unnamed reviewer was. "How the [nuns'] ... different personalities doing all the hard manual as well as spiritual labour at the school, work together to achieve the goal of guiding, teaching and disciplining these lovable bush children without head-on, destructive clashes is told in this powerful, topical play whose action takes place in the incredible isolation and chill of the north, but generates a warmth of togetherness which can only be found when all work unselfishly for the common good." A CBC press release on

Figure 1. Sister Balonika and Telegraph Jim go fishing. Production photograph from *Sister Balonika*, with thanks to the CBC.

April 15, 1969, reported an audience for *Balonika* of 1.7 million—the biggest audience for a ninety-minute *Festival* production since 1964. It had an "Enjoyment Index" of 83, topping the very popular series *Wojeck*, and was seen as a high note on which to end the long run of the prestigious *Festival*. Unlike most ephemeral television drama, this script was also published in 1973 as a study text for schools—doubling the ironies in the drama itself, since it would have been studied in schools far removed from the conditions the residential school represented. The book came out in the early 1970s, when a few texts that reflected not only theatre but also radio, television, and cinema were appearing in classrooms.

The first line of dialogue belongs to school bus driver and handyman Forty Horse Johnson: "Okay you kids, we're all going to the new jail today. All out, eh. All out."[18] The bureaucracies that run the school have not noticed that there are no playgrounds, no handyman to fix things, no money for new clothes for the children, many of whom have nothing, and little for good food—and that the nuns have no more than the children and also have to work sixteen-hour days. However, atypically for a residential school at that time, there is no corporal punishment and no rule that the children must use English only, even though the Sister Superior, Sister Grace, and even Sister Balonika cannot speak their languages. Brothers and sisters are not parted. The children speak "Indian" among themselves, and an English dialect similar to the one St. Pierre had established in *Cariboo Country*.

Unlike *The Education of Phyllistine*, *Sister Balonika* shows children successfully resisting acculturation. For her First Communion, Telegraph Jim—Nancy Sandy, who had also played Phyllistine—insists on wearing a beautiful porcupine headband, as well as the little white crown of starched veil each girl has made for herself. Sister Superior makes an issue of it— "It looks like something in a moving picture"—completely misidentifying something precious worn to honour a special occasion with a Hollywood costume cliché. However, the much more experienced bishop asks: "Porcupine or bird quill? ... Beautiful work ... Perfect work ... Daughter of *the* Telegraph Jim? ... Two Telegraph Jims. I thought one was all the territory could stand." She is the daughter of a famous trapper who happens to be in jail, which is why she is in school. In contrast to Phyllistine's experience, over the months this confident child, Telegraph Jim, has not essentially changed in any way but manages instead to combine in some fashion what she has learned in both cultures, an intrinsically hopeful statement.

But there are two serious structural flaws in the film. One is that, only four scenes before the end, the audience is presented with Balonika's inexplicable and sudden mental collapse when, through her carelessness with matches, Sitkum, a brain-damaged child, sets the school on fire. As badly burned children emerge, Sister Superior leads a dangerous rescue of the four children still inside, then tends to the rest. Balonika, who has just been fishing with Telegraph Jim, slowly approaches the burning school in complete denial. "The school isn't burning. There's nothing wrong." Balonika, who has been the source of joy in the children's lives with her guitar and her playful support, cannot cope. Given the context of *Cariboo Country*, *Phyllistine*, and another *Festival* special, *How to Break a Quarterhorse*, I do not think this is intentionally racist in any way. Nevertheless, her failure comes out of nowhere. As a well-prepared and therefore effective plot twist, Sister Superior's gifts of organization and narrow focus are shown to support her actions in the crisis. Sister Superior rolls in mud puddles before she enters the flaming school. She is the one who knows that there are thirty-six cans of condensed milk in the grocery order to use for burns. To Balonika, who is mechanically administering mouth-to-mouth resuscitation and refuses to stop, she says sharply: "'That one is dead. Dead, you idiot. We haven't any time for the dead. Come over and help the ones who are burned' ... *Sister Balonika does not move. She remains, kneeling, hands in her lap, beside the body of Annabelle Joe.*" In contrast, Balonika's instantaneous breakdown is ill prepared and not in keeping with the resilient, energetic, gifted, and sometimes wiser character presented to this point, and it comes across as improbable. Months later, back in the mother house, the Mother Provincial orders Sister Balonika to return to the school. Guilt about her carelessness in not securing the matches, her inability to help Sister Superior in the crisis, and above all the deaths of the children have paralyzed her emotionally and spiritually. When she says, "I have not refused to go," Mother Provincial replies: "'Provided you could retain your role as Our Lady of Sorrows ... You make me sacrilegious. You irritate me beyond countenance. Do you think you are the only woman in the world who has experienced guilt?' *No answer.* ' ... Under your vow of obedience ... At Donjek Ridge School, Sister Veronica, you will laugh. And you will sing. And you will be merry, Sister Veronica.'" Sister Balonika: "I will try." Provincial: "*spacing every word*, 'You ... will ... obey.'"

The last scene, which is clearly intended to show Balonika beginning to find a way to reintegrate into the life of the school, is also problematic. She arrives late to the confirmation service and slips into the back of the church. Sitkum, who has been sedated, recognizes her and welcomes her with a fragment of the song Balonika has taught the children: "Michael Row the boat ashore. Hallelujah."[19] As the service drones on, Telegraph Jim, clearly bored, starts the first line of the first verse of the song: "The Chorten Rifer is wite and coe [the Jordan River is wide and cold]. Hallelooya !" Gathering Sitkum and then the others in the song, to the amusement of the bishop, she continues, "It chills the boty but it warms the soul." After the children sing another chorus "in full voice," he asks Sister Balonika to come up as they do a second verse. "*Sister Balonika comes and stands before them. She does not sing but she stands with her hands forward, down and open toward them. A smile is on her face*," as they sing the verse about an ancient symbol of death and rebirth: "Did you hear what old Jonah said ... When they thought he was dead ... I was takin' me a ride ... in that big old whale's inside." Telegraph Jim, using Balonika's words, exhorts them to "Use your lips and your tongues. Don't sing like Intians and Englishmen."[20]

St. Pierre indicates that the young actors must convey that the children are not necessarily singing for Sister Balonika: "*Each one is singing for his own personal enjoyment, hearing his own voice among the multi-tude.*" Each one, given a voice by Balonika, is supposed to be reasserting his or her individuality within the context of a residential school, but that is not a stage direction even a mature actor can carry out. It was certainly not evident to me when I repeatedly viewed the film. Meanwhile, only Sister Superior notices and is anguished by the fact that Sitkum has reverted to his catatonic state, alone, twitching. The stage directions direct that she say the following line *"under the burden of the long, hard and unreward-ing years,* 'Sitkum. Oh Sitkum dear.'" Then Balonika, *"motherlike folds her arms around him. The children still pay no heed for they are singing. Sitkum roughly elbows his way out of the nun's arms. She lets him go. He walks to the wall of the chapel and stands there, the world's loneliest child. His face is pressed in a corner, his arms are behind his head. FADE TO BLACK ON SISTER BALONIKA'S FACE. She is kneeling. Her hands are in her lap. She is looking at Sitkum. Against closing titles we hear, but do not see, Telegraph Jim singing alone. Without resonance because no walls sur-round it ... rendered not for an audience* [which includes the viewers] *but rendered only for the satisfaction of the singer herself,* 'We are marching on / En singing as we ko / To the promis' lan' / Where the living waters flow ... '"

While admitting that some problems are irremediable, it is made clear that the fact that the children's individuality has not been crushed or com-promised is also intended to be the salvation of Sister Balonika. In turn, she will still bring added warmth to the school. Eventually, she will even be able to live with her guilt. But the question is, how credible is that transformation? Sitkum's inability to ever be part of the community grounds the drama in a more universal reality of our collective inability to heal some wounds, including Balonika's. But since her earlier failure was not prepared for, her reintegration into the school loses its force, with the unintentional result that stereotype is reinforced: the white nun saves what can be saved from the "Indian" nun's carelessness and subsequent paral-ysis.[21] The drama has failed to create a multidimensional yet coherent protagonist, leaving the film a series of vignettes about a residential school that has had many of the rough edges removed.

Where the Spirit Lives

Where the Spirit Lives, broadcast in 1989 and still available in video stores, was a bridge, on the subject of residential schools, between *Sister Balonika* in 1960 and *North of 60* in 1992. Mary Young Leckie, one of the pro-ducers of *Where the Spirit Lives* and wife of its writer, said: "We did not set out to tell the story from a Native perspective. The film signifies white

people asking for forgiveness."[22] Although the issues raised by generations of children affected by residential schools is rendered more palatable
by setting the film in the 1930s, a printed coda tells the audience, who are
feeling good that Komi and her little brother have escaped, that the last
school was closed in 1988—a salutary shock that closes the gap. The fact
is that, according to a government site, "Most residential schools ceased
to operate by the mid-1970s but the last federally-run residential school
in Canada closed in 1996."[23]

Four representative children provide different clues of what the impact
of residential schools on their adult lives will be. Rachel, Komi's gentle
friend, is sexually abused by the matron and dies running away—she has
no future. Esther, a monitor who had mocked Komi (renamed Amelia) as
a "bush Indian" but came to respect her rebellion, cannot run away with
Komi on her second, successful escape attempt because she is too accul-
turated. "This has always been my home. I'm too scared." Yet she will
likely find that she belongs in neither world when she leaves. George, an
older boy who has shared dreams about "Hawaii" with Komi as he taught
her to read a map, finally rises in his wrath and beats up the sadistic master who is about to thrash her little brother. Our last sight of him is in
handcuffs waiting for the RCMP to take him away. In his case, as in so many
others, the burning anger felt by some residential school survivors, when
it has no outlet and is often fuelled by alcohol, lands him in jail again and
may even be visited on family members. But the viewer is left to extrap-
olate the future of Esther and George. Komi's future is not what the Reverend Buckley, who recognizes her potential for leadership, says it will
be—a "descent back into the mud" as a sexual plaything. Komi finds the
strength to flee with her little brother only because she knows her family
is alive and because, as even Buckley recognizes, she is a natural leader
with the capacity to plan and the determination to carry out her plan. She
is not an average child. In fact, she could be the ancestor of Michelle
Kenedi, the protagonist of *North of 60*.

North of 60

North of 60 is a unique series in many ways. One is that it shows residential schools' aftermath for adults. Early in the series, in Episode 12, "Sisters of Mercy," by Rebecca Schechter—who won a Gemini for it—Michelle
is confronted by Sister Simone, the headmistress who beat her, cut off her
hair, humiliated her, and made her say in front of the other children, "My
father's a drunk, my mother's a whore." Yet she barely remembers Michelle.
The same sister, who taught English, had encouraged Michelle's brother

Peter, the band chief with an MBA, to excel academically and was his "all-time favourite teacher" who encouraged him to be the best he could be. As is often the case, Michelle has told nobody of what happened to her—not even Peter. They struggle over an essay that Hannah, Michelle's daughter, is writing for an NWT contest. In a one-on-one session with Hannah, Sister Simone contradicts what Michelle had told her, that traditional hunting had not changed for thousands of years. Sister Simone points out that the Dene had no iron, knives, or scrapers and lived in the Stone Age. "You even got words from us. *Maasi* [the word for thank you] comes from the French," with the strong inference that the idea of thanks is foreign to the Dene. Later, Michelle tells Hannah firmly that *maasi* sounds the same but does not come from the French and that real history comes not from books but from the stories their ancestors have passed on.[24] Reality in this fiction is embedded in oral history, as it is for all First Nations peoples, a reality acknowledged in several recent court decisions.

When Hannah withdraws from the contest, Sister Simone barges in on Michelle at home. She tells her bluntly that she won't let her daughter enter, "because what you made her write is garbage." After Hannah hears them exchange words, then give her contradictory instructions, she runs from the room. Sister Simone says, "You still have to turn everything into a fight. Even at your daughter's expense!" and slams the door as she leaves.

At this point, the dramatic conflict still looks like a battle of cultural narratives centred on a teacher who suited one child and not his sister. When Peter, ever the diplomat, tries to explain Michelle's anger to Sister Simone, and when Hannah hands in her newest version of her essay without her mother's knowledge, Michelle is further isolated from her family. Schechter has disarmed the majority of her audience, who in 1992 might have been been more unaware of the complexity of the issues raised by residential school than they are now. She encourages the viewers to rationalize along with Peter and the rest of the community, who simply want to forget, drawing them further into the issue itself. But when Peter, angry about Hannah being forbidden to enter her essay, returns with Sister Simone, reality hits home. Michelle, in a tightly controlled voice, says to her, "Tell him about the bath of ice cubes." Reaction shot of Peter, appalled. With a small smile, Sister Simone replies: "I honestly don't remember. I had hundreds of girls ... some just as difficult as you." Unknown to Sister Simone, Hannah is listening as Michelle, in a strained but clear voice, replies: "Tell him how you herded us into the gym in the middle of the night. Tell him how you made me say, 'My father is a drunk, my mother is a whore, God is the only one who loves me,' over and over in front of everyone." Sister Simone, quietly and with conviction: "What did you want? To stay in the Stone Age? We had to break your connection with the past. I knew who you were and what you were ... I only wanted the best for you." As she turns to leave, she turns back and says, "When the time comes I can answer for it," reminding the viewers once again of her religious vocation. The next day, as mother and daughter watch her leaving town, Hannah remains puzzled that her mother is not rejoicing. Hannah: "She's gone, Mom. Isn't that what you wanted?" Michelle: "I wanted her to say she was sorry." This was some years before the churches and the parishes were sued, long before the federal government acknowledged that there was a problem to be addressed, and long before some of the churches apologized.

Michelle is a survivor who has made an orderly life for herself in the RCMP, but only after a struggle with alcohol. Peter has been truly "educated" at St. Anne's in useful academic skills that allow him to go to university. Like Tomson Highway and Phil Fontaine, the fictional Peter has gone on without apparent difficulty to acquire real qualifications for life with the band or in the wider world. Unlike others, he was not sexually abused. *North of 60* does not get into that territory. Even this remarkably truthful series does not show the range of abuse perpetrated and the failure to educate in even a rudimentary way at some, though not all, residential schools. The reality was that residential schools very often "graduated" students with grade three or four skill levels. Often, students were trained in manual labour and housekeeping and were expected to work half-days maintaining the buildings and growing food for themselves and the teachers to eat.

This episode launches one of the major themes in *North of 60*, the ongoing impact of residential schools on people's lives and on whole communities. Lynx River has had so much trouble with alcoholism that it has declared itself a dry town. Wedding celebrations are toasted in grape juice. There are many other passing references to the aftermath as the series progresses, including Peter's workaholic tendencies, which cost him his wife and child; his desire to prove himself over and over and to compensate somehow for the fact that he could not protect Michelle as a child; Michelle's selective memories; her shame that her parents were "bush Indians"; and her troubled relationship with Hannah, which, though resolved, demonstrates the effect of lack of parenting in her own childhood. In Lynx River, many kids have grown up without fathers.[25]

Residential school is also the focus in other episodes. In Episode 42, "Ties That Bind," by Thomas King, of Greek and Cherokee heritage, Peter is trying to decide whether to leave Lynx River for a powerful job in

Ottawa when a small boy appears, seen by two elders and Peter but no one else. Peter frantically tries to find him. At last he catches up with him and embraces him—it is his terrified ten-year-old self about to be hauled off to residential school. Peter decides to stay in Lynx River. In the less successful companion episode (83), "Peter and the Wolf," by Drew Birch, when Peter is deciding to run for the legislature of the NWT, he has a confusing set of supernatural encounters. The episode finally becomes coherent when his dead father and mother talk with him about his estrangement and his feelings of shame about them. When he says he should have come home for his mother's funeral, his father nods yes and his mother hugs him. His father then tells him: "You were forced to live in two worlds. You were torn in two, a wound that will never heal ... Perhaps the next generation, the grandchildren ... " He does not finish the sentence, but the implication is that Peter has responsibility for that next generation. Yet he will always be in pain. The dialogue is also a little too expository, but at least there are no easy words about healing.

My last example is in *Distant Drumming* (2005) the latest, perhaps last *North of 60 Mystery*, where an ex-priest visits Lynx River seeking forgiveness from Daniel Deela for what he had done to him in a residential school years before. The priest's past comes out after he is murdered when Michelle and a younger colleague, Marjorie, an ex-Mountie who is promoting tribal policing, visit Daniel in search of the murderer. In flashback, Daniel, who is a successful father, guide, and hunter, tells them that the priest shook and often beat the children and in an act of sadism violently destroyed his carefully hidden drum, a gift from his father and his only link with home. Flash-forward in Daniel's account to his angry refusal to forgive the priest anything and the priest's stumbling exit into the bush, where he is murdered by another Native man, a stranger to Lynx River. Later, Marjorie says to Michelle, who is putting flowers on Hannah's grave, that both her generation, who escaped residential schools, and Michelle's, who endured them, "blame ourselves for everything," and that her generation needs to remember the bad memories of those older than themselves, as well as the good. The Dene cultural advisors on the first-season episode "Sisters of Mercy" were Nick Sibbeston, Eleanor Bran, and Leo Norwegian. Thirteen years later, Eleanor Bran was also the cultural advisor on *Distant Drumming*. The movie shows that Daniel, like Michelle, Peter, Komi, Telegraph Jim, and perhaps even Phyllistine, can survive to become adults who keep some of their heritage intact—but that the bitterness does not vanish and the ground-in self-hatred is an enemy that is never fully defeated.

Some, though not all, of the adult survivors in this television series, as in real life, make new lives for themselves. But the teachers, who represented the will of the dominant society that all "Indians" assimilate, are also shown as going on obliviously or asking for a too easy forgiveness. For those who were locked into residential schools, justice is elusive, restoration problematic. As widely reported in the papers and on the CBC, in 2005 the government of Canada continued to spend tens of millions of dollars over several years on a bureaucracy that was intended to "fast track" claims of survivors of residential schools while paying out almost nothing to those people, many of whom are old, ill, and poor. However, the process was relaunched in May 30, 2005, with the appointment of a special mediator, a retired Supreme Court judge. Phil Fontaine's response, as a survivor and leader, was reported as follows: "The day's agreement marks a 'turning point' in relations with Ottawa. 'We are turning the corner on the tragedy of residential schools,' Fontaine said, dedicating the day not only to survivors, but also those who have already died. 'The emphasis is on fair and just compensation,' he added, 'but most importantly on healing and reconciliation.'" An agreement in principal was signed on November 20, 2005, and announced on November 23, one day before a major conference of the Assembly of First Nations, the premiers of all the provinces and territories, and the prime minister.[26] A genuine settlement was finally reached and received court approval on March 21, 2007. After an opt-out period, it began to be implemented on September 19, 2007.

The damage done can only be acknowledged and compensated by the dominant society. But, ironically, it cannot be undone by those who created the schools. Rather, it must be undone by the victims themselves, as *Where the Spirit Lives* and *North of 60* show. These CBC programs, broadcast from 1964 to 2005, which addressed this painful issue in carefully researched detail, may have helped in a small way to change the minds and even the hearts of viewers. Working not with documentary but rather with the emotional power of fiction, they tried to educate the viewers about the complexities of some of the issues raised by residential schools. Through television drama, as well as many other means, self-respect in First Nations, Métis, and Inuit peoples may thus be reinforced by a growing respect from the rest of us.

Notes

1 Reported in Patten, "Programs on Residential Schools." Simply made and very affecting, the two-part "Residential Schools: Moving beyond Survival" was made by Newsworld, APTN, and VisionTV, all of which showed them within an eight-day period in primetime. All three had a panel with an open forum, and APTN and Vision followed the programs with call-in shows. APTN also provided contact numbers for viewers.

2 "The Government of Canada operated nearly every school as a 'joint venture' with various religious organizations. On April 1st, 1969, the Government assumed total responsibility for the school system, although churches remained involved for some years in many instances" (www.irsr-rqpi.gc.ca/english/history.html, accessed June 21, 2005). The home page, www.irsr-rqpi.gc.ca/english, begins, "The web site deals with subject matter that may cause some readers to trigger (suffer trauma caused by remembering or reliving past abuse). The Government of Canada recognizes the need for safety measures to minimize the risk associated with triggering." Another section, at www.irsr-rqpi.gc.ca/english/statistics.html, reports, "It is estimated there are 86,000 people alive today who attended Indian residential schools."

3 Producers Heather Golden, Eric Jordan, Mary Young Leckie; executive producer Paul Stevens; director Bruce Pittman; writer Keith Ross Leckie. Made "with the co-operation of the Spirit Lake Band."

4 Miller, "Where the Spirit Lives."

5 The website http://archives.cbc.ca/IDC-1-70-692-4006/disasters_tragedies/residential_schools/clip4 (accessed October 18, 2007) provides a clip of Fontaine first making the charges on the CBC's national news on Oct 30, 1990, one of a set of radio and television clips in the online CBC Archives on the subject. No longer available, www.presbyterian.ca/assemblyoffice/council/IRSAgreementAnnouncement.html presented the agreement of one denomination that ran two schools. Other denominations and Catholic and Anglican dioceses face much bigger settlements and a few dioceses have gone bankrupt. See also www.anglican.ca/Residental-Schools/resources/primer.htm (accessed October 18, 2007).

6 J.R. Miller's *Shingwauk's Vision*, the most comprehensive scholarly work on the subject to date.

7 Miller, *Turn Up the Contrast*, 68–90.

8 The 2001 Vancouver International Film Festival provides notes for two screenings of the film at www.viff.org/viff/a_press (accessed October 23, 2007). The short story version, written after the television drama, appears in *Smith and Other Events: Tales of the Chilcotin*, by Paul St. Pierre. St. Pierre said that the drama was grounded in fact.

9 CBC's *Beachcombers* (1972–90), which was an important precursor to *North of 60*, had been one of the first series in the world—and it was seen around the world—to feature an Aboriginal character, Nick's employee and then partner Jesse Jim, a Coast Salish who grew up and got married on the show.

10 Played by Chief Dan George, who got his first acting job as the recurring character in *Cariboo Country*.

11 See five chapters of background on and analysis of the series in Miller, *Outside Looking In*.

12 A version of my analysis of the third *North of 60* movie special, *Dreamstorm*, is posted at www.wintertime.com/OH/nof60.html (accessed October 23, 2007).

13 All quotations here and elsewhere, unless noted, come from notes taken on viewing the films before or after they were catalogued at the National Archives or from my off-air study tapes.

14 "The Chinook Jargon word for 'Indian.' ... At present it is generally considered to be offensive," according to theYinka Dene Language Institute website, www.ydli.org/langs/siwash.htm (accessed October 18, 2007). See also www.billcasselman.com/cwod_archive/siwash_updated.htm (accessed October 18, 2007), where its current racist use is documented in pictures and text.

15 Keately and St. Pierre decided against a different voice-over narration on the shot that painted a bleak future for Phyllistine. See Miller, *Rewind and Search*, 102. More details about the making of *Sister Balonika* and *Cariboo Country* are to be found there as well.

16 At http://archives.cbc.ca/IDC-1–73–1062–5914/politics_economy/jean_chretien/clip3 (accessed October 18, 2007). And www.turtleisland.org/discussion/viewtopic .php?t=535 (accessed October 23, 2007) demonstrates that the white paper is still a subject for discussion.

17 *Performing Arts in Canada* 6 (2) (May 1969).

18 St. Pierre, *Sister Balonika* (production notes), 8. This text also has useful stills from the film. St. Pierre, with a characteristic shot of wry, dedicates it to "those who can distinguish between people and causes." The book is not a copy of the script used by the producer/director for shooting the film—the stage directions are as full as those of George Bernard Shaw's published plays, while directions in working television scripts are minimal. I have seen the program twice, most recently at the National Archives, where all the material discussed in this chapter is deposited. However, since the published script is the form in which the original is most easily accessible to the readers, I will refer to the script.

19 A very popular folk song (origins unknown) in the 1960s that was sometimes sung at political rallies.

20 On September 10, 2001, CBC's *The National* broadcast a documentary on Don Freed called " Our Very Own Songs." Freed has spent several years getting Dene, Cree, and Michif schoolchildren to make up and sing their own songs about what has happened to them in their lives, where they live, stories, and daily events. One of them commemorates Sister Lea, who was buried with nineteen children after their school on "Mission Hill" caught fire. She went back in to save them and also died. The song says that if her spirit is still there, it is friendly.

21 Being from a First Nation did not guarantee empathy with the children. See "Cree Nun Sentenced for Abusing Students."

22 Greer, *TV Times* supplement to the *St. Catharines Standard*.

23 At www.irsr-rqpi.gc.ca/english/history.html (accessed October 18, 2007).

24 As the NWT Dene website, www.cancom.net/~dehchofn, confirmed in October 2005 when I inquired about the source of the word.

25 A fact alluded to wryly in Don Burnstick's "Redskin" routine, caught on film by Drew Hayden Taylor in his 2000 NFB film, *Redskins, Tricksters and Puppy Stew*.

26 Of the 13,785 Indian residential school claimants who filed claims against the government of Canada through the Alternative Dispute Resolution and/or litigation process, 2,430 have had their claims resolved. Launched in June 2003, the ADR process has received 1,687 applications, with 197 resolved. The awards for physical abuse or wrongful confinement ranged from $250 to $3,500. Leaders of the First Nations complained that a lot of money had been spent on the process but very little had reached survivors. By 2005, the process was under review and a new

settlement was on the horizon. The final settlement hammered out in March 2007 can be found at www.reglementpensionnatsindiens.ca/English.html (accessed October 22, 2007). The website for people with claims is www.reglementpensionnats indiens.ca/English.html (accessed October 22, 2007).

References

Canadian Press. "Cree Nun Sentenced for Abusing Students." *St. Catharines Standard*, June 25, 1999.

CBC Times, March 22–28, 1969.

Greer, Sandy. Cover story, *TV Times*. In the *St. Catharines Standard*, Oct 28, 1989.

"Mediator Named to Residential School Talks." CTV Online, May 30, 2005. Available at www.ctv.ca/servlet/ArticleNews/story/CTVNews/1117471492250 _112880692. Accessed October 22, 2007.

Miller, J.R. *Shingwauk's Vision: A History of Native Residential Schools*. Toronto: University of Toronto Press, 1996.

Miller, Mary Jane. *Turn Up the Contrast: CBC Television Drama Since 1952*. Vancouver: University of British Columbia Press and CBC, 1987.

———. *Rewind and Search: Conversations with the Makers and Decision-Makers of Canadian Television Drama*, Montreal and Kingston: McGill-Queen's University Press, 1996.

———. *"Where the Spirit Lives:* An Influential and Contentious Television Drama about Residential Schools." *American Review of Canadian Studies* (Spring/Summer 2001): 71–84.

———. *Outside Looking In: Viewing First Nations Peoples in Canadian Dramatic Television Series*. Montreal and Kingston: McGill-Queen's University Press, 2008.

Patten, Cheryl. "Programs on Residential Schools Elicit Strong Viewer Response." *Windspeaker*, March 2001.

Performing Arts in Canada 6 (2) (May 1969).

St. Pierre, Paul. *Sister Balonika*. Production notes and study outline by Leonard Peterson. Agincourt, ON: Book Society of Canada, 1973.

St. Pierre, Paul. *Smith and Other Events: Tales of the Chilcotin*. Norman: University of Oklahoma Press, 1994.

Vancouver International Film Festival, 2001. Available at www.viff.org/viff/a_press. Accessed October 22, 2007.

Yinka Dene Language Institute. At www.ydli.org/langs/siwash.htm. Accessed August 29, 2005.

Filmography

The Beachcombers (CBC, 1972–90)

Cariboo Country (CBC, 1960)

CBC Archives (October 30, 1990): http://archives.cbc.ca/IDC-1-70-692-4006/ disasters_tragedies/residential_schools/clip4

The Education of Phyllistine (CBC, 1964)
North of 60 (CBC 1992–97)
North of 60 Mysteries (CBC, 1999–2005)
Our Very Own Songs (CBC, *The National*, 2001)
Redskins, Tricksters and Puppy Stew (National Film Board of Canada, 2001)
Residential Schools: Moving Beyond Survival (Newsworld/APTN/VisionTV, 2001),
      dir. Drew Hayden Taylor
Sister Balonika (CBC, 1969)
Where the Spirit Lives (CBC, 1989)
Wojeck (CBC, 1966–68)

PART THREE

Mapping Geographies

JOHN MCCULLOUGH

Representations of Urban
Conflict in *Moccasin Flats*

I n the past decade, Saskatchewan has established itself as an active site of regional and international film and television production. The province's participation in Global Hollywood includes numerous movies of the week, Terry Gilliam's feature film *Tideland* (Canada/UK, 2005), the hit sitcom *Corner Gas* (Prairie Pants Productions/CTV, 2003–), the multicultural sitcom *Little Mosque on the Prairie* (WestWind Pictures/CBC, 2006–), and a wide range of cable television products, including *Incredible Story Studio* (Vérité Films/CTV, 1997–2002,), *My Global Adventure* (Mind's Eye Productions, 2001), *renegadepress.com* (Vérité Films, 2004–), and the extraordinary *Moccasin Flats* (Big Soul Productions, 2003–05), which features stories about First Nations youth in Regina, the capital of Saskatchewan.

Created and produced by First Nations women and shot on location with an abundance of exterior footage, *Moccasin Flats* provides a glimpse of the social issues that give shape to life in a city that has become identified, along with Saskatoon, Winnipeg, and Edmonton, as a site of social crises featuring racism, poverty, crime, violence, addiction, and regional underdevelopment in Canada. The theme of underdevelopment haunts these cities, providing proof of capitalism's indifference to and exploitation of uneven development. In these cities, evidence of "progress" and "civilization" exist alongside underdevelopment and devolution: here, the possibility presented by a wired virtual business sits next to dustbowl and apartheid standards of poverty, disease, and hopelessness. According to this evidence, the only democratization to have happened in late capitalism is the democratization of poverty, leaving us with a world that one observer describes as a "planet of slums."[1] *Moccasin Flats* represents this situation in unsparing detail, which may have been too much to gain wide

support, but it is also an articulation of the diverse aspirations of Indigenous youth, who are suspended between eroded and colonized traditions
and a globalization that threatens to abandon them.

The Regina location is interesting, given the recent success of *Corner
Gas*, which features comic Brent Butt and a cast of "yokels" in stories
about small-town Saskatchewan. Despite being shot in and around Regina,
with exteriors shot in the town of Rouleau, south of the city, and interiors shot in the government-funded sound stage in the city's "knowledge
corridor," as well as on set in Rouleau, *Corner Gas* uses the location principally as a generic Prairie setting and relies on well-worn sitcom tropes:
the father is the butt of most jokes, the cops are hapless, the mayor is con-
niving and petty, and a variety of minor characters take turns playing the
village idiot. In this sense, it finds its mirror image on the East Coast in
Trailer Park Boys, (Trailer Park Productions, 2000—) and its precursors
would include *The Beachcombers* (CBC, 1972–90). In these shows, the
"region" plays out as exotica that can be capitalized as an international commodity. In some cases, the shows also serve the tourism industry, as show
locations become vacation and tour destinations. Typically, the shows'
themes and storylines involve quotidian events and humorous misunderstandings, all drenched in a redemptive humanist sentimentality. Unlike
most popular US television shows—and previous generations of Canadian television drama, such as *Night Heat* (Grosso Productions,1985–89)
or *Street Legal* (CBC, 1986–94)—which feature stories situated in large
urban centres, Canadian television now typically sells itself by exoticising
regionalism.

This process is consistent with Doreen Massey's (1994) view that, in
globalization, the local and the regional are not necessarily effaced and in
many cases become intricately coordinated with the metropolis. It echoes
as well David Harvey's (2001) point that globalization demands the cap-
italization of the margins and local products, and this process of com-
moditization is distinguished by the rapid development and exploitation
of all resources within reach. This happens with great intensity in the
realm of culture, in which new forms of communication allow for the
rapid transportation of product from the regions or margins to the centre. For regions, media industries have often been perceived as "cash cows,"
particularly in areas where traditional industries have disappeared or been
downsized. It is regularly argued that media industries offer relief for such
regional economic restructuring and it is in the region's best overall interests to develop strategies to attract media productions, including promoting the location, reducing labour costs, and building state-of-the-art

production and post-production technology and facilities.[2] Ben Goldsmith and Tom O'Regan (2005) have shown how the recent construction of studio facilities worldwide is a consequence of the globalized media industry and is directly linked to the emergence of lively competition among various jurisdictions vying for regional film and television investment. Immersed in global competition, Canadian regional television production also has to deal with centralized power in the form of distribution networks. Serra Tinic (2005) has presented the case that Canadian regional productions continue to suffer from centralized control and that this is an aspect of the structural contradictions inherent in Canadian television production, in which regional stories and perspectives are often eclipsed by the complex negotiations required to "green-light" regional production. In Regina, for instance, the local television production industry is the result of, among many things, a weak Canadian dollar, the construction of a sound stage and post-production facilities, local university- and college-level film and video training, various tax credits, and programming quotas. The success of several productions from the region is testament to the "jurisdictional advantage" that the region developed in the late 1990s and the early years of the twenty-first century.

Moccasin Flats has to be seen from the perspective of this regional industry development and as part of the recent history of regional Canadian television productions generally, including *Corner Gas*, *Riverdale* (CBC, 1997–98), *Trailer Park Boys*, *Da Vinci's Inquest* (Barna-Alper Productions/CBC, 1998–2005), and *Road to Avonlea* (CBC/Disney/Sullivan Entertainment, 1989–96). These shows have all found success in niche markets, and their producers have been successful in exploiting specific structural advantages in the "new international division of cultural labour."[3] This is in contrast to previous Canadian media industry history, which was dominated by public and publicly funded broadcasting dedicated to nation building and in which regionalism and regional representations are seen as fundamental to national diversity, democratic representation, *and* federalism. This history, which includes shows such as *The Beachcombers*, *The Forest Rangers* (CBC, 1963–65), *King of Kensington* (CBC, 1975–80, CBC), *North of 60* (CBC, 1992–96), *Jake and the Kid* (CBC, 1995–99), and *Drop the Beat* (CBC, 2000), tends to privilege public service and "social message" programming, which often gives the shows a pedantic tone, particularly in comparison with US television.

Moccasin Flats is a fascinating mix of all of these histories and influences. It was created and produced by the independent firm Big Soul Productions, whose founders are two First Nations women, Jennifer Podemski

and Laura J. Milliken. Though young, these producers have a signifi-
cant track record in Canadian regional media production, including
Podemski's acting work in *Lost Child* (US, 2000), *Dance Me Outside*
(Canada, 1994) and the television show *The Rez* (CBC, 1996–97). She
was also a producer on the television series *Seventh Generation* (Big
Soul Productions, 2001–04). Milliken is a producer with extensive cred-
its and a past member of the board of directors of Toronto Women in
Film and Television.

Big Soul Productions used tax credits and other state-sponsored inducements associated with the Regina location to gain a cost advantage during
production and, in focusing on First Nations themes and characters, the
producers enabled access to national distribution through the Aboriginal
Peoples Television Network. The show's first season was groundbreaking
on a number of levels—it was APTN's first commissioned drama, the pilot
episode was a hit at the Sundance Film Festival, and it was the first APTN
show to "cross over" to the arguably mainstream cable channel, Showcase. But its uncompromising depiction of downtown Regina did not flow
well with commercial television beyond First Nations and specialty channels, and the show was renewed for only eight episodes in each of its second and third years. To connect with a youth and First Nations audience,
the show positioned itself as both a commercial and public service product, attempting to use the language of popular entertainment to communicate with and ultimately empower mass audiences. The show took the
form of a half-hour drama, which is a program type that has been previously successful with other Canadian teen and youth dramas; for instance,
The Kids of Degrassi (CBC, 1982–86), *Degrassi Junior High* (Playing With
Time, 1987–91), and *Drop the Beat*. As well, the show mixes neo-realism
with non-realist styles in a hybrid aesthetic that is emblematic of much
Canadian television programming.[4] Institutionally, then, the show can be
seen to borrow a variety of television conventions to serve a community
empowerment function, on the one hand, and an international commodity function on the other.

The show is unique in its use of a variety of principles of neo-realism,
including location shooting. I focus on this aspect primarily because *Moccasin Flats* is set in downtown Regina, a city that is usefully understood
in the context of geographical materialist urban studies, particularly the
concepts of "burn-out," policing, class-based and racialized urban planning,
and suburbanization. *Moccasin Flats* takes Regina's colonial history as a
given, and a large part of its aesthetic success lies in its documentation of
the degradation of human life that this colonial legacy bequeaths to the con-

temporary residents of the area. In fact, the show's ultimate lack of success in finding a large international audience may have to do with its refusal to whitewash the social crisis that is the consequence of Regina's geopolitical history. Because the show treats its location as a function of social relations, and specifically as an environment of class and racial disequilibrium, its tone is in striking contrast to more commercially successful regional Canadian shows like *Da Vinci's Inquest*, *Trailer Park Boys*, and *Corner Gas*. These shows are connected to the tradition of Canadian naturalism, in which the characters' psychological makeup is influenced by and reflected in the natural environment—here, the regions give rise to the character types that populate the shows as though they are part of the environment like the wheat or the fish that surround them. By contrast, *Moccasin Flats* uses its geography in a materialist fashion to describe how, in capitalism, underdevelopment creates a series of contradictions that the characters have to work through. For instance, Dillon (Justin Toto) has a basketball scholarship but feels as if he is abandoning his friends by accepting it. But he also feels that he will be cheating himself if he doesn't take this opportunity to get out of the city and the dead ends he foresees. The history of colonialism and underdevelopment that Regina embodies is made manifest in the choices presented to Dillon—in both cases, the result is repressed desire. But it is not as though the natural environment had anything to do with his underdevelopment—that is the result of capitalism. The different fates of these regional shows suggest that there are various shades of localism and realism that play well in Global Hollywood.

The structure and effects of colonialism, and now possibly neo-imperialism, are well represented in Regina's urban planning. Given minimal geographical barriers, the colonial engineers and social planners applied the grid mercilessly, and, as Brian Stockton's Saskatchewan Trilogy has highlighted, the role of social and geographical engineering is a significant aspect of Saskatchewan's history and its residents' identity. Not surprisingly, beyond its role as a colonial fortress and settlement, Regina has no cultural tradition or natural significance. It is a train town in the most unforgiving manner—the tracks divide the city into a variety of sections, all of which function to remind the residents that there is a "right" and "wrong" side of the tracks. Even though the CPR passenger trains no longer go through it, the city space remains partitioned according to the colonial needs of the railway: industrial zones are adjacent to the tracks, working-class neighbourhoods surround the lines, and police forces are located along the length of the main lines. This repressive urban geography is emphasized by the CPR property that runs through downtown and serves to contain poverty, violence, and disenfranchisement in the neigh-bourhoods north of the railway, an area of the city known as North Cen-tral. The tracks, then, play a significant role in themes as diverse as personal identity, community solidarity, urban planning, and policing, and it is notable that it is this urban space that *Moccasin Flats* illuminates.

Regina was built as a CPR train town and was designated the capital of the North-West Territories in 1882. In 1885, the colonial government, represented by Lieutenant-Governor Edgar Dewdney, tried and hanged Louis Riel in the city. Fifty years later, state repression was again showcased in the city when in 1935, in the midst of the Great Depression, the anti-poverty On-to-Ottawa Trek was brutally derailed in the Regina Riot. These are provocative illustrations of how the state has used its control of space in Regina in unmistakably militaristic ways, and it is imperative to see that, as well as being a physical space, the railway corridor is a conceptual and cultural space that has helped legitimate colonialism to the present day. The city's colonial heritage continues to encourage conservative definitions of urban geography. "South of the tracks," and especially "the south end," are still phrases used to designate the residential and recreational space of the city's professional middle class and social elites. This division reflects the logic of financiers and entrepreneurs who, in the 1880s, invested in the lands that lay south of the proposed trans-Canada CPR track. In fact, in Canadian train towns that are divided east to west by the track, the south side of the downtown and the original built environment will typically represent a distinct class privilege over the north side. A good example of this is seen in Noam Gonick's film *Stryker* (Canada, 2004), where the story begins in the train yards in the north end of Winnipeg and the action, featuring First Nations and working-class gangs, happens around the north end of Main Street, miles from the city's middle-class neighbourhoods to the south and in the suburbs.

In Regina, the literalness of this mapping has encouraged those with social aspirations to avoid ending up "north of the tracks." With suburban-ization in the 1960s, core houses tended to enter into a cycle of short-term ownerships, absentee landlordism, and reduced market value—the standard US burn-out patterns. Services declined or disappeared. Along streets such as Dewdney Avenue, Albert Street, and 4th Avenue (i.e., from blocks numbered, north to south, 1100 to 1500), until the 1970s there were a variety of grocery stores, butchers, bakers, medical offices, convenience stores, and light industrial businesses. In the late 1970s, the development of affordable family-size houses in the suburbs, and the suburbanization of most industry, gutted what is now known as North Central of working-

Figure 1. A city divided: this shot establishes the train tracks as central to the show's themes as well as its mise-en-scène.

class paycheques and the core became associated with underdevelopment and dilapidation.[5] Land costs and rents were depressed, the area's tax base shrank, and a variety of social housing in-fill, including low-income housing and halfway houses, was introduced. Schools were closed or downsized; for example, Albert Public School and Scott Collegiate.

The stories in *Moccasin Flats* take place in this neighbourhood, with the "new" Albert School and Scott Collegiate, now partially a police precinct, prominently featured. The show's depiction of North Central corresponds to the actual history of the space, which in the 1960s became populated by people who had migrated to the city from depreciated rural contexts, including First Nations people from nearby reserves who had moved to the city to avoid high levels of poverty, disease, and joblessness. From the 1970s on, North Central is not only about class war but is also profoundly about racialized conflict, and this provides a substantial amount of material for the show.

The show's fidelity to this urban geopolitics is evident in the way the characters, and our feelings about them, are mapped onto their primary location in the street grid. Jonathan (Landon Montour), when he is dealing, operates out of a bunker in the 100 block, on the extreme north end of North Central. But when he starts to turn his life around, and when he wants others to think he is rehabilitated, he lives in a house at 1077, which is located between 4th and 5th Avenue, the heart of North Central. While this seems like a move in the "right" direction, we also know that this is still a troubled community because we overhear characters make calls for paramedics who are told to get to "Cameron and 5th" or "4th Avenue," just around the corner from where he and his family are trying to build a better life. In the show, as in the city, the bigger the paycheque, the higher the street address, the best example being Corporal Strongeagle (Andrea Menard), a First Nations cop who lives in the 2400 block, which, being south of College Street, is on the cusp of "living in the south end."

The goal of getting to the south end, which is treated like an escape for the residents of North Central, is also part of the logic behind representing Dillon and Sarah's (Kristin Friday) meetings on the shore of Wascana Lake, which lies south of downtown and, with Wascana Creek, forms a water barrier between the two halves of the city. Though they never get to the south side of the park, the south shore is always present in the background as a horizon. The profound meaning of these sequences lies in the additional fact that this background includes the legislative buildings on the south shore, suggesting that the characters' dreams of success are intertwined with the colonial history that those buildings ultimately represent. These shots imply that the characters are to colonial history what figure is to ground. Though the dialogue never comments on this relationship, the *mise en scène* consistently uses the legislative buildings as background, in large part because of their architectural prominence in the city. For instance, in the opening episode of the third season, Red (Ron Harris) and Candy (Candace Fox) are walking toward the camera along a railway track. In this telephoto shot, which compresses distance into a visually dense but shallow composition, the legislative buildings loom at the vanishing point in eerie soft focus and the shot can be read as a visual collapsing of three orders of geopolitics in the area: the histories of First Nations, the establishment of capitalism on the plains via the train, and the omnipresent apparatus of the state.

In an effort to control the mobility of both the poor and people of colour in Regina, house prices and rental rates have been used to block movement. This can be seen in the cathedral area, one of the city's "buffer zone" neighbourhoods that have been usefully deployed at various times to absorb advances from the north. As sites of gentrification, these areas slow down the movement of poverty to south of the tracks by artificially inflating the value of land and rents. The result is that the city centre is understood as the battleground between two material and ideological worlds. In *Moccasin Flats*, this is represented in the difficult conversations and confrontations, at downtown locations, between the First Nations

Figure 2. A cognitive map of Regina: Wascana Lake serves as a moat and the Government Buildings serve as a literal and figural backdrop for First Nations youth.

social worker and the police officer, as well as the tensions that arise between Matthew (Mathew Stroneagle) and Red at Betty's house, which is in the 2200 block. These are accurate representations of the tensions that arise in downtown, where real estate and land are used to prohibit southern expansion of the underdevelopment associated with North Central. In fact, the standoffs between middle-class characters, which represent these real-life conflicts, not only occur in the downtown but are also introduced by shots of the twin glass and steel towers at 12th Avenue and the Scarth Street mall, framed to look as though they are confronting each other as giant combatants in a chess game.

Regina's rigorous grid, defined by class and racial identity, is not only a representation of what has developed but is also a template upon which Reginans cast their dreams and aspirations. For instance, in season one of *Moccasin Flats*, Dillon finally convinces Sarah to go to the movies with him and they are seen at the Galaxie Cinemas, a new addition to the old Normanview Mall, which was one of the early suburban malls built to service working-class "white flight." The meaning of this brief scene becomes clear when the viewer realizes that, in Regina, you have to get out of North Central to go to a cinema, and this makes a trip to the movies like a trip to another planet. In another episode, Corporal Strongeagle is signified in part as a sellout because she lives in a house in the 2400s, indicating that she lives well south of North Central. But, in a very decisive way, the show also suggests that her life is now troubled by what are represented as middle-class concerns—failed relationships, identity crises, and fear of professional failure. Her very success in leaving North Central is the source of her anxiety about her place out of the neighbourhood. She resolves this conflict, temporarily, by doing community policing in North Central, but when the budget dries up—another deft representation of the consequences of underdevelopment—her superior, who is also Native but much more committed to assimilation, orders her back into uniform and back to HQ. The second season ends with her, in uniform, shooting a youth in the community centre where she used to do her community outreach work. As with much of the tragedy in the show, the tone is ironic, and this invites consideration of the contradictions of underdevelopment, including the theme of alienation.

In the show, and in the city itself, getting "to the right side of the tracks" has significant inducements. In a manner that leaves no room for confusion, the city's "jewels" are kept in the south end and what remains on the north side of the tracks, especially in the core, is its own inducement to "get south." Houses are poorly maintained and rentals are controlled by a handful of slumlords who each own dozens of properties. In the show, the white New Age drug lord is a character who approximates the loathsome quality of slumlords in underdeveloped areas. What the show tends to miss is the extent of the structural inequality in the area. For instance, there are no grocery stores in the core area, no butchers or bakers, but the city's two hospitals and police HQ and its neighbourhood outreach precinct—attached to what remains of Scott Collegiate—are located there, as are the casino and the horse track, as well as a variety of liquor stores, pawn shops, fast food outlets, and sex trade stroll zones. A "cognitive map" of the area, in the sense that Fredric Jameson has developed this term, would represent this underprivileged status, but also the various layers of institutional power and structure that give shape to the community.[6]

This concept provides a useful way of thinking about the numerous shots of the neighbourhood that grace the opening of each episode and various scene transitions. Some of the shots are meant to depict underdevelopment as degradation—for example, shots of abandoned houses—but many of the shots also suggest that North Central provides a radical challenge to those who think that development and "progress" are the only way to secure society, solidarity, and human progress. For instance, the people on bikes, the pedestrians on the streets, and the children hanging out around their houses with their friends, parents, and pets all imply that, outside of the crises that capitalist relations engender, there is always potential for human community.

The unforgiving nature of the grid and the socio-political meaning of the CPR line are not always depicted. But in one episode, in which the prostitute, Danna (Danna Henderson), shoots up with the CPR tracks as a backdrop to the action, we have a rich display of the range of problems that the train tracks introduced. As a train blows through town, Danna is picked up, in a stupor, by one of the show's faceless villains, who induces her to "party" with him. Here, the tracks on her arm are an extension and logical outcome, the show seems to argue, of the tracks of the CPR. In Regina, the main line parallels Danna's "mainlining" and her addiction parallels the poisoned, residual colonial social imaginary that prevails in the city. The show's attention to detail is routinely very precise, and this fidelity to Regina's space is useful for a general audience to the extent that it allows every viewer the opportunity to understand how Canadian Prairie cities "work." But for an audience that knows Regina, the effect of this realism is not only geo-political but also inflected with a curious poetic. For instance, in the above scene, the placement of the character is crucial, as she—and the camera and viewers—are clearly on the north side of the tracks, looking to move beyond this colonial barrier. But with the tracks and a security fence blocking her way to the south end of town, even she realizes that the quest is impossible, given that it is encrusted with more than a century of violent repression. And the drugs don't help her escape, because they leave her incapacitated and vulnerable. As we see her drive away with the john, we understand that she is being absorbed back into North Central. The predictable outcome, for those marked by the city's racist and classist legacy of underdevelopment, is to become obsessed with mainlining by the main line, which ultimately only serves to confirm the rigid social structure that survives.

Moccasin Flats, then, represents local social problems as connected to the history of colonial rule in the region, but these representations also point in the direction of political struggles that are common to dispossessed populations globally. To this end, the show borrows much of its style from American popular culture that features subaltern youth and their strategies of resistance. Paula Massood has described this style as a "hood film" chronotope that is "focused on young male protagonists, included in an inner city *mise en scène*."[7] By featuring First Nations b-boys, rappers, gangsters, pimps, hookers, and dealers, all of whom seem to reflect a contemporary global image of life in ghettos as it is represented in popular culture, the show connects subaltern youth identity through urban style and themes of capitalist exploitation. But the show combines this chronotope with representations of First Nations youth who are connected to cultural traditions that include drumming, powwow, and Aboriginal spiritual practices. The show's strategy is to indicate that these connections between contemporary urban life and traditional practices are highly contradictory, in both positive and negative ways.

Matthew, for instance, is a drummer and powwow dancer, but he is also a rap music producer and promoter. His character's identity is regularly revealed in stories that contrast traditional values and community solidarity with the everyday realities of contemporary capitalism and the various types of exploitative relations it encourages. On several occasions, Matthew's commitment to tradition and community solidarity encourages him to disavow his responsibilities regarding safety and appropriate ethical behaviour. When he is promoting the rapper Red, for instance, out of a sense of fraternal honour he turns a blind eye to Red's involvement in Jonathan's crystal meth operation and is thus seemingly partially responsible for several ODs in the community. On the other hand, his traditional connections, which he attributes to his upbringing by his aunt Betty (Tantoo Cardinal), give him a perspective that sees beyond the hyperbole of the local gangsters. In this way, he can provide some substantial advice to his friends, in particular Dillon, who chooses to go to university on the basis of Matthew's encouragement.

Thus, the contradictions that the show represents not only provide a recognizable portrait of life in Regina but also encourage young viewers in similar situations to comprehend their lives as complex and full of contradictions. In this way, the show serves a pedagogical role and, to the extent that the producers see the show as containing lessons about appropriate behaviour and good life choices, it can be seen to be part of the Canadian public service media tradition, much of which has been adopted by the show's host broadcaster, APTN.

In large part, though, the representation of the contradictions faced by the characters leads to significant impasses in how to think about a solution, as despair characterizes the tone of most of the series. It is a sign of the courage of the producers that, in choosing to follow a realist aesthetic trajectory, they have avoided compromising a materialist understanding of the spatial arrangements of the city, and, in the process, they have likely paid the price of producing a form of social criticism that is difficult to sell to the mainstream. In fact, the second and the third seasons show evidence of having been altered by the pressure of "ratings"—in particular, the tone of the third season seems less critical and more in line with the

Figure 3. Neo-realist style: location shooting and unstaged daily life.

liberal humanism of popular commercial television in Global Hollywood. As I have argued, the neo-realist portrayal of Regina leads to a series of relatively convincing representations about the contradictions facing Indigenous youth in underdeveloped regions throughout the world. Principally, this is achieved through an accurate depiction of the spatial arrangements in the city. But this leads to a series of narrative and character developments that, by the end of the second season, are hopelessly difficult to manipulate into a positive story about Aboriginal youth in Canada. Given that one of the goals of the show is youth empowerment, the realist approach seems to have inherent difficulties in the sense that there is no happy ending for any of the characters. To the extent that facing the reality of the situation does not provide affirmative stories about life in the Prairies, *Moccasin Flats'* alternative is to depict the negative consequences of illegal activity. For instance, Jonathan's crazed mental state and his imprisonment serve as deterrents to First Nations youth, who might justifiably feel that the gangster's solution to the contradictions of capitalism is preferable to the confusion experienced by Matthew, Sarah, Dillon, and Candy.

To teach the lesson that crime does not pay, the show regularly uses anti-realist techniques, particularly to undermine the power of criminals and gangsters. Through the second season, Jonathan is increasingly bothered by his unconscious, which is represented as an unbridled doppelgänger played by Ryan Rajendra Black. Here, the show creates a rich intertextuality that references cinema history—for instance, *Fight Club* and

German expressionism—and Canadian television programming—Ryan Black is recognizable to viewers as one of the young stars of *The Rez*. Jonathan's double usually appears when he is feeling emasculated by the breakdown of his family life, which is crumbling because of his guilt over lying about his criminal activities. He continues to deceive his son and the boy's mother, Tara (Sarah Podemski), while he compensates for his lack of involvement in the family by providing material well-being. But this is based on his production of crystal meth and an aggressive turf war with other dealers. Inevitably, his duplicity leads to a series of complications and his mental health degenerates into a series of paranoid and jealous delusions. In these sequences, the camera angles are canted and the lighting is highly stylized, in a clear attempt to differentiate this type of criminal character as scary and volatile. Jonathan is represented as facing a diminishing range of options, and it is clear that this is part of the heritage of being poor and Aboriginal in Regina but also very much a part of his particular solution to that situation. In this way, he is contrasted to his longtime buddies Dillon and Matthew, who choose different survival plans. The implication of the show is that Jonathan's reaction to his environment is understandable but not morally justifiable. So, while we understand that his identity is going to reflect the general indifference and lack of compassion of his surroundings, the deceit and duplicity that are part of his reaction are not condoned. The double, then, becomes the force that ruins his life, and one of the lessons is that drugs, crime, and associating with gangsters all lead to delusional behaviour and, as in the case of Jonathan, prison. The double is given the name Devlin Day, which clearly illustrates the Christian moral dichotomy that organizes this story development. For Red, who has been deceitful in his own regard, the same lesson is registered when he panics, hides out in a paranoid state of fear, and is ultimately shot at his debut concert. Similarly, as Danna gets increasingly hooked on crystal meth, her mental anguish is exaggerated and her performance becomes increasingly ghoulish and somnambulistic. All these representations share a similar formal style that borrows from the agitated and emotionally transparent tradition of expressionism, and the use of this strategy suggests that the show is fundamentally interested in a representational mode that places realism as the norm and expressionist style as an indicator of individuated crisis and abnormality. The style of *Moccasin Flats*, then, offers an example of popular culture in which realism is used as a critical cultural form.

Loretta Todd has recently described her film *Kainayssini Imanistaisiwa (The People Go On)* (Canada, 2004) as a form of meditation about and

Figure 4. Expressionist style: Jonathan's alter-ego Devlin Day (Ryan Rajendra Black) becomes menacing in high-contrast lighting.

reclamation of the land. This cultural strategy is peripheral to but in response to colonial rule. In contrast to the colonial system of land treaties, which still organizes life for Aboriginal populations in the North, cultural representations of the land serve as tactics for reclamation and repatriation. In a variety of ways, Todd suggests, the land, and First People's contradictory connections to it, are invoked and recalled in contemporary Aboriginal art and cultural practice.

I would extend this description to *Moccasin Flats*, and I would borrow the term "literalist" from filmmaker Thom Andersen's work on Los Angeles, *Los Angeles Plays Itself* (US, 2004), to describe the style of literal spatial representation in the television show. From this perspective, the tracking shots along the streets of North Central are not only attempts to describe the historical-materialist arrangements of colonial space, as I have suggested, but figural reclamations of space that before the middle of the nineteenth century was considered "Indian land." Nowadays, to reclaim the land, Aboriginal artists participate in revisionist histories of the land—recording it and reconfiguring its meanings—telling stories in ways that are contrary to the colonial record. Associated with this strategy and crucial for its continuation is the training of First Nations youth, and here *Moccasin Flats* also has to be recognized as a socio-political milestone, given that it was a significant employment and youth empowerment project for North Central. The show developed out of Big Soul's RepREZentin' training project, which Milliken and Podemski have used in producing both *Seventh Generation* and *Moccasin Flats*. Essentially a government-funded initiative, RepREZentin' is designed to train youth for employment in media industries and is integrated with the federal Job Start/Future Skills training program. Its success suggests an intriguing way to imagine media as a political and economic force in the struggles of global Indigenous peoples.

In light of the way *Moccasin Flats* reclaims the Great Plains for First Nations people, the space of *Corner Gas* has to be re-evaluated as not only the site of happy and funny white simpletons, but the site of colonialism and theft of resources. One of the ironies of this is that in *Moccasin Flats*, the First Nations residents are bound by the city but rarely have cars, while the residents of rural Dog River are almost exclusively white and congregate around the gas station, where cars and the logic of transportation dominate the landscape. The contrast between these two images, both cognitive maps of southern Saskatchewan, is the legacy of colonial rule on the Prairies, a space that is organized by the logic of "the grid" of transportation science, topographical rationalism, and land speculation. No matter how popular *Corner Gas* is by comparison, the images that *Moccasin Flats* captures—by tracking endlessly through the streets of North Central, running around basketball courts and playgrounds, following cyclists and pedestrians up the heat-drenched alleys, panning across the upper windows of rental properties—resonate as profound articulations of the show's geopolitical context, an achievement that is fundamentally connected to the show's realism and use of neo-realist techniques. This aesthetic choice is connected to a political and community-oriented project, and the combination of neo-realism and political modernism suggests that *Moccasin Flats* may be an incipient form of radical political culture that is connected to cultural and political movements that have been recently shaping the "left." These developments would principally include groups affiliated with what are described as anti-globalization movements, in which issues of Indigenous land rights and criticisms of the ideology of development echo ideas that *Moccasin Flats* represents. The show's ultimate demise may indicate that the empowerment function of television, usually a local activity, is a hindrance to international sales. This is frustrating, because part of *Moccasin Flats*' radical appeal lies in the fact that its stories and representations of underdevelopment have global and international significance, if not mainstream acceptance. Globalization could encourage cultural flows, connections, and communications, and in those cases where *Moccasin Flats* is broadcast on other national Indigenous networks—for example, the recently created Aboriginal networks in New Zealand and Australia—one can imagine alternative programming finding a place in global media. But, given that global culture is typically a capital affair, mainstream popularity serves as the initial filter for cultural goods trying to sell themselves internationally. In very direct ways, *Moccasin Flats*' dedication to realism may have limited its popularity with mainstream audiences, who were uncomfortable with frank representations of poverty and racism as it exists in the middle of the so-called First World.

Notes

1   Davis, "Planet of Slums."
2   Christopherson, "Divide and Conquer."
3   Miller et al., *Global Hollywood* 2.
4   Hogarth, *Documentary Television in Canada*.
5   Levin, *City History and City Planning*.
6   Jameson, *The Geopolitical Aesthetic*.
7   Massood, "City Spaces and City Times," 200.

References

Christopherson, Susan. "Divide and Conquer: Regional Competition in a Concentrated Media Industry." In *Contracting Out Hollywood: Runaway Productions and Foreign Location Shooting*, edited by Greg Elmer and Mike Gasher, 21–40. Lanham, MD: Rowman & Littlefield, 2005.

Davis, Mike. "Planet of Slums." *New Left Review* 26 (March–April 2004): 5–34.

Goldsmith, Ben and Tom O'Regan. *The Film Studio: Film Production in the Global Economy*. Lanham, MD: Rowman & Littlefield, 2005.

Harvey, David. *Spaces of Capital: Toward a Critical Geography*. New York: Routledge, 2001.

Hogarth, David. *Documentary Television in Canada: From National Public Service to Global Marketplace*. Montreal and Kingston: McGill-Queen's University Press, 2002.

Jameson, Fredric. *The Geopolitical Aesthetic: Cinema and Space in the World System*. Bloomington: Indiana University Press, 1992.

Levin, Earl A. *City History and City Planning: The Local Historical Roots of the City Planning Function in Three Cities of the Canadian Prairies*. Published PhD thesis. Winnipeg: University of Manitoba, 1993.

Massey, Doreen. *Space, Place, and Gender*. Minneapolis: University of Minnesota Press, 1994.

Massood, Paula J. "City Spaces and City Times: Bakhtin's Chronotope and Recent African-American Film," In *Screening The City*, edited by Tony Fitzmaurice, 200–15. New York: Verso, 2003.

Miller, Toby, Nitin Govil, John McMurria, Richard Maxwell, and Ting Wang. *Global Hollywood* 2, rev. ed. London: British Film Institute, 2005.

Tinic, Serra. *On Location: Canada's Television Industry in a Global Market.* Toronto: University of Toronto Press, 2005.

Filmography

The Beachcombers (CBC, 1972–90, Canada)

Corner Gas (CTV/Prairie Pants Prod., 2003, Canada)

Dance Me Outside (David Webb and Bruce McDonald, 1994, Canada)

Da Vinci's Inquest (CBC/Barna-Alper Prod., 1998–2005, Canada)

Degrassi Junior High (Playing With Time Prod., 1987–91, Canada)

Drop the Beat (CBC, 2000, Canada)

Fight Club (1999, US), dir. David Fincher

The Forest Rangers (CBC, 1963–65, Canada)

Incredible Story Studio (CTV/Vérité Films, 1997–2002, Canada)

Jake and the Kid (CBC, 1995–99, Canada)

Kainayssini Imanistaisiwa (The People Go On) (2004, Canada), dir. Loretta Todd.

The Kids of Degrassi (CBC, 1982–86, Canada)

King of Kensington (CBC, 1975–80, Canada)

Little Mosque on the Prairie (CBC/WestWind Prod., 2006–, Canada)

Los Angeles Plays Itself (2004, US), dir. Thom Anderson

Lost Child (2000, US), dir. Karen Arthur

Moccasin Flats (Big Soul Productions, 2003–05, Canada)

My Global Adventure (Mind's Eye Prod., 2001, Canada)

Night Heat (Grosso Prod., 1985–89, Canada)

North of 60 (CBC, 1992–96, Canada)

renegadepress.com (Vérité Films, 2004–, Canada)

The Rez (CBC, 1996–97, Canada)

Riverdale (CBC, 1997–98, Canada)

Road to Avonlea (CBC/Disney/Sullivan Entertainment, 1989–96, Canada)

Saskatchewan Trilogy (2002–06, Canada), dir. Brian Stockton

Seventh Generation (Big Soul Productions, 2001–04, Canada)

Street Legal (CBC, 1986–94, Canada)

Stryker (2004, Canada), dir. Noam Gonick

Tideland (2005, Canada/UK), dir. Terry Gilliam

Trailer Park Boys (Trailer Park Productions, 2000–, Canada)

GLEN LOWRY

Da Vinci's Inquest

Postmortem

People talk quietly over coffees and cigarettes. An actress playing a panhandler does a crossword puzzle by the light of the tent. An extra dressed in a short red leather skirt, her breasts spilling out of her tank top, takes a light from a uniformed officer, who flashes her his badge. They laugh, and talk about how much work there is in the film industry this season in Vancouver.[1]

When the CBC announced on February 13, 2006, that it would not renew *Da Vinci's City Hall* (2005), *This is Wonderland* (2004), or *The Tournament* (2005) for the fall season, it effectively cancelled its entire primetime drama lineup. For viewers and critics, the network's decision to wipe the slate clean came as a surprise, especially in relation to *Da Vinci's City Hall*. Developing out of producer Chris Haddock's awarding-winning *Da Vinci's Inquest* (1998–2004), which had viewers in "45 nations in five continents," US syndication, and significant market saturation, *Da Vinci's City Hall* was the continuation of one of the longest-running primetime dramatic series on Canadian television, and one might reasonably have expected the CBC to keep the series in rotation for more than one season. "When the *Da Vinci* TV show followed Campbell's career from the coroner's office to city hall," however, "not enough viewers followed suit," and the network did not wait around to see if the ratings would improve, pulling the plug halfway through the first season.[2]

The cancellations were seen as the result of a change of command at the CBC: "Industry observers suspect that the newcomers want to put their own stamp on next season's drama."[3] Weak ratings, compared to CTV's hit *Corner Gas* (2004–),were blamed on the CBC lockout and the consequent late start of the fall 2005 season. Nevertheless, the question of whether the show failed to attract audiences because it was poorly promoted or poorly conceived remains open for debate.[4] What is clear is that, in the context of English-language programming and the emergence of BC's film and television industry, the cancellation of *Da Vinci's City Hall* marked the end of an era. The much-loved Dominic Da Vinci, played by Nicholas Campbell, transcended his character to become a presence off set in the Vancouver media and on the streets of the Downtown Eastside—Vancouver's own King of Kensington, Don of the DTES—and is set to enter the annals of Canadian TV.

Breaking with tradition, choosing not to foreground BC's natural environment—"Beautiful British Columbia"—as earlier BC-based shows such as *The Beachcombers* (1972–90) or *Danger Bay* (1985–90) had done, *Da Vinci's Inquest* generated quality television that focused on Vancouver's inner city. Capitalizing on the resources of BC's burgeoning film and television production industry and on Vancouver's emergence as a global urban centre, Haddock and the creators of the series produced aesthetically engaging, politically charged representations of life (and death) on the streets of the DTES. As Serra Tinic demonstrates in *On Location: Canada's Television Industry in a Global Market*, the inception of *Da Vinci's Inquest* was linked to a new CBC policy to produce more Canadian programming from regions outside a 150-kilometre radius of the Toronto headquarters, a policy that helped fuel the growth of the BC film and television industry during the 1990s. Tracking this development, Tinic argues, "In British Columbia, film and television production and tourism are multimillion-dollar industries that are integral components of the province's larger economic globalizations strategy and goal to establish Vancouver as a world class, or global, city." Her research shows: "In 1997 the television and motion picture industry spent directly an estimated $700 million in Vancouver, an increase of $100 million from 1996. During that year, the BC Film Commission provided services to $2.7 billion worth of productions (one-third of the potential market) and confirmed Vancouver's status as the third-largest production centre for American movies and television series [i.e., after Los Angeles and New York]."[5]

In this context, *Da Vinci's Inquest* exemplified the possibilities of Vancouver's burgeoning industry and its limitations. If, as Tinic contends, "Vancouver provides a strategic location from which to examine the relationships among regional, national, and global cultural productions," then *Da Vinci's* representation of Vancouver provides a key site with which to think through certain relationships between cultural production and the cultural artifact, economics and aesthetics, industry and series.[6]

In 1996, the CBC announced it was going to "Canadianize" its schedule within two years, and, as a direct result of the new mandate, the premier episode of *Da Vinci's Inquest* aired in 1998. According to Tinic, the CBC's choice of *Da Vinci's Inquest* over four other projects demonstrated a lack of interest in shows that "address the specificity of the 'place' of Vancouver."[7] Further, she argues, "The network's final decision to proceed with *Da Vinci's Inquest*, a 1990s version of *Quincy* [1976–83] merged with Britain's *Cracker* [1993–95], reinforced the enduring sentiment that Toronto's definition of regional production was primarily concerned with setting rather than social and cultural specificity in prime time." For Tinic, the series' representations of Vancouver's inner city "emphasize the generic markers of any crime or murder-mystery program."[8] According to this somewhat problematic argument, there is little portrayed on *Da Vinci's Inquest* that is intrinsic to Vancouver itself, except perhaps its geographical backdrop—the mountains and the ocean hovering above or floating behind generic shots of Vancouver's gritty downtown streets, alleys, and infamous SROs (single-room occupancy hotels). In fact, as Tinic and others point out, what makes Vancouver special as a location is its easy adaptability. Vancouver is an exceptionally good place for crews to work because there is a large variety of locations available: forests, ocean, mountains, city, farmland—everything from glaciers to "shooting galleries"—are all within half an hour from downtown.[9]

The situation is, however, more complicated than this. Inasmuch as the intersections of local specificity and the overwhelming forces of globalization define Vancouver as a particular urban locale, within the nation and beyond, they do so in a manner that tends to mark the built environment for a relatively short time, more or less in passing, and then they become invisible beneath the surface of the transient city. British Columbia's relatively small population, dependence on a resource-based economy, and geopolitical function as a "national terminus" and/or gateway between North America and Asia, together with the complex dynamics of civic, provincial, national, and international institutional and governmental interventions in different socio-economic relations, all impact its cultural production, and, I would argue, following Henri Lefebvre and the social geographers who have taken up his argument, the "social space" imagined and/or reproduced therein. Cultural specificity per se involves not only geo-historical facts but also—and more to the point—a dialogics of cultural act and practice. Markers of "place," to use Tinic's term, on the other hand, tend to emphasize a more positivistic, recognizable view of Canadian culture and/or geography. Linked as the concept is to a hegemonic regionalism, "place"—as opposed to "space"—tends to invoke a fixed set of cultural determinants that reflect external, predominantly centralist notions of Canadian culture and fail to account for the contradictory nature of culture. Entering Vancouver as social space at a particular historical juncture, *Da Vinci's Inquest* was both local and timely despite the obvious generic antecedents (*Wojek, Quincy, Cracker,* etc.) it brought to bear, and this made the series interesting for audiences in Vancouver and in other parts of the nation or across the globe. The ghost of Canada's and BC's colonial past—racialized revenants who are ubiquitous and invisible on Vancouver streets—haunt *Da Vinci's Inquest,* providing it with aesthetic and political relevance exceeding intentionality.

Inserting itself into a growing discourse around the struggles of this inner-city neighbourhood, *Da Vinci's Inquest* focused on the work of City Coroner Dominic Da Vinci, a hard-living, hard-edged, mumbling but socially progressive everyman modelled on real-life Senator Larry Campbell, the former Vancouver mayor and ex-city coroner. With Larry Campbell's expert assistance as a consultant and writer, *Da Vinci's Inquest* was able to bring this mainstay of genre TV to life for primetime audiences. In so doing, the series became a confluence of real-life social issues and the emergence of an unfolding political drama. Delivering well-directed, well-scripted, and well-photographed episodes featuring some of Canada's best independent actors, writers, and directors, the series was able to rise above its initial conception as a hybrid of stock, US-style police procedurals. In turn, *Da Vinci's Inquest* provided an engaging reflection of Vancouver's local situations and cultural politics, more or less as they were unfolding. David Spaner contends that *"Da Vinci's Inquest does for television what Vancouver filmmakers such as Bruce Sweeney and Lynne Stopkewich do for movies—provide a quality alternative to the schlock produced by Vancouver's US-based film and TV industry."*[10] Drawing on a pool of independent talent—linked to if not entirely dependent on the US-funded, schlock-producing local industry that had grown up during the 1990s—*Da Vinci's Inquest* successfully challenged decades-old assumptions about the characteristically low quality of primetime Canadian television drama. Avoiding the pitfalls of trying to reproduce the look and feel of the larger-budget US counterparts, the show staked out a territory of its own. "With more links with the indie film scene than anything else on North American television," the series was able to harness local forces and to change the look of English-language television in Canada.[11]

Act One: Little Sister

Everybody's looking for a pattern. Shit, it's random. Take a look out the freakin' window—it's chaotic. That's the pattern: there's no pattern. What's in the woods today that I can kill, that's all.[12]

In their blues-tinged, jazz-inflected portrayals of life and death on Vancouver's streets, the creators of *Da Vinci's Inquest* demonstrated a canny ability to capture real-life historical events as they unfolded. During its seven seasons, the series was able to spin narrative from a number of local stories while or even before they played out in the mainstream media. Not only was the series able to hitch a ride on Larry Campbell's rising popularity among the people of Vancouver and in the media, the series' representations of the disappearance and serial murder of women on the DTES—"Vancouver's missing women"—was also timely.

The first three episodes ("Little Sister," Parts 1, 2, and 3), which were directed by well-known Canadian filmmaker Anne Wheeler and aired on October 7, 14, and 21 in the fall of 1998, string together a narrative focused around the violent death of a number of women who were victims of a serial killer. Taking the metaphor of "dead drunk" to an extreme, these episodes portray a necrophiliac murderer who uses his victims' weakness for alcohol and their vulnerability to allow his crimes to go undetected. The violence depicted in these episodes, while only obliquely related to actual incidents, evokes the tragedy of Vancouver's "missing women" and locates the series within an emerging controversy around violence against women in the DTES.

By the beginning of the second season, when Wheeler returned to direct the first two episodes ("Cinderella Story," Parts I and II), the "missing women" had become a full-blown news story, with police offering a reward for information on the women and *America's Most Wanted* featuring the story during US and Canadian primetime.[13] Wheeler's feminist sympathies, and the timeliness of her episodes, helped to position the series in relation to early representations of Vancouver's "twenty-eight missing women"—the fact that this number that would continue to grow to more than sixty gave *Da Vinci's Inquest* an uneasy relevance.[14] The initial episodes comprised an early source, albeit fictional and imaginative, for information about the situation and the Vancouver Police Department's deplorable lack of response to it while establishing *Da Vinci's Inquest* in the midst of an emerging media maelstrom.

In "Little Sisters, Part 1," Dominic Da Vinci decides to follow up on a comment from the pathologist, Sunita "Sunny" Raman (Suleka Mathew), who notes that the toxicology results from a dead woman found in the harbour at the beginning of the show fits with a succession of cases involving women dying of apparent alcohol overdoses. Against the wishes of his boss and colleagues in the police, Da Vinci goes back to open the files, this proving himself willing to look for a pattern of homicidal violence where his predecessors have seen only the effects of chronic abuse and abjection—or as veteran cop Leo Shannon (Donnelly Rhodes) puts it, "chaos." Deaths that were ruled accidental, written off to addiction or misadventure, were in fact, it turns out, the work of a serial killer, Charlie (Eric Peterson), who has been murdering women for thirty years.

Impatient with the progress of the homicide investigation, Da Vinci goes under cover. Detectives Mick Leary (Ian Rhodes) and Angela Cosmos (Venus Terzo) watch through binoculars in disbelief as Da Vinci, in disguise, enters a local diner to gather evidence. Chatting up the murderer, Da Vinci claims to know Charlie from high school: "My bulldog use to crap on your lawn." Da Vinci's working-class banter and affected accent prove convincing: he gets samples of fish and chips that he believes will match the undigested food found in the stomach of the victim, Roxanne. Despite the fact that the "undercover" scenario is extreme—heavy-handed—it does help to establish a key aspect of Da Vinci's character. It suggests that Da Vinci has an ability to form relationships with people from all walks of life. He is as comfortable on the streets as he is in the office of the coroner, if not more so. In a symbolic plot twist, Da Vinci eats some of the evidence, which he finds out contains a rare parasite, and becomes infected with one of the same pathogens as the victims.

As the series develops, it becomes apparent that Dominic Da Vinci is an antihero. He suffers from vices of his own. The ethical sanctity of his quest to solve the misidentified murders is occluded by an inability to escape his own troubled past. As the storyline develops through the first three episodes, it is difficult to determine whether Da Vinci is guided by compassion or jealousy, ethical conviction or personal anger. Viewers are left to question whether he is driven by spite for his ex-wife Patricia (Gwynyth Walsh), pathologist of record for the cases in question, or by jealousy of Patricia's new flame and his boss, Chief Coroner James Flynn (Robert Wisden), who had initially ruled the women's deaths "accidental." Either way, Da Vinci's determination flushes out a serial killer, announcing the new city coroner as a champion for the forgotten and the downtrodden denizens of Vancouver's DTES.

In addition to introducing the series' principal characters and setting the narrative tone, the early episodes establish a clear filmic aesthetic for the series. Wheeler lifts Vancouver's Downtown Eastside to a level of cin-

Figure 1. Da Vinci's investigations took him to Vancouver's seamy underbelly. Image courtesy of Haddock Entertainment.

ematic beauty and helps to provide the show with a strong sense of location. Imbuing Vancouver's gritty streets with a patina of degeneration that was to become characteristic in the years to follow, she places Da Vinci within a particularized urban landscape. The dilapidated storefronts, teeming alleys, inhospitable single-room occupancy hotels, and local diners of the city's neglected inner-city neighbourhood are more than crime scenes; they become quotidian spaces in which the lives of the characters take place each week. The district around the coroner's office is portrayed as dangerous and vibrant. Inviting viewers into Da Vinci's world, Wheeler's camera works in concert with Haddock's scripts both to humanize the stories it tells and at times to retell them.

Characteristically, almost generically for this type of crime drama, the camera seems to be in constant motion, roaming the downtown streets on foot or by car, swinging high above the port from a crane, or zooming in on different urban landscapes from a distance. Yet compared with the frenetic cinematography of *Hill Street Blues* (1981–87), *NYPD Blue* (1993–2005), or *Law and Order* (1990–), there is a serenity to Wheeler's camera work, which works with the soundtrack to create a look and feel based loosely on a cool jazz aesthetics of the 1950s. The long telephoto shots and context-setting pans of dimly lit streetscapes and interiors, used in conjunction with a soundtrack that carefully mixes snippets of conversation, soft jazz lines, and environmental noise, produce a strongly voyeuristic effect that, rather than repelling or disorienting viewers, tends to seduce or draw us in. Picking up on conventions of film noir, Wheeler's camera holds our focus on banal details from the surroundings—cranes hovering above the Vancouver port, a forgotten alley, Da Vinci's coffee cup. Rather than standing out against the backdrop of their urban surrounding, the characters, particularly the men, blend in, their features, hair, and wardrobe tending toward the disheveled rather than the polished and the plastic. Da Vinci's grey suits and nondescript trench coats are reminiscent of Sam Spade, Philip Marlowe, or Mike Hammer.

Reinforcing the uncanny tension between the familiar and the abject— working the hinge that Freud argues joins the *heimlich* and *unheimlich*— the *Da Vinci's Inquest* aesthetic established by Wheeler and Haddock early on in the series underpins a fascination for the intersections of the humane and the barbaric that make up the core of the city. Beyond the fact that these episodes rehash grisly "true crime" dramas that are more or less lifted from the pages of the *Vancouver Sun*, what is remarkable about the way the storyline is developed by the creators is that it establishes an extended sense of kinship around the victims, a figurative bond that links the pathologists, police, and, I would argue, the viewer, with the murdered women.

As a counterpoint to the narrative thread involving the arrival of Roxanne's brother in Vancouver to claim his sister's corpse and seek justice for her murder, we are also introduced to the murderer's mother and the family's long history of violence. The recent murders are part of a pattern that began with the disappearance of a local girl thirty years earlier, when Charlie was a teenager. Following Da Vinci's lead, the police unearth the girl's remains, buried beneath the dirt floor of a garage behind an unremarkable Vancouver house. This not only links the violent present to the past, but it also reverses a dominant topology of fear. Rather than finding that the situation on the DTES is caused by the intrusion of some foreign element or being, the detectives find the roots of the problem in the home(l)y environs of Vancouver's tree-lined streets. Roxanne comes to Vancouver from an unspecified reservation elsewhere in BC; the murderer, Charlie, is born and raised here. And it is his violent past, not her degeneration, that returns to haunt the centre of the city. Thus, *Da Vinci's Inquest* recreates a kind of West Coast gothic in which evil is buried just below the surface of Vancouver's streets, not off in the forests. The little sisters' murders are not the consequence of an extrinsic force recently arrived in the city but of something in the ground upon which the new Vancouver is being built.

These opening episodes suggest that the missing women are not an unfortunate side effect of some new process of alienation but part of an old history. Contrary to a widespread belief that their disappearance or death might be the product of their own reckless behaviour, figured in the initial lack of interest in these cases by the coroner's office or the police, or for that matter the result of a dehumanizing globalization of Vancouver's growing sex and drug trades, these episodes trace the roots of the crime back to a pattern of violence that begins with Vancouver's middle class during the 1960s. They take viewers back to an earlier period in Vancouver's history when the city was just beginning to emerge as a modern urban centre, a period prior to its entrance into a global economy. Placed within a historical context, then, we might say that the violence depicted here, while dependent on the DTES as a stage, predates the neighbourhood's emergence as an epicentre of urban poverty in Canada.

Wheeler and Haddock establish a link between Da Vinci and both the victims and the perpetrators. Da Vinci's own vices and everyman demeanour place him alongside, rather than as morally superior to, those living and dying in the DTES. In this regard, alcoholism serves an important aspect of Da Vinci's character. At the end of the first episode, in a bar with his police colleagues, Da Vinci falls off the wagon with a recklessness akin to that of the murdered women. Furthermore, in a telling conclusion to the "Little Sister" episodes, Da Vinci meets up with a new girlfriend, an academic psychologist who provides him with a paper on "sex and death," which are, as she puts it, his "favourite subjects." While he pours her a drink, she describes the killer's pattern, which Da Vinci ironically appropriates. Her explanation of the murderer's imagined MO becomes a script for seduction. Da Vinci the recovering alcoholic, and cuckolded husband, turns out to be an unrepentant womanizer. His mimetic repetition of this violent pathology in the comfort of his own living room and in the company of this young woman provides an unnervingly flippant commentary on the preceding three episodes.

The subplot in these initial episodes involves Da Vinci's confronting another series of deaths: the suicide of a middle-class father who inadvertently poisons his family in the process of killing himself. The story of this "dumb, stupid prick," as Da Vinci calls him, provides a balance to the murder narrative and reinforces the notion that violence exists within families and is as much the product of stupidity as it is of sinister intent. The job of the coroner involves both high-profile murder cases and inane, quotidian bad luck. In this way, *Da Vinci's Inquest* collapses the boundaries separating internal and external forces—the private and local are as dangerous as the public and foreign.

In the later seasons, especially season six, when Da Vinci bid unsuccessfully for the position of police chief, and season seven, when he enters the mayoral race, *Da Vinci's Inquest* shifts the focus away from Da Vinci's work as a coroner, particularly as it relates to the spectacular and gruesome serial murders, and onto civic politics. While he remains committed to "saving the living by attending to the dead," more of Da Vinci's energy seems to go into furthering his social agenda. A vocal proponent for North America's first government-sanctioned "safe injection site" and advocate for the establishment of an official red-light district, Da Vinci moves from being an artist of the macabre to a social visionary. Following the trajectory of the later seasons into *Da Vinci's City Hall*, we might say that Dominic Da Vinci takes what he learns on the streets and in the alleys of the DTES across town to the halls of power. Mirroring an emergent political climate in Vancouver, the fictional coroner becomes a vehicle for primetime viewers to identify and imagine alternatives to serious social ills. Paralleling the historical rise of Larry Campbell to the position of Vancouver mayor, Da Vinci's career swerves into civic office, moving the series away from the procedural to the political, a transition that culminates in the emergence of *Da Vinci's City Hall*, which springs phoenix-like from the ashes of *Da Vinci's Inquest* following season seven. In the process, however, Da Vinci moves from one genre of television to another, and in so doing, the series shifts focus from the Vancouver streets and the everyday struggles of its denizens to the machinations of civic politics and the more rarefied spaces of public office.

Act Two: Vancouver

Cameras pan city blocks of boarded up businesses, thriving pawnshops, small grocery and coffee shops, single-room occupancy welfare hotels, drug dealers' turfs, and drug users' doorways. What the cameras fail to record are brightly painted wall murals and satirical graffiti; curtained windows, roof gardens and flower boxes in hard-won social housing projects; and the schools, drop-in centres, clinics, missions, churches, parks, and playgrounds that announce that the Downtown Eastside is home for many—sometimes briefly, sometimes for a lifetime.[15]

A key element in the success of *Da Vinci's Inquest* is linked to the creators' ability to blur the boundaries between the news and entertainment and to deliver a winning mix of facts and fiction from the streets of Downtown Eastside Vancouver. For Haddock, "Vancouver is a central character in the show." He says: "That's where we've succeeded. The more specific you get, in dealing with things on location, the more universal and genuine it becomes."[16] The wisdom of Haddock's approach is clear in the critical accolades *Da Vinci's Inquest* has enjoyed and in the series' longevity. The show's success suggests a strong appetite for its urban aesthetic and history-based narratives focused on real life-and-death situations in a neighbourhood infamous for high rates of sexual abuse, substance abuse, HIV/AIDS and hepatitis infection, crime, and grinding poverty. For seven seasons, *Da Vinci's Inquest* demonstrated a near-prescient ability to ride a growing wave of international interest in the DTES as a primary site of urban decay and the devastating effects of poverty and alienation.

To understand the rhetorical power of *Da Vinci's Inquest*, it is important to recognize something of the social situation it draws on. In a recent study of the DTES in relation to women who live and work there, Leslie Roberston and Dara Culhane provide useful insight. Focusing on the epicentre of the DTES, Robertson and Culhane describe the situation in this way:

> The corner of Main and Hastings Streets has recently been dubbed the corner of "Pain and Wastings." Since 1997, when the City of Vancouver Health Department declared a public health emergency in response to reports that HIV infection rates among Downtown Eastside residents exceeded those anywhere else in the "developed" world, this corner has become a focal point for emerging local, national, and international debates about the causes of, and solutions to, widespread practices of illicit intravenous drug injection and the spread of HIV/AIDS.[17]

While Robertson and Culhane don't deny that the area faces deep-seated social problems, they argue that well-publicized or accepted "truths" about the DTES negatively impact those who are living and working there. The media attention, riddled as it is with stereotypes about women, Aboriginals, teenagers, mental health patients, and victims of various forms of abuse, is to the detriment of the neighbourhood.

The health and social problems in the DTES are complex, and many of the causes for them extend back to the early history of the city. As Roberston and Culhane, among others, have shown, coming to terms with the situation in the DTES involves understanding the complicity of a much broader public. As Da Vinci comes to recognize, the cure to the social ills of the DTES exist outside the neighbourhood itself, across town in city hall, or over in Victoria, or back in Ottawa. Thus, the series reflects, consciously perhaps, the work of academics and researchers such as Culhane and Robertson, Neil Smith and Jeff Derksen, Nick Blomley and Jeff Sommers, Shlomo Hasson and David Ley, and others, whose work demonstrates how the geography of the DTES extends beyond the boundaries of a neighbourhood. Representations of this neighbourhood, which tend to fixate on the poverty and abjection of its residents rather than the larger social processes involved, have arguably become a further detriment to the health and well-being of people who live there. To understand this area might entail a look beyond the spectacle of abjection to an analysis of the way visible poverty is instrumental to the movement of large sums of money through it in illegal and illicit commercial enterprise.

Unwittingly perhaps, *Da Vinci's Inquest* becomes both a benefactor and victim of the historical contexts with which it is so intimately linked. While the 1990s mark a dramatic shift in the nature of the social problems in the DTES, and a notable shift in the discourse, the roots of the neighbourhood's troubles go back to the beginning of the twentieth century and Skid Row, a ghetto on the edge of Vancouver's port where predominantly male workers—longshoremen, fishers, merchant marines, loggers, miners, and mill workers—would rest and recreate between stints at sea or up in the mines and forests of BC's north and central interior. On the edge of Chinatown and Japantown, and an easy walk to the black community in Hogan's Alley, this neighbourhood has always been characterized by its links to racialized communities. Thus, the multiplicity of shots of the port, streetscapes, cafes, and SROs that comprise the recognizable settings of *Da Vinci's Inquest* carry the patina of this infamous past. The city's few remaining neon signs—remnants of a time when Hastings and Granville glowed in a wash of neon reds, blues, and greens—and fashionably outmoded restaurants—the Only Cafe or the Ovaltine—visually define the series' *mise en scène*. These visual reminders of an era when many of the denizens of the DTES would be men on their way to or from "the skids" resonate with the muted jazz of the musical soundtrack, infusing the series with a high level of nostalgia.

This nostalgia tends to elide the bond *Da Vinci's Inquest* has with the historical emergence of Vancouver's burgeoning sex and drug trades. During the 1990s, with the shift in public awareness of HIV/AIDS and a growing incidence rate among intravenous drug users, much higher than that within the city's gay communities, Canadian television audiences were being subjected to renewed fears about the spread of HIV/AIDS. In the media, the "epidemic" that was seen to be raging on the DTES exemplified its status as a "Third World" enclave in the midst of the fastest-growing and most expensive city in Canada, and by association "the First World." A well-rehearsed moral panic over prostitution and alcoholism fed into a new and much more volatile fear of the lethal mixing of degenerate sexuality and rampant drug use. If, as Robertson and Culhane suggest, the Vancouver Health Department and other government offices were responsible for drawing attention to the DTES among researchers and health care professionals, it was the media who brought these concerns home to Canadian viewers.[18]

Da Vinci's professional interest in death and urban decay fits into a larger hysteria about the DTES. Contextualizing the media's fixation on "The Worst Block in Vancouver," as 100 West Hastings Street was dubbed, geographers Jeff Sommers and Nick Blomley describe a polarization of wealth and an increasing isolation of the DTES from the rest of the city. Their research suggests that the median income in the DTES fell from "nearly half [the national average] in 1970 to less than a quarter in 1990," while during the same period, it grew nearly five times larger in the rest of the city.[19] Connecting this growing economic disparity with moral panic over HIV/AIDS, Sommers and Blomley write, "Both IV drug use and the disease were then conflated with the signs of growing poverty and marginality, such as homelessness, begging, and "squeegee kids," all of which had become increasingly visible in the downtown peninsula and inner city neighbourhoods over the 1990s." Eventually, they suggest, this led to a "pathologization of the poor turned into the pathologization of an entire neighbourhood."[20] This old port-side neighbourhood, the architectural heart of historic Vancouver and a mere stone's throw from the touristy cobblestone streets of Gastown, quickly became "ground zero" for seemingly all current urban nightmares. Vancouver's DTES had become Canada's Detroit, despite the fact that the economy was booming throughout the rest of the city and suburbs surrounding it.[21]

The DTES imagined in *Da Vinci's Inquest* is part of a larger creative and critical discourse that simultaneously problematizes the political alienation of the neighbourhood while paradoxically feeding on it. Inasmuch as the DTES becomes a major site for the international traffic of narcotics and other illicit commodities, it becomes a commodity in its own right. It is easy to be cynical about primetime English-language Canadian television, especially in the context of its ability to deal with the types of social issues raised in *Da Vinci's Inquest*. Yet the desire to represent urban decrepitude, or to see it represented on television, is an important driving force behind

Da Vinci's Inquest and its positive reception. The news media, echoing statements by the show's writers, actors, and producers, repeatedly characterized the series in terms of its "political" engagement with difficult social concerns.

In a short essay for *Saturday Night* magazine, the show's first intern, writer Esta Spalding, recounts her experience of being on set for a shoot "along one of the 'kiddie strolls,' in this case a two-block stretch of a dark, industrial warehouse zone where johns are guaranteed to find the youngest girl prostitutes."[22] The "stroll," like the "low track," another infamous stretch of the DTES known for street-level sex trade, was a key location for *Da Vinci's Inquest*. Spalding describes her own struggle with the reality that she has been hired to research and write about for the show. Titled "Working Girls," her piece depicts a paradoxical connection between the show's actors, writers, and producers and the sex-trade workers they represent. Working with a timeworn analogy between theatre and prostitution, Spalding's essay points to the socio-economic reality that underwrites the show. Ironically, perhaps, the economic disparity and social isolation the show sets out to capture is the very situation that makes the series possible, or at least financially viable. The show's desire to represent or in some way document the difficulties of living on the street in the DTES, Spalding's article suggests, might also be understood as feeding into the problem. During production, the shoot forces Vancouver's sex and drug trades to move a little farther down the block: "The real working women aren't far off. Tonight we've taken over their corner, so they've moved down a block or two. They're the ones without jackets, perched on stiletto heels, cold and teetering and only half there." By way of conclusion, Spalding writes: "Watching it all from the periphery, it's moments before I realize that one of the women standing on the edge of the light isn't an actress at all. She's a working woman who's left her corner of the street for a few minutes. I watch her drain her paper cup and take a final drag from her cigarette, then she tosses the cup into a dumpster and walks back into the night."[23]

Thinking about this series in the context of Canadian culture and television, it is easy to read into Spalding's uneasiness. If the success of *Da Vinci's Inquest* hinges on the producers' knack for fitting its skid row forays into Vancouver's urban politics, then a key facet of this success is linked with the show's ability to locate itself within the nationalist project backing the series, financially and ideologically. Symbolically, Da Vinci's political success, despite his commitment to the welfare of individuals living on the DTES, many of whom are socially and economically alienated because of race, gender, class, age, sexuality, and mental health, is contingent on his ability to find support in Ottawa.

Following the narrative trajectory of *Da Vinci's Inquest* through *Da Vinci's City Hall*, we find an increasing connection between the coroner and the federal government. As momentum for a career in city hall builds, Da Vinci's success depends on his ability to find favour with Liberals in Ottawa for establishing a safe injection site and developing a red-light district. In season seven, Da Vinci literally goes to bed with a federal bureaucrat. Returning to his old philandering ways, established in the very first episodes of the show but downplayed in subsequent seasons, Da Vinci becomes romantically involved with Claire (Leanne Adachi), who counsels him on his bid to be mayor. Their personal relationship symbolically reinforces Da Vinci's alignment with the federal Liberals. His new friends help overcome opposition to his plans from municipal and provincial politicians and their supporters, and Da Vinci's focus drifts away from the specificity of the DTES.

On the level of ideology, Da Vinci's movement into the political arena and away from more quotidian matters of life and death on the DTES suggests a problematic concession to neo-liberalism. This is not to say that municipal and provincial governments are any less complicit with a neo-liberal agenda, only that Da Vinci—and with him the series itself—abandoned the social situation that gave the series its political edginess. Taking, for example, the "Little Sister" episodes discussed earlier, the series seems to take a dramatic departure from some of the earlier aspects of the show's main character and the narratives that evolve around him. In the earlier episodes, Da Vinci distinguishes himself by being willing to concentrate on the fine details of his cases and championing the rights and dignity of victims and their families. In the later, politically focused episodes, and in seasons six and seven in particular, his ambitions get the better of him and he becomes embroiled in the give and take of political life. The series shifts focus away from the city and onto the man.

Act Three: Postmortem

> The reconstruction of central urban neighbourhoods is increasingly embedded in the circuits of global culture and capital. Above all, the central city has become a field of capital accumulation—production as well as consumption—with inner urban landscapes increasingly transformed into the factories of spatial change.[24]

In the tradition of the best of English-language Canadian television dramas represented by programs such as *Wojek*, *North of 60*, and *Human Cargo*, *Da Vinci's Inquest* provides Canadian audiences with gritty realism, on the one hand, and a more believable response to difficult social situations on the other. To put it in slightly different terms, *Da Vinci's Inquest* satisfies a desire to see liberal humanism revitalized, set against the backdrop of an increasingly inhuman urban landscape. The creators of the series carve out a space on primetime English Canadian television that is more contradictory or contentious, more politically engaging than the big-budget alternatives produced by "the networks" to the south. *Da Vinci's Inquest* taps into an apparent need on the part of viewers to see something recognizably "Canadian" but categorically different from what they are used to seeing.

Thus, a key facet of the show's success is that it allows viewers to see Vancouver as Vancouver, rather than as some unnamed American city. Accustomed as we are to seeing Canadian cities and neighbourhoods standing in as generic backdrops in low-budget productions—for example, *Smallville* (2001–), *McGyver* (1985–92), *The X-Files* (1993–98), and countless movies of the week, which traditionally have been paid for by the American networks for distribution in the US and then piped back across the border for Canadian audiences—viewers could take comfort, even genuine pleasure, in having access to "recognizably Canadian situations and settings."[25] Unlike US counterparts such as *Hill Street Blues*, *Law and Order*, *Homicide: Life on the Street* (1993–99), or *NYPD Blue*, all of which tend to rely on more stylized settings and name-brand actors, *Da Vinci's Inquest* was able to harness local events to mass appeal. Attending to stories more or less as they were unfolding, the creators of *Da Vinci's Inquest* kept the series relevant to various audiences and a developing realpolitik.

Encoded as the urban space in which weekly episodes take place and the wellspring for the majority of storylines explored in it, particularly those involving drug abuse or the sex trade, Vancouver's DTES was instrumental in helping *Da Vinci's Inquest* distinguish itself as a unique cultural object. As critics have suggested, part of the genius of the show was the way in which the city itself became a character. However, it is also important to note that these same locations and neighbourhoods are in part the result of economic forces that have made BC into a viable location for North American film and television production. In turn, these forces have played a crucial role in making *Da Vinci's Inquest* a profitable export.

Situating the series within the social-cultural matrix it represents creatively, and addressing the series' apparent ability to capitalize on local violence, critics need to separate the hype generated in local and national media, which to a large extent has been supported if not fostered by the series' creators, from the show's own discursive complicity with a neoliberal rationalization of Vancouver's urban core within networks of global

Figure 2. By the time Da Vinci moved from the coroner's office to the mayor's office, the show had lost its critical edge. Image courtesy of Haddock Entertainment.

capital. Situating *Da Vinci's Inquest* within the cultural production of Vancouver, rather than seeing it in more general nationalistic terms, allows us to understand the series as part of an emergent discourse that links remarkably diverse modes of articulation and performance. Borrowing the concept of "scaling" from Smith and Derksen's writing about globalization and the gentrification of the DTES, I want to suggest that part of the problem with *Da Vinci's City Hall*—and to a lesser extent this is also true of the final season of *Da Vinci's Inquest*—is that it attempts to rescale the axis of the political to the level of the nation. Rather than locating Vancouver within an urban–global dynamic, the cultural-political scope of the series allows itself to become circumscribed by outmoded national and regional relationships. It loses sight of a vital representational drive that comes to the fore in the earlier seasons. Shifting focus away from the DTES and onto Da Vinci's political career, it moves from an unfolding social imaginary and onto the psychological struggles of a powerful individual.

The cancellation of *Da Vinci's City Hall*, ultimately the demise of *Da Vinci*, was the product of more than simple ill will at the CBC. The series' declining ratings were exacerbated by its own representational strategies. Figuratively and literally, the DTES that Da Vinci grew to represent has begun to disappear under the forces of gentrification. The historical situations that gave the show its edge were no longer current: the "missing women" were found to have been murdered, and the murderer was in police custody; Larry Campbell had left civic politics—after serving as the mayor of Vancouver, Campbell stepped down to become a senator in Ottawa. Furthermore, the combined forces of gentrification and economic expansion had dramatically altered Vancouver's urban landscape and changed the BC film and television industry. Neither Vancouver nor the DTES are what they were when Da Vinci entered the scene in 1998.

If, as Smith and Derksen have argued, "cities have become rescaled as production platforms" for global capitalism, then it is important to recognize Vancouver's DTES in relation to the forces of neo-liberalism.[26] The DTES was not forgotten; instead, it was and is the product of a large-scale reorganization and redistribution of both capital and culture. If "cities can be seen as the new factories of the global economy, making everything for global consumption," then we are left to wonder about the audience's appetite for *Da Vinci's Inquest* and its stories of Vancouver's drug and sex trades. To think of the DTES in relation to globalization and Vancouver's links with other urban sites around the world necessitates our addressing difficult questions about the relationships between cultural production and economic exploitation. Contrary to its initial success, *Da Vinci's City Hall* abandoned the unstable social energies of urban Vancouver in favour of a more stable hero. Attempting to gain political power, Da Vinci underwent a change and became embroiled in a more or less predictable struggle for political power and office, which took him too far from the streets and the neighbourhood that made the series interesting to viewers in the first place. Coming to terms with the series' political horizons is crucial to understanding not only the implications of the show vis-à-vis the politics it imagines for itself, but also something of the larger geopolitical forces within which it was embedded. In this sense, the producers' desire to give voice to situations and people otherwise disenfranchised in the mainstream media—a source of its rhetorical force and ultimately its downfall—took the series to the limits of nationalist cultural production. Reading *Da Vinci*'s shift in focus away from the police procedural and onto the political requires consideration of the series as a commodity for global consumption, especially in the context of its increasing popularity. Following the logic of global capitalism, the series, which began as a product geared at predominantly Canadian audiences, entered a global marketplace, where it was made to confront new and different situational pressures.

Contrary to its self-conscious radicalism and almost flippant anti-Americanism, especially in representations of resistance from US authorities to Da Vinci's plans for the safe injection site and red-light district, the show's success came to rely on its ability to reproduce American-style politics and political figures for a growing international audience.[27] For viewers in Canada, the US, and elsewhere, Da Vinci's anti-conservative and anti-Republican, if not anti-American, sentiments offer respite from more stridently patriotic and socially conservative fare available on the big US networks.

Looking at the figure of the main character himself, we can see that the show moved away from the realization of Da Vinci as a troubled everyman, a drinker and philander who suffers from his own self-destructive behaviour. The subtext of the earlier episodes suggested that Da Vinci's lack of restraint had cost him his marriage and nearly his career. In Episode 2, the chief coroner tries to get Da Vinci to drop his investigation by reminding him that he only got the job as a favour, a last chance. In the later seasons, however, Da Vinci's personal weaknesses, which initially place him among those he seeks to help, have more or less disappeared. His drinking and his sexual proclivities are firmly under control, and as I suggested in the preceding section, he has learned to use sex to further his career. A more powerful individual, perhaps, Da Vinci has cleaned up his image for mass consumption. He is no longer a drunk. His ex-wife and child have disappeared from the picture. In fact, Da Vinci's personal life is almost entirely eradicated in favour of his career and political ambitions. Contrary to his earlier edgy defiance, Da Vinci has become a shinier, safer commodity for export. He is removed from the city and the streets that gave him life and becomes a mere reflection of the series itself.

Notes

1 Spalding, "Working Girls," 38.
2 CBC News Online, "*Da Vinci* Cancelled."
3 Ross, "Two Acclaimed CBC Dramas to Be Cancelled."
4 For a discussion and analysis of the CBC's new direction, see MacDonald, "Drama Queen No More."
5 Tinic, *On Location*, 30.
6 Tinic, *On Location*, 30.
7 Tinic, *On Location*, 91.
8 Tinic, *On Location*, 92.
9 Peter Babiak notes: "Peddling domestic locations to lure film crews pushed out of foreign neighbourhoods is a duplicitous practice, but not too surprising in an ideological state apparatus like the BCFC, whose only submission under 'Community Service' is a registry for property owners to advertise their homes and offices to

location scouts. Like a floozy hitching its own pretty skirt, the commissars keep a photo library of 'a variety of residential areas, back alleys, office towers, stunning mountains, glaciers, castles, country roads, wild westcoast beaches' to seduce even more film companies to BC" (*West Coast Line*, 128). See also Gasher, *Hollywood North*.

10 Spaner, *Dreaming in the Rain*, 123.

11 Spaner, *Dreaming in the Rain*, 123.

12 This is spoken by Leo Shannon (Donelley Rhodes) in the "Little Sister" episode in the first season of *Da Vinci's Inquest* (1998).

13 For a discussion of the coincidence of the opening episode of the second season and the case of the missing women, see Bailey, "CBC Mixes Reality of Prostitution with Fiction."

14 For more on domestic melodrama and Wheeler's depictions of patriarchal and colonial violence, see Lord, "States of Emergency."

15 Robertson and Culhane, "Introduction," 19.

16 Gill, "Dissecting Da Vinci."

17 Robertson and Culhane, "Introduction," 18.

18 Robertson and Culhane, "Introduction."

19 Sommers and Blomley, "The Worst Block in Vancouver," 42.

20 Sommers and Blomley, "The Worst Block in Vancouver," 21.

21 Parallels between the two sites are developed in Stan Douglas's *Every Building on 100 West Hasting* and *Le Detroit*, the latter an exhibition featuring images of Detroit's heroic modern industrial architecture in ruins.

22 Spalding, "Working Girls," 38.

23 Spalding, "Working Girls," 38.

24 Smith and Derksen, "Gentrification Generalized."

25 Museum of Broadcast Communications, "E.N.G.," at www.museum.tv/archives/etv/E/htmlE/eng/eng.htm (accessed May 1, 2006).

26 Smith and Derksen, "Gratification Generalized."

27 See MacDonald, "Made in Canada."

References

Babiak, Peter. "Rising Stars and Dead Metaphors." *West Coast Line* 36 (2): 128–29.

Bailey, Ian. "CBC Mixes Reality of Prostitution with Fiction." *Calgary Herald*, September 8, 1999: B9.

Blomley, Nick. *Unsettling the City: Urban Land and the Politics of Property*. London: Routledge, 2004.

CBC News. "*Da Vinci* Cancelled." CBC News Online, February 14, 2006. Available at www.cbc.ca/bc/story /bc_da-vinci20060213.html. Accessed January 10, 2008.

Freud, Sigmund. "The Uncanny." In *The Standard Edition of the Complete Psychological Works of Sigmund Freud*, Vol. XVII, edited and translated by James Strachey, 219–52. London: Hogarth, 1953.

Gasher, Mike. *Hollywood North: The Feature Film Industry in British Columbia*. Vancouver: UBC Press, 2002.

Gee, Dana. "Dominic One of TV's Unforgettable Characters." *Vancouver Province*, February 14, 2006.

Gill, Alexandra. "Dissecting Da Vinci: TV's Most Popular Coroner Is the Construct of Three Guys." *Globe and Mail*, November 9, 2002.

Hasson, Shlomo and David Ley. "The Downtown Eastside: One Hundred Years of Struggle." In *Neighbourhood Organizations and the Welfare State*, edited by Hasson Shlomo and David Ley, 172–204. Toronto: University of Toronto Press, 1994.

Lefebvre, Henri. *The Production of Space*. Translated by N. Donaldson-Smith. Oxford: Basil Blackwell, 1991.

Lord, Susan. "States of Emergency in the Films of Anne Wheeler." In *North of Everything: English Canadian Cinema Since 1980*, edited by William Beard and Jerry White, 312–26. Edmonton: University of Alberta Press, 2002.

MacDonald, Gayle. "Made in Canada, Big in Syria," *Globe and Mail*, December 18, 2001: Review Section.

———. "Drama Queen No More." *Globe and Mail*, February 25, 2006.

Museum of Broadcast Communications. "E.N.G." Available at www.museum.tv/archives/etv/E/htmlE/eng/eng.htm. Accessed May 1, 2006.

Robertson, Leslie and Dara Culhane. "Introduction." In *In Plain Sight: Reflections on Life in Downtown Eastside Vancouver*, edited by Leslie Roberston and Dara Culhane. Vancouver: Talonbooks, 2005.

Ross, Val. "Two Acclaimed CBC Dramas to Be Cancelled." *Globe and Mail*, February 13, 2006. Available at www.theglobeandmail.com/servlet/story/RTGAM.20060213.wxwonder13/BNStory/Entertainment/home. Accessed May 1, 2006.

Smith, Neil and Jeff Derksen. "Gentrification Generalized and Rescaling the Cultural." Unpublished essay.

Sommers, Jeff and Nick Blomley. "The Worst Block in Vancouver." In *Stan Douglas: Every Building on 100 West Hastings*, edited by Reid Shier, 18–58. Vancouver: Contemporary Art Gallery/Arsenal Pulp Press, 2002.

Spalding, Esta. "Working Girls." *Saturday Night*, November 1999.

Spaner, David. *Dreaming in the Rain: How Vancouver Became Hollywood North by Northwest*. Vancouver: Arsenal Pulp Press, 2002.

Tinic, Serra. *On Location: Canada's Television Industry in a Global Market*. Toronto: University of Toronto Press, 2005.

Filmography

Corner Gas (Prairie Pants Productions/Three Thirty Five Productions/CTV, 2004–)

Cracker (A&E/Granada, 1993)

Da Vinci's City Hall (Haddock Entertainment, 2005)

Da Vinci's Inquest (Haddock Entertainment/CBC, 1998–2004)

Danger Bay (Sunrise Films, 1984–89)

E.N.G. (Alliance Communications/CTV/Telefilm, 1990–94)

Hill Street Blues (MTM/NBC, 1981–87)

Homicide: Life on the Street (Baltimore Pictures/Fatima Productions/MCEG/Sterling Entertainment/NBC, 1993–99)

Law and Order (Wolf Films/Studios USA Television/NBC/Universal,1990–)

McGyver (Henry Winkler/John Rich Productions/Paramount, 1985–92)

NYPD Blue (20th Century Fox/Fox Television/Steven Bochco Productions, 1993–2005)

Quincy, M.E. (Glen A. Larson Productions/Universal, 1976–83)

Smallville (Tollin Robbins Productions/Millar Gough Ink/Warner Bros./DC Comics/Smallville Films, 2001–)

The Beachcombers (CBC, 1972–90)

The Tournament (Adjacent 2 Entertainment, 2005)

This is Wonderland (Indian Grove Productions/Muse Entertainment Enterprises/Alice Productions (Muse), 2004)

The X-Files (20th Century Fox/Ten Thirteen Productions, 1993–2002)

JEN VANDERBURGH

Imagining National Citizens
in Televised Toronto

ramatic television programming has pride of place in discourses of cultural nationalism in Canada. So entrenched is the belief in drama's abilities to consolidate a sense of "culture" that funding strategies are rhetorically said to be a component of national defence.[1] This link between television drama and the advocacy of a particular, unified version of Canadian nationhood is a foundational tenet of the Canadian Broadcasting Corporation, for whom the project of "national culture" is its raison d'être.[2] But the CBC's challenge in producing "national" drama is that television production is contingent on place. "The nation," in other words, is an impossible televisual location. To create "national drama," location has had to signify the nation.

One technique used by the CBC has been to frame locations as "national" microcosms. These locations tend to be cohesive, geographically and culturally isolated from other communities. Sometimes they are situated in the temporal past, outside of contemporary time and space, a strategy that intensifies the location's allegorical impact.

The CBC's second, more nuanced approach has been to situate drama in a recognizable contemporary location. This approach to narrativizing location is dialectical, since it inflects the "national" allegory with located specificities. Overwhelmingly, for this latter purpose, the city of Toronto has been the CBC's location of choice.[3]

By now, we know that consigning authorship to the CBC should be framed as a problematic. The institution has not functioned as a monolith, nor has its drama been consistently authored.[4] Yet these caveats do not obviate the claim that tendencies are observable across the CBC's dramatic content. If anything, the non-monolithic claim makes the implications for the tendencies we may find more compelling. This is because the

CBC's existence as a discursive project—as opposed to a fact of nature—derived from multiple sites of authorship does not preclude its intrinsic status as a social mechanism that has actual effects on the conceptualization of both a "Canadian imaginary" and everyday life. Discourse and "the social" are in this way mutually constitutive. This is the lens through which I view Toronto's characterization, its aesthetic, and its performative function as a dialectical site within CBC's "national" dramas.

In this context, the imaginary Toronto of CBC dramas, the aesthetic of which represents a simulacrum of "the nation," also functions as a barometer of a "national public." A "public," like the Toronto of CBC dramas, and the CBC itself, is both a discursive construction and an actual social fact. That is to say, there is an actual audience being heralded by CBC programs, and the everyday experiences of people take place within a discursive yet operational understanding of a "Canadian nation." The specificities of the material and historical convergence of CBC Television in 1952 and Toronto's postwar cosmopolitanism entrenched Toronto's semiotic function within a particular nation-building project distinct from Radio-Canada's use of Montreal. What I hope this chapter makes clear is the extent to which the CBC's conceptualization of Toronto has mediated and recorded "national" social anxieties.

Over time, Toronto's dialectical significance as a site of national allegory and located social specificity in CBC drama exposes an increasing ambivalence to the nation-building project. Deliberate, and articulated in fragments through policies, this project can be defined as an investment in a particular vision of Canadian nationhood that privileges unity, a "cultural mosaic," and shared social policies. Its cultural and ethnic orientation is dominated by the English language and British and American cultures, and is inflected to varying degrees by the French language and Québécois, immigrant, and Aboriginal cultures. This particular understanding of what constitutes the CBC's conceptualization of Canada has effectively colonized the abstract space of television in the interests of a singular Canadian nation-state.

Since the inception of CBC Television, Toronto drama has emphasized ethnic tensions, inequality, and even the paranormal—a far cry from a singular imagined community. But the historical scope of these Toronto dramas reveals a significant change: a gradual trajectory of the citizen's alienation from national social policies. In the remainder of this chapter, I offer symptomatic readings of three popular CBC dramas—*Wojeck* (1966–68), *The King of Kensington* (1975–80), and *Seeing Things* (1981–86)—intended to be emblematic of three decades of CBC drama located in Toronto. My argument is that these programs bear witness to a decline in the ability of the "citizen" protagonist to effect changes in policy. These expressions of the citizen's agency are tied to place. In the 1960s, *Wojeck*'s Toronto characterizes citizens as social actors with the agency to develop policy in response to the city's deficiencies, as determined by actual lived experience. By the 1970s, the model of community governance articulated in *The King of Kensington* evidences a naturalized understanding of national policy as immutable and incapable of responding to the diverse needs of its citizenry. In the 1980s, *Seeing Things* characterizes national policy as being so far removed from citizen intervention that only the paranormal can contravene the rational efficiency of "public" bureaucracies. This trajectory, made observable in CBC drama, leads me to consider what this increasing divide between the citizen protagonist and national policy implies about the experience of "national citizenship" in public life.

Wojeck

CBC's first major series filmed on location in Toronto, *Wojeck* is premised on the career of Toronto city coroner Steve Wojeck.[5] The series' discursive thrust positions Wojeck's insatiable quest for moral justice and policy reform against the seemingly insurmountable, sometimes indifferent, but ultimately benevolent bureaucracy of Canadian politics, the legal system, and law enforcement. The narrative privileges Dr. Wojeck's "common sense," which results in systemic change for the "public good." Since the plot of each episode revolves around the investigation of a death in an effort to prevent a similar death in the future, the series is built on a blend of the popular anti-establishment discourses of the late 1960s and the nationalist perspective of the CBC.[6] The show's inquests and investigations build cases for change: for better safety measures in the auto industry ("Swing Low, Sweet Chariot"); for standardized and impartial inspections of working conditions on construction sites ("Tell Them the Streets Are Dancing"); for controls on food safety and alcohol ("Another Wonderful Day" and "A Dime Harry Doesn't Need"); for reducing disparity in medical treatment ("Thy Mother a Lady, Lovely and Bright"); and for preventing insurance fraud in the conduct of homes for the aged ("Listen! An Old Man is Speaking"). Although failures of the social system are acknowledged in *Wojeck*, hegemony, as it is articulated in the series, ultimately serves the public interest. Legislation and procedure, which as municipal, provincial, and national practices are shown to be mutable and receptive to popular opinion, might be said to be the real heroes in each episode.

In *Wojeck*, the practices of governance and the regulation of public institutions are conceptualized as a work in progress for which all citizens are held responsible. Steve Wojeck, though exceptional in his commitment to his work as a public servant, is considered an average Canadian of middle-class income and Polish Canadian descent. If legislative change is positioned as one aspect of social advocacy in *Wojeck*, change in public opinion is considered its complement. In many episodes, where "the system" falls short of treating "the public's" ills, *Wojeck* advocates a shift in the public's collective consciousness to improve a chronic problem. In these episodes, viewers are invited to sympathize with individual characters whose deaths or crises represent the need for communal awareness and attitude adjustment. "The Last Man in the World" features an Ojibwa man, new to Toronto, who is driven to suicide by systemic racism. "You've Been Very Kind" warns that religious counselling should not act as a substitute for the medical treatment of depression. Dr. Wojeck confronts his Catholic faith in the two-part episode "The Cold Smile of Strangers" when the failure to address the question of abortion is held accountable for the death of a woman who received a badly administered illegal abortion and the imminent demise of an otherwise healthy young girl. And in "After All, Who's Art Morrison?" the homosexuality of a respected public figure is demonstrated to be incompatible with a homophobic public perception of masculinity.

Ideologically, *Wojeck* departs from the conventions of television drama at the time in both US drama and studio dramas produced at the CBC. The series, for example, disrupts binaries between the state and the individual, the personal and the bureaucratic, and "right" and "wrong" that provide conventional reference points in dramatic narrative. Also unusual is *Wojeck's* tendency to encourage viewers to split empathetic subjective identifications between the lawmakers and law enforcers and society's victims in the same episode. In "All Aboard for Candyland," an episode that exposes the failings of a system that identifies drug addiction as a criminal rather than medical issue, the ideal viewer's sympathy shifts between Dr. Wojeck; his wife, Marty; the Crown attorney; a young junkie; and a suicidal heroin dealer/addict/nursery school teacher. Rather than achieving clarity, the episode foregrounds the difficulty of allocating blame for systemic social problems and the necessity of resolving them in a holistic manner in which all parties, citizens and policymakers alike, take responsibility for the common good of a society characterized as efficient yet humane.

Within this set of episodes, Toronto features prominently as a location in which to enact social-problem dramas of national significance.

Toronto thus functions as a microcosm.[7] Just as Michel de Certeau describes the experience of viewing New York City from the 110th floor of the World Trade Centre, a perspective removed from the fray that makes clear the mastery of space, so do *Wojeck*'s opening sequences in seasons one and two feature extended panoramic establishing shots of Toronto highways at night.[8] The movement of cars, reduced in nighttime aerial composition to fragments of light in motion, emphasizes Toronto's connectivity, creating tension between incoming and outgoing movement. This view of Toronto's arteries connects the city with flow in much the same way as Harold Innis's (1956) theory of staples, where communication pathways are imagined as essential symbolic tools for conceptualizing the unity of the Canadian nation. At the same time, *Wojeck's* Toronto panoramas imply the randomness of its narratives: that this city is filled with as many stories as there are characters, each one representative of and reliant upon the operation of a communal social unit. The tension between individual stories and their shared Toronto landscape implies that people are at once special and ordinary.

Characters, as fictitious citizens, emerge out of obscurity and frequently return to it by episode's end. Bruno Gerussi's character, Mario, for example, in "Tell Them the Streets Are Dancing," is initially inaudible as he walks toward the camera amid the ambient noise of street and pedestrian traffic. As Mario achieves visual and narrative prominence, his issue is addressed by official judicial inquiry and leads to policy reform. The episode concludes with an aerial shot of Mario and his girlfriend, dancing together on an empty neighbourhood street. As Mario fades from prominence, the camera's trajectory emphasizes his narrative journey from obscurity to visibility in Toronto—an aesthetic representation of how fairly he has been treated by its social structure. The city's initial monolithic appearance is tempered by the efforts of individuals within its administration who work to make it humane. *Wojeck* thus naturalizes a characterization of Toronto based on an active collective of individuals committed to a form of social progress to which national policy is responsive.

The use and specificity of recognizable Toronto locations in *Wojeck* demystifies the bureaucratic process of national governance. In tandem with Toronto's allegorical function, the specificity with which Toronto is characterized in *Wojeck* legitimates actual space by virtue of its narrative articulation. Implicitly, the characterization of Toronto mimics the narrative journey of each episode's guest star, resolving in the equilibrium of the collective unit. When one person is oppressed, the series argues, the collective suffers. Likewise, when an injustice is compensated, the city reflects equilibrium. In "The Last Man in the World," considered by many to the best episode of the series, the aesthetic treatment of Toronto spans from frenetic to meditative, parallel to the resolution of systemic racism that the character, Joe Smith, encounters. An Ojibwa-identified man from Moosenee, Joe is not an official band member because he was adopted. His status makes him ineligible for social programs and compensation. The episode begins abruptly, apparently midway through a nighttime street brawl outside Toronto's Hotel Waverly and Silver Dollar Room bar. The bar signs feature prominently in the sequence, their pulsating lights echoing the intensity of the dramatic action. Camera shots are mainly hand-held close-ups with a narrow depth of field that appears shaky and disorienting. Camera angles depict Joe in fragments as he knocks down a police officer with a punch. Amid the large crowd assembled, Joe's violence aligns our sympathy with the wounded police officer and the hegemonic system that he represents. Paired with the flashing lights of the bar sign and the spasmodic editing of the street fight, Joe's anger seems hysterical and unjustified and his subsequent arrest warranted.

After Joe hangs himself in his jail cell, his story is revealed in the diegetic present of Dr. Wojeck's investigation, supported by a series of flashbacks illustrating Joe's initiation in Toronto. Through Wojeck's investigation, what begins as an individual problem, Joe's lived experience in Toronto, becomes established in the narrative as a systemic problem with the Canadian Indian Act. Wojeck's comment that "one of these days … this country's going to hang itself with red tape" secures a literal connection between Joe's suicide by hanging and the state of "the nation" under current policies. As the episode concludes with Wojeck's inquest and the presumption that Joe's death will result in actual social change, order is restored at the local level within the city. The police sergeant whose negligence allowed Joe access to the belt by which he hung himself is reprimanded. A friend raises funds to put toward Joe's burial, and a small group, observed in an aerial shot that emphasizes the location in the city, gathers in the sunshine to bury Joe with dignity. In contrast to the opening sequence, shot at night, this daytime sequence implies that, with light cast upon it, Joe's situation has been recognized.

The characterization of Toronto in *Wojeck* thus functions to demonstrate the humanity and responsiveness possible in a bureaucracy that serves its citizens. Policy in *Wojeck* is conceived as coming from the ground up, inspired by actual lived experience, represented by case workers like Dr. Wojeck and society's "victims," such as Joe Smith. As a broadcaster with a specified national interest, the CBC demonstrates with *Wojeck* the relevance of social reform on actual experience and, likewise, the relevance

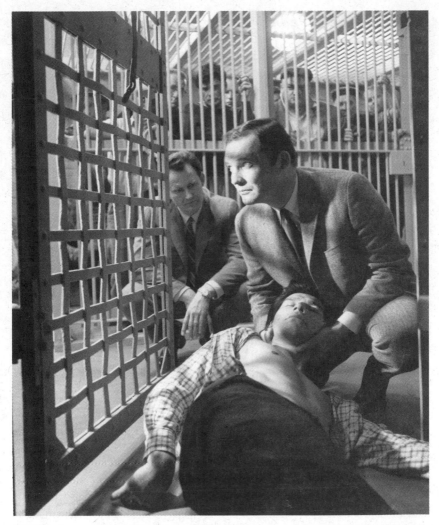

Figure 1. Coronor Steve Wojeck (John Vernon) investigates the hanging death of "that Indian," Joe Smith (Johnny Yesno), in "The Last Man in the World." Photo used with permission from CBC Archives.

of actual experience to national policies. Toronto's twofold function within the narrative is to provide a dynamic backdrop and characterization of a location that echoes, as in pathetic fallacy, the narrative action and to provide an allegory of "the nation" to which the series refers. Echoing the excitement and anxiety of 1960s urban discourses, Toronto is characterized as the axis around which Canadian social problems circulate. It is framed as the heart and conscience of a "nation" that is responsive to its citizens.

The King of Kensington

Wojeck's utopian vision of citizen agency in Toronto's collective urban problematic was challenged in the next decade by *The King of Kensington's* articulation of identity politics. The decision to locate the series in Kensington Market, a specific enclave of the ethnic working class, subdivides Toronto and, by implication, "the nation" into categories of belonging that are premised on politics and agency.[9] Whereas *Wojeck's* defining metaphor for Toronto is mobility—literally, in terms of an aesthetic of highway and street landscapes, and figuratively, in terms of the possibilities for class mobility within a unit wherein citizens have agency to mediate policies—*The King of Kensington's* Toronto emphasizes stasis. The Kensington Market neighbourhood of the series is characterized by the community's internal mechanisms, which have been derived to provide agency to citizens who feel as if they do not have agency outside the community. In this way, the location is defined as a response to civic, provincial, and federal government—quite a tall order for a situation comedy.

In terms of its semiotic context, the series is emblematic of a turn in the 1970s for CBC drama to conceptualize Toronto less as an urban fiction intended to narrativize national policy issues through stories about law enforcement, the medical community, journalism, or politics and more as a social network of lived experiences, conceived as, and differentiated by, neighbourhood. Developed for mass appeal, the series heralds its audience not by explicitly dealing with policies and broad social themes, but by conceptualizing "national address" through the fictional rendering of the private life of a citizen, in this case Larry King, the series' main character. A Kensington Market convenience store owner (turned community centre director in season five), King's character, played by Al Waxman, serves in both name and practice as the social and humanist leader of his community. Implicitly, Kensington Market functions as a microcosm of larger community, the Canadian nation. Whether *King's* mediation references Canada's "two solitudes" symbolized as a hockey game ("Hockey Night in Kensington"), urban crime ("The Purse Snatcher"), or immigration ("Variety Store"), the series models—to use the language of its ideology—a working-class, grassroots, "commonsensical" approach to governance. Within the discursive approach to community leadership upheld in the series, individual circumstances take priority over policies and bureaucratic networks and practices, which are alternately framed as dehumanizing, inefficient and ineffective, and discriminatory to minority and middle- to low-income citizens. Larry King's approach to community is thus subversive in that he provides actionable solutions to contravene the impenetrability of procedure; for example, bank financing ("Variety Store," "Movin' On") or police investigation ("Purse Snatcher"). However, it should be clarified that Larry's intervention does not pose a threat to the dominant social order because he works within its existing systems on behalf of the disenfranchised. Personified by "King" Larry, the series posits, often with self-reflexive caveats to the English-speaking, white male–identified position of privilege it adopts, a liberal humanist ethics as the cornerstone of governance. The series overtly criticizes Canadian policies when they contravene the show's ideology (e.g., a national unemployment crisis in "Variety Store," official language policies in "King's First Date" and "Hockey Night in Kensington," and the state of national health care in "Counter Attack").

Larry King's centrality to the series is held in tension with a sense of the significance and primacy of location. The relationship constructed between Larry and Kensington Market is dialectical, which is to say that the character of King and the character of the market mutually inform one another. Structurally, Larry's store contributes one physical piece of the market, which reciprocally, if narrowly, supports the existence of Larry and his family. Thematically, Larry is perpetually saving aspects of the market community. Formally, this takes place as Larry allays potential crises in each episode: for example, the community Thanksgiving dinner ("Kensington Achievement Award"), the hockey and baseball teams ("Hockey Night in Kensington" and "The Prom"), family conflicts ("Big Brother"), or finances and careers ("Central Tech Tiger," "Variety Store," and "Movin' On"). Although Larry narrowly avoids a community crisis in each episode, his perspective is not characterized as objective, nor does he function as a deus ex machina, descending from a privileged position of insight in order to solve the narrative conflict. Larry's principle space within the diegetic location reinforces the tension between his dual roles as participant/instigator and community mediator.

The home that he shares until season four with his wife, Cathy, and mother, Gladys, is a two-storey apartment located on top of the variety store in which he works, on Pembroke Street, in the heart of Kensington Market. The configuration of Larry's home space signifies his and his family's embeddedness in the community. Larry's space becomes private in vertical proximity to the street. The variety store, which opens directly to the street, functions as a public space, while the living area, connected by doors to the street to the store, is an intermediary space between public and private life. Inviting peripheral characters to this space is intended to remove them momentarily from their problem in public life. Examples include King's giving a teenage tomboy beauty tips before her prom ("The Prom"), encouraging a recovering alcoholic to reconnect with his family ("Big Brother"), and counselling a couple to get married ("The Best Man"). King's bedroom, used sparingly as a location in the series, is generally reserved as a respite for private discussions between Larry and Cathy, most notably in the sequence where Cathy explains why she is leaving the marriage ("Cathy's Last Stand"). But even this space, the most private of King's locations, can be penetrated. In one episode ("The Prom"), King receives a phone call in bed from a troubled teenager and King bemoans the fact that when his wife sneezes in his bedroom, his mother blesses her from the next.

As *King's* diegetic configuration of space indicates, it is not Larry King or Kensington Market as independent entities, but rather their interaction that is the subject of the series. Larry not only reacts to problems that arise in Kensington Market, but as a participant in the community, he often creates obstacles, too, either through misunderstanding or well-intentioned interference. In keeping with the humanist ideology of the series, resolution of the primary conflict in each episode always directly favours a community ideal, often at the expense, literally or figuratively, of Larry. In the final episode of season three, "Cathy's Last Stand," Larry is asked by his wife to help her leave the marriage so she can "find out who she is." Larry's personal sacrifice is necessary to benefit a dominant late-1970s feminist ideal, which is that the institution of marriage is inherently patriarchal, thus subsuming the identity of the woman.

Within *King*, Kensington Market's discursive function contradicts popular expectations of its significance within the Canadian nation. Whereas the historical fact of the market's economic "poverty" encourages the perception of the community as reliant on the social safety net of the nation, the fictionalized market community exemplifies models of alternative or cooperative living and working arrangements. Inadvertently, this network benefits the nation by modelling a community whose self-sufficient practices bypass the federal system and bureaucratic systems, particularly financial and social institutions such as banks, counselling facilities, and legal mediation. The community's autonomy is naturalized in the series. With the exception of Cathy's significant departure, success in the context of community is an end in itself and the characters do not desire more. This tendency is observable in a variety of examples. Sports victories that occur in the community ("Central Tech Tiger," "The Prom," "Hockey Night in Kensington") do not lead to championships outside the community. Success in education and business is defined by the extent to which it meets

Figure 2. Larry (Al Waxman) and Cathy King (Fiona Reid)—CBC television's "it" couple of the 1970s—were all smiles until Cathy left to "find herself" at the end of season four. Photo used with permission of CBC Television Archives.

the basic needs of existence and provides a service to the community, rather than igniting capitalist desires or economic upward mobility. Attempts at entertainment, such as Larry's brief foray into stand-up comedy ("The Comic" and "Kensington Achievement Award"), are meant to entertain the community as an end in themselves. Validating the integrity of the Kensington community, episodes frequently use upwards of twenty community extras and realistic-looking, episode-specific set locations, creating the look of an authentic community and cultivating and legitimizing a Kensington Market aesthetic.

Although location is an important feature of the sitcom genre generally, it typically borrows from the semiotic discourse of a place previously established in narrative (e.g., New York or Los Angeles) to give the series a sense of realism by eliciting a cultural shorthand of place. For *King*, there was at that time no comparable mythology of Toronto, nor a text base on which narrative associations could be made. Rather than foregrounding location to make the series appear authentic or to evoke a place-based semiotic shorthand that was virtually nonexistent at the time for Toronto, the series does the reverse: it creates a narrative mythology for Toronto, making a community identifiable by virtue of its narrativization. By providing a cognitive map of Kensington space and community, the series legitimizes the experience of living in a Toronto neighbourhood by articulating the experience in narrative form. Whereas the sitcom genre typically universalizes themes and issues, *King* takes issues "universal" to the sitcom and localizes them and, in doing so, makes explicit reference to its macro (national) and micro (community) contexts.

King's location as an enclave determined by class and ethnicity reflects an increasing cultural preoccupation in the 1970s with identity politics and a critique of the emerging rhetoric of multiculturalism.[10] As "national drama," *Wojeck's* liberal humanist vision for "the nation," so representative of 1960s discourses that measure the health of a community by the rights of the individual, is challenged by *King's* 1970s-inflected perspective that structures of power are relational and institutionalized. Whereas *Wojeck's* Toronto is unified, *King's* Toronto is subdivided into neighbourhoods, at best, or ghettos, at worst, defined by class and ethnicity. *Wojeck's* aerial establishing shot of the city, which implies the mobility, abstraction, and equity of its citizen protagonists, is in contrast to *King*, whose establishing sequence fixes its protagonist firmly at street level within the daily life of a particular section of the city.

These are not merely aesthetic distinctions. Changes to the characterization of Toronto in "national" drama testifies to changes to the conceptual model with which the Canadian national problematic is imagined.

Whereas *Wojeck*'s Toronto connotes the potential for the nation-building project, *King*'s Toronto perceives this project skeptically, as inadequate to address the actual needs of "national" citizens. The series' characterization of Toronto models explicitly located community formations as an alternative way for citizens to experience agency.

Seeing Things

With *Seeing Things*, CBC's dramatic comedy about a Toronto crime reporter with extrasensory perception, the skepticism that characterizes *King's* 1970s ambivalence toward the nation-building project becomes entrenched in an ironic approach. It proposes, with tongue firmly in cheek, that if the institutional conglomerate known as "the nation" cannot adequately serve its citizens, perhaps the paranormal could be harnessed to help. The characterization of Toronto's spiritual essence as earnestly dedicated to social justice and the welfare of its citizens draws on the city's puritanical reputation. As University of Toronto physicist Leopold Infeld wryly wrote, Toronto in the 1950s was "perhaps the finest place in which to die, especially on a Sunday afternoon when the transition between life and death would be continuous, painless and scarcely noticeable."[11]

Twinned with Toronto the Good's reputation as deadly boring is the use of Toronto as "dead" space, as the negated space of American location shooting where, since the 1970s, the city has been notoriously disguised as anyplace else. *Seeing Things* was created in part to respond to this practice. David Barlow, the co-creator of *Seeing Things*, was specifically asked by John Kennedy, then head of CBC Drama, not to make Toronto look like Seattle.[12] Produced with the overt intention to capture a Toronto-specific aesthetic and discourse, *Seeing Things* not only asserts the city's specificity, but it quite literally gives a "dead" city a soul that speaks from its negative space. That this voice is characterized as an intervention advocating on behalf of citizens reifies the understanding of the citizen as disenfranchised.

This reading differs somewhat from pioneering writing on *Seeing Things* by Lianne McLarty, who considers the series' preoccupation with "marginality" to be first and foremost an Innisian comment on Canada's status in relation to American and British popular cultures, products, and economies.[13] While the series remains consistent with a longstanding Canadian tradition that uses narrative to illustrate structural, "centre/margin" relations of culture, McLarty suggests that the particular innovation of the series is to use the "strategy" of "self-conscious television." Its methods essentially foreground and subvert the colonizer's tools—American television conventions—in telling the story of the effects of cultural and televisual colonization.

While there is much validity to this interpretation, I believe it overlooks the centrality of Toronto's locatedness to the show's signifying practices and the way its specific understanding of marginality compares to a trajectory of other CBC dramas. My claim is that *Seeing Things* not only comments on Canada's marginal status as a cultural and ideological producer. The show's anxiety also refers to the increasing marginality of local citizens to the policies and structures that comprise their nation.

Inspired by play and the paranormal, evoking approaches to city space established by the surrealists and the situationists, *Seeing Things* promotes a discourse that questions purely empirical approaches to social formations. In the series, a Toronto aesthetic is conceptualized around the tension inherent in the coexistence of the urban uncanny and the intense rationalism of the structures upon which the modern urban and "national" formations are predicated. The term "uncanny" is used here to evoke Freud, but also to refer more generally to what is incomprehensible. By superimposing the uncanny on rational structures such as policy and law, *Seeing Things* foregrounds the extent to which these seemingly divergent discourses are embedded in conceptualizations of the urban and the way they seem to exist in the city of Toronto to comic effect.

Seeing Things adheres to a narrative formula. Each episode revolves around a murder investigation, to which the protagonist, Louie Ciccone, contributes by interpreting three clairvoyant visions. Louie's visions are consistently demarcated within the narrative. Occurring three times per episode, each vision builds on the previous one and becomes increasingly decipherable. Foreshadowed by a consistent audio cue, images slightly obscured by a gelled lens are intercut with an extreme close-up of Louie's eyes, accentuated by large-framed glasses. Louie's ability to "see" is undermined by the frequency with which he wrongly interprets his visions. His initial interpretation of his visions is either incomplete or misleading, prompting the murder investigation to change course.

In startling contrast with contemporary Toronto's adoption of cellphones and Internet communication, *Seeing Things'* Toronto is analogue. To speak with someone in the Toronto of the series, characters must either be in proximity to one another or they must talk through phone wires, an act that confines the body to a wall or a desk with a handset receiver. Louie's ability to access information through extrasensory perception, therefore, has material significance within the narrative structure of the series. The ability to receive communication without a visible medium

Figure 3. Louis Del Grande hams up the paranormal in a publicity photo for *Seeing Things*. Photo used with permission from CBC Television Archives.

makes Louie himself a medium of communication, or, as the results of an assessment of Louie's telepathic potential label him, "a medium medium."

The Toronto of *Seeing Things* is conceptualized as painfully rational and without subtext. This concept translates directly to the show's structure. Humour, for example, is derived from the absurdity of superimposing the conventions of American or British detective shows on Toronto, a strategy that McLarty refers to as "self-conscious television." In "Defective Vision," an attempt is made to smuggle Louie to a secret location at gunpoint by covering his head with a paper bag. When the bag is removed, Louie immediately recognizes the location as the Balalaika, a restaurant where he had recently taken his ex-wife, Marge, for her birthday. In an effort to convince Louie that he is in a secret location, one of his captors insists that the restaurant only *looks* like the Balalaika. Another captor is quickly disarmed by Louie's genuine praise of the perogies and the price of the dinner special. Not only do villains in *Seeing Things* appear to be role-playing, unsuccessfully emulating crime show conventions, but the transposition of these conventions to Toronto is contextualized as comical. In this episode, as in others, comedy tempers threats of violence. The gun used to hijack Louie turns out to be a fake and the captors' intimidating qualities are offset by their desire to hear Louie praise their restaurant.

This example, typical of a comic sequence based on destabilizing conventions, also demonstrates how Toronto is framed as benign in relation to other cities. The joke that Louie immediately recognizes his secret location plays on the presumed absurdity of being lost in Toronto. Such humour reifies an understanding of Toronto's notoriously hyper-rational urban planning and also acknowledges the city's relatively provincial status in global terms.[14] Toronto is not the *flâneur's* nineteenth-century Paris or the detective show's gritty American city.[15] In the rational Toronto, there is considerably less romance, less opportunity to wander, get lost, or be hidden. After all, there are, as Louie's abduction reminds us, very few Russian restaurants. But however unsuitable Toronto appears when conventions of the detective genre are imposed upon it, it would be wrong to claim that Toronto is "feminized" in a binary relationship with failed phallic conventions. It is true that the combination of the city of Toronto and crime show conventions is the primary structural basis for comedy in the series, but it is specifically the combination that is ridiculous, not Toronto.

Although the authorities do fall short of arriving at "truth" in the series, thereby valorizing Louie's ESP to augment rational legal procedures, the system as a whole is revered by those who participate in it and by those whom it prosecutes. Louie is not a substitute for civic, provincial, and national bodies of authority, the police and the legal system. His intervention as a local urban actor is a gesture of located citizenry.[16] Louie, for example, does not carry a gun, sign of the phallic power of the police; instead, he disarms criminals with objects from the everyday, such as cakes or sandbags. In remaining a reporter, not a vigilante, Louie's structural function supports the legal system to which he hands over captured criminals for prosecution in each episode.

But within the discourse of the show, the legal system, organized as it is to expedite the pursuit of justice, often overlooks the "truth," which is where the supernatural intervenes. Due process and orderly procedures conducted by the police and the law are performed within the realm of the rational and observable. By the same logic, naturalized in the series, what seems irrational and unseen cannot be processed by governing systems. It is thus a system predicated on positive rather than negative space. The American model articulates this bias as "innocent until proven guilty." Louie, through his ESP, serves as a mediator to bring intangible truths, "felt" but not otherwise witnessed, into the realm of the positive and provable.

Louie's "visions" begin inexplicably when he attempts to resign from the newspaper to restore his marriage. The sudden appearance of the paranormal counteracts Louie's rational decision to resign from the *Gazette*. Structurally, then, the visions transform Louie's work as a Toronto reporter into a "calling" of ethereal significance with local implications. The visions become naturalized as the expression of an abstract force—an advocate for citizens who are not adequately served by governing institutions. Toronto's character is positioned as this "paranormal," its Protestant earnestness and commitment to social justice asserting itself. Far from being merely irrational, the paranormal expressed through Louie's visions is ideologically informed and advocates an empirical truth. Its purpose is to account for the factors that impede "justice," thereby augmenting existing systems of social governance.

Not only does this paranormal social conscience reside specifically in the negative space of dramatic Toronto, but the choice of Louie as its medium ensures that outcomes will be reported publicly in the local newspaper. Guided by a paranormal force positioned as Toronto's conscience, Louie is an urban intervention within a plethora of civic, provincial, and national policies and bureaucracies. In other words, the paranormal functions to monitor the effectiveness of social process in the city, replacing the role of policy reform. In contrast with *Wojeck*'s 1960s optimism for the care of citizens within the framework of "nation," *Seeing Things*, two decades later, bears witness to a more cynical view of policy in practice. Although Toronto maintains its function as an allegory for the nation in *Seeing Things*, the series takes a negotiated stance on how the citizen fares within the nation-building project and privileges "the local" as the site with the greatest potential for the welfare of citizens.

Conclusions

This reading of three CBC flagship dramas produced over three decades suggests a shift in the way "national" citizenship has been dramatized in Toronto. It witnesses a trajectory in the perception of national social policy from "common sense" in the 1960s to impenetrable social obstacle by

the 1970s and into the 1980s. In addition to articulating the discursive construction of "common sense" aligned with the protagonists of these dramas, further analysis would yield insights about the signification of class
and gender in the construction of these ethnically marked protagonists as
"citizens." While these series use Toronto as a constant semiotic framework
within which to negotiate relations to a "national" social formation, particularly in terms of social policy and lived culture, the relation of "the citizen" to the signifier appears to have changed significantly in three decades.
Wojeck's citizen is charged with constructing community by adopting and
amending policies, whereas the comedy of *King* is derived from making do
within seemingly impermeable bureaucratic paradoxes. In *Seeing Things*,
the regulation of Toronto has morphed beyond the empirical into the
abstract space of the paranormal. Could this sense of a dislocated location
be one of the symptoms of Toronto's emerging "global" status, which
begins to privilege a culture of urbanity and transnational capital over the
nation-state? Or could it be that decision-making practices with regard to
policies that affect everyday urban life are perceived to have become so far
removed from citizens and from tangible frameworks of space and time
that these processes appear to occur within the paranormal?

This narrative that I identify across a body of CBC drama is inextri-
cably linked with Toronto's current characterization as an allegory for the
nation. What, for example, are the implications of *This Is Wonderland*'s
(2004–06) citizen characters, for whom agency and advocacy is found at
the local level largely outside and seemingly in spite of "the law" and
other provincial and national governing policies? Contrast this disenchant-
ment with *Wojeck*'s optimism about the national project, where local
Toronto catastrophes resulted in local inquests intended to inform provincial and national policy change. CBC's recent Toronto flagship legal drama
continues the trajectory of characterizing social policy away from *Wojeck*'s
"common sense" toward "nonsense," its title, *This is Wonderland*, evoking the topsy-turvy world of Lewis Carroll. Overwhelmed by bureaucracy
and the pace of urban life, both lawyers and clients in *Wonderland*, in the
interest of compassion, naturalize the subversion of policy as a matter of
practice, gleaning rational solutions from the insane. Movement away
from the promise of policy to a distrust of the rational and bureaucratic
implicitly confounds the perceived relations of the CBC and its "national"
citizenry.

Though the CBC has always been at arm's length from government in
principle, its dramatic programming has habitually been dismissed on
charges of federal didacticism. To imply that the CBC has been sufficiently

organized to do so as a singular monolith is, I believe, to give the institution more credit than is due. This argument also does not adequately account for the variation that we find in its expression of a national problematic, both within the institution and in its programming. Authorship remains a contentious issue with respect to the CBC, yet I do not believe that this ambiguity about where meaning is produced discounts the presence of tendencies across its dramatic programming. That is to say that, while the CBC has no psyche and its signature dramas have not been centrally authored or even necessarily produced in-house, it remains an institution dedicated to a particular understanding of nationhood. Both the institution and especially the content of its dramas have engaged in a dialectic with its mutually constitutive and equally discursive construct: the climate of its "national public."

It is also deeply ironic that at the same time that the CBC is accused of being an instrument of nation building, it is itself subject to government whims. Over the span of time that this chapter explores, policies in the form of funding cuts, government reviews, and the CRTC's and Telefilm's increasing support of private broadcasters and producers have frustrated the institution fundamentally.

In this sense, I do refer to the institution as singular. Is it inconceivable to think of the CBC as a subject in this way? Could it be that the shift that this chapter identifies in CBC drama, from optimism to skepticism of the viability of the nation-building project and in the agency of the national citizen, somehow also reflects the institution's "subjective" ambivalence toward government? Is it possible to postulate that these dramas function as barometers of both a "national public" and an institutional climate?

If so, it might begin to explain why CBC drama has been taking up the position of the jilted "national citizen."

Notes

1   The concept of dramatic production as a national defence against US cultural imperialism is explicit in commission reports from the 1950s and becomes an implicit part of arguments used to sustain Telefilm and, recently, to "Save our CBC." In the fall of 2003, the union for Canadian television actors, ACTRA, staged highly publicized—and televised—protests against threats to cut the Canadian Television Fund, and also to encourage the CRTC to increase the minimum requirements of Canadian content, underscoring the rhetorical conflation of the production of drama as cultural defence and an important element of the economy. J.M. Bumsted maintains that the cultural defence argument originated as an economic strategy. See Bumsted, "Canadian Culture in Peril," 21–28. Frank Peers outlines the classic case that nationalism and the free market are social forces in conflict. See Peers, "The Nationalist Dilemma in Canadian Broadcasting."

2   As a result, Radio-Canada has become more than the French-language version of the CBC. It is structurally and culturally an entity unto itself.

3   The CBC's approach is contrary to the one Sarah Matheson rightly identifies, primarily in industrial television that uses Toronto as a site on which to "project placelessness." See Matheson, "Projecting Placelessness," 117–39. In other work, Matheson explores how the Toronto station Citytv uses city space to conceptualize "civic membership." See "Televising Toronto," 70–81.

4   Mary Jane Miller's work on the CBC depicts the organization as a network of actors—for example, changing creative decision makers, policies, funding conditions, cultural industries, and regions—which complicates the idea of attributing authorship to the CBC. See, for example, *Turn Up the Contrast* and *Rewind and Search*.

5   Miller notes that Toronto's "grainy and particularized sense of place" begins as a trend with *Wojeck* (*Turn Up the Contrast*, 48).

6   Miller, *Turn Up the Contrast*, 66.

7   Matheson develops the idea of Toronto's symbolic function as national microcosm. See Matheson, "Ruling the Inner City," 46–62.

8   de Certeau, "Walking in the City," 126–33. In season one, the "celestial" perspective is from Highway 427 and in season two from the Gardiner Expressway.

9   Matheson's comprehensive article "Ruling the Inner City: Television, Citizenship and *King of Kensington*" argues compellingly that Toronto is intended to function as a "symbolic image of a unified image of Canada." While Matheson's reading is excellent, I consider the use of *King's* Kensington Market to be less optimistic in terms of its endorsement of the locale's potential to serve as "a national ideal." Though I agree that the comedy does provide a degree of "reassurance," its critique of class and ethnic status is at times biting and, I believe, much more provocative than is typically acknowledged.

10 See Matheson, "Ruling the Inner City," 52.

11 As quoted in Carpenter, "That Not-So-Silent Sea," 250.

12 Telephone conversation with David Barlow, October 2005.

13 See McLarty, "Seeing Through Things," 46–48, and "*Seeing Things*," 102–09.

14 Toronto is planned on a grid system.

15 However, Matheson argues that the aesthetic of one of Toronto's local television stations, Citytv, enables the armchair *flâneur*.

16 This reading of Louie as a local actor differs from McLarty's, whose characterization of Louie references the "national." She writes, "In contrast to the American model, Louis [sic] seems to be yet another example of the traditional English Canadian male hero, the somewhat ineffectual, awkward, perennial adolescent" (McLarty, "*Seeing Things*").

References

Bumsted, J.M. "Canadian Culture in Peril." *The Beaver*, February–March 1991: 21–28.

Carpenter, Edmund. "That Not-So-Silent Sea." In *The Virtual Marshall McLuhan*, edited by Donald F. Theall, 236–61. Montreal and Kingston: McGill-Queen's University Press, 2001.

de Certeau, Michel. "Walking in the City." In *The Cultural Studies Reader*, edited by Simon During, 126–33. New York: Routledge, 1993.

Innis, Harold. *The Fur Trade in Canada*, revised edition. Toronto: University of Toronto Press, 1956.

Matheson, Sarah. "Projecting Placelessness: Industrial Television and the 'Authentic' Canadian City." In *Contracting Out Hollywood: Runaway Productions and Foreign Location Shooting*, edited by Greg Elmer and Mike Gasher, 117–39. Lanham, MD: Rowman & Littlefield, 2005.

———. "Televising Toronto: The Construction of Urban Space in City-TV." *Spectator* 18 (1): 70–81.

———. "Ruling the Inner City: Television, Citizenship and *King of Kensington*." *Canadian Journal of Film Studies* 15 (1): 46–62.

McClarty, Lianne. "Seeing Through Things." *Canadian Forum*, August–September 1985: 46–48.

———. "*Seeing Things*: Canadian Popular Culture and the Experience of Marginality." In *Communication Canada: Issues in Broadcasting and New Technologies*, edited by Rowland Lorimer and Donald C. Wilson, 102–09. Toronto: Kagan and Woo, 1988.

Miller, Mary Jane. *Turn Up the Contrast: CBC Television Drama Since 1952*. Vancouver: University of British Columbia Press, 1987.

———. *Rewind and Search: Conversations with the Makers and Decision-Makers of CBC Television Drama*. Montreal and Kingston: McGill-Queen's University Press, 1996.

Peers, Frank. "The Nationalist Dilemma in Canadian Broadcasting." In *Nationalism in Canada*, edited by Peter Russell, 252–67. Toronto: McGraw-Hill, 1966.

Filmography

The King of Kensington (CBC, 1975–80)
Seeing Things (CBC, 1981–86)
This Is Wonderland (CBC, 2004–06)
Wojeck (CBC, 1966–68)

SARAH A. MATHESON

Realism and Community in the Canadian Soap Opera

The Case of *Train 48*

On July 1, 2005, Train 48 rolled into a Burlington, Ontario, GO Train station. The doors opened and the busy commuters exited onto the platform. Having finally reached its destination, this would be the train's final journey. After three seasons, the popular Canadian soap opera, *Train 48*, had been cancelled, leaving many devoted fans wondering about the fate of their favourite characters, whose daily commute between Toronto and the suburbs provided a range of dramatic conflicts.

While many loyal viewers were surprised by the seemingly abrupt end to the series, the demise of *Train 48* is unfortunately in keeping with the history of the soap opera genre in Canada. While there have been attempts to establish long-running daytime dramas, producers have had little success in creating programs that have been able to sustain the loyal viewership and routine viewing patterns necessary to maintain a daily serial drama. Despite the fact that soap operas are a truly international genre, it is not a form typically associated with Canadian television traditions. According to Robert C. Allen, "No other form of television fiction has attracted more viewers in more countries more regularly over a longer period of time than has the serial."[1] In light of the global popularity of serial dramas, the dearth of Canadian soaps, as well as the limited critical work available on the genre by Canadian scholars, is striking. With more than 300 episodes of *Train 48* produced and aired, this series was a hopeful example of the possibility that a domestic soap opera might have some longevity. However, despite its disappointing cancellation, *Train 48* was a landmark series in Canadian television, with more episodes produced than any other Canadian soap. Therefore, while three seasons is a relatively brief period, especially when compared to US soaps, many of which extend more than fifty years, *Train 48* is nonetheless a significant series when we consider the precarious place of the genre in the larger context of Canada's broadcasting history.

This chapter examines *Train 48* in the context of Canadian television traditions, focusing on the significance of realism and community in the program. While the soap opera may not be a genre typically associated with realism, perhaps because of its emphasis on fantasy and excess, Anna McCarthy points out that realism is a key critical concept in analyzing national variations of the genre. According to McCarthy, "Variations in the production and reception dynamics of realist forms in soap opera tend to demarcate national differences within the genre."[2] Therefore, the social realism of Britain's *Coronation Street* and its depiction of working-class life, she argues, is distinguished by critics and viewers from the emotional realism identified in American soaps, demonstrating how national versions of soap opera are often identified with varying types and forms of realism.[3] The realism associated with *Train 48* is in keeping with a Canadian tendency to blend reality and fiction and represents an interesting example of a quite different way realism may be brought to bear on the genre. This program is an ideal example of the "hybrid realism" associated with a Canadian approach, as it combines elements drawn from the soap opera with the conventions of reality television. The series focuses on typical soap opera themes—romance, family, infidelity, and so on—and relies on a serial narrative structure characteristic of the daytime drama. At the same time, the program borrows techniques from reality-based formats, including the conversational structure of the talk show.

This chapter analyzes *Train 48* as a hybrid series, exploring how factual and fictional formats and public and private narratives are combined to present a specific depiction of community situated in the context of contemporary urban life.[4] The series' merging of these different generic codes and conventions offers a reworking of the idea of community within modern urban culture. In the context of the explosion of Toronto as the so-called megacity and in relation to broader discourses on urban life, *Train 48* offers an interesting reimagining of community in the midst of these changes.

Production Context

In her overview of soap operas in Canada, Mary Jane Miller points out that despite the popularity of domestic soaps on Canadian radio, the genre has not had much of a presence on Canadian television. One key factor Miller identifies as having contributed to the genre's absence from Canadian TV screens is cost. She writes, "The reason that there are no Canadian television soap operas on the CBC or CTV appears to be that the private net-works find it much cheaper to import the problems of Middle America than to invent new ones in North Bay or Battleford."[5] In terms of the history of soap opera in Canada, therefore, the context within which *Train 48* emerged was fairly bleak, as previous attempts had had limited success.[6]

Train 48 debuted in June 2003, during a time of wide popular discussion of a serious "crisis" facing Canadian TV drama. Changes in 1999 to Canadian content regulations expanded the definitions of priority programming to include current affairs and entertainment magazine programs, allowing private broadcasters to substitute these more cost-efficient genres for more expensive domestic dramas. Then, in February of 2003, finance minister John Manley announced a $25.5-million cut to the Canadian Television Fund, throwing the industry into a tailspin and leaving many productions without financing. Some established series, such as *Red Green, This Hour Has 22 Minutes*, and *The Eleventh Hour* appeared to face uncertain futures. After intense lobbying by the industry, a $12.5-million advance was returned to the fund. However, the dialogue about the worsening state of Canadian drama continued, as did calls for increasing financial support for the production of domestic dramatic programming.

In terms of its production and financing, *Train 48* reflected the pressures and complications of this era. It did not rely on any government grants or funding from the CTF. The budget was approximately $35,000 per half-hour episode, which is about one-fifteenth of the typical cost of thirty minutes of Canadian primetime drama.[7] Promoted as "Instant Drama," *Train 48* was loosely scripted, as writers outlined character, theme, and conflict and performers improvised the dialogue. The show was taped in the morning, edited in the afternoon, and broadcast the same evening, and all of the dramatic action takes place on one set. Executive producer Steve Levitan described it as "the future of television drama—in this country at least. This show is to TV drama what Henry Ford was to cars."[8] Critics frequently mentioned the minimal production values, the simple set, and the low-budget quality of the program in general. The "no frills" look and feel of the production can be viewed as a response to the financial pressures facing Canadian TV drama at this time. The innovative quality that critics pointed to was in part related to producers' success in undertaking a popular drama without government subsidies. Dierdre McMurdy notes that the current popularity of "low-fat" programming like reality-based shows and reality TV–style shows such as *Trailer Park Boys* and *Train 48* are responses to prevailing trends in US television but also adhere to a cost-efficient business model ideal for the production of "low-cost content."[9] Both of the above series can be viewed as creative responses to the financial constraints of television production in Canada. They adopt the familiar codes and conventions characteristic of popular—and relatively inexpensive—US reality-based programming yet provide unique takes on the genre. They self-consciously play with the strategies and expectations associated with reality TV and in so doing encourage a different kind of engagement with the form.

Train 48 was based on the Australian series *Going Home*, and therefore was also representative of a global trend toward purchasing successful formats from elsewhere and adapting them for domestic viewership. Recent examples of formats adapted for a Canadian market include *Canadian Idol, Project Runway Canada, Canada's Next Top Model*, and *Are You Smarter Than a Canadian 5th Grader?* According to Albert Moran, the licensing of television formats provides a measure of predictability. The adaptation of "tried and tested" formats is appealing to producers who believe that these new versions are likely to repeat the success of the original.[10] According to Levitan, this was crucial to pitching the idea of *Train 48* to Global Television, as he was able to demonstrate previous success. In an interview, he says: "I had lunch with a programmer at Global and I said I want to do a show featuring eight characters on a train going home from work every day. We will do a show a day. And she laughed and said, 'You can't do that, nobody's done that.' And I said they've done it in Australia, and I can show you tapes of it."[11] In an increasingly unstable and uncertain era in television, the adaptation of a proven formula was viewed as a lower-risk approach to production.

The series may also be looked at as one shaped by the realities of convergence within the current Canadian television industry. The program was intertwined with a number of CanWest interests. It was broadcast daily on Global Television and weekly updates were featured in CanWest newspapers in the "Commuter Diary" column written by Rebecca Eckler. Characters were often seen reading the *National Post* and, in selected episodes, Eckler was situated as an extra in the background. Global TV weatherman Anwar Knight performed a cameo on the show, weaving *Train 48* into the larger fabric of Global programming. Viewers were also encouraged to provide feedback about where they thought the narratives should go, and to suggest topics and cast their votes in polls, they were directed to the *Train 48* website on CanWest's Canada.com. CanWest advertising executives used the series as an example of the company's "cross-promotion and cross-selling ... convergence strategy."[12]

The tense state of television production in Canada and the context of the multi-interest, convergence-oriented approach of CanWest helped shape the form and structure of *Train 48*. Cheaply produced, based on a proven formula, not reliant on government funding, and intertwined with a variety of media outlets, this program clearly reflects the realities of the marketplace. The cancellation of *Train 48* also appears to reflect these continuing tensions within Canadian television. In explaining their decision to end the show, Barbara Williams, Global's vice-president of programming and production, is quoted as saying, "After more than 300 episodes, we believe that *Train 48* has come to the end of its natural life."[13] The suggestion that the series had simply "run its course" is a fairly curious statement, considering that a central characteristic of the soap opera as a genre is its "open" narrative structure, its resistance to closure, and its seemingly infinite nature.[14] *Train 48* was replaced by *ET Canada*, a substitution that may reflect changes in Canadian content regulations, which seem to have prompted the appearance of a number of new entertainment magazine programs on a variety of networks. It may also speak to this continuing "crisis" of drama on Canadian television more generally as broadcasters appear to abandon more innovative kinds of programming, such as *Train 48*, in favour of more standard, formulaic, and perhaps more lucrative TV fare.

Train 48: Form and Structure

In reviews in the popular press, critics described *Train 48* in ways that emphasized its hybrid nature and suggested its blending of reality and fiction. It was variously portrayed as a program that "ambitiously mixes 'reality' with drama and improvisation,"[15] a "reality-based soap opera,"[16] and a "blend of current events, soap opera intrigue and elements of reality television."[17] In interviews, Levitan recounts his initial response to viewing the Australian version: "It felt to me at first like this couldn't be a bunch of performers acting this stuff ... This must be somebody who smuggled a handicam into a real train."[18] He sought to recreate a similar hidden-camera feel in *Train 48*, which he says is "a drama that feels real as opposed to a reality show that feels fake."[19]

These descriptions of *Train 48* suggest that the realism of the program can be attributed in part to its adoption of the conventions of reality TV. Rather than making an explicit "claim to the real," as we find in reality television, the realism of *Train 48* is associated, as Levitan's comments suggest, with a feeling or sensibility that is conveyed through the program's representational elements. The series has been likened to popular "docu-soaps" *Big Brother* and *The Lofters*, a correspondence that is undoubtedly related to the program's co-optation of the textual and aesthetic strategies of the docu-soap. *Train 48* utilizes an observational mode, with a shaky hand-held camera conveying the documentary realism associated with the fly-on-the wall style of the docu-soap.[20] It also works to produce a voyeuristic perspective characteristic of this form. According to Levitan, "The show is designed to make viewers feel like voyeurs watching the events unfold during their own commutes."[21] The scenes are often shot over the characters' shoulders, providing a perspective intended to mimic the experience of a commuter eavesdropping on private conversations and duplicating the voyeuristic pleasures critics have associated with reality-based programming. The unscripted storylines and improvised dialogue further contribute to the sense of spontaneity and replicate the seeming "naturalness" of the docu-soap.

The realism associated with *Train 48* may also be linked to the ways current events are integrated into the narratives. The quick production schedule allowed for characters to respond to current events the same day, creating a sense of immediacy. Characters discuss timely issues ranging from the SARS crisis to mad cow disease to promises broken by the Ontario McGuinty government to the influence of thin celebrities on teenage girls' self-esteem, offering personal responses to larger social and political debates. In this way, *Train 48* also draws on the conversational structure of the talk show as characters explore different perspectives on contemporary issues. A number of public figures also made cameo appearances on the program. For example, following the controversy surrounding her fallout with Prime Minister Paul Martin and the Liberal Party, former cabinet minister Sheila Copps did a guest spot on the show. The introduction of the topical creates the sense that these characters' lives unfold within a larger public sphere, as they engage with some of the same issues and events affecting viewers' own lives. It situates personal dramas within the context of a shared public world.

As a hybrid, *Train 48* also adopts the serial narrative structure of the traditional "open" soap opera, reflecting the ways the program combines techniques borrowed from these more fact-based formats—the docu-soap, the talk show—with the narrative structure and dramatic concerns of fictional formats. The narrative structure of the series replicates the soap opera's multiple, intertwined storylines, complicated backstories, and frustration of closure. It also focuses on typical soap opera themes, similarly revelling in the exposing of secrets, intimate revelations, and personal confessions. Moreover, like the traditional soap opera, *Train 48* is primarily dialogue driven, privileging talk over action. The confined setting of the train means that events taking place in these characters' lives are largely relayed through conversation. Therefore, while *Train 48* adopts the aesthetic strategies of reality TV, producing a sensibility that approx-imates the realism of that form, its narrative structure and thematic pre-occupations are indebted to the more traditional soap opera.

The inclusion of material drawn from the day's headlines contributed to what one critic described as *Train 48*'s "near-live nature."[22] This sense of immediacy is not only related to the series' references to events taking place outside this fictional world, but is also related to its cultivation of a sense of the "live" that suggests another type of realism at play. The real-ism of television, according to a number of scholars, has often been bound up with the medium's ability to broadcast events live. Critics and theorists have argued that TV insists on an ideology of liveness and a sense of imme-diacy.[23] Even when programs are pre-recorded, TV is imbued with a sense of continuity with the "now," consistently identifying itself as happening in the present tense. Misha Kavka and Amy West argue that it is in this "zone of immediacy" that reality TV functions. This temporal experience, they argue, is key to the way that reality TV constructs a "socially mean-ingful 'real.'" They write: "The social relevance of Reality TV lies in its cre-ation of intimate viewing communities, but this is an intimacy that cannot be understood without a closer examination of the temporal (and spatial) aspects of immediacy. The aim here is to show that Reality TV pursues inti-macy (emotional closeness) through immediacy (temporal closeness), cou-pling the proximity of the 'here' with the urgency of the 'now.'"[24] In their analysis of *Big Brother* and *Survivor*, Kavka and West highlight the impor-tance of this temporal dimension to the programs' production of the "real" and its construction of social intimacy.

In soap opera, John Corner identifies a similar temporal dimension that contributes to a certain sense of the "real." He writes, "Viewers typ-ically experience episodes of their favourite soap opera as a routine engage-ment with an imagined world running concurrently with their own real one."[25] He argues that the pace of the soap opera seems to unfold at the same pace as the everyday life of the viewer, which encourages a sense of correspondence between the soap world and the "real" world that is fur-ther reinforced by the dailiness of the soaps themselves.[26]

These perspectives have relevance for *Train 48* in that its depiction of community is related to how a sense of temporality is manufactured. Crit-ics described the unpredictable nature of the program, which offered view-ers "the pleasure of watching instant storytelling invented on the fly."[27] The notion of "instant drama" suggests not only a cheap, quick production style but also a temporal element that produces a sense of the now. This "near-live" aesthetic, produced through the timeliness of current events and

Figure 1. The cast of *Train 48*. Photo courtesy of Protocol Entertainment Inc.

the spontaneity of the improvised performances, creates the impression of an intimate social space that corresponds with a larger public sphere that is in step with our own.

An analysis of a representative scene from *Train 48* reveals how the program brings together various elements drawn from a number of different genres and invokes a connection to a wider public sphere. In one episode, Dana, a hip lesbian musician, is seated across from David, a young gay doctor, when Jesse, a young, newly out lesbian, approaches and sits down. Jesse provokes a discussion about the difficulties involved in being gay in the city by explaining her recent run-in with a rude waitress in a local restaurant. The three discuss their different feelings about prejudice, offering contrasting viewpoints and relaying their own experiences. Dana argues that Jesse's feelings of mistreatment are not because she is gay, but rather because she is obnoxious and demanding. Jesse responds, "I may be gay, but I still need condiments." David is more sympathetic and describes his own daily struggles with homophobia. While Jesse vows to continue her struggle against intolerance, David says that he is too tired and too old to keep up the fight. The conversation shifts to the problems of adoption for gay couples, as David and his partner have been discussing starting a family. Reference is made to Canada's new surrogacy laws, which will make it more difficult for couples to use this option (in later episodes, Dana volunteers to serve as their surrogate). Throughout this conversation, it is revealed that Jesse and Dana had a brief affair and that David is currently facing murder charges. An emotionally charged storyline focused on private issues and personal confessions is framed by a larger social and political context. The discussion unfolds as a debate, with the obviously improvised dialogue lending the scene a casual, spontaneous, conversational feel. Different sides of the issue are explored and reference is made to political debates and new legislation. At the same time, there are revelations of a past romance that bring in a complicated backstory, and the scene ends with a cliffhanger as Jesse contemplates the surprising revelation of David's murder case. This scene demonstrates well the programs' hybrid nature, combining the realism associated with reality TV and current affairs programming, structured around a more traditional soap narrative, with moments of comedy thrown into the mix. The aspects of daily routine associated with both commuter culture and the soap opera, combined with the timeliness of its referencing of current events, reinforces the notion that there is a temporal correspondence between this fictional world and the "real" world.

Redefining Public and Private

Staging private dramas within the context of a larger public sphere reflects the series' refiguring of the relationship between public and private, something that is related to the program's generic influences. According to Laura Stempel Mumford, the "ruling dynamic" of soap operas is "the public exposure of private feelings and experiences."[28] In her analysis of the public–private dimensions of the genre, Mumford argues that soaps enact a redefinition of these spheres that initiates a "collapse of the private into the public."[29] John Dovey similarly argues that the form of reality TV

Figure 2. *Train 48* promotion. Photo courtesy of Protocol Entertainment Inc.

represents a refiguring of public–private relations: "The new formats of contemporary factual TV that have appeared are characterized by a shifting understanding of what constitutes the acceptable domains of the private and the public."[30] In the case of the docu-soap, it appears that privacy no longer exists, as the everyday actions and interactions of the participants are subjected to the public gaze of the camera. The surveillance perspective of the docu-soap further blurs the distinctions between public and private. Likewise, the talk show is a genre that depends upon public disclosure of the private and personal. *Train 48*'s emphasis on talk and confession over action suggests an interesting connection with the therapeutic narrative that a number of television critics have identified as a key feature of daytime talk shows. In framing private confessions around public issues, the program often used these characters' personal narratives to explore, but not always resolve, the larger issues it tackled through its storylines.[31]

In all of these forms, therefore, the boundary between public and private is redefined, and critics have understood the significance of this blurring in different ways. What the commentators share, however, is the view that this blurring has specific consequences for how community is portrayed. Critics have emphasized the significance of community to the soap opera, arguing that a definitive feature of the genre is its focus on particular communities of interrelated characters. Mumford links the genre's undermining of the distinctions between public and private to its yearning for a particular type of community: "While it is true that soap opera communities make secrecy impossible and require characters to submit their experiences to constant public scrutiny, the programs also replicate nostalgic fantasies about the intimacy of the traditional family or small town."[32] And Gray Cavender suggests that reality TV's invocation of community appeals to a nostalgic past and may possibly also contribute to an undermining of community.[33] Regardless of their critical stances, scholars have offered analyses that highlight the importance of community to these forms.

The Train as a Liminal Space

Train 48 is a series similarly occupied with the question of community. Unlike these other forms, however, *Train 48* does not offer fantasies of a nostalgic return to the small town or the "fully self-sufficient family."[34] Nor does it represent the retreat from the public sphere that Dovey describes. *Train 48*, while enacting a similar collapse of public and private, departs from these forms by offering a different understanding of community: the train is represented as a kind of liminal space, a space "betwixt and between."

Drawing on Victor Turner's notion of the liminal character of ritual, critics have suggested the relevance of liminality to various forms of popular culture. In the context of television studies, for example, Horace Newcomb and Paul Hirsch have emphasized the liminal quality of television as a medium. They focus specifically on Turner's notion of the liminal as an "'inbetween' stage, when one is neither totally in nor out of society. It is a stage of licence, when rules may be broken or bent, where roles may be reversed, when categories may be overturned."[35] Their concept of television as a "cultural forum" considers television a kind of cultural ritual. Drawing on work by Peter Brooks and Clifford Geertz, John Docker notes the liminal quality of melodrama, which exists between the rules of everyday society and as a place where those things that are repressed—e.g., emotions, fears, conflicts—may be expressed.[36] In terms of genre, the hybrid nature of *Train 48* implies a similar ambiguity and "in between" quality. However, it is in terms of its representation of space that the series thematizes this sense of liminality.

In the context of urban culture, Lauren Langman and Katie Cangemi define liminal spaces as "alternative realms" that exist apart from the social structure: "It [the liminal] represents a period of ambiguity, a marginal and transitional state. The liminal stands apart from the usual as illness stands in opposition to the typicality of health. Liminal realms are times and sites of freedom, agency (empowerment), equality, license, and spontaneity."[37] Liminal spaces in cities, they argue, are "ambivalent and ambiguous, located between local and global markets, between private value and public use, between home and work, culture and commerce."[38]

This characterization of liminal space in the city and in different forms of popular culture seems to reflect well the way space is represented on

Train 48. The train never reaches its destination (until the final episode). The train is positioned somewhere between the downtown and the expansive exurbs, a place anchored neither in the city nor in the suburbs. An analysis of the opening sequence conveys this sense of a liminal space. The sequence consists of a fast-paced montage of shots depicting different trains and landscapes: exterior shots of a train in the station in front of the Royal York Hotel, an interior shot of Union Station, shots of trains moving in various directions, different images of platforms, train tracks, tunnels, and signals; there are daytime and evening shots, industrial, rural, and urban landscapes, and so on. Opening sequences typically operate to establish a setting and context for a series. Here, that context is rooted in the urgency of commuter culture, reflecting the quick pace of travel. It is also vague in terms of grounding the drama in a particular location. Brief shots of easily identifiable Toronto landmarks offer a fleeting suggestion of place. However, the jumble of images defies a stable sense of locality. Instead, this montage conjures a more ambiguous setting, moving through urban, suburban, and rural spaces. The sequence suggests a transitional space and conveys the sense of mobility rather than fixed place.

Inhabiting a space marked by liminality, the characters on *Train 48* are not bound by the hierarchies of the workplace or the structures of the family. They are essentially a group of strangers brought together by the daily routine of the commuter experience, yet occupying a space temporarily freed from the constraints of the social structure. As a liminal space, the train becomes a place where the expression of those things not usually socially sanctioned is permitted. Characters freely reveal a range of personal secrets: Zach confesses to his affair with his brother's girlfriend; Pete reveals his infidelity with Mag, who is his fiancée's wedding planner; Seymour discusses his problems being intimate with his new love, the transgendered Christine; and so on. It is a space of conflict where, it seems, anything can happen. Separated from co-workers and kinship ties, these strangers' anonymity affords them the freedom to express what is seemingly taboo in their everyday lives.

Televising Commuter Culture

Setting, therefore, is crucial to *Train 48*'s depiction of community. The space of the GO Train is the series' only location, eschewing the traditional soap settings of the home and the workplace. Linking downtown districts with surrounding exurbs, the commuter train operates as a powerful symbol of the suburban lifestyle. The series' evocation of Toronto emerges within the context of the controversial 1998 amalgamation of its twelve boroughs, merging metropolitan Toronto with the surrounding suburban communities to form a large centralized municipality dubbed the megacity. The debates surrounding the megacity conflict were figured as a struggle between urban and suburban values and spurred renewed anxieties about the relationship between the suburbs and the city, as amalgamation appeared to erase the distinctions between the two. The "real" city of Toronto, it was feared, would disappear, and the city would give way to the bland, commercial culture that many believed characterized suburban life. The Greater Toronto Area has witnessed astounding growth in recent years, and the breakneck speed of the spread of suburban sprawl in Toronto and other places has provoked further popular dialogue about the significance of this transformation of the city.[39] This debate has included anxieties about the consequences of sprawl on health, on the environment, on the nature of community, and on families. Suburban living has become synonymous with sprawl and, in the context of debates over the megacity, is now more than ever figured within popular discourse as a threat to the continued livability of the city.

Cultural critics have often characterized suburban life as antithetical to established forms of community, linking the growth of sprawl to a decline in civic life. In *Suburban Nation*, for example, Andres Duany, Elizabeth Plater-Zyberk, and Jeff Speck describe the "disjunction between the private and public realms" in which "more and more citizens seem to be withdrawing from public life into the shelter of their private homes."[40] Accompanying suburbanization, they argue, is the "decline in the civic arts of conversation" and the waning of social space.[41] Matthew Lindstrom and Hugh Barlting note a similar connection between suburban life and the disappearance of civic culture. They write, "Sprawl has also been implicated as a culprit in the larger social malaise of civic disengagement ... society over the past 30 years has become more individualistic and less concerned with notions of community."[42] Commuter culture is emblematic of this disjunction as suburban dwellers attempt to traverse the growing distance between work and home and as the juncture where the fissure between public and private life widens.

Reading *Train 48* in this context, the commuter train functions as a symbol of suburban culture, deeply implicated in the routines of the daily journey between work and home. Characters are connected through routine, meeting each other each day as they travel home. Commuter trains are rarely imagined as places of sociability and are more likely conceived of as a place of estrangement. However, as Simon Ward points out, trains also symbolize "'the dream of connection,' a network of rails connecting disparate regions" and operate as "a powerful symbol of collectivity, particularly at times of political and national transition."[43] In the midst of a rapidly expanding metropolis, the train operates as a symbol of connection and collectivity on a number of levels: enabling commuters to overcome the vast geographical separation of work and home, city and suburb, but also in terms of the potential it offers for social connection as well.[44] Unlike the aggressively individualistic, private character of the automobile, the train offers up the possibility of a different kind of commuter culture, one that is not in conflict with concepts of community. Drawing on Raymond Williams's concept of "mobile privatization," Margaret Morse describes the "non-space" of the freeway, which produces a unique sense of isolation and connection.[45] In contrast, the commuter train offers the potential of a mobile *public* space.

This is what *Train 48* seems to appeal to: the possibility of a reconfigured public space that, in its collapsing of the boundaries between public and private and in terms of its liminal quality, seems to temporarily reconcile the divides that are at the heart of suburban culture. Critic Shanda Deziel noted the ways *Train 48* seemed to contrast with popular conceptions of the commuter experience when she wrote: "Strangers on commuter trains rarely acknowledge the fact that they see each other every day. Engaging other passengers in meaningful conversation is out of the question. But on *Train 48*, a new Canadian TV show about commuter culture, a twice-divorced pharmaceutical executive, a redneck construction worker and a lesbian musician/hairdresser can be found sharing secrets of their love life, debating current affairs and gossiping about other regular train riders."[46] *Train 48* represents the commuter train as a social space marked not only by personal disclosure but also by civic engagement. The lost art of conversation is seemingly rekindled as characters share their private lives with strangers, but also reflect on politics and current events. The result is an eclectic mix of intimacy and civic discourse, a liminal realm where the public and private merge.

Deziel's description of the diversity of the characters also invokes the heterogeneity associated with liminal spaces, where hierarchies are temporarily levelled. Characters from varied backgrounds and professions intermingle, evoking an impression of equality. In this sense, *Train 48* does not represent a nostalgic return to a lost sense of community by recreating the small town or dramatizing the integration of the family. Rather, it suggests the possibility of a temporary social intimacy within a space where this does not typically exist. It suggests a liminal space, a space of transition that is temporarily freed from the divisions, anxieties, and obstacles associated with a sense of collectivity and community in contemporary urban life.

Conclusions

As a hybrid, *Train 48* is emblematic of a tendency on Canadian TV to blend reality and fiction. In form and structure, it was shaped by specific industrial conditions and constraints that contributed to its appearance in the media marketplace. However, it also offers a compelling refiguring of the concept of community in contemporary culture. By combining factual and fictional formats and public and private narratives, *Train 48* depicts a symbolic social space that gains specific resonance when examined in the context of broader discourses on urban life. By reading the series' textual and aesthetic strategies in the context of popular anxieties about suburban living, I have attempted to suggest some of the larger implications of the program's representation of space and place. The space of the train is deeply implicated in the problematic milieu of commuter culture and all it implies about the transformation of metropolitan areas. Its liminal quality appeals to the imagined possibility, however transitory, of a reconfigured social space within this realm.

Notes

1   Allen, "Making Sense of Soaps," 243.
2   McCarthy, "Realism and Soap Opera," 50.
3   McCarthy, "Realism and Soap Opera," 49–52.
4   Bondebjerg identifies the combination of public and private narratives and factual and fictional forms as a key characteristic of the hybridized, "true-life-story" genres in shows such as *Rescue 911* and *America's Most Wanted* and their blurring of the public and private spheres. See Bondejborg, "Public Discourse/Private Fascination."
5   Miller, *Turn up the Contrast*, 119.
6   There have been a number of brief efforts to produce soap operas in English Canada. Miller identifies the CBC's *Scarlett Hill* in 1962 as an early attempt. This program was not, she says, a traditional soap opera but a daily serial with a new story each week. In 1974, the CBC broadcast *The House of Pride*, a half-hour primetime serial drama, and in 1979 aired the continuing daytime drama *Country Joy*. Both of these were also short-lived. Through the 1970s, there were also a number of "hybrid" series that drew on soap conventions and combined these with elements drawn from the talk show, comedy, sitcom, and crime program forms (Miller, *Turn Up the Contrast*, 119–124). In the early 1990s, the context of co-production spawned two ambitious yet disastrous soap operas: *Family Passions* (Germany–Canada) and *Foreign Affairs* (Canada–Netherlands–Argentina). Later that decade, *Riverdale*, modelled on *Coronation Street*, aired but was cancelled after three seasons because of financial pressures. Currently, OMNI's evening serial drama, *Metropia*, appears to be promising.

7   Atherton, "*Train 48* or Train Wreck?"

8   Nestruck, "Meet the Conductor."

9   McMurdy, "Reality Hits Home."

10   Moran, *Copycat TV*, 20–22.

11   Niedzviecki, "Buying into Franchise TV."

12   Shecter, "E-Newspapers."

13   As quoted in Strachan, "Global's *Train 48*."

14   Allen distinguishes between "open" and "closed" soap operas. According to his definitions, open soap operas never reach a final conclusion, whereas closed soap operas are from the outset working toward an ultimate resolution. See Allen, "Making Sense of Soaps," 250–55.

15   Menon, "Sex and Current Events on *Train 48*."

16   Strachan, "*Train 48* Unlike Anything Else."

17   Vallis, "Your Daily Commute."

18   Atherton, "Global's New Show."

19   March, "All Aboard."

20   For a full description of the realism and style associated with the docu-soap, see Bruzzi, "Observational-Fly-on-the-Wall-Documentary" and "Docusoaps."

21   Vallis, "Viewers Will Plot Storylines."

22   Atherton, "A Lot Can Happen."

23   Caughie, *Television Drama*, 99. See also Feuer, "The Concept of Live Television."

24   Kavka and West, "Temporalities of the Real," 136–37.

25   Corner, *Critical Ideas in Television Studies*, 59.

26   Corner, *Critical Ideas in Television Studies*, 59.

27   Fulford, "Drama Worth Catching."

28   Mumford, *Love and Ideology in the Afternoon*, 49.

29   Mumford, *Love and Ideology in the Afternoon*, 49.

30   Dovey, *Freakshow*, 21.

31   See, for example, Shattuc, *The Talking Cure*.

32   Mumford, *Love and Ideology in the Afternoon*, 63.

33   Cavender, "In Search of Community," 154–72.

34   Feuer, "Narrative Form," 112.

35   Newcomb and Hirsch, "Television as a Cultural Forum," 505.

36   Docker, *Postmodernism and Popular Culture*, 254.

37   Langman and Cangemi, "Globalization and the Liminal," 145–46.

38   Langman and Cangemi, "Globalization and the Liminal," 146.

39   Other cities, most notably Hamilton, Halifax, and Montreal, have undergone a similar amalgamation that has prompted comparable debates about urban space. Therefore, while I am situating *Train 48* in the specific context of Toronto, the anxieties that the show addresses have wider relevance.

40   Duany, Plater-Zyberk, and Speck, *Suburban Nation*, 42, 59.

41   Duany, Plater-Zyberk, and Speck, *Suburban Nation*, 63.

42   Lindstrom and Bartling, "Introduction," xxiii.

43   Ward, "Train and Nation," 13. Ward analyzes the German soap opera *CityExpress* and offers some thought-provoking ideas about the soap opera genre, public space, and community that have interesting correspondences with *Train 48*.

44   In Canada, this linking of the railway with discourses of social connection is taken even further, as communication theorists have often drawn an analogy between broadcasting and the forging of the Canadian railway. As a nation-building tech-

nology, the railway brought together geographically dispersed regions of the country, encouraging trade and communications and engendering a greater sense of identity and shared purpose. Parallels have been drawn to broadcasting in terms of linking the nation and offering the possibility of a similar sense of connection and greater sense of collectivity. A quote from Marc Raboy illustrates this familiar discourse: "Where in the nineteenth century, the railroad was central to the project of creating Canada, in the twentieth, broadcasting was essential to maintaining it" (Raboy, "Canada," 162).

45 Morse, "The Ontology of Everyday Distraction."
46 Deziel, "Strangers on a Train."

References

Allen, Robert C. "Making Sense of Soaps." In *The Television Studies Reader*, edited by Robert C. Allen and Annette Hill, 242–57. London: Routledge, 2004.

Atherton, Tony. "Global's New Show a Mix of Drama, Reality." *Leader-Post* (Regina), May 31, 2003: A14.

———. "*Train 48* or Train Wreck? Global Takes a Chance on a Soap Opera That's Shot Without a Script and Aired on the Same Day." *Halifax Daily News*, June 1, 2003: 27.

———. "A Lot Can Happen on a Train." *Sudbury Star*, June 6, 2003: B6.

Bondebjerb, Ib. "Public Discourse/Private Fascination." In *Television: The Critical View*, 6th ed., edited by Horace Newcomb, 383–400. New York: Oxford University Press, 2000.

Bruzzi, Stella. "Observational-Fly-on-the-Wall-Documentary" and "Docusoaps (Accidental Footage)." In *The Television Genre Book*, edited by Glen Creeber, 129–34. London: British Film Institute, 2001.

Caughie, John. *Television Drama: Realism, Modernism and British Culture*. Oxford: University of Oxford Press, 2000.

Cavender, Gray. "In Search of Community on Reality TV: *America's Most Wanted* and *Survivor*." In *Understanding Reality Television*, edited by Su Holmes and Deborah Jermyn, 154–72. London: Routledge, 2004.

Corner, John. *Critical Ideas in Television Studies*. Oxford: Oxford University Press, 1999.

Deziel, Shanda. "Strangers on a Train." *Maclean's*, June 9, 2003: 77.

Docker, John. *Postmodernism and Popular Culture: A Cultural History*. Cambridge: Cambridge University Press, 1994.

Dovey, John. *Freakshow: First Person Media and Factual Television*. Sterling, VA: Pluto Press, 2000.

Duany, Andres, Elizabeth Plater-Zyberk, and Jeff Speck. *Suburban Nation: The Rise of Sprawl and the Decline of the American Dream*. New York: North Point Press, 2000.

Feuer, Jane. "The Concept of Live Television: Ontology as Ideology." In *Regarding Television*, edited by E. Ann Kaplan, 12–22. Frederick, MD: University Publications of America, 1983.

————. "Narrative Form in American Network Television." In *High Theory/Low Culture: Analyzing Popular Television*, edited by Colin MacCabe, 101–14. New York: St. Martin's Press, 1986.

Fulford, Robert. "Drama Worth Catching." *National Post*, June 10, 2003: AL1.

Kavka, Misha and Amy West. "Temporalities of the Real: Conceptualising Time in Reality TV." In *Understanding Reality Television*, edited by Su Holmes and Deborah Jermyn, 136–53. London: Routledge, 2004.

Langman, Lauren and Katie Cangemi. "Globalization and the Liminal: Transgression, Identity and the Urban Primitive." In *The City as an Entertainment Machine*, edited by Terry Nichols Clark, 141–76. Oxford: Elsevier, 2004.

Lindstrom, Matthew J. and Hugh Bartling. "Introduction." In *Suburban Sprawl: Culture, Theory and Politics*, edited by Matthew J. Lindstrom and Hugh Bartling. Lanham, MD: Rowan & Littlefield, 2003.

March, Catherine Dawson. "All Aboard the Improv Express." *Kingston Whig-Standard*, May 29, 2003: 30.

McCarthy, Anna. "Realism and Soap Opera." In *The Television Genre Book*, edited by Glen Creeber, 49–54. London: British Film Institute, 2001.

McMurdy, Deirdre. "Reality Hits Home for TV Producers." *The Gazette* (Montreal), February 19, 2004: B3.

Menon, Vinay. "Sex and Current Events on *Train 48*." *Toronto Star*, June 4, 2003: F01.

Miller, Mary Jane. *Turn Up the Contrast: CBC Television Drama Since 1952*. Vancouver: University of British Columbia Press, 1987.

Moran, Albert. *Copycat TV: Globalisation, Program Formats and Cultural Identity*. Bedfordshire, UK: University of Luton Press, 1998.

Morse, Margaret. "The Ontology of Everyday Distraction: The Freeway, the Mall and Television." In *Logics of Television: Essays in Cultural Criticism*, edited by Patricia Mellencamp, 193–221. Bloomington: Indiana University Press, 1990.

Mumford, Laura Stempel. *Love and Ideology in the Afternoon: Soap Opera, Women, and Television Genre*. Bloomington: Indiana University Press, 1995.

Nestruck, J. Kelly. "Meet the Conductor: *Train 48*'s Head Honcho Producer Emerges from the Shadows." *National Post*, August 28, 2003: AL4.

Newcomb, Horace and Paul M. Hirsch. "Television as a Cultural Forum." In *Television: The Critical View*, 5th Edition, edited by Horace Newcomb, 503–15. Oxford: Oxford University Press, 1994.

Niedzviecki, Hal. "Buying into Franchise TV." *Globe and Mail*, August 7, 2003: R3.

Raboy, Marc. "Canada." In *Television: An International History*, edited by Anthony R. Smith, 162–68. Oxford: Oxford University Press, 1998.

Shattuc, Jane. *The Talking Cure: TV Talk Shows and Women*. New York: Routledge, 1997.

Shecter, Barbara. "E-Newspapers with Built-in Video Coming: CanWest Sees Boost for Advertisers." *National Post*, April 3, 2003: FP7.

Strachan, Alex. "*Train 48* Unlike Anything Else on TV." *Vancouver Sun*, June 3, 2003: C2.

———. "Global's *Train 48* Makes Its Final Run Next Month." *Edmonton Journal*, June 3, 2005: G5.

Vallis, Mary. "Your Daily Commute Comes to Television." *National Post*, February 27, 2003: AL6.

———. "Viewers Will Plot Storylines for New Show." *Edmonton Journal*, March 2, 2003: B8.

Ward, Simon. "Train and Nation: *CityExpress*—The Soap Opera." *Journal of Popular Culture* 34 (3): 9–26.

Filmography

Are You Smarter Than a Canadian 5th Grader (Insight Productions, 2007–)
Big Brother (US) (CBS, 2000–)
Canada's Next Top Model (Temple Street Productions, 2006–)
Canadian Idol (Insight Productions/CTV, 2003–)
The Eleventh Hour (Alliance Atlantis, 2002–05)
Entertainment Tonight Canada (CanWest Global Communications, 2005–)
Going Home (SBS/McElroy Television, 2000–01)
Project Runway Canada (Insight Productions, 2007–)
Survivor (Mark Burnett Productions, 2000–)
The Red Green Show (S&S Productions, 1991–2006)
This Hour Has 22 Minutes (Salter Street Films/Alliance Atlantis/Halifax Film, 1992–)
Trailer Park Boys (Trailer Park Productions/Topsail Productions, 2001–)
Train 48 (Protocol Entertainment, 2003–05)
U8TV: The Lofters (Alliance Atlantis, 2001–02)

KIRSTEN EMIKO MCALLISTER

Human Cargo

Bridging the Geopolitical
Divide at Home in Canada

The United States and Canada are facing external threats related to international terrorism, transnational crime, and drug and people smuggling. These common concerns make it paramount for both countries to work together to develop a coordinated strategy ... [to] strengthen their security ... [and respond] to threats of terrorism, criminality and contraband.[1]

H*uman Cargo* (2004) is a six-part miniseries that "takes current world events and brings them ... into [Canadian] living rooms with human faces, human voices."[2] Broadcast on CBC Television in August 2004, the award-winning series explores anxieties surrounding the Canadian refugee system in an age of transnational crime and terrorism.[3] Following the fates of six refugee claimants from international "hot spots" including Burundi, Afghanistan, Honduras, and China, the series delves into difficult questions about the ability of the Refugee Board of Canada to distinguish "bona fide" from "bogus" refugees—questions that are the basis for more troubling concerns about whether Canada should be accepting refugees at all.

Ripped from Reality

Human Cargo draws the audience into the world of refugees by promising to be close to reality. The characters and scenes are literally "ripped" from news stories about illegal immigrants, right-wing politicians, terrorist bombings, human trafficking, and overcrowded refugee camps. Feeding into "Fortress America's" affective economy of fear,[4] this is a world in crisis.[5] It is a world where more than ten million people fleeing civil war, ethnic cleansing, and political persecution threaten every year to flood across our borders.[6]

Human Cargo also plays into the anxieties and pleasures of action-packed films like *Tears of the Sun* (2003) and *Black Hawk Down* (2001), as well as television shows like 24 and *Alias*. These productions manage simmering public anxiety by isolating the source of violent disorder overseas in the "Third World" and Eastern Europe. Audiences are assured that the collapsing world order—read American imperialism—can be saved by eradicating spreading networks of terrorists, transnational criminals, and corrupt politicians.

But in contrast to sensational news stories and action thrillers, *Human Cargo* traces the complicity of the "West" in the global spread of violence and political chaos. The series reveals the investment of Canadian corporations and government officials in unstable political regimes that force millions to flee their countries every year. In this regard, *Human Cargo* belongs to a new genre, what I will call the *geopolitical complicity drama*. This genre examines the role of democratic Western countries in geopolitical crises, challenging the way popular media productions construct underdeveloped regions of the world as threats to world order. In this genre, the flow of transnational capital, information, people, and commodities, far from creating a "global village," has created a complex set of local–national–global interconnections that make each of us, at the most personal levels, complicit with the violence occurring at home and abroad.

The British television miniseries *Traffik* (1989) is arguably one of the first productions in this genre. Directed by Alastair Reid, *Traffik* explores the way international drug trafficking connects individuals living across the globe, including the families of a British politician, a German businessman, and an impoverished Pakistani farmer. The decisions each character makes have unforeseen and often devastating consequences for the other characters living thousands of miles away and feeds into social and economic problems, whether drug addiction in Britain or opium farming in Pakistan. Stephen Soderbergh directed *Traffic* (2000), the North American version of *Traffik*, more than ten years later.[7] It traces how drug trafficking connects families in the United States and Mexico, causing social ills in both countries. More recent productions in this genre include the CBC/BBC miniseries *Sex Traffic* (2004), Lifetime miniseries *Human Trafficking* (2005), and films like the British/German co-production *The Constant Gardener* (2005) and the independently produced *Syriana* (2005).

Like these productions, *Human Cargo* traces how global investments and political corruption connects the fates of individuals in "Third" and "First World" countries. At the same time, insofar as *Human Cargo* aims to criticize Canada's role in the global refugee crisis, the series falls within the tradition of Canadian docudramas, dramatizing events based on "real social problems" and adhering to the CBC mandate to address socially relevant issues.[8] The production notes also make it clear that the series works along the lines described by Hogarth as "a forum for journalistic activism ... to interpret and pass judgment on contemporary social life."[9]

This chapter assesses the techniques *Human Cargo* uses to encourage the audience to critically interpret and pass judgement on Canada's role in the global refugee crisis. The first section of the chapter considers *Human Cargo*'s use of conventions from television dramas to make connections between Canada and atrocities in countries in the economic south. I argue that the use of multiple storylines allows audiences to identify with characters from both sides of the geopolitical divide, especially characters from underdeveloped countries. In addition, I examine the emotionally powerful trope of the family, also typical of television miniseries.[10] The main dilemma that all characters face involves either the separation or the breakdown of their families. As a common theme, the family serves to "humanize" the characters, though it presents a limited heteronormative trope for the nation.

In the second section of the chapter, I examine the use of dramatic and realist techniques to increase the audience's investment in the characters. For example, the series increases the emotional impact of the characters by getting established Canadian actors from well-known television programs to play the roles. *Human Cargo* also draws on controversial racist events specific to British Columbia to heighten the intensity of the conflicts. This factor has the potential of critically engaging citizens whose views about refugees and immigrants have been shaped by these events. The series also authenticates its portrayal of refugees by using Third World actors, which, as I argue, raises issues about voyeurism.

In the third section, I consider the role that "bearing witness" to refugee testimonies plays as a formal device for transformation. It is through bearing witness that one of the main characters, Nina Wade, a right-wing politician, begins to question her racist views. Audience members are also encouraged to "bear witness" to the atrocities refugees have undergone in regions that, although geographically distant, are closely interconnected with each of us through our political and economic decisions.

Multiple Storylines, Global Interconnections

Human Cargo uses a number of well-established dramatic conventions to make interconnections between Canada and atrocities committed in the economic south. The use of multiple characters with intersecting storylines is taken directly from dramatic television series.[11] Audiences are

Figure 1. Moses Buntu, his sister, Odette, and her family in Tangoma. Still from *Human Cargo* (2004), courtesy of Howe Sound Films.

encouraged to identify with the personal struggles and individual limitations of characters from the Third and First Worlds. In stark contrast to films like *Black Hawk Down* and *Tears of the Sun*, as well as television shows like 24, where Third World and Eastern European characters are backwards, barbaric, and/or bomb-bearing threats, the series works to break down the psychic dichotomies between the West and the rest. In fact, in the portrayal of the two main characters, *Human Cargo* reverses the good/evil dichotomy, making Moses, the "African" man, the most sympathetic character and Nina, the white Western woman, a reactionary racist.[12]

The storylines of Moses Buntu and Nina Wade are given the most narrative weight. The closure of the series depends on Moses' ability to overcome external obstacles including civil war and captivity, as well as Nina's ability to overcome crippling personal obstacles such as xenophobia and the desire for power. We follow both characters from the moment their lives are turned upside down in the first episode to the moment when they meet in Canada. The audience is introduced to Nina Wade when she loses her seat as a member of Parliament in a by-election in Vancouver; we are introduced to Moses Buntu when civil war erupts between Hutus and Tutsis in Burundi.[13]

In the first episode, the lives of Nina and Moses could not be more separate. They live on different continents. Nina is a politician with power-

Figure 2. The defeat of Nina Wade in a Vancouver by-election. Still from *Human Cargo* (2004), courtesy of Howe Sound Films.

ful connections living in a wealthy Vancouver neighbourhood with her radical daughter, Helen, who disdains her mother's right-wing views. Moses is a schoolteacher in the village of Tangoma and the devoted uncle of his sister's children. The conflicts that the characters face also seem completely unconnected: the loss of a by-election in Vancouver and civil war in Burundi.

But as the series progresses, the connections between the Third and First World tying Nina and Moses together become evident. For example, the audience is introduced to the interconnections when Helen decides to join a relief agency, Pax Terra, in Burundi. When civil war breaks out, Nina seeks help from her lover, Peter Fowler, to rescue Helen. Peter has just left his post as the prime minister's aide and returned to the corporate world. As a personal favour to Nina, he makes arrangements to fly Helen out of Burundi through one of his companies, the Canadian-owned Trillium Goldmines.[14] The seemingly innocuous personal and corporate networks linking lives in Canada and Burundi become political when they intersect with the storyline of Moses.

With the eruption of civil war, Trillium hires Tutsi soldiers to round up men in Moses' village to work as slaves. The soldiers kill Hutu villagers, burn houses, and force women and children, Moses' sister and her children among them, to leave the charred remains of their homes. Far from being a good corporate citizen that rescues Canadians stranded in disaster zones, Trillium exploits political crises, taking brutal measures against innocent civilians to protect its interests. There is no doubt about the complicity of Canadian managers: they turn a blind eye when the soldiers execute villagers to keep everyone compliant. After Trillium destroys Moses' village, separates his family, and enslaves him in the mine, where he is also tortured, he manages to escape and thus becomes one of the millions of refugees fleeing for their lives.

Human Cargo shows the devastating impact of the global interconnections on families. Not unlike what Jane Feuer calls the "trauma drama," *Human Cargo* is concerned with resolving the traumas of the family.[15] All the characters in *Human Cargo* are caught up in the struggle to reunite families who have been physically separated or emotionally alienated from each other. But, unlike trauma dramas, *Human Cargo* does not, as Gitlin argues, "displace social debate into the tropes of victim and villain ... crisis and rescue."[16]

The connections between the families of Moses and Nina occur by chance when Helen ends up in the same refugee camp where Moses' sister, Odette, and her children have taken shelter. But rather than bringing relief to Odette and the other refugees, Helen brings disaster. For example, when Odette's young son, Noba, falls under the influence of a gang that demands food supplies from Pax Terra, naïve and arrogant Helen confronts the gang leader despite the pleas of her co-workers to back down. As tensions mount, Tamara, Helen's lover, who also works for Pax Terra, intervenes. Amid the confusion, Noba accidentally fires his gun and shoots Tamara.

Helen is portrayed in a critical light here. Her attitudes, actions, and motives seem to be based on the colonial fantasy, à la Angelina Jolie in *Beyond Borders* (2003), where middle-class white Westerners save "helpless Africans."[17] For example, although Helen is clearly distraught at the death of Tamara, it does not dampen her desire, notably her desire for "others."[18] Almost immediately after Tamara bleeds to death, Helen accepts comfort from Eyob, a brilliant young Ethiopian doctor with the promise to be "the future of Africa." Their intimacy transforms into a relationship and Helen finds emotional stability. But the political conditions around them spiral out of control and Eyob is killed when a large shipment of food arrives and Noba's gang brazenly sabotages the delivery trucks. In the confusion, Eyob is shot. Helen and her co-workers barely manage to escape, leaving Eyob behind and engulfed by panicking refugees.

It is as if all relationships are doomed in the refugee camp. Not only are Tamara and Eyob killed, but it is also where the gang forces Noba to shoot Odette, his mother. This is one of the dramatic climaxes of the film, and an example of how the series conveys the emotional impact of the civil war through the melodramatic breakdown of family relationships rather than just relying on graphic depictions of murder and mutilation. The tragedy of civil war involves the tragedy of the family, most notably the murder of a mother by a son.

The deaths of Odette, Tamara, and Eyob also raise questions about the role of sexual and racial others. In conventional mainstream narratives, sexual and racial others are disposable, being either subservient or threatening to the hero.[19] To what extent does *Human Cargo* reproduce the construction of sexual and racial others? The answer is not straightforward. By the time Odette is murdered, the audience has had sufficient time to invest in her character, making her death, as mentioned above, one of the climaxes of the series. She is one of the few characters who is motivated by a strong sense of justice, even if it entails taking measures against her children. But this is exactly where Odette is rendered "other." When she fails to convince Noba to leave his gang, she takes drastic measures. Both terrified and incensed by his fascination with guns and violence, weeping, she cuts off his "trigger" finger.

Given that the refugee camp is outside the regular rule of law and no longer under the jurisdiction of any nation-state, Odette has little recourse to stop the proliferation of violence within her family and in the camp. As Odette's child, Noba remains her possession and thus under her law. The law of the family—and, implicitly, the nation—requires Odette to protect Noba, yet if he violates the family (social) contract, she must also punish him. But once Noba joins the company of men, Odette's matriarchal power is nullified. The series in fact suggests that all men in positions of power act outside the rule of law, whether they be Canadian politicians or Tutsi military captains. This gendered discourse on law and violence reproduces essentialist notions of women as nurturers caring for the family/nation and men as violent competitors, making it difficult for women to step out of their roles without being severely punished.

Regardless, the act of cutting off Noba's finger moves dangerously close to reproducing racialized images of "tribal violence."[20] Consider how the audience would respond if Nina were to cut off Helen's finger. It would be unthinkable. Yet it is used to frame Odette as an "African" woman who resorts to physical mutilation to control her son. This image is reinforced when she takes Noba to Pax Terra's health clinic. Eyob wants to reattach Noba's finger, but Odette replies, "I gave [the finger] to the ancestors." But there are other ways for a viewer to read Odette's statement against the narrative. Note that her recourse to "the ancestors" is out of character. When confronted with life-threatening circumstances in previous scenes, she never sought guidance from "ancestors," or for that matter "the Virgin Mary." It is possible to read Odette from a subaltern position if we consider the context. She makes her statement to Eyob, an Ethiopian doctor, not one of the Western aid workers, who might dismiss her as a superstitious "African." Yet, as a Pax Terra worker, Eyob still represents the (neo)colonial authority on whom her survival depends. She thus cannot risk explaining that she cut off Noba's finger in a desperate attempt to stop further gang violence. But as someone from a former colony, Eyob is less likely to accept her statement at face value. He might instead recognize her attempt to ironically use a Western myth about "superstitious Africans" to evade questioning that could require her to submit to (neo)colonial punishment.[21] In this context, "I gave it to the ancestors" takes on another meaning, one that ties Eyob and Odette together in their knowledge of (neo)colonial oppression.

It is more difficult to read Odette's representation as a mother from a subaltern or feminist position. The audience is encouraged to identify with Odette as a mother desperately trying to protect the moral order of the family against the violence of men acting outside of the law.[22] This means that when Noba kills Odette he is also symbolically killing "Mother Africa," the bearer of social and moral order.[23] As a result, when the son who represents "future generations" kills his mother, the camp collapses into complete disaster and everyone must flee.

In this context, Helen's efforts to create "alternative" families, first with Tamara and then with Eyob, should offer an alternative to the violent order of the heteronormative family.[24] But even though Tamara and Eyob are presented as characters with depth and integrity, deeply caring for Helen despite her naïve arrogance and destructive actions, they are quickly killed off. Moreover, Helen's heterosexual relationship with Eyob is given more significance: their brief relationship results in a child. The way Tamara is quickly forgotten trivializes the significance of her love— and sacrifice—for Helen. Yet at the same time, the way Helen's desire quickly shifts to Eyob makes her desire appear recreational and opportunistic. This points to another way to read the deaths of Tamara and Eyob: Helen is the threat. As a privileged middle-class woman who views the world as her playground, she leaves a trail of destruction among the progressive causes and people that she most respects. The deaths of Tamara and Eyob are inevitable outcomes of her naïve and arrogant fantasies about saving the world.

But in the terms set by the heteronormative family, Helen's relationships with both characters are forbidden and dangerous. At the level of the narrative, their deaths restore "order" insofar as they violently end the "abnormal" unions and impel Helen to return "home" to Canada and take up her position as a middle-class heterosexual woman. Thus, while the family is an emotionally powerful way to humanize characters, as a trope it designates conservative—and deadly—gendered roles.

Blending "Reality" and Fiction: The Emotional Charge of Authenticity

Like *Traffik*, *Traffic*, and *Sex Traffic*, what makes *Human Cargo* especially compelling is the way it blends fictional and non-fictional genres to create emotionally charged characters and scenes. By "ripping" characters and events from news headlines, the series feeds into the recent fascination with shows that promise proximity to "reality," to the "authentic," delivering the emotional intensity and vulnerability that, it could be argued, we have difficulty finding in our everyday worlds. But as Bill Nichols wrote in 1991, documentary realism can in fact effectively utilize dramatic conventions such as protagonists and narratives based on "problem/solution" to make convincing portrayals of events, people, and arguments.[25] In other words, what captures the effect of the "real," or, more specifically, gives events or characters the quality of being "live" or "authentic," is highly mediated.[26]

At another level, *Human Cargo* gives characters and events ripped from the news emotional charge by using iconic Canadian actors who also have roles in other CBC miniseries, including *H2O* (2004) and *Intelligence* (2006–07). Moreover, these actors play characters similar to the characters they play in well-known shows like *Da Vinci's Inquest* and *24*.[27] As in other long-running series, whether the *EastEnders* or *Street Legal*, these characters have taken on a life of their own in the popular imaginary, coming to embody prototypical figures.

Perhaps the most well-known television actor in *Human Cargo* is Nicholas Campbell. He plays Jerry Fischer, the human rights lawyer who represents Moses. After eight seasons playing Dominic Da Vinci, the coroner in *Da Vinci's Inquest* and then the mayor of Vancouver in *Da Vinci's City Hall*, Campbell has arguably come to embody the Canadian prototype for an outspoken, anarchic public figure fighting for the rights of the disenfranchised.

Like Campbell's character in *Da Vinci's Inquest*, Jerry Fischer works in the world of law, confronting injustice and corruption on a daily basis. Committed to fighting for the underdog, like Dominic, Jerry thrives on challenging authorities and finding loopholes in the system to protect his clients. Jerry also has problems keeping his work and personal lives separate, prioritizing his clients over his family. This results in conflicts with his wife, Charlene. The conflicts are given extra emotional charge by using Leslie Hope to play Charlene. Hope played a similar character in the first season of the television series 24: Teri Bauer, the wife of Jack Bauer, a Counter Terrorist Unit agent responsible for national security. Like Teri, Charlene struggles with Jerry's inability to put his family ahead of his public duties. The tense emotional dynamics between Teri and Jack are transposed onto the relationship between Charlene and Jerry, increasing the intensity of their family dysfunctions. *Human Cargo* thus gives news headlines the emotional charge by using well-known actors who have become figures in the popular imagination.

Shot on location in Vancouver, *Human Cargo* also adds an element of realism by making references to the city's changing social and cultural landscape. Unlike international co-productions that Serra Tinic argues tend to erase the specificity of place to appeal to a global market, *Human Cargo* is compelling in part because it draws on conflicts over the urban landscape that feed off racial animosities rooted in the history of British Columbia.[28] These animosities were stirred up in the 1990s when Hong Kong immigrants moved to Vancouver and began purchasing properties in wealthy, primarily "white" Westside neighbourhoods. As if taken straight out of Vancouver's real estate pages, there is a scene in *Human Cargo* where prospective buyers are viewing Nina's spacious Arts and Crafts house. Nina recognizes two Asian women. Just a few weeks previously, she had angrily accused them of cheating in a game of tennis, drawing on old stereotypes that Asians are incapable of understanding civilized British notions like "fair play." As the women comment on her house, Nina overhears them saying that the house is worthless and should be torn down—with echoes of sensational news stories about Hong Kong immigrants tearing down houses considered historical landmarks, playing into old fears about Asians invading Vancouver with a foreign culture that threatens the cultural (British) landscape.[29]

The hostility against Asians forms the backdrop for Nina's racist views, such as her comments in a televised speech after Sanjay Desa defeats her in a federal by-election:

We were defeated not so much by a candidate as by a vote committed to a minority segment of our population ... In ... two districts alone ... more than 50 per cent of the population is non-Canadian, and the result is that more and more ... the conflict and the tumult and the social ills that beset the people from these foreign lands, largely in the most underdeveloped parts of the world, are now being fought out in the streets of Vancouver.

There is nothing new about the views expressed in Nina's speech. Fears about Asians and other immigrants "taking over" the province date back to the early 1900s.[30] But at a formal level, *Human Cargo* mobilizes these fears, giving them a shape in the form of Nina Wade. As a narrative device, it personifies the racist dimension of popular views about immigrants and refugees. Audience members who have internalized elements of anti-Asian discourses will likely identify with some of Nina's reactionary statements. Yet when she puts her views into action, it is difficult not be repulsed by the consequences. For example, ripping another controversial headline from the news, the series shows Nina's response to a cargo ship of illegal Chinese immigrants that the government does not prevent from entering Canadian waters.[31] She is outraged and leaks the story to the media. The publicity pressures the government to force the overcrowded ship back out to sea, where it sinks, drowning everyone on board. Nina thus becomes implicated in their deaths. This is a critical turning point for Nina, who finally begins to fathom the repercussions of her hateful views. To her credit, she does not avoid the blame, accepting her role in the disaster as if to encourage audience members to consider the repercussions of their own racist views.

Human Cargo also draws on the discourse of "authenticity" to increase the credibility of the Third World actors.[32] For example, the CBC website describes how the experiences of the actors playing refugees are similar to the identities of their characters. Bayo Akinfemi, who plays Moses Buntu, "draws on his own experience with the Canadian immigration process to bring enormous depth and dignity to the character."[33] The website describes Akinfemi's experiences as a Nigerian who was initially denied immigrant status when his Canadian-born wife tried to sponsor him. According to the website, after two years of separation, Akinfemi entered Canada under a pseudonym and applied for refugee status. Like his character Moses, "Akinfemi approached the authorities with facts about his true identity ... [and, to his surprise the] Immigration Department [granted him permanent residence status]."[34] Highlighting the similarities between Akinfemi and his character suggests that, rather than an actor, the audience is viewing an actual "refugee." In this way, *Human Cargo* purports to use subjects whose experiences guarantee the audience proximity to reality.

But hiring actors who guarantee a level of authenticity can raise troubling ethical issues, especially if they portray victims. It is useful to compare *Human Cargo* to the miniseries *Sex Traffic* (2004), which follows the plight of two sisters from Moldova, Elena and Vera Visinescu, who are sold into sexual slavery. In a Canadian Press article, Tim Arsenault underlines "the authenticity" of the actresses playing the two sisters: "Anamaria Marinca and Mara Popistasu ... [their] natural performances are outstanding ... [they] have never done any film work. They were both right out of theatre school in Romania."[35] Since they have little acting experience, a viewer might wonder how skilled they are at distancing themselves from their roles, underlining their "naturalness" and their "innocence," just like the "innocence" of their characters, who believe they are travelling to London for jobs in the service industry. Their lack of experience and "innocence" implicitly promises a more "realistic" portrayal of the graphic scenes of violent rape and murder. In other words, the website suggests that the audience is witnessing real feelings of terror and helplessness as the actors perform scenes of rape for the camera.

The exploitative use of the authenticity in *Sex Traffic* raises questions about the use of the authenticity of the actors in *Human Cargo*. While the website identifies Acharki and Akinfemi as "Africans," their nationalities are not used to increase the veracity of traumatic scenes of torture and sexual exploitation.[36] The CBC website and *Human Cargo*'s promotional material present both as highly trained actors, which underlines to the audience that they are watching them "act" rather than "enact" terror and humiliation.

Moreover, Acharki and Akinfemi do not play victims, unlike Marinca and Popistasuin, who play terrified, helpless females. For example, while Marinca's character, Elena, is constantly devising ways to escape with her sister, she always fails, placing them both in greater danger.[37] Her agency is thus rendered self-destructive. In contrast, Moses and Odette demonstrate their inner strength by actively resisting captors while protecting those around them. But nor are they presented as heroes: Odette fails to stop her son from joining "rebels" and Moses is forced to kill in order to survive.

In its efforts to heighten dramatic effects, *Sex Traffic* reproduces troubling fantasies of human agency. It is the liberal-lefty white British charity worker, Daniel Appleton, who "saves" Elena when he finally couples with her in the conclusion. As Elena is passed between pimps, customers, and finally to Daniel, the idea that women are sexual property exchanged between males is reinforced:

The British producer Derek Wax of *Sex Traffic* states that the intention was a realistic portrayal of a seamy, ruthless underworld [that] pulls no punches. There are many scenes of nudity and perhaps the most graphic rape scene to air on conventional television. But because it's about punishment and control, not sensuality ... such images are not gratuitous. We felt we needed to be true to that moment ... The reason why the girls are anally raped is because they don't want to get them pregnant because they're less useful to them.[38]

What Wax describes as the need "to be true to the moment" is a naïve and disturbing commitment to realism. Most of the rape scenes are shot from the perspective of male aggressors, showing in detail how they violate young women. This places the viewer in the disturbing position of the rapist, dominating, violating, and terrifying the victim under the guise of criticizing sex trafficking. Graphically depicting rape scenes from the point of view of the rapist reproduces the violent relation between the victim and the aggressor, placing viewers in the position of sadistic voyeurs where they identify with the perpetrator.[39] If the purpose of the series is to "educate" audiences and challenge our relation to subjects made vulnerable by transnational forces, it is necessary to carefully consider visual and narrative strategies used to convey violence, rather than using realist techniques to sell it to international audiences.[40] Given that the market cum audience for many of the young women from Eastern Europe includes the UK and North America, the distribution of *Human Traffic* to these same markets is hardly reassuring.

Resolutions: Testimonies and Transformations

I have argued that *Human Cargo* challenges popular media representations of refugees as external problems, in particular as potential threats to national security. Like a number of recent television series and films on transnational trafficking, *Human Cargo* traces the role that Western countries such as Canada have in forcing refugees to flee their homelands. These productions challenge the dichotomy between democratic First World and supposedly backwards Third World countries.

Like *Traffik*, *Traffic*, *Syriana*, and *The Constant Gardener*, the solution in *Human Cargo* does not involve a hero who saves the "natives" or destroys Third World "evil." In fact, as is usual in the Canadian tradition, none of the characters offer a resolution. All of the characters' storylines have open-ended, ambivalent conclusions with dark undertones.[41] As described above, most of the characters with integrity, whether Odette, Tamara, or Eyob, are killed off. Jerry Fischer, the refugee lawyer who fights for the rights of the disenfranchised, is also killed. The media is complicit, covering up Jerry's death and framing him as belonging to human trafficking rings and terrorist cells. This suggests that there are far more dangerous networks working behind the scenes than "bogus refugees" sneaking across the Canadian border. Even more ominous, just when the series concludes, Naila, a Muslim refugee Jerry tries to help, ends up giving a terrorist cell the information they need to conduct a major attack on Vancouver sometime in the near future. A physician, Naila enters Canada illegally, searching for her husband, who is also educated. She is horrified to learn he has joined a terrorist cell. But when she discovers that the security agents have killed him, she releases the information to her dead husband's associates. By concluding the series with terrorists aiming to unleash a major disaster, a narrative that disturbingly draws on reactionary representations of Muslims circulating in the media, the audience is left with anxious questions rather than reassuring answers.

If there is any resolution, it lies in the hands of Nina Wade when she comes face to face with Moses Buntu during his refugee hearing. Nina's final decision is shaped by a process of transformation that begins in the first episode of the series: bearing witness to the testimonials given by refugees. Replicating the real-life testimonials as closely as possible, *Human Cargo* adheres to the procedures set out by the Immigration and Refugee Board: "Refugee protection determination ... [is] one of the most difficult forms of decision-making ... [Claims] are often complex. Claimants, speaking through an interpreter, are usually not at ease in their role as witnesses ... The events they describe happened in faraway countries, frequently in the midst of civil strife, and their allegations are often impossible to document. As a result, it can be very difficult to distinguish between false and genuine claims."[42] The final determination of whether a claim is "false" or "genuine" occurs in the hearing, face to face with the claimant. But the process is much more complicated than simply determining the "truth."

This is where *Human Cargo* is innovative. Drawing on the genre of courtroom dramas, the testimonials given by the refugees in *Human Cargo* are intensely emotional, involving the disclosure of events that are painful and difficult to recount. And like witnesses in courtroom dramas, it is as if the refugees return to the moment when the events occurred. According to experts in the area of trauma studies, the act of retelling accounts of horrific violence, painful losses, and cruelty does in fact involve a "reliving, a reoccurrence of the event."[43] This places the members of the refugee board, such as Nina, in a position to "bear witness." To fully bear witness

Figure 3. Moses Buntu and his lawyer, Jerry Fischer, during the refugee hearing. Still from *Human Cargo* (2004), courtesy of Howe Sound Films.

entails participating "in the account given ... [In their] role as the interviewer of survivors ... [they also participate in] the reliving and reexperiencing of the event."[44]

But as Nina demonstrates, witnessing refugees "relive" traumatic experiences does not necessarily garner sympathy. In Nina's first hearing, with a Sri Lankan refugee, she is dismissive and sarcastic, telling the refugee, "I am sorry, Canada is not here to hold your hand." She vehemently takes the position that refugee claimants are lying. As Judith Lewis Herman writes: "It is very tempting to take the side of the perpetrator. All the perpetrator asks is that the bystander do nothing ... [The] victim ... asks the bystander to share the burden of pain."[45] Testimonies can threaten witnesses' assumptions about their world as a just and safe place.[46] To bear witness can raise questions about their involvement in governments, corporations, and consumer practices and their beliefs.

Insofar as bearing witness requires witnesses to question themselves, there is the possibility for transformation. By the time Nina assesses the case of Li Dan-Ye, she is finally able to bear witness. In this scene, care is taken to convey Li's trauma, starting with her account of how a state-run hospital cut her unborn baby out of her womb. She recounts her horror when a nurse insisted afterwards that "there [never] was [a] baby." Despite being visibly moved by Li's case, the evidence forces Nina to reject her claim. No longer able to maintain a safe distance through scorn and denial, Nina is shaken, admitting that "what happened to her was appalling."[47]

When it comes to Moses' case, Nina's personal and political connections to Burundi make it difficult to accept his account. His file implicates Peter Fowler's mining company in atrocities. When Nina attempts to discredit Moses with information she illegally gathers from the Burundi government, Moses' lawyer, Jerry Fischer, challenges her violation of protocol, forcing her to continue the hearing. Whenever she tries to challenge Moses, rather than discounting him, more details are disclosed about the horrific persecution he underwent. She learns, for example, about his torture and the execution of his neighbours by soldiers hired by Trillium Goldmines.

The audience could identify with Nina or judge her. But after viewing the atrocities and painful losses Moses underwent over the six episodes, it becomes difficult to identify with Nina. Even Nina abandons her position that all refugee claims are "bogus." Essentially, her ability to bear witness depends on whether she can question her racist assumptions and the corporate and government networks that tie her to Burundi through Peter Fowler. In the end, despite pressure from Peter, she grants Moses refugee status.

Conclusions: The Family, the Nation, and Politics

If *Human Cargo* had ended with Nina's transformation and Moses' new home in Canada, it would have had a neat conclusion, transforming a complex political problem into the personal struggle of two characters, one who overcame the external obstacles of civil war and another who overcame the internal obstacles of racial hatred. But when Nina holds a press conference to call for an investigation into the government's involvement in Burundi, she turns the problems into public issues. She also publicly admits to violating the protocols of the refugee board and announces her resignation, as well as her decision to remove herself from public life. What distinguishes Nina from her lover is that she does not condone murder and enslavement, showing that, in the end, she has integrity. At the level of narrative, Nina's final acts seem to suggest that justice is still possible. It could be argued that *Human Traffic* is about the transformation of Nina Wade, a right-wing Canadian politician, giving hope about recuperating Canada's role as an arbitrator in international conflicts.

But at another level, Nina's retreat from public life seems defeatist. When Helen returns from Burundi, she also retreats from politics. In the safety of her mother's house, she relives her traumatic experiences, blurting out shocking racist statements: "They should drop a bomb in the middle in Burundi—they should just start over … you were right." When she discovers that she has conceived a child with Eyob—that she has returned with "human cargo"—she exclaims, "Your daughter has brought back a souvenir from deepest darkest Africa!" Mother and daughter appear to have reversed positions. Again, the series is harsh on Helen, portraying her as a spoiled middle-class child who reacts badly when she realizes that her ability to freely cross borders—sexual and national—has been curtailed. This is a bleak statement about the next generation of Canadians.

The removal of Nina and Helen from the world of politics could be seen as "punishment": the domestication of women who transgress their gender roles. Perhaps the limitation of *Human Cargo*, as I have argued above, lies with the main trope: the family. The effort of all the characters to save their families encourages the audience to make emotional investments in each of them. But the family in its most conservative configuration is the site of normative values regarding sexuality, racial bloodlines, and gender roles. It is also a powerful metaphor for the nation, and in accordance with the terms of this trope, for Nina and Helen to reunite as a family, as women they must retreat from the world of politics, which was the source of their conflict.[48]

In conclusion, *Human Cargo* engages the popular imaginary, ripping its stories from news headlines and dramatic productions about refugees, terrorists, and civil war. But rather than just presenting the refugee as a figure of fear, it also presents Western democracies as a source of global violence. In this way, *Human Cargo* follows the Canadian mandate for documentary television to "faithfully and creatively represent … the real conditions in which [Canadians] live … formally empowering them by engaging the civic and aesthetic skills they need to participate in cultural affairs."[49] But in a global world where governments are corrupt and the media feed off the affective economy of fear, it is not so clear where those skills can be employed effectively anymore. But at least, unlike international co-productions such as *Sex Traffic*, whose scenes of rape cross borders as easily as trafficked women and children, *Human Cargo* encourages the audience to question their own complicity in the global refugee crisis. While the series does end up reproducing some of the more reactionary images circulating in the media, notably of Muslims, by refusing to offer closure—killing off characters who could seek resolutions, including the human rights lawyer, activists and politicized women—audience members are left to seek their own resolutions, hopefully in the larger worlds they live in.

Acknowledgements

Many thanks to the following individuals: Glen Lowry, for feedback on earlier drafts of the chapter; Linda Svendsen, who kindly provided a copy of *Human Cargo* and indulged my questions; Sue Baek of Howe Sound Films, who generously provided stills from the series; and Sylvia Roberts, the liaison librarian for the School of Communication at Simon Fraser University, who provided invaluable assistance in research.

Notes

1 Citizenship and Immigration Canada, at www.cic.gc.ca/english/pub/border2000/border2000.html (accessed January 28, 2006).
2 Hugh Beard, *"Human Cargo:* Production Notes."
3 The awards include seven Geminis and six Leos. See www.cbc.ca/humancargo/awards.html (accessed January 10, 2008).
4 Massumi, "Fear"; Ahmed "Affective Economies"; Horsti, "Global Mobility and the Media."
5 See the Campaign against Racism and Fascism, "Fortress America," at IRR News, www.irr.org.uk/2003/august/ak000002.html (accessed April 20, 2006).
6 United Nations High Commissioner For Refugees, "The World's Stateless People: Questions and Answers, Report," 2004, at www.unhcr.ch/cgi-bin/texis/vtx/home (accessed April 20, 2006).
7 One of the few articles on these productions is Shaw, "'You Are Alright, But ...,'" 211–23.
8 Hogarth, *Documentary Television in Canada,* 6. Following through with a mandate to involve and educate citizens, the CBC made a website for *Human Cargo* that organized online forums as well as public gatherings across Canada to discuss refugee issues. In addition, the website has links to refugee organizations and non-profit organizations that provide information and ways to become involved.
9 Hogarth, *Documentary Television in Canada,* 87.
10 Miller, "Inflecting the Formula," 112; Paget, *No Other Way to Tell it,* 132.
11 Miller, "Inflecting the Formula," 111.
12 It is important to note that the series presents Nina as a complex character, making it possible to sympathize with her, even if only a little, as a woman struggling to succeed in the male world of politics and as a single mother struggling with the scorn of her progressive daughter.
13 It is significant that the writers selected Vancouver for the "refugee story" of Moses Buntu. Historically, communities established by black Canadians, African-Americans, and Caribbean Canadians, as well as immigrants and refugees from Nigeria, Somalia, and other African countries, have established themselves in Central Canada, Quebec, and the Maritime provinces. *Human Cargo* points to a change in the demographics. Gibril Koroma states: "According to the 1996 Statistics Canada census figures, there were only 6,095 Africans in Vancouver in 1996 but the 2001 census revealed that the number has quadrupled to 24,700 Africans ... due to changes in Canada's immigration policy ... especially in the 1980s at the height of Africa's civil wars. Canada took in, on compassionate grounds, thousands of refugees from Sudan, Ethiopia, Eritrea, Somalia; and more recently from Liberia, Sierra Leone and the two Congos." See Koroma, "Canadian Cultural Policy and the African Diaspora."

14 Or so it is suggested—exact details about the involvement of corporations and government bodies are not disclosed, but evidence suggests that, behind the scenes, there is a network working to control events.

15 Feuer, as quoted in Paget, *No Other Way to Tell It*, 133.

16 Gitlin, as quoted in Paget, *No Other Way to Tell It*, 133.

17 Fair and Parks, "Africa On Camera," 40, 41.

18 Gilman, "Black Bodies, White Bodies"; Stoller, *Race and the Education of Desire*.

19 Shohat and Stam, *Unthinking Eurocentrism*.

20 Fair and Parks, "Africa on Camera," 40.

21 Even if it is difficult to critically read against the racialized stereotype of tribal violence, we need to consider, regardless of our views on mutilation, if Odette's act is in fact less "barbaric" than our democratic methods of punishment, whether death by electrocution or locking individuals up in crime-infested jails.

22 Gledhill, *Home Is Where the Heart Is*.

23 Boehmer, *Stories of Women*; Yuval-Davis and Anthias, *Woman-Nation-State*.

24 Wall, "Going Out to the Straight Community."

25 Nichols, *Representing Reality*, 71, 19.

26 Nichols, *Representing Reality*, 184.

27 For example, Nina Wade is played by Kate Nelligan, who has been nominated for Gemini and Academy Awards for her roles in television miniseries such as *Blessed Stranger: After Swiss Flight 111* (2001) and *The Cider House Rules* (1999) and a Gemini Award for her role in *Margaret's Museum* (1996). Helen Wade is played by Cara Pifko, who starred in the now discontinued Canadian dramatic series *This Is Wonderland* as a young legal aid lawyer.

28 It is interesting to note that *Sex Traffic*—as well as the more recent production *Human Trafficking*, on the trafficking of children and women—became widely available as DVDs in January 2006 and April 2006, respectively. Both are co-productions. According to Linda Svendsen, while Alliance Atlantis had the distribution rights for *Human Cargo*, arrangements have only just been made, after much work and negotiation, to release the series as a DVD with another company.

29 See Mitchell, *Crossing the Neoliberal Line*; Cavell, "The Race of Space."

30 See Adachi, *The Enemy That Never Was*.

31 It refers to a controversial incident in 1999 that involved a ship of illegal Chinese immigrants landing on the Queen Charlotte Islands. This event also resonates with similar stories about illegal Chinese migrants in Europe and the United States, as well as historical incidents like that of the *Komagata Maru*, when Canadian officials refused entry to a steamship with 376 immigrants from British India in 1914. See the documentary *Continuous Journey* (2004), directed by Ali Kazami.

32 Nichols, *Representing Reality*, 150.

33 "The Stars: Bayo Akinfemi," at www.cbc.ca/humancargo/stars_akinfemi.html (accessed January 10, 2008).

34 "The Stars: Bayo Akinfemi," at www.cbc.ca/humancargo/stars_akinfemi.html (accessed January 10, 2008).

35 Arsenault, "No Holds Barred for Sex Traffic."

36 En route to the refugee camp, a man demands that Odette sexually "pay" for the water from his well, though the rape is not shown. We only see her enter his house and, afterwards, her attempts to hide her distraught state from her children.

37 For debates on representing trafficked women, see Agustín, "Migrants in the Mistress's House"; Lindstrom, "Regional Sex Trafficking in the Balkans Transnational Networks in an Enlarged Europe," 45–52.

38 Canadian Press, "CBC Uses Holiday Weekend to Air Sex Traffic."
39 Radstone, "Social Bonds and Psychical Order," 61.
40 See Cornell, ed., *Feminism and Pornography*; Hesford and Kozol, eds., *Just Advocacy?*
41 Miller, "Inflecting the Formula," 108; Tinic, "Going Global," 178. ˙
42 Immigration and Refugee Board of Canada, "Frequently Asked Questions." www.clc.gc.ca/english (accessed January 26, 2006).
43 Laub, "Truth and Testimony," 69
44 Laub, "Truth and Testimony," 69.
45 Herman, *Trauma and Recovery*, 7.
46 Herman, *Trauma and Recovery*, 72.
47 It could be argued that while the series sympathetically portrays a refugee claimant from Mainland China, this does nothing to question negative discourses regarding "rich Asians."
48 Virdi, *The Cinematic Imagination;* Morley, *Home Territories;* Yuval-Davis and Anthias, *Women-Nation-State.*
49 Hogarth, *Documentary Television in Canada*, 6.

References

Adachi, Ken. *The Enemy That Never Was.* Toronto: McClelland & Stewart, 1976.

Agustín, Laura. "Migrants in the Mistress's House: Other Voices in the 'Trafficking' Debate." *Social Politics: International Studies in Gender, State and Society* 12 (1): 96–117.

Ahmed, Sara. "Affective Economies." *Social Text* 22 (2): 117–136.

Arsenault, Tim. "No Holds Barred for Sex Traffic." *Tuned In*, 2004. Available at Wendy Crewson: Sex Traffic Articles, http://wendy-crewson-fan.tripod.com/id125.html. Accessed January 28, 2008.

Beard, Hugh. "*Human Cargo:* Production Notes." Force Four Entertainment (November 2003).

Boehmer, Elleke, ed. *Stories of Women: Gender and Narrative in the Postcolonial Nation.* Manchester: Manchester University Press, 2005.

Canadian Press. "CBC Uses Holiday Weekend to Air *Sex Traffic.*" Available at Wendy Crewson: Sex Traffic Articles, http://wendy-crewson-fan.tripod.com/id125.html. Accessed January 28, 2008.

Cavell, Richard. "The Race of Space." *New Formations* 31 (1997): 39–50.

Cornell, Drucilla, ed. *Feminism and Pornography*. New York: Oxford University Press, 2000.

Fair, Jo Ellen and Lisa Parks. "Africa On Camera: Television News Coverage and Aerial Imaging of Rwandan Refugees." *Africa Today* 48 (2): 35–57.

Gilman, Sander. "Black Bodies, White Bodies: Toward an Iconography of Female Sexuality in Late Nineteenth Century Art, Medicine and Literature." In *"Race," Writing, and Difference*, edited by Henry Louis Gates Jr., 223–61. Chicago: University of Chicago Press, 1985.

Gledhill, Christine, ed., *Home Is Where the Heart Is*. London: British Film Institute, 1987.

Herman, Judith Lewis. *Trauma and Recovery: The Aftermath of Violence from Domestic Abuse to Political Terror*. New York: Basic Books, 1992.

Hesford, Wendy, and Wendy Kozol, eds. *Just Advocacy? Women's Human Rights, Transnational Feminisms, and the Politics of Representation*. New Brunswick, NJ: Rutgers University Press, 2005.

Hogarth, David. *Documentary Television in Canada: From National Public Service to Global Marketplace*. Montreal and Kingston: McGill-Queen's University Press, 2002.

Horsti, Karina. "Global Mobility and the Media: Presenting Asylum Seekers as a Threat." *Nordicom Review* 24 (1): 41–54.

Koroma, Gibril. "Canadian Cultural Policy and the African Diaspora: A Study of Four African Cultural Organizations in Vancouver." Honours Project, School of Communication, Simon Fraser University, Burnaby, BC, 2004.

Laub, Dori. "Truth and Testimony: The Process and the Struggle." In *Trauma: Explorations in Memory*, edited by Cathy Caruth, 61–75. Baltimore: Johns Hopkins University Press, 1995.

Lindstrom, Nicole. "Regional Sex Trafficking in the Balkans Transnational Networks in an Enlarged Europe." *Problems of Post-Communism* 51 (3): 45–52.

Massumi, Brian. "Fear (Spectrum Said)," *Positions* 13 (1): 31–48.

Miller, Mary Jane. "Inflecting the Formula: The First Seasons of *Street Legal* and *L.A. Law*." In *The Beaver Bites Back? American Popular Culture in Canada*, edited by David H. Flaherty and Frank E. Manning, 104–22. Montreal and Kingston: McGill-Queen's Press, 1993.

Mitchell, Katharyne. *Crossing the Neoliberal Line: Pacific Rim Migration and the Metropolis*. Philadelphia: Temple University Press, 2004.

Morley, David. *Home Territories: Media, Mobility and Identity*. London: Routledge, 2000.

Nichols, Bill. *Representing Reality: Issues and Concepts in Documentary*. Bloomington: Indiana University Press, 1991.

Paget, Derek. *No Other Way to Tell it: Dramadoc/Docudrama on Television*. Manchester: Manchester University Press, 1998.

Radstone, Susannah. "Social Bonds and Psychical Order: Testimonies." *Cultural Values* 5 (1): 59–78.

Shaw, Deborah. "'You Are Alright, But ... ' Individual and Collective Representations of Mexicans, Latinos, Anglo-Americans and African-Americans in Steven Soderbergh's *Traffic*." *Quarterly Review of Film and Video* 22 (2005): 211–23.

Shohat, Ella and Robert Stam. *Unthinking Eurocentrism: Multiculturalism and the Media*. London: Routledge, 1994.

Stoller, Ann Laura. *Race and the Education of Desire: Foucault's History of Sexuality and the Colonial Order of Things*. Durham, NC: Duke University Press, 1996.

Tinic, Serra. "Going Global: International Coproductions and the Disappearing Domestic Audience in Canada." In *Planet TV: A Global Television Reader*, edited by Lisa Parks and Shanti Kumar, 169–85. New York: New York University Press, 2003.

———. *On Location: Canada's Television Industry in a Global Market.* Toronto: University of Toronto Press, 2005.

United Nations High Commissioner for Refugees. "The World's Stateless People: Questions and Answers, Report," 2004. Available at www.unhcr.ch/cgi-bin/texis/vtx/home. Accessed April 20, 2006.

Virdi, Jyotika. *The Cinematic Imagination: Indian Popular Films as Social History*, New Brunswick, NJ: Rutgers University Press, 2004.

Wall, Derek. "Going Out to the Straight Community: Television and Heteronormative Logics in Representations of Homosexuality." *Group Identities on French and British Television*, edited by Michael Scriven and Emily Roberts, 119–25. New York: Berghahn Books, 2003.

Yuval-Davis, Nira and Floya Anthias, eds., *Woman-Nation-State*, London: Macmillan, 1989.

Filmography

24 (Imagine Television, 2001–)
Alias (Touchstone/Bad Robot Productions, 2001–06)
Beyond Borders (Mandalay Pictures/Paramount, 2003), dir. Marlin Campbell
Black Hawk Down (Jerry Bruckheimer, 2001), dir. Ridley Scott
The Constant Gardener (Potboiler Productions, 2005), dir. Fernando Meirelles
Continuous Journey (2004, Canada), dir. Ali Kazami
Da Vinci's City Hall (CBC, 2005–06)
Da Vinci's Inquest (CBC, 1998–2005)
H2O (CBC, 2004), dir. Charles Binamé
Human Cargo (Force Four Entertainment/Howe Sound Film, 2004), dir. Brad Turner
Human Trafficking (Granada/Big Motion Pictures, 2005), dir. Christian Duguay
Intelligence (CBC, 2006–)
Sex Traffic (CBC/Channel 4, 2004), dir. David Yates
Syriana (Warner Bros./Section Eight, 2005), dir. Stephen Gaghan
Tears of the Sun (Lobell Productions/Mike Lobell/Cheyenne Enterprises, 2003), dir. Antoine Fuqua
Traffic (USA Films, 2000), dir. Stephen Soderbergh
Traffik (Channel 4, 1989), dir. Alistair Reid

List of Contributors

Marusya Bociurkiw is assistant professor of media theory in the School of Radio and Television Arts at Ryerson University in Toronto. She is the author of four literary books, including *Comfort Food for Breakups: The Memoir of a Hungry Girl* (Arsenal Pulp Press, 2007). She has been producing films and videos in Canada for the past fifteen years, including, most recently, *Flesh and Blood: A Journey between East and West.* Her monograph on Canadian television, *Feeling Canadian: Nationalism and Affect on Canadian Television,* is forthcoming from Wilfrid Laurier Press.

Michele Byers is assistant professor in Sociology and Criminology at Saint Mary's University. She has written extensively on television, youth, and identity. In 2001, she was awarded a SSHRC grant to study the *Degrassi* series and the production of youth and Canadian identity. In 2004, she was awarded a second SSHRC grant to engage in a broader study of television, film, and the production of Canadian youth cultures. She is editor of *Growing Up Degrassi: Television, Identity and Youth Cultures* (Sumach Press, 2005).

Lyle Dick is the West Coast historian with Parks Canada in Vancouver. He is the author of 70 publications on topics in Canadian and American history, historiography, and Arctic history, including the book *Muskox Land: Ellesmere Island in the Age of Contact* (University of Calgary Press, 2001). He was awarded the Harold Adams Innis Prize for Canada's best English-language book in the social sciences in 2003. His published work includes several detailed investigations into the relationships of narrative form and Canadian history, including earlier articles on the books and visual content of the CBC series *Canada: A People's History.*

Zoë Druick is associate professor in the School of Communication at Simon Fraser University, where she teaches courses in media, film, and cultural studies. She is the author of *Projecting Canada: Documentary Film and Government Policy at the National Film Board* (McGill-Queen's University Press, 2007) and has published articles on documentary film, educational media, and cultural policy in *Television and New Media, Studies in Documentary Film, Canadian Journal of Film Studies*, and *Canadian Journal of Communication*. Her current work involves an investigation of the links between documentary and democracy.

Derek Foster is assistant professor in the Department of Communications, Popular Culture and Film at Brock University. His PhD dissertation (Carleton University, School of Journalism and Communication, 2004) studied the evolution of squeegeeing as a controversial social issue through the lens of rhetorical theory. His recent publications focus on a wide variety of communication media studied as visual rhetoric and contesting discourses surrounding reality television.

David Hogarth is associate professor in Communication Studies at York University. His research is concerned with the history and current state of documentary in Canada and worldwide. He is the author of *Documentary Television in Canada: From National Public Service to Global Marketplace* (McGill-Queen's University Press, 2002) and *Realer Than Reel: Global Dimensions in Documentary* (University of Texas Press, 2006). He is now researching the political economy of independent documentary production.

Aspa Kotsopoulos is senior policy analyst in Television Policy and Applications at the Canadian Radio-television and Telecommunications Commission (CRTC). In 2004 she received her PhD in Communications from Simon Fraser University, where her dissertation was nominated for a Governor General's award. She has published articles about Canadian television in various journals and anthologies, and has taught courses in film and media studies.

Glen Lowry teaches in critical and cultural studies at Emily Carr Institute for Art + Design + Media in Vancouver. A specialist in contemporary Canadian literature and culture, he edits *West Coast Line*. His recent published work looks at the limits of cultural nationalism in relation to racialized writing, 20th-century poetics, photography, and contemporary art. He is currently working on a collaborative Research Creations project on the uncanny mirroring of Vancouver's urban waterfront in the desert West of Dubai, United Arab Emirates.

Sarah A. Matheson is assistant professor in the Department of Communications, Popular Culture and Film at Brock University. Her research and teaching interests are in film and television studies, with a recent focus on reality television in Canada and the U.S. and issues surrounding taste and popular culture. She has published several articles on the representation of Toronto on English-Canadian television.

Kirsten Emiko McAllister is assistant professor in the School of Communication at Simon Fraser University. She has published in the areas of cultural memory, visual culture, and political violence, focusing on Japanese Canadian internment camps. Her more recent research focuses on refugees and discourses of inclusion and exclusion. Some of her publications include articles in *Visual Studies* and *Cultural Values* and a book co-edited with Annette Kuhn, *Locating Memory: Photographic Acts* (Berghahn, 2006).

John McCullough teaches in the Department of Film at York University. He has a PhD in social and political thought and was the first coordinator of the graduate programs in interdisciplinary studies in fine arts at the University of Regina. His current research includes analysis of popular Hollywood films, Canadian regional television production, and First Nations in film and television.

Mary Jane Miller is Professor of Dramatic Arts Emerita at Brock University. She is the author of *Turn Up the Contrast: CBC Television Drama since 1952* (University of British Columbia Press and CBC, 1987) and *Rewind and Search: Conversations with Makers and Decision Makers of CBC Television Drama* (McGill-Queen's University Press, 1996). She is completing the forthcoming book *Outside Looking In* for McGill-Queen's University Press, about the representation of First Nations people in series television.

Julie Rak is associate professor in the Department of English and Film Studies at the University of Alberta. She is the author of *Negotiated Memory: Doukhobor Autobiographical Discourse* (2005) and the editor of *Auto/biography in Canada: Critical Directions* (2005). She is co-editor (with Jeremy Popkin) of *On Diary*, a new translation of recent essays by Philippe LeJeune (University of Hawaii Press, 2008) and co-editor (with Andrew Gow) of *Mountain Masculinity: The Life and Writings of Nello (Tex) Vernon Wood on the Canadian Rockies, 1911–1938* (Athabasca University Press, 2008). She is the editor of a special issue of *The Canadian Journal of American Studies* on popular auto/biography (forthcoming 2008). Julie has published on popular culture,

Canadian culture and autobiography theory most recently in *English Studies in Canada*, *biography*, and *Life Writing*. Her current book project is about mass-produced memoir and biography in print and on television in North America.

Katarzyna Rukszto is assistant professor in the Department of Sociology at Wilfrid Laurier University. Her current research examines representational politics of museums and heritage sites, particularly those that focus on military history, war, and national identity. She is also revising a book manuscript on the Heritage Minutes.

Jen VanderBurgh is a SSHRC Postdoctoral Fellow in the Department of Film and Media at Queen's University, where she working on a manuscript that compares national approaches to archiving and teaching television. Her other research concerns representations of urbanity as a problematic of nation, culture, and technology in Canadian film and television. She has published in the *Canadian Journal of Film Studies*, *Topia*, *Quebec Studies*, and the *Encyclopedia of the Documentary Film*.

Index

Books in the Film and Media Studies Series
Published by Wilfrid Laurier University Press

The Young, the Restless, and the Dead: Interviews with Canadian Filmmakers / George Melnyk, editor / 2008 / xiv + 134 pp. / photos / ISBN 978-1-55458-036-1

Programming Reality: Perspectives on English-Canadian Television / Zoë Druick and Aspa Kotsopoulos, editors / 2008 / x + 344 pp. / photos / ISBN 978-1-55458-010-1

Harmony and Dissent: Film and Avant-garde Art Movements in the Early Twentieth Century / R. Bruce Elder / forthcoming 2008 / 462 pp. / ISBN 978-1-55458-028-6